The Millennium Book of Prophecy

The Millennium

Book of Prophecy

777 Visions and Predictions

from Nostradamus, Edgar Cayce, Gurdjieff,

Tamo-san, Madame Blavatsky, the Old and New Testament Prophets and 89 others

John Hogue

HarperSanFrancisco

A Division of HarperCollinsPublishers

Produced by Ron Tanner for Byron Bay Media Pty Ltd.
Design by Annelies Jahn, Ik'on graphic design Sydney Australia.
(based on a concept by John Hogue).
Production Assistant: Rebecca Townsend.
Printed by Tien Wah Press (Pte.) Ltd, Singapore.
1
FIRST EDITION
Library of Congress Cataloging-in-Publication Data
Hogue, John
        The millennium book of prophecy / John Hogue...1st ed.

        Includes bibliographical references.
        ISBN 0-06-251077-0 (pbk)
        1. Prophecies (Occultism) 2. Twentieth-century Forecasts.
I, Title
BF1809. H64   1994
133.3–dc20   93-45558
                                                                 CIP

94 95 96 97 98 SIN 10 9 8 7 6 5 4 3 2 1

Contents

x............**HOW TO READ THIS BOOK**
How the Prophecy Indexing Works
How to Find a Prophet's Biography
A Note on Narrative Voice
Prophecy Index Glossary

xiv........**INTRODUCTION:** TERROR AND HOPE
Prophecy at a Glance

20........**PART ONE:** A CROSSROAD AT THE END OF TIME

21...........**INTRODUCTION**
Latter-Day Dateline

24..........**CYCLES OF TIME**
Living on the Cusp of Time
The Second Millennium
The Last Popes
The Wheel of Dharma has Stopped!
Kali Yuga

37...........**PURIFIED BY FIRE**
The Final Warnings

42..........**SIGNS IN THE SKY**

44.........PART TWO: TOMORROW OF FEAR
       Introduction
       The Four Horsemen of the Apocalypse
          — The Four Hellriders of Doomsday

48..........THE FIRST HELLRIDER: OVERPOPULATION

52..........THE SECOND HELLRIDER: EARTH TRAUMA
       Introduction
       Heap of Trouble
       Gassed Planet
       The Great Drought
       Global Deluge
       A Greenhouse or an Icehouse Effect?
       Both Fire and Ice Spell F-A-M-I-N-E !
       Quakes, Shifts and Shakes
       A Map of the Post-Shift World

84..........THE THIRD HELLRIDER: THE LEMMING SYNDROME
       Introduction
       The Seven Final Plagues

              "Dis-ease" 1: Blood, Plague
              "Dis-ease" 2: Waters of Death
              "Dis-ease" 3: Hidden Poisons
              "Dis-ease" 4: Plague from the Skies
              "Dis-ease" 5: Depression, Hopelessness
              "Dis-ease" 6: The Opiate of False Prophets
              "Dis-ease" 7: Do You Realize You Are the Plague?

104.........THE FOURTH HELLRIDER: THE THIRD WORLD'S WAR
         Introduction
         Will to Catharsis
         Disarming Dreams
         New Age Weapons
         The Northern and Southern Blocs
         Triumvirate of Terror
         Nuclear Bush Wars
   Armageddon: When the Euphrates Runs Dry
                 Armageddon: When the Food Runs Out
                 Armageddin' Ethnic
                 Armageddon: A War of International Terrorism
                 Fail Safe Armageddon
                 Armageddin' Ecological: When the Supersystems Break Down
         The Second Holocaust
         World War III? — World War Free-for-All!
         From Cold War to Nuclear Winter

153.........AND THE HORSE THEY ALL RIDE: A NIGHTMARE UNCONSCIOUS
         Four Dimensions of a Nightmare
         What Makes Prediction So Predictable?
         The Doomsday Body Count

164......PART THREE: TOMORROW OF BLESSINGS
       Introduction

172.........IS THERE A BRIDGE TO UTOPIA?
       Introduction
       Bridge One: Invention
       Bridge Two: Meritocracy
       Bridge Three: Russia Is the Hope of the World
       Bridge Four: Commune Earth
       Bridge Five: The Humanitary-Industrial Complex
       Warning! There Is a Dark Side to Aquarius

214.........DEATH OF THE PAST
       Prologue
       Going, Going, God?
       Nuclear Family, Nuclear War
       The Rat Race: A Society of Homo "Hamster" Sapiens
       Nationalism: The Global Penitentiary System
       Man Divided Against the Self

252........SPIRITUAL REBELLION
       Introduction
       Religionless Religion
       Homo Novus
       Meditation: Therapy for Madhouse Earth
       The Critical Mass of Enlightenment

316.........."WITHIN"

320........EPILOGUE: EVER NOW

322........APPENDIX: THE SEERS' ENCYCLOPEDIA

340........BIBLIOGRAPHY

343........ACKNOWLEDGEMENTS

How to Read This Book

The Millennium Book of Prophecy explores the lives and visions of history's greatest prophetic seers. Whether ancient or modern, pagan or Christian, these adepts of future-sight moved beyond the social and historical framework of their times to paint a common vision of what is in store for us in this final and climactic decade of the twentieth century. The picture they collectively paint contains brush-strokes of both terror and of hope.

Within the pages of this book are 777 visions from 102 prophetic sources. It is the most comprehensive gathering of prescient visions yet published. It reveals for the first time the shared revelation of history's great seers that our survival into the next century may depend on the partial or complete re-examination of our current belief systems.

If their message is heard, then we who are living in the final years of a long and violent age have the key to give our children the potential for endless tomorrows.

HOW THE PROPHECY INDEXING WORKS

The Millennium Book of Prophecy is structured as a prophetic anthology. Just as the prophets often sampled the future out of linear sequence, so the reader can dip into any section at random and absorb its image and message.

All predictions are in italics. Roman type enclosed in brackets is used to streamline my interpretation of a prophecy, or indicate additions or changes I have made to the text of a prophecy to explain, clarify, or correct a quotation's grammar. For example:

"*He* [man] *will come to take himself to the corner of Luna* [the Moon] *where he will be taken and placed on alien land.*"

Changes or clarification by the prophet appear in italic type within brackets or parentheses.

"*Then these united or upon an equitable basis, would become or could become, powers (for good); but there are many interferences...*"

The name of the prophet appears after every prophecy, followed by the actual or estimated date of the prediction in parentheses. For example:

Madame Blavatsky (1888)

Prophets often collected and indexed their predictions in books and religious scriptures. In such cases you will find the name and date of the prediction, followed by an abbreviated code for the book's title and the prediction's indexing. For instance:

St John of Patmos (AD 81-96) Rev 16:12

"Rev 16:12" stands for St John's Book of Revelation, Chapter 16, Verse 12. This abbreviated indexing is decoded in the **Prophecy Index Glossary** appearing at the end of this introduction. There one can find the source of the prediction quoted.

HOW TO FIND A PROPHET'S BIOGRAPHY

It has been my observation for the past twenty years as a writer and interpreter of prophecy that a narrative gets bogged down when it weaves predictions with too much biographical information on the prophets. Often it can be found that people view prophecies in two steps: first, they want to know what's going to happen; second, after that desire is fulfilled they want to know more about the person making the predictions. *The Millennium Book of Prophecy* uses its

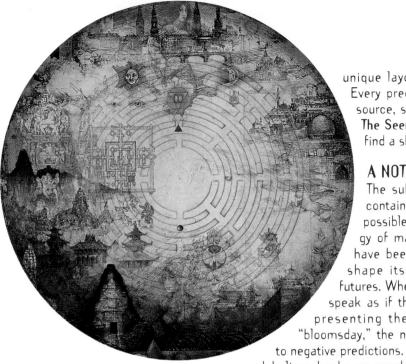

unique layout design to satisfy both desires. Every prediction is followed by its author or source, so the reader can turn at any time to **The Seers' Encyclopedia** in the Appendix and find a short biography of the prophet quoted.

A NOTE ON NARRATIVE VOICE

The subject of prophecy is big enough to contain as many contradictions as there are possible destinies. I have written an anthology of many slants and points of view and I have been compelled to make my narrative shape itself around all of these potential futures. When on the subject of doomsday, I may speak as if there is no hope for tomorrow. While presenting the possibility of a future-friendly "bloomsday," the narrative may run completely counter to negative predictions.

I believe books on prophecy have suffered in the past from trying to make solely objective sense out of events unborn. Therefore, I have tried to place the essential messages of this book within an entertaining and thought-provoking interface of pictures, text, prophecies and graphics.

There are many layers to this work. It may read differently each time the cover is cracked. Each two-page spread will contain many graphic fingers pointing to essential truths about the right use of prophecy, but never once will that essential key be described directly, since the search for it is in part the key itself. In short, my narrative is both verbally and pictorially *occult*.

I define this word by its original meaning, the one that mystics and alchemists always intended, and not the meaning given by dictionaries and modern psychics, which is "secret" or "hidden." Rather, I use the same definition intended by the master to the disciple in search of truth — that which is "occult" is the essential reality beyond dialectics, beyond judging, and above what we have been taught is good and evil, right or wrong. That which is "occult" is neither moral nor immoral nor even amoral. Occult truth is transmoral. No one is hiding it. In fact we are hiding from it. We are it! It is not secret, it is simply something that anyone who is being honest with you will never dare express directly in conventional language. It cannot be expressed in that way. "It" is vast and subtle all at once; therefore, like my narrative, it contains all contradictions.

Another important guideline I must make here is that if there are prophetic insights in this book it is a blessed accident. If you experience moments of true insight within these pages it is only because I must have been out of the way to allow them to flow through to you.

It has been my experience that no person — or better, no *personality* — has intelligence. It is only when one's limiting *persona* is out of the way that a state of true intelligence functions. Otherwise the *personas* of prophets and their interpreters, including myself, may impart their biases rather than true insights.

It is my hope that you will remember this final guideline as you examine the following pages. It is essential for the fullest enjoyment of this work.

Prophecy Index Glossary

Only the full title and original publication date are included here. Check the Bibliography for further information. The name of the author is recorded if the prophecies were collected in an anthology or if the prophet changed his pseudonym, as is the case with Osho and Da Avabhasa.

Ambres (channeled by Sturé Johannson)
Amb   *AMBRES:* 1987

Sri Aurobindo
Savt   *Savitri: A Legend and a Symbol:* 1990 (13th printing)

Da Avabhasa (aka "Bubba," or "Da" Free John, Da Kalki and Da Love Ananda)
Bdy   *The Enlightenment of the Whole Body* by Da Free John: 1978
Garb   *Garbage and the Goddess* by Bubba Free John: 1974
Scien   *Scientific Proof of the Existence of God Will Soon Be Announced by the White House!* by Da Free John: 1980

Bahá'u'lláh
Aqd   *Kitáb-i-Aqdas* (The Most Holy Book): 1973

'Abdu'l-Bahá
Wis   *The Wisdom of 'Abdu'l-Bahá:* 1911
Prm   *Promulgation of Universal Peace:* 1982
Slc   *Selections from the Writings of 'Abdu'l-Bahá:* 1978
Gpb   *God Passes By* (Shoghi Effendi): 1944

Roger Bacon
Epsc   *Epistola de Secretis* (Epistle of Secrets): 1269

BIBLE CODES:
Old Testament Books
Ez   Ezekiel
Jo   Joel
Jer   Jeremiah
Zek   Zechariah
Is   Isaiah
Mic   Micah
Dn   Daniel
New Testament Books
Rev   Revelation
Mt   Matthew
Lk   Luke
Mk   Mark

Madame Blavatsky
ScDoc   *The Secret Doctrine:* 1888

Edgar Cayce
Note on the Readings: His 14,246 trance sessions are indexed by the subject's case number and the hyphenated number of the reading, for example: №301-4. For further investigation of the readings you can contact the Edgar Cayce Foundation, Virginia Beach, VA, USA.

Cheiro
Cwp   *Cheiro's World Predictions:* 1926 (Revised in 1931)

David Goodman Croly
Glmps   *Glimpses of the Future:* 1888

Andrew Jackson Davis
Pen   *The Penetralia:* 1856

Deguchi Nao
Omo   *Omoto-Shin'yu* (Omoto Prophecies): 1900

G.I. Gurdjieff
Lfe   *Life Is Real Only Then When "I am": All and Everything/Third Series:* 1930
Beelzb   *Beelzebub's Tales to His Grandson* (3 Vols): *All and Everything/First Series:* 1924-1927

Mira   *In Search of the Miraculous* by P.D. Ouspensky: 1915-1917 (Statements of Gurdjieff recorded and edited by P.D. Ouspensky)

Hermes Trismigistus
Asc III   *Ascliepus III* by Hermes Trismegistus: AD 150-270

J. Krishnamurti
Liah   *Life Ahead:* 1963

Mohammed
Qur   *The Holy Qur'an:* AD seventh century

Ruth Montgomery
Aby   *The World Beyond:* 1971
Wbf   *The World Before:* 1976
Amg   *Strangers Among Us:* 1979
Alns   *Aliens Among Us:* 1985
Hrd   *Ruth Montgomery Herald of the New Age:* 1986

The Mother
Conv   Conversations — Published in "The Bulletin of Sri Aurobindo International Centre of Education" in 1931

Michel Nostradamus: from *The Centuries*
C	(Century, or Volume)	There are initially ten Centuries of usually 100 quatrains a piece. Nostradamus wrote duplicate quatrains as well as fragmentary Centuries 11 & 12.
Q	(Quatrain)	
Q dup	(duplicate Quatrain)	

Osho (aka Acharya Rajneesh, or "Bhagwan Shree" Rajneesh)
BofR   *The Book of Rajneeshism:* 1984
DtoL   *From Darkness to Light:* 1985
DiSutra   *The Diamond Sutra:* 1977

DtoD   *From Death to Deathlessness:* 1985
FtoT   *From the False to the True:* 1985
GFutr   *The Golden Future:* 1987
GrCh   *The Greatest Challenge: The Golden Future:* 1987
Hari   *Hari Om Tat Sat:* 1987
HiSp   *The Hidden Splendor:* 1987
Htmc   *Hansa To Moti Chugai (Hindi)* 1979
Ltus   *The Land of the Lotus Paradise:* 1984
LTst   *The Last Testament:* 1985
Myst   *The Path of the Mystic:* 1986
NewD   *The New Dawn:* 1987
Omph   *Om Mani Padme Hum:* 1987
Psyc   *Beyond Psychology:* 1986
RajB IV   *The Rajneesh Bible, Vol 4:* 1985
RajUp   *The Rajneesh Upanishad:* 1986
Razr   *The Razor's Edge:* 1987
RbSp   *The Rebellious Spirit:* 1987
Rebl   *The Rebel:* 1987
Soc   *Socrates Poisoned Again After 25 Centuries:* 1987
Trns   *Transmission of the Lamp:* 1986
Watr   *The Sound of Running Water:* 1976
Womn   *A New Vision of Women's Liberation:* 1987
ZnPr   *Zen: Path of the Paradox, Vol II:* 1979

The Hindu Puranas
Mat-P   *Matsya Purana:* cAD 330
Vis-P   *Visnu Purana:* cAD 900

Tamo-san:
Awkw   *Lecture for the Awakening of the Whole World:* May 1989
Moor   *Moor the Boat:* 1957
Look   *Look Here!* discourse: Summer 1960
Trshr   *Opening of the Treasure House, Beginning of the Enlightenment:* 1989

Alan Vaughan
Ptrns   *Patterns in Prophecy:* 1973

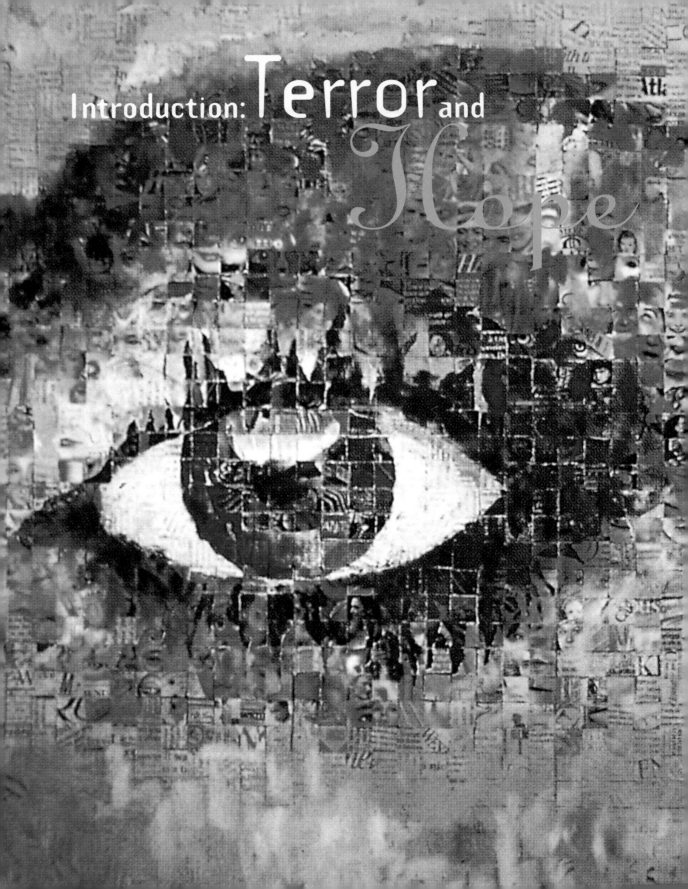

Introduction: Terror and *Hope*

I have already faced the end of my world.

It happened on Ash Wednesday, the first day of Lent, in 1981. I was preparing to drive to my girlfriend's house in Laguna Beach for dinner. Just as I was about to leave, I sensed a vastness hovering over me — a premonition of impending death. It became so tangible it froze me at the threshold. I stood motionless for sixty seconds of forever; then something pushed me into action. I fumbled for my car keys and headed off. Ten minutes later, death met me in a hurry. A station wagon ran a red light at fifty-five miles an hour and slammed into the driver's door of my compact car.

Glass and steel ripped apart like garments.

The paramedics say I was unconscious for twenty minutes. They had given me up for dead and were working on the other driver. When they were finally preparing to saw me out of the wreckage, they noticed my slumped body stir with life.

Twenty minutes or twenty centuries made no difference to what had been "me" in the ruined car. All meaning was discarded with the din of shredding metal and shattered glass falling away. My consciousness was launched into an ocean of golden silence.

Perception of myself was everywhere and nowhere, running at a million years a moment. I remember hovering over parents and friends who never saw me. I wasn't there. And I did this "not there-ing" with as much reality as I had "done" the physical body. I looked through my girlfriend's eyes and saw her hands cutting carrots for the meal we would never have. Her hands suddenly stopped. She put down the knife and folded her fingers thoughtfully.

There were other beings "not there-ing" in the golden silence. They cast the impression, like turning on a light, that I was home and there was no need to return "down there."

But somewhere in the lower vibrations of the space/time continuum, a pair of eyes opened. My mind re-engaged. Coolness, and a restfulness I have never felt before, encompassed the form that was the only thing left unbroken in the car. I felt like a time traveler returning from a million-year journey, inwardly silent and centered.

Someone was tapping on the glass. An ashen-faced paramedic gaped at me through the window and yelled, "Can you get out?!"

"Sure," I said evenly, as if he had only asked me for the time.

I found the door handle and walked away from death.

Prophets explain that through techniques of deep prayer, trance or meditation — and sometimes even through a severe shock — they can have a glimpse of a higher vista of consciousness, where the horizon of time stretches far beyond the present moment.

The objective mind cannot always repress the psychic in us. And in some rare moments the fantastic even leaves its calling card at a skeptic's door. I remember how I tried to reach out to those I loved after the collision propelled me into the golden light. Later on I asked my girlfriend what she was doing at the time of the accident.

"I was in the kitchen," she said, "cutting some carrots for dinner, when suddenly something stopped me. I knew you weren't coming...that something terrible had just happened."

Facing life's ultimate threat of change — death — has given me a deep sense of gratitude, not only to the mystery that continues to give me life, but also to the sixth sense that sent me a premonition of danger. If I had been more self-observant, and more open to my own prescience, I might have respected that premonition and avoided a circumstance that almost killed me.

I contend that we all suffer from prophet's block. Most of us have been programmed to act like ostriches, to hide our heads from premonitions of change. A premonition of apocalypse — whether personal or global — may be a blessing in disguise. We can use precognition as an alarm to wake up in time and steer our destiny out of harm's way.

2

Prophecy at a Glance

NOW has been seen before. There are documented prophecies in hundreds of books spanning the history of this subjective art over the last 10,000 years. For decades, premonitions bureaus in America and England have recorded hundreds of certified cases of people accurately predicting the future.

The orthodox scientist dismisses any sincere study of the paranormal as a pseudo-science. Current scientific expertise concerns itself with matter, a word defined in its Latin roots as "to measure." But many phenomena around us, like the universe itself or the potential of human intelligence, have no yardstick. Can it be denied that these mysteries exist simply because we cannot quantify and measure them? Is it not pseudo for a purely rational scientist to attempt an objective measurement of the subjective? That is a contradiction in terms.

At present, the art of psychic prediction is an enigma beyond our rational understanding. Be that as it may, the following time line of documented forecasts from the last 10,000 years is enough proof that the accuracy of prediction extends beyond any pseudo-scientific lucky guess.

The time has come to reassess our limits and to reawaken the prophet within us all.

The End of the Last World Before Noah's Flood

This is when the trouble started. Everything they [the people] needed was on this Second World, but they wanted more....The people began to quarrel and fight, and then wars between villages began. Still there were a few people in every village who sang the song of their Creation. But the wicked people laughed at them until they could sing it only in their hearts. Even so, Sótukknang [the Lord of the Universe]...appeared before them.

"Spider Woman tells me your thread is running out on this world," he said "...I have decided we must do something about it. We are going to destroy this Second World just as soon as we put you people who still have the song in your hearts in a safe place."

So again, as on the First World, Sótukknang called on the Ant People to open up their underground world for the chosen people. When they were safely underground, Sótukknang commanded the twins, Pöqánghoya and Palöngawhoya, to leave their posts at the north and south ends of the world's axis, where they were stationed to keep the Earth properly rotating.

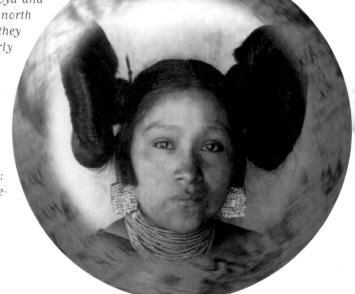

The twins had hardly abandoned their stations when the world, with no one to control it, teetered off balance, spun around crazily, then rolled over twice. Mountains plunged into seas with a great splash, seas and lakes sloshed over the land; and as the world spun through cold and lifeless space it froze into solid ice.

This was the end of Tokpa, the Second World.

The Book of the Hopi as recounted by
**Oswald White Bear Fredericks
and recorded by Frank Waters**

According to Hopi Indian legend, the world has already ended three times. Long before Noah's Ark and a biblical four-cornered world, the Indians of prehistoric North America were aware that the Earth is round. Ice destroyed the world before Noah. Flood destroyed the Hopi world of Noah's contemporaries. Modern Hopi shamans say fire will be the destroyer of our current world — sooner than anyone would like to think.

— BEFORE 6500 BC

Prehistoric Nuclear War

A single projectile, charged with all the power of the universe; an incandescent column of smoke and fire as bright as 10,000 suns [from] a shaft fatal as the rod of death.

Endowed with the force of thousand-eyed Indra's thunder: It was destructive to all living creatures....Hostile warriors fell to the earth like trees burnt down in a raging fire....Elephants...fell to earth uttering fierce cries...burnt by the energy of that weapon.

A substance like fire has sprung into existence...blistering hills, rivers and trees. All...are being reduced to ashes....You cruel and evil ones, drunk with pride, through that iron bolt you shall become exterminators of your race.

The Mahabharata: Ancient Hindu poem

Nuclear cruise missiles of antiquity?

   Dr Robert Oppenheimer, chief scientist in the creation of the atomic bomb, believed it possible that a nuclear war was fought in the twilight of prehistory. He was well versed in Hindu legends chronicling the appearance of a new and unknown weapon, used at the climax of an antediluvian world war called the *Mahabharata*, where whole races were *burned beyond recognition* and survivors suffered what appears to be radiation sickness: *Their hair and nails fell out.*

— BEFORE 4500 BC

The Great Flood

I will cause it to rain upon the Earth forty days and forty nights; and every living substance that I have made will I destroy from off the face of the Earth.

The Book of Genesis

...heavy rain fell from the sky by night and day. Men tried to climb the houses but the houses submerged. The sky fell down...

Popul Vuh: Bible of the Mayan Indians

Mankind had gone back to mud.

Babylonian records of the Flood

Ancient peoples of Asia, Europe and the Americas share predictions and accounts of a great flooding of the Earth. When looked at collectively as in Charles Berlitz's book, *Doomsday 1999*, a conclusion could be drawn that the legendary island continent of Atlantis was more fact than myth. Its catastrophic plunge beneath the waves in one terrible night may have been the source of Noah's Flood.

The Battle of Salamis

...all-seeing Zeus grants Athena's prayer
that the wooden wall not only shall not fail,
but will aid you and your children...
Divine Salamis, you will bring death to
women's sons.

Aristonice: Pythia of Delphi

Athens, the cradle of Western rational thinking, was facing annihilation by Xerxes' Persian hordes. The time had come to give logic a break and consult the Oracle of Delphi. The Athenians sought in her poetry a divine omen of victory for the Greek fleet gathering off Salamis. Admiral Themistocles interpreted her correctly that the wooden walls of his galleys would make many a Persian mother weep for her sons drowned off the island of Salamis.

"Beware the Ides of March!"

At the onset of 44 BC, after the death of his arch-rival, Pompey, Julius Caesar seized the reins of power from the crumbling Roman Republic. Caesar scarcely had time to celebrate his victory. Vestricius Spurinna, a Forum temple priest — fresh from examining the entrails of a sacrificial beast — came to warn him: "Beware the Ides of March." Spurinna was convinced that March 15 boded evil for the new dictator. Against this and many other portents of doom, Caesar was drawn like a magnet to his fate. On March 15, Senators conspiring to assassinate him set the political bait; they promised they would vote him king if he visited the Senate that day. As Caesar climbed the steps of the Senate, he passed Spurinna and remarked, "The Ides of March have come." "Yes, Caesar," responded the priest, "come but not gone." A few minutes later Rome's most illustrious dictator lay dead and bleeding from twenty-three knife wounds.

— AD 0 to 33

The Birth and Death of Christ

The birth of Christ, his entry into Jerusalem upon a donkey, and the details of Christ's crucifixion were foretold by Hebrew prophets between 500 and 1,000 years before these events happened.

But thou, Bethlehem Ephratah, though thou be little among thousands of Judah, yet out of thee shall he come forth unto me that is to be the ruler in Israel: whose goings forth have been from of old, from everlasting.

Micah (c. 721 BC) Mic 5:2

Rejoice greatly, O daughter of Zion; shout, unto thee: he is just, and having salvation; lowly, and riding upon an ass...

Zechariah (c. 160 BC) Zek 9:9

For dogs have encompassed me: the assembly of the wicked have enclosed me; they pierced my hands and my feet. I may tell all my bones: they look and stare upon me. They part my garments among them, and cast lots upon my vesture.

The Psalms 22:16-18

— AD 70

The Karma of the Crucifixion:

The Destruction of Jerusalem

Thine enemies shall cast a trench about thee, and compass thee round, and keep thee in on every side, and shall lay thee even with the ground, and thy children within thee: and they shall not leave thee one stone upon another: because thou knewest not the time of thy visitation.

Y'shua (AD 30-33) 19:43-44

Pre-destiny missed?

According to the prophet from Galilee, this Old Testament prediction was misinterpreted by a prophetically-biased Sanhedrin. The orthodox Hebrews desired a warrior Messiah rather than a prince of peace and may have crucified their savior. Thirty-seven years after the blood of Y'shua dried upon the Cross, blood flowed in the streets of Jerusalem when the Romans crushed a Jewish rebellion. Three legions lay siege to the city and encircled it with a trench so no citizen could escape. The people of the Holy City put up a heroic fight, but in time all their defenses were systematically wiped out. The last defenders retreated into the Temple of Solomon, where they met death by fire and blade. The inhabitants who had not died from famine and plague were drawn and quartered by the legionaries; the men and the old were slaughtered, the women and children were sent into slavery. Then the entire city was razed except one bleak tower, left as a tombstone to mark where Jerusalem had once been.

The Coming of the *Lost* White Brother

At the height of the Aztec Empire, a collective vision existed among priests and citizens alike that bearded visitors from across the eastern sea would soon appear on their shores. All native American peoples of that time shared a vision of the return of Pahána, the lost white brother. The Hopi Indians said that if Pahána returned with the symbol of the cross, this showed he had not kept a balance between his inventions and his spirit and he would bring a holocaust upon the native Americans. A string of evil omens assailed the Aztec Empire at the advent of the white brother. There was famine, an eclipse, an earthquake and the cold light of a comet bathing the capital city for several months. All were seen as omens of imminent doom.

In 1507 King Montezuma — the Aztec Napoleon and empire builder — went to Tlillancalmecatl (the place of heavenly learning) to divine the meaning of these premonitions. Occultists placed before him an ash-colored crane. While in trance, Montezuma peered at a vision reflected in the mirror-like crest of the bird's head and saw the firmament beset by flaming torches. The flames melted into a vision of massed invaders astride large deer. (No Aztec had ever seen horses.) At the same time, Pranazin, Montezuma's sister, fell in a death-like faint. On recovering her senses, she described a vision of great ships from the east, crowded with alien men in strange attire, with metal casques atop their bearded heads.

Her dream men were destined to plant their cross banners upon the rubble of the Aztec Empire. In 1520 Aztec nightmares became reality when Hernando Cortés, leading a marauding army of mounted conquistadors, seized and destroyed the Aztec Empire.

The Execution of Montmorency

The Lily of the Dauphin will proceed to Nancy.
The Elector of the Empire as far as Flanders.
A new prison for the great Montmorency,
Outside the usual place delivered up
to famous punishment [clere peyne] **C9 Q18**

The French prophet Michel Nostradamus (1503-1566) could transmit detailed futures in very few words. In the first two lines he identifies the next and future French ruler, who would use the title *Dauphin* before coronation. He also mentions the city of Nancy, which was liberated in 1633 by the same king, Louis XIII. Line two tells us the reason: to free Philip Christopher von Sötern, the *Elector* of the Holy Roman Empire, who was imprisoned near *Flanders* (Brussels).

Lines three and four take a retroactive look at the execution in 1632 of the popular governor of Languedoc, Montmorency. Nostradamus calls him *the great*, the nickname of this popular hero who was tricked by Cardinal Richelieu into supporting Louis' idiot brother in his claim for the throne. Montmorency was condemned to die at the newly constructed Hôtel de Ville. The prophet correctly calls it a *new prison* and *outside the usual place* for execution.

Louis' punishment of Montmorency was indeed famous at the time. Even the Queen of England and the Pope pleaded for leniency on his behalf, but to no avail. The original words for *famous punishment* are *clere peyne*. The swordsman who beheaded the governor was named Clerepeyne! All this was seen by Nostradamus over seventy-five years before it happened.

8

— 1789 to 1794
The *French* Revolution

At about AD 1800 great tribulations will come. Arrogance and vanity will rule the world. Cocks will arise in France, and they will break the lilies, kill monarchs and oppress the Christian faith and the Church. Priests and servants of the Church will be reduced to misery, the young led to atheism, and republics will be established in the whole world... **Pastor Bartholomaeus (1642)**

People will be stirred up against their king....Paris was never in such great trouble. **(C6 Q23)**

...From the enslaved people, songs, chants and demands. The Princes and Lords are held captive in prisons. **(C1 Q14)**

...conflict will take place at the Tuilleries by the 500....Fire and bloody slicing [during]...the advent of the common people....The Christian Church will be persecuted more fiercely than ever it was in Africa, and this will last to the year 1792 which they will believe marks the renewal of time. **Nostradamus (1555-1557) Excerpts from C9 Q34, C9 Q20 & Epistle**

The cock was the symbol of the French republicans; the lilies, the symbol of the *fleur-de-lis* upon royal livery. An anti-god religion called The Cult of Reason was established by the new republic. The French Revolution spread republicanism around the European world. The Tuilleries didn't even exist when Nostradamus foresaw it being stormed by 513 Fédérés, better known as the Five Hundred Marseillaise. The Church was disbanded, the monks and nuns guillotined or thrown out on the streets. Also 1792 was the year the revolutionaries believed marked the beginning of a new age. They celebrated this by replacing the old Christian calendar with a new one.

— 1800 to 1815
The Rise and Fall of *Napoleon*

An Emperor will be born near Italy... Napoleon was born in Corsica off the Italian coast.

...He will cost his Empire very dearly....He is less a prince than a butcher. **C1 Q60**

From simple soldier he will attain to Empire...Italy, Spain, and the English tremble; he will be greatly attentive to foreign women. **C4 Q54**

Napoleon's greatest lovers were Josephine, born in the Caribbean; Marie Walenska, a Polish princess; and his second Empress, Marie-Louise — Austrian.

For fourteen years he will hold his tyranny... **C7 Q13**

Napoleon ruled as First Consul, then later as Emperor of France, from 1800 to 1814. He fell from power as a result of his disastrous Russian campaign of 1812, of which the prophet said:

...The kingdom rushes to great misfortune....A mass of men approach from Russia. The destroyer ["Neapalluon" in Greek] will ruin the old city: he will see his Roman empire quite desolated....He would not know how to extinguish the great flame... **C4 Q82**

Moscow was set on fire. Napoleon's army was forced to desert the charred ruins at the onset of the Russian winter.

BONAPARTE

...Ready to fight he will desert. The chief adversary [Russia] will be victorious. The rear guard will make a defense, those who falter dying in the white country. **C4 Q75**

Napoleon deserted the remnant of his retreating army, which was destined to die, almost to a man, in the snows of Russia.

In the third month...the boar and the leopard meet on the battlefield...

In June 1815, three months after his escape from exile, Napoleon — who Nostradamus calls the boar — fought the Duke of Wellington at Waterloo. Napoleon called Wellington the Leopard of England.

...The fatigued leopard looks up to heaven and sees an eagle playing with the sun. **C1 Q23**

...[They] will appear to the victor...neither bugle nor cries will stop the [French] soldiers. In time liberty and peace is achieved through death... **C1 Q38**

At Waterloo, Wellington's battered army had withstood every French attack. At sunset, Napoleon hurled his own Imperial Guard in one final charge. As the French attack mounted the ridge, the Duke and his men could see the brass eagles atop the standards of Napoleon's Old Guard swinging against the setting sun. Moments later an English volley shattered their charge. The French were routed.

...The great empire will be exchanged for a little...petty place...[to] which he will come to lay down his scepter. **C1 Q32**

Napoleon was exiled to the tiny island of Saint Helena, where he died in 1821.

Selections from **The Centuries** by Nostradamus (1555-1557)

— 19th CENTURY

Wars and Revolutions

The Napoleonic Wars

Prussia and Russia will divide Poland among themselves. Fulfilled in 1793.

In 1805 a war will break out between France and Austria, and if Austria will not make peace, she shall lose everything.

Austrian forces were routed by Napoleon at Austerlitz in 1805. Francis I quickly sued for peace and saved his empire.

A year later, in 1806, war between Prussia and France will begin. In 1807 another war, this time between France and Russia, will break out.

Napoleon fought and defeated Prussia in 1806. His forces collided with the Russians in 1807.

The 1848 Pan-European Revolution

In 1848, a terrible revolution will spread over all Europe. Kings and emperors will descend from their thrones.

Europe did experience widespread revolutions in 1848. The French king Louis Philippe was deposed. **THE PROPHECY OF WARSAW (made by a Polish monk in 1790)**

The Industrial Revolution

Horses Put Out to Pasture

Horses will be kept for pleasure and ornament, nothing more, in the days to come.

Moll Pitcher (1780s)

Discovery of Electricity and Radio Waves

When the animal tamed by man begins to speak after great efforts and difficulty, the lightning so harmful to the rod will be taken from the earth and suspended in the air. **Nostradamus (1555)**
C3 Q44

Railroads, Cars and Planes

Iron roads will be built, and iron monsters will bark through the wilderness. Cars without horse and shaft will come, and men will fly through the air like birds. **Stormberger (18th century)**

The Internal Combustion Engine

Carriages will be moved by a strong and beautiful and simple admixture of aqueous and atmospheric gases easily condensed, so simply ignited, and so imparted by a machine resembling our [steam] engines, as to be entirely concealed and manageable between forward wheels.

Andrew Jackson Davis (1856)

Radio and Television

...magnificent music conducted on wires hundreds of miles away will play at the instigation of man. **Moll Pitcher (1780s)**

The Helicopter

Instruments of flying may be formed in which a man, sitting at his ease and meditating on any subject, may beat the air with his artificial wings after the manner of birds.

Roger Bacon (thirteenth century)

International Air Travel

...aerial cars...will move through the sky from country to country; and their beautiful influence will produce a universal brotherhood of acquaintance. **Andrew Jackson Davis (1856)**

Man on the Moon

He [man] will come to take himself to the corner of Luna [the Moon] where he will be taken and placed on alien land. **Nostradamus (1557) C9 Q65**

1912 —

The Sinking of the Titanic

One evening in 1897 Morgan Robertson, retired sailor and writer of short stories, began to unravel the mental knots of his all-day writer's block. As he relaxed, he felt the familiar presence of what he called his "astral writing partner" take the helm and cast him adrift in an ocean of images. A vision for a new story coalesced through the imagined fog and icy waters of the North Atlantic. A great ocean liner on her maiden voyage, her three twisting screws pushing 75,000 tons at twenty-five knots, cleaved the chilled waters on a collision course with an iceberg!

Robertson saw the name *Titan* on her bow, and knew this 800-foot ocean liner would have nineteen watertight compartments, giving both passengers and crew the illusion that she was unsinkable. The folly of such a claim would reveal itself when, on slicing her bow against the unseen iceberg, *Titan* would sink and 3,000 of her passengers would drown because there were only twenty-four lifeboats.

Robertson set to writing *The Wreck of the Titan, or Futility* his fictional chronicle of the ultimate maritime disaster, which was to take place in the mid-Atlantic on a moonless April night. Fiction became reality 14 years later. On her maiden voyage, the *Titanic* cut the icy waters of the North Atlantic off Newfoundland, her three propellers churning 66,000 tons at twenty-three knots toward an unseen iceberg. There were only twenty-two lifeboats aboard, since the 883-foot ocean liner was considered unsinkable. In spite of her designer's arrogant claim, the collision with the iceberg had sliced open three of her sixteen watertight compartments — one too many to survive. The *Titanic* and a majority of her 2,224 passengers faced an icy death on the moonless night of 14 April 1912.

— 1 AUGUST 1914

World War I

When in the outskirts of the forest the iron road will be finished, and there the iron horse will be seen, a war will begin, to last for twice two years. It will be fought with iron fortresses that move without horses, and with powers that come from the earth and fall from the sky.
Stormberger (eighteenth century)

The day World War I began was pinpointed two centuries before it happened by a simple and reclusive cowherd in the Bavarian forests bordering Czechoslovakia. On 1 August 1914, a new railroad line between Kalteneck and Deggendorf (running on the edge of Stormberger's forest) officially opened — the day the hostilities began. The war did last four years and saw the introduction of terrible new weapons such as mines *from the earth*, poison gas *falling from the sky* and tanks — *iron fortresses that move.*

Rasputin and the Death of the

Gregory Rasputin, mystic hypnotist, faith healer and womanizing monk, had great influence over the Czar and Czarina because of his miraculous cure of the young heir to the Russian throne, the hemophiliac Prince Alexi. As the year 1916 drew to a close, the "mad" monk sensed his own impending death. A prophecy made eleven years earlier, when he met the palm reader Count Louis Hamon, must have fed his own premonition. The English count, better known as "Cheiro," was also a master hypnotist. After fighting an unsuccessful battle of hypnotic wills, Cheiro broke off, declaring that Rasputin would be poisoned, stabbed and shot. He also saw the monk being thrown into the icy waters of the Neva river and left beneath the ice to die.

In a letter written in December of 1916, Rasputin wrote to the Czarina predicting his own murder would take place before New Year's Day 1917. He promised the Czarina that her family would flourish if he was killed by peasants, but if he was killed by princes she and all her family would die within two years.

Around Christmas time, Rasputin was poisoned, shot and thrown beneath the ice of the Neva by Russian princes. Czar Nicholas II, the Czarina and all their children were shot by Bolshevik guards on 16 July 1918, little more than a year-and-a-half after Rasputin's murder.

The Stock Market Crash

Right after this horrible war there will come a time when money will have no value. For 200 guilders not even a loaf of bread will be available, and yet there shall be no famine. Money will be made of iron, and gold shall become so valuable that for a few gold coins a small farm can be bought. **Stormberger (eighteenth century)**

After World War I, Germany experienced a catastrophic economic depression. For a time, the German mark was almost worthless, inspiring the more eccentric to paper their walls with banknotes. Stormberger had prophesied the minting of money and inflation 200 years before anyone had a clue about such things, let alone an eighteenth-century cowherd.

[He] will have a great amount of moneys to care for. In the adverse forces that will come then in 1929, care should be taken lest this, without the more discretion in small things, be taken from the entity. (№2723-1) **Edgar Cayce (a trance reading made in 1925 for a businessman)**

In the spring of '33 will be the real definite improvements. (№311-8)

Edgar Cayce (a reading made in 1931 about the Depression)

Though Edgar Cayce was known as the "sleeping prophet" for his habit of giving trance readings while reclining unconscious on a couch, most of his clients didn't take his sage future advice lying down. Many fortunes were saved through his advice prior to the Stock Market Crash of 1929. He was also correct about the economy improving by 1933. That spring, a new president, Roosevelt, and a New Deal for the USA were inaugurated.

— 1939 to 1945

World War II

When...?

Great discord. Warfare will arise...unions will be split apart including England and the Mesopotamia of Europe [France] in [19]45 and others to '41, '42, and '37.

Nostradamus (1557) Epistle

Germany broke its Non-aggression Pact with Russia in 1941; America broke relations with Japan and Germany that same year. In 1936-1937, Hitler openly opposed the Treaty of Versailles by re-occupying the Rhineland and instigating full-scale re-armament.

Why...?

This treaty is not a peace, but an armistice of twenty years. **Marshal Foch, French general, commenting on the Treaty of Versailles (1919)**

The interval between world wars...

Two or three decades after the first great war will come a second, still greater war. Almost all nations of the world will be involved. Millions of men will die, without being soldiers. Fire will fall from the sky and many great cities will be destroyed. **Stormberger (eighteenth century)**

The perpetrator...

The ruler [Hitler] will avail himself of the spirit of discord and will enter other countries by force to govern over them...exceedingly great shall be the suffering in the countries devastated by him...new signs will arise [the swastika]. As he had come, he will go, leaving the world in chaos. **Pastor Bartholomaeus (c. 1642)**

When America will enter the war...

The only likelihood will be in 41....This too — if the people pray, and live as they pray — will pass... **Edgar Cayce (1939) №1949-1**

Hiroshima and Nagasaki...

Near the harbors within two cities, there will happen two scourges the like of which was never before seen. Famine, pestilence within [radiation?], people put out by the sword. They cry for help from the great immortal God! **Nostradamus (1555) C2 Q6**

And peace...

... to be established in 44 and 45. **Edgar Cayce (1941) №1152-11**

Earthquakes of this Century:

As seen by Edgar Cayce

We do not find that this particular district [San Francisco] in the present year will suffer...While portions of the country will be affected, we see these will be farther east than San Francisco — or those south, where there has not been heretofore the greater activity.

(January 1936: №270-35)

UPDATE: The town of Bishop in central California, south-east of San Francisco, suffered a severe earthquake on 10 May 1936.

As has oft given, Jupiter and Uranus influences in the affairs of the world appear the strongest on or about October 15th to 20th...there may be expected...violent wind storms — two earth-quakes, one in California and another in Japan — tidal waves following, one to the southern portion of the isles near Japan!

(August 1926: №195-32)

UPDATE: Heavy storms slammed into the Kuril Islands near Japan on 14 and 15 October. Earthquakes hit Japan on 19 and 20 October. Three tremors shook California between 22 and 26 October.

Cayce believed that major earth changes would rack the world until 1998. They would begin after 1958, when, he says:

The Earth will be broken up in the western portion of America... (1934: №3976-15)

When there is the first breaking up of some conditions in the South Sea [South Pacific]...or in the Mediterranean, and the Etna area, then we may know it [the earth change] *has begun.* (1932: №311-8)

UPDATE: In 1961 Alaska, suffered one of this century's worst quakes. Mountains shifted an average of five feet. The sea floor rose fifty feet in some offshore areas. In 1963 the island of Bali in the South Pacific suffered a major quake, and a new volcano appeared off Java over the remains of Krakatoa. In 1960 Morocco had a quake that lifted the offshore Mediterranean seabed 3,000 feet! Mt Etna erupted violently in 1959, rising twenty-five feet.

16

— 1963

The Assassination of John Kennedy

In 1952 Jeane Dixon stood in deep prayer before the statue of the Virgin Mary at St Matthew's Cathedral in Washington DC. The astrologer and prophetess, already respected for predicting India's independence and the death of President Roosevelt, was suddenly gripped by what would become one of history's most well-known forecasts. She says she saw the dark church interior lit by the brilliant sun-soaked image of the US White House with the shimmering numbers 1-9-6-0 hovering above it. Pulled like a magnet, her consciousness floated toward the main door, where a young man with striking blue eyes stood upon the threshold. An inner voice impressed upon her that this young man, a Democrat, would be elected President in 1960 and was destined to die violently while in office.

In 1956 she described her vision to Jack Anderson, the publisher of *Parade Magazine*, beginning what would become the most pre-documented prediction in history. Dixon's further visions were reported to credible witnesses: one in October 1963 foresaw shadow hands representing death removing the Vice President's name plate from his office door. Later she saw the letters "o" and "s" for the beginning and "d" for the end of the assassin's name — (Os)wal(d).

During November of 1963, Dixon's friends noticed her increasing concern about her premonition of doom for the young President. She even tried to warn him through her White House contacts, but to no avail. On the 22nd, while lunching with friends at the Mayflower Hotel in Washington, she suddenly became so distraught that she couldn't touch her food. "Something dreadful is going to happen to the President today," she declared.

Around that same moment, at a sixth-floor window of the school book depository in Dallas, Texas, Lee Harvey Oswald and perhaps several other assassins positioned around Dealy Plaza, were taking aim at President Kennedy's motorcade.

Back at the Mayflower Hotel, Jeane Dixon and her friends were finishing lunch. The orchestra suddenly fell silent. The conductor announced that someone had just taken a shot at the President. Her friends tried to comfort her, saying that he must have avoided danger. "No," she replied, "the President is dead...you will learn that he is dead."

— 1968 to 1969

Atlantis Resurfacing!

Evidences of this lost civilization are to be found in the Pyrenees and Morrocco on the one hand, British Honduras, Jucatán and America upon the other...especially, or notably, in Bimini and the Gulf Stream... **Edgar Cayce (1932) №364-3**

Poseida will be among the first portions of Atlantis to rise again. Expect it in sixty-eight and sixty-nine (1968, '69). Not so far away! **Edgar Cayce (1940) №958-3L-1**

In 1968 a diving expedition was arranged to explore what seemed to be symmetrically-shaped stones off the island of Bimini. The divers discovered what appeared to be marble pillars. Also awaiting them in the turquoise Caribbean waters was a great road, or esplanade, fashioned out of giant blocks in the manner of Incan masonry. The formation disappeared and reappeared along the ocean floor for 3,000 feet. Since then, towers, stairways, walls and even pyramids have been discovered around other Caribbean islands and on the sea floor beneath the Gulf Stream off the coast of the eastern USA.

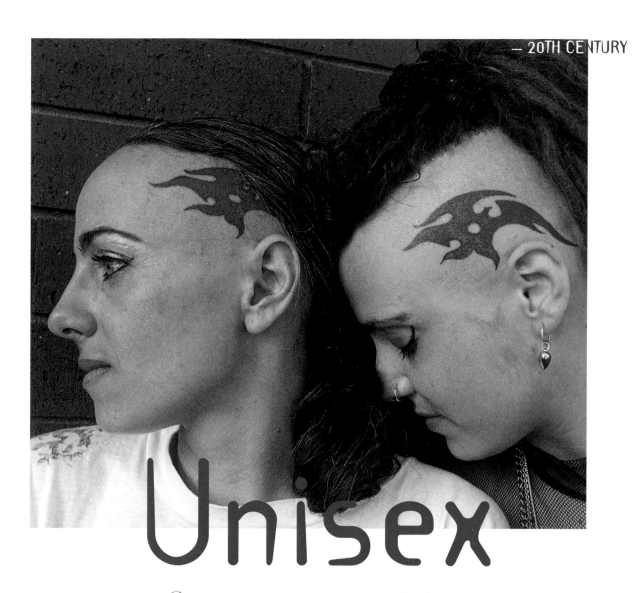

Unisex

And now a word in uncouth rhyme
Of what shall be in future time:
For in these wondrous far-off days,
The women shall adopt a craze
To dress like men and trousers wear,
And cut off their locks of hair.

Mother Shipton (c. 1561)

The *Poisoning* of a Pope

When the great Roman's tomb is found, the day after a pope shall be elected. The Senate will not approve of him. His blood is poisoned in the Sacred Chalice.

[He] will be mocked by his electors; this enterprising and prudent person will suddenly be reduced to silence.

He who will have government of the great cape will be led to execute in certain cases. The twelve red ones will spoil the cover. Under murder, murder will be perpetrated.

They will cause him to die because of his too great goodness and mildness. Stricken by fear, they will lead him to his death in the night.

Selections from *The Centuries* by Nostradamus (1555-57). Excerpts from: C3 Q65, C10 Q12 & C4 Q11

The prophet wrote a most shocking chronicle of future papal intrigue. He foresaw a pope elected soon after the unearthing of St Peter's Tomb from beneath the Vatican. The tomb was discovered in 1978, the year Pope John Paul I was elected by the College of Cardinals. Though the public loved Gianpaolo's sunny smile and simple humanity, the conservative Cardinals were enraged by his radical reforms. He died a month after his coronation, the details of his passing shrouded forever in secrecy. It was divulged by certain intimate sources that he was found dead in his bed the morning he planned to expose the Vatican Bank scandal. Cardinal Villot, head of the Vatican Curia — the Papal Cabinet of twelve Cardinals — had removed from the Pope's lap the papers listing the crimes and people to be dismissed, along with the bottle of Effortil on his night stand that John Paul used to alleviate his low blood pressure. According to investigative reporter, David Yallop, author of *In God's Name* (Bantam), Villot passed false information to the press and made sure the Pope's body was embalmed before an autopsy was performed. From his vantage point beyond time, Nostradamus implicates these twelve red ones as the Pope's murderers.

— 1986

The Chernobyl Disaster

It is here that the great conflict will occur — America, Russia...the time is not far off....The Lady [vision of the Virgin Mary] extended her hands in a protective gesture over a region that seemed to me to be the Ukraine. And I saw an infernal fire raging above, to the left of me, in Russia. It appeared to me to be the result of a great explosion that erupted from the earth. The lady said: "And so you see, nothing remains." And looked upon what was virtually a deserted plain.

Seen by a girl from Holland between 1945 and 1954

A ghost town exists in Russia. Open doors creak in the wind, which whispers in weeds that border roads and choke vegetable gardens. The surrounding unmanaged fields grow wheat that no living person can ever use for bread. This is the town of Pripyat, a once-teeming Ukrainian settlement of 45,000 set in the shadow of Chernobyl nuclear reactor number four. The explosion, which covered large areas of Europe with radioactive dust, left a gaping hole that has been sealed with 300,000 tons of concrete and 6,000 tons of lead. The wound is bandaged but the festering sore continues. Between thirty-one to 7,000 people died from the short-term effects of radiation. Future victims wait in the queue, with seemingly healthy bodies brewing cancers. Chernobyl's silhouette in the silent Ukrainian countryside stands as its own prophecy of other hazards awaiting us in the nuclear age.

The Cold War Ends

A clash with the "barbarians" will weaken America but put it into alliance with Russia. In fact, the clash may already have happened, being dubbed the cold war, the Korean Police Action and Vietnam. The alliance with the Soviet Union should follow soon but with America in a weaker position than now. **Alan Vaughan (1973) Ptrns**

One day the two great leaders will be friends: their great power will be seen to grow. The new land [America] will be at the height of its power; to the man of blood the number is reported...

The East shall quake for fear of those two brothers of the North who are yet not brothers... **Nostradamus (1555-1557). Excerpts: C2 Q89 & Epistle**

By the 1980s two Cold War superpowers, up to their necks in nuclear weapons, had reached parity in the race to see which country had the greatest destructive potential. The numbers game of nuclear and conventional arms reductions for the coming 1990s may be implied by Nostradamus. The *man of blood* could be Gorbachev, who carries a bloody birthmark on his head and is responsible for the reforms that brought a thaw to the Cold War and an opening for American/Russian friendship.

In the original prophecy, Nostradamus uses the word *demis* for friend. His often-applied device of altering correct spelling and punctuation to make a play on words implies either the meaning "*demis*" — to halve, to set apart; or *d'amis* — friend; in other words, what he wrote later on in his Epistle to Henry II of France, as the *brothers who are not yet brothers*.

Nostradamus appears to view today's promises of disarmament with caution, and in other prophecies warns that the first steps toward a US-Russian alliance at the end of the 1980s may collapse by the mid-90s in a nuclear war. Even if a Pollyanna would like to see the combined destructive force of our nuclear bombs reduced by 90 percent, she couldn't rest easy about a future free of nuclear war. If there are still enough bombs to kill every human being once rather than the current 800 times, that's more than enough!

Part One: A Crossroads

at the *end* of Time

The ancient cultures have each had their unique concepts of time. The Mayan astrologer of pre-Colombian Mexico calculated epochs as precisely as modern science with its computerized mathematics. The Hindu priest-astrologer recorded the position of stars as they appeared in our skies over 90,000 years ago. They clocked passages of time so vast that one million years is but a quiver in Brahma's eyelid. Contrary to this leisurely drift down a Gangean river of time, the priestly timekeepers of Western cultures, such as the Christian apostles, wait impatiently for salvation to come at the end of their relatively tiny millennium.

Astrologers the world over pin their system of time upon silent stars, perhaps unaware that their counterparts in other ages gauged their own invisible clocks by the movement of sky and Earth. Yet as sure as the stars have no mindfulness of the projections we make upon them, and as steady as is the glow of their cold light on our self-fashioned ages of glory and folly, a reckoning has been set within each human concept of time. A moment has been preordained by some mysterious synchronicity, when all the great clocks of the centuries will tick no more. Without their knowing, these ancient diviners have all ascertained approximately the same moment for the end of time. It is coming very soon — somewhere around the Judeo-Christian calendar year of AD 2000.

In Egypt there stands a prophecy in stone. The Great Pyramid of Giza, built between 2500 and 3000 BC, is more than a megalomaniac's mausoleum. It is a measurement of time spanning the entire Adamic Age, from Adam and Eve's exile from the Garden of Eden during the era of Genesis 6,000 years ago to the present. Esoteric archaeologists posit that the ascending passageway leading deep inside the great stone edifice to the King's Chamber is not only the tunnel to a pharaoh's tomb but also a symbolic time line as well, pinpointing important dates in human history. It is generally believed by esoterics that each "pyramid inch" (approximately one standard inch) running along the ascending passageway corresponds in time to one Judeo-Christian year. Each change in the passageway's design signifies an important milestone in Adamic history.

We observe the first significant date after escaping the blinding light of the Egyptian sun and stumbling down a dark and stuffy corridor. Soon we meet the cramped beginning of the ascending passageway to the King's Chamber. Our walk upward through time begins with pyramid inch 1,486, which is said to correspond to the year Moses led the tribes of Israel out of Egypt and Pharaoh's charioteers took a bath in the Red Sea (1486 BC). We crawl for a seemingly interminable period up through this ancient stone version of an air conditioning duct, at last emerging in the spacious stairway called the Grand Gallery. The entrance to this awesome flight of steps corresponds to the year AD 33, which witnessed the crucifixion of one of the many Jewish claimants to the title of Messiah, provoking the birth of Christianity.

After a long ascent, we haul ourselves over a giant stone step marking 1844, the year Christian Millerites mistakenly believed the world would end. In fact, 1844 did see the violent end of the Mormon prophet Joseph Smith, who was arrested and jailed "for his own protection" and then murdered by his orthodox Christian jailers "for their protection."

We leave the Grand Gallery behind and begin the final, latter-day leg of our journey. We shuffle on flat ground through a tight access way and past an antechamber finally arriving at the King's Chamber itself. Architectural esoterics say this last plateau beyond the ascending passageway represents the final scene of the Adamic Age when all the accumulated learning and "bad karma" sown in the past will be reaped. From the great step onward, each pyramid inch represents a month rather than a year, as time and historical events take on a new density and begin a final acceleration toward the end, not unlike the candle which flames most brightly just before it burns itself out.

First we crawl through the short passage into the antechamber which marks the beginning and end of our slaughterhouse century's First World War: August 1914 to November 1918. Next we gingerly duck through another entry way signifying the year 1936, when a shift in the Earth's magnetic core was due — one that would trigger a catastrophic slide of the Earth's crust by 1998, according to American prophet Edgar Cayce.

Once through the last passage, we stand inside our final destination: the stark enclosure housing an empty sarcophagus. Even the more down-to-the-dig archaeologists theorize it may not ever have been intended for a pharaoh's remains, but was instead a symbol of the

LATTER-DAY DATELINE

Are we living in the latter days before the end of the world and the advent of Christ? That is what most televangelists declare, while they hedge their bets with a quote from Matthew 24:42: *Ye know not what hour your Lord doth come...*
Dating a future event has been one of the hardest feats of prophecy. Only a handful of daring seers have stood the test. Their predictions for the twentieth century and beyond are listed in the time line that runs throughout Part One.
Our common future seems destined to die out in one final surge of dates, breaking on the shores of the next millennium.

resurrection of a future Messiah scheduled to appear in the Egyptian priesthood's version of the Second Coming.

Most interpreters of pyramid prophecy claim that the final measurement between the entrance of the chamber and the opposing wall represents the latter-days before the end of the world. It is the time when mankind will either begin a new stage of evolution in consciousness or suffer a global suicide. The entrance of the chamber marks inch 1,953, the time some prophets say that the emergence or re-birth of Osiris, the Egyptian Christ, should have occurred. Whether we have yet to recognize a new Christ-Osiris walking among us, only time will tell. However, if by giving an inch fate will take a mile's worth of dates, then 1953 also marks the death rattle of the Adamic Age. Measuring the final steps of our journey brings us smack into the opposite wall of the King's Chamber by September of 2001, when time, as the Egyptian priest knew it, will stop.

The 1990s pinpoint the final millisecond before the cosmic hour is up. Berosus, the great Chaldean astronomer of the second century BC, set his alarm for the year 25,872. His priestly doubles in 4th Dynasty Egypt measure the final tick of their sidereal digital by computing the sum of the crossed diagonals of the Great Pyramid, giving us the total of 25,826.6 pyramid inches. This means end-time could happen any time between the year 2000 and September 2001!

The Persian Mythratic calendar of 3,000-year cycles sets the time for the forces of good and evil to battle it out once and for all at the close of this century. The last Celtic Druid 500-year cycle ends around 2000. The Teutonic tribes of ancient Germany, like their Viking and Celtic neighbors, share similar prophetic visions about the coming end-time. They use variations on a theme called Götterdämmerung (The Twilight of the Gods), a time when heaven and earth are destroyed by a final battle and its residual ecological catastrophes.

The Cabalistic-Hermetic schools, which once formed an occult underground throughout the Christian Era, predict doomsday at the end of their grand calendar of 7,000 years — that's AD 2000; the Tibetans call it quits after fourteen incarnations of their patron saint Chenrezi as the Dalai Lama, their spiritual-political ruler. The fourteenth and current Dalai Lama has considered filling his post by ballot, which would break the spiritual tradition of searching for the true reincarnation of Chenrezi. Custodians of the Tibetan occult sciences grumble that the last true expression of the soul of Chenrezi was the thirteenth Dalai Lama, who died in 1932.

Those who believe that the cycles are only closing a great chapter in human history and then resume their course without much fanfare should be warned: Very few of the most accurate seers from the closing Adamic Age view a tomorrow beyond the first decade of the next century. There are two possible reasons for this: either we will destroy all our tomorrows with either a nuking or a thorough polluting of Earth, or the prophets of the Adamic era are blocked by a subconscious fear and loathing of the upcoming changes that must precede our entry into the next great era.

AD 1900 —

AD 1910 —

1900	1902	1904	1910	1911	1912
"Evil Century"	Edward VII	British invade Tibet	Death of Edward VII	Chinese leave Tibet	The sinking of the
–Nostradamus	crowned	– Lama-astrologers	– Cheiro (1902)	– Lama-astrologers	Titanic
(1555)	– Cheiro (1902)	(before 1850)		(c. 1850)	– Cheiro (1911)

24

Islam will end the day a man walks on the lamp of the night! (the Moon): A prediction-in-jest attributed to Mohammed. The faithful of Allah, like the rest of us, saw the seemingly impossible fulfilled when men walked upon the "lamp of the night" in 1969. Could this signify that the Islamic Apocalypse has begun? Arab terrorist factions have been actively seeking nuclear and chemical weapons since 1969. Add to this the nuclear and chemical arms race between Israel and its neighbors and one might see this prophecy come true before 2000.

Like to know when the world will end? Here are some dates proffered by Christianity: 996, 1186, 1533, 1665, 1866, 1931, 1945, 1954, 1960, 1965, and 1967. Christian prophets have gambled on more dates for doomsday than any other religion. Their next cry of "wolf!" won't be a solo, but just another wail in a chorus singing a song of doom for 2000.

AD 1920 —

AD 1930 —

| 1914-1918 World War I – Lama-astrologers (c. 1850) | 1920 Hoover not chosen as US President – Evangeline Addams (1920) | 1921 Enrico Caruso dies – Evangeline Addams (1921) | 1927-29 Mussolini seizes Libya – Cheiro (1925) | 1929 Stock Market Crash – Edgar Cayce (1925) | 1933 The New Deal – Edgar Cayce (1929) |

According to Masoudi, a medieval Coptic historian, the Great Pyramid of Giza was built by King Surid to preserve the spiritual and mathematical knowledge of Egypt in a giant stone scripture that would weather not only the coming great flood but a future world conflagration as well. Esoteric scholars claim that the Pyramid chronicles life from the time of Adam and Eve to the year 2001, when the world, as we are told by Surid's dream interpreters, will be destroyed by fire coming from the constellation of Leo.

THE PYRAMID

Berosus the Chaldean Astronomer (second century BC) consigns us to Satan's space odyssey when the current sidereal precession of equinoxes draws to a close by 2001. He sees all terrestrial life and limb consumed by fire during a planetary alignment in July of that year. The fire will be followed by a great flood in October when, by his calculation, the same planets are conjoined in Capricorn.

BABYLON

Lord Buddha said that the Wheel of Dharma, which creates the momentum needed for a global search for truth, requires a new buddha (awakened one) to give it a fresh spin every 2,500 years. He divides the cycle into five 500-year intervals punctuated by a significant loss of momentum in the spiritual evolution of man. The first revolution starts around 500 BC with a push from Gautama Buddha; orbit number two pushes off the BC standard for a lunge into AD standard time with Christ; revolution three sees a weaker spin between AD 500-700, while China turned Buddhist and Islam was born; in AD 1000 Europe became Christianized and Asia turned Buddhist; an ever-more anemic turn of the Wheel around 1500 witnessed the birth of Sikhs and Protestants. The momentum of truth will grind to a halt by 2000.

THE WHEEL OF THE DHARMA

Western astrologers map the stars' influence on man's actions by what is defined as the Great Cosmic Year. This is the time it takes the Sun to retrograde through all the twelve tropical constellations of the zodiac — 25,970 years. It takes the sun 2,160 years to back-pedal one cosmic month through each constellation. The current Cosmic Month, better known as the Piscean Age, is divided into four cosmic weeks of roughly 500 years. The Sun takes seventy-two years to retrograde one degree. This cosmic day has a feminine (night) and a masculine (day), each of thiry-six years. At present we are in the late afternoon of the masculine phase, where our actions will bring karmic reactions at the onset of the night phase in 2008. At that time, humanity could experience a spiritual rebirth or destroy itself.

WESTERN ASTROLOGY

Don't celebrate if 2000 passes without incident. According to the Mayan Indians of ancient Mexico, the calculators of one of the most accurate calendars ever created, time will run out on us by the year 2012.

MAYAN CALENDAR

AD 1940 —

1935	1936	1937-1945	1938	1939	1941
Last Dalai Lama born	Modern construction techniques	War of Second Antichrist (Hitler)	War threatens the whole world	World War II	US enters war
– Lama-astrologers (c. 1850)	– Mother Shipton (c. 1550)	– Nostradamus (1557)	– Polish monk (1790)	– Evangeline Addams (1931)	– Edgar Cayce (1939)

Astrology is not an objective science. It is a science of allegory, symbolism. It is a poetic language that uses the stars as its vocabulary. Astrology's essential function is to catch the drift of universal forces and communicate how they influence the body, mind and spirit of man. Throughout the book I will return to this cosmic metaphor in an effort to describe elemental and spiritual forces caught somewhere between objective and subjective definitions.

When a mystery can't be approached objectively, poetry and myth can bring one closer to its existential truth. Astrology-speak is one language to explain the twilight zone between matter and spirit. When the flow of individual and impersonal events requires it, I will weave planetary nouns with constellation participles, and link the subject and predicate with verbs of a Jungian and archetypal flavor.

Astrology is also a poetry about time. Its stanzas are measured by the movement of the stars. One epic poem runs along in twelve stanzas — or twelve constellations of the zodiac. A recitation takes 25,970 years, by non-sidereal calculation, completing a cycle called the Great Cosmic Year. Each stanza runs for 2,160 years — the time it takes one constellation to ascend over the skies in a precession of equinoxes. We call each stanza a cosmic month. Each of these "months" forms a human era, or epoch, where history's positive and negative potentials are given astrological exposition.

A correct reading of this poetry will allow us to travel the road map of the human ego. Astrology believes that the entire spectrum of human history, with all its drama, tragedy and humor, takes on a certain collective focus which changes roughly every 2,000 years. Our present stanza-age is entitled Pisces the Fish. It began around 2,000 years ago with the life of Y'shua Bar Joseph, whose new religion, as foretold in Matthew 16:4, would be known by the Piscean sign of the "fish-man." The symbol of the fish was used by early Christians until an expanding hierarchy of priests systematized the religion, dropped the fish and changed the Jewish name of its founder to a Grecian misnomer — Jesus Christ.

The Piscean Age just loves religious hierarchies, secret societies, lonely monks in lonelier monasteries. The planet Neptune represents its archetypal forces. Through its ruling planetary "noun," the sentences of Pisces are shaped by the verbs of dreams and adjectives of contemplation punctuated with spiritual transcendence.

There is a dialectic in every reading of the cosmic stanza. To best understand the language of astrology in unlocking the future, it must be explained that each cosmic month has its darker side, which must be given equal attention if we are to avoid being trapped under its unconscious influences. The darker side of Pisces loves dictatorial theocracies, espionage, hidden enemies, and at the very worst, reveres illusions over truth. Characteristic of a Piscean Age are the dreams of imaginary heavens and hells, the surrender of intelligence to father figures and the worship of death cults. It is also blighted by superstitious religions, blind faith, and the complete denial of hidden enemies, the primary one being the straightjacket of conditioned personality we

AD 1950 —

1943	1945	1947	1950	1953-2001	1958-1998
Battle of Kursk – Edgar Cayce (1943)	World War II ends – Edgar Cayce (1941)	Partition of India – Jeane Dixon (1946)	Tibetan Apocalypse: Chinese invade – Lama-astrologers (before 1850)	World Teacher emerges; end times begin:- Pyramid Prophecy (3000 BC)	Christ (consciousness) appears on Earth – EdgarCayce (c.1934)

Living on the Cusp of Time

all are taught to strap our uniqueness in. The Piscean nightmare is hidden behind every morality, every law and knee-jerk tradition that has outlived its use in human evolution, yet is blindly worshipped unto doomsday.

Pisces is the twelfth and final constellation in a grand cosmic cycle, so the Fish Era also stands for the culmination of all of our actions and reactions for just under 26,000 years. If we were dinosaurs, then the 90s would be the final decade of the human Cretaceous Era. It is the time of death and transcendence. It is no wonder that so many prophetic time cycles are coming to an end in these final years of not only a cosmic month but also a great cycle of centuries. It includes in its final quarter the history of known civilization — the great Adamic cycle of centuries, which began in prehistoric paradise with biting from Eve's apple and ends with all of us eating it by the year 2000.

The passing of an astrological age is akin to the final moments of a dying man. Just before the slide from life, the deceased-to-be often experiences what appears to be a miraculous recovery. In the same way, many of the strongest influences of a dying age enjoy a final flare-up before expiring. If my interpretation of stellar poems is correct, then the wave of fundamentalism in Christianity, Hinduism and Islam, as well as the sudden upsurge of nationalistic and ethnic fervor we see today, do not denote a renaissance of old values but presage their final demise within the space of a few decades.

If the 1990s are seeing an unprecedented return to conservative values and a return of millions to the church/mosque/temple, it does not bode well for Piscean love of father/god, shepherd/sheep figures in the future. The new millennium will not be Christian, at least in the way most traditionally Piscean interpreters project. In the next millennium Christians will be far less "fishy." They will be ruled by a new planet, Uranus, the deprogrammer, the archetypal force defined by astrologer and author Jeff Green as "freedom from the known."

The next age, the first stanza in the next cosmic poem of time, will be the Age of Aquarius. It is symbolized by the spiritual master as water bearer. He imparts impersonal and oceanic consciousness to cleanse humanity's dramas. What flows from his urn is not water, but electric blue vapor. His gift is that which cannot be grasped but experienced. He is atmosphere, enlightenment.

Aquarius is also symbolized by two parallel zigzag lines representing the life force potential of humanity. They are serpents of subtle, immaterial power. One is positive, the other negative. They must forever be in balance; otherwise disaster will follow. They are the Western version of kundalini — the serpentine double helix running up through the spine of our invisible and more subtle spiritual bodies. It is an energy passageway through which sex is transmuted to super consciousness. It is no wonder that the Age of Aquarius was christened by the sexually free 1960s; however, sexual freedom is only the beginning. What began with orgies, free love, and free sex gurus will end in the transformation from biology to beatitude.

AD 1960 —   AD 1970 —

1958-1998	1960	1963	1968	1968	1972
Catastrophic land changes – Edgar Cayce (1931)	Young Democrat becomes US President – Jeane Dixon (1952)	Kennedy assassinated – Jeane Dixon (1963)	First ruins of Atlantis discovered off Bimini – Edgar Cayce (1940)	Cultural Revolution reaches peak – Edgar Cayce (c. 1932)	War of 3rd Antichrist begins – Nostradamus (1557)

The serpents of Aquarius symbolize the sign's bridge between opposites. Aquarius is the dance instructor of intimate enemies in a rumba paradox. Where Pisces, the dreamy old sage, holds his yin and yang fishes, symbolizing our slippery dramas flip-flopping in a crucible of black and white dialectics, Aquarius will see polarities become complementaries. Psychic Uri Geller and metaphysical debunker James Randi will make up. Today's scientist will be tomorrow's mystic.

The new age has its darker potential too: the next twenty-century stanza of time may sing a song of irreconcilable polarization if great awareness and heart-fulness are not applied to keep Aquarius' extreme forces of chaos and structure in balance. The kundalini of the world will awaken around the year 2000. Snakes can be dangerous. A sudden jolt to our collective conscious mind will either bring on an experience of impersonal enlightenment to man, or collective insanity. Just as Pisces began and closed the last Cosmic Year, Aquarius will plant karmic seeds in mankind which will burst into blossom or tangle mankind in weeds 250 centuries hence.

It is popularly believed that the new age officially begins in the year 2000. However, this doesn't mean that one parties on 31 December 1999 in the Piscean Age and wakes up with a cosmic hangover the next morning in the Age of Aquarius. The influences of astrological eras overlap for several hundred years' duration in what is called a cusp.

Aquarius is only at the commencement of his reign. War, destruction, bloodshed, and famine are the instruments of his purpose...by which he destroys convention and enthrones "the new" on the ruins of the old. **Cheiro (1925) Cwp**

AD **1980 —**

1975 World Teacher's message goes West – Madame Blavatsky (1888)	1978 Poisoning of Pope John Paul I – Nostradamus (1555)	1982 Beginning of the end of Kali Yuga (Hindu Apocalypse) – Indian astrologers	1984 Gorbachev heads USSR & perestroika begins – The author (1983)	1985 AIDS recognized as world plague – Nostradamus (1555)	1986 Cold War ends – Polish monk (1790)

Today could be called the most schizophrenic period in history. Our split personality stems from a tug-of-war between the cosmic influences of the dying Piscean Age and the upstart Aquarian age, which began eclipsing its predecessor around the 1750s and will influence our destiny as much as fifty percent between 1990-2012. Simply put, this means our thoughts and actions in the next few years will be pulled backwards by Piscean

The Age of Aquarius

sentiments of orthodox faith, invisible gods and romantic dreams — American and otherwise — while equally strong and rebellious vibrations from Aquarius will push us headlong toward a destiny of revolution, a quest for truth at all costs and a demand for paradise — now or never!

It must be remembered that Hitler and Big Brother are the darker, reactive side effects of Aquarius. The coming psychic trauma brought about by the loss of the past and the plummeting into the new may cause history's heart to miss a beat by the year 2000. As far as prophecy is concerned, it is not certain whether history's heart will start again. Great awareness will be needed as each of us walks on the razor's edge of time. The paper-thin bridge across the prophetic nightmares of the 90s heads us for the Aquarian potential of knowing truth as our own. One wrong step and we fall into the abyss of mind control and mass insanity.

Out of chaos stars are born.

Friedrich Nietzsche

AD 1990 —

1987
Final stage of Iran-Iraq
War begins
- Nostradamus (1555)

1988
Soviet pullout from
Afghanistan
- Nostradamus (1555)

1989
US-Soviet friendship
begins
- Nostradamus (1555)

1991-1999
Worldwide drought
& ecodisasters
- Nostradamus (1555)

1993-2002
World War III and/or
a Spiritual Revolution
- Nostradamus (1555)

The Second Miller

Back in the 990s, the Christian world held its breath. It was believed that Judgment Day would come 1,000 years after the birth of Christ. Medieval preachers interpreted the biblical hordes from the north — from Gog and Magog — to be the fearsome Vikings ransacking their towns and churches. Present-day Sunday school teachers are just as adamant that the Gog-Magogians are the Russians — perestroika and a thawing Cold War aside. On the other hand, today's believers in virgin births and the rumors of virgin births have one up on their first-millennium counterparts. They haven't missed the linchpin that unleashes the true Apocalypse: not only must the Jews first return to the Holy Land and re-establish Israel, but also the Temple of Solomon must be rebuilt. In 1989 the petitions for a new temple were so numerous that even the Israeli Ministry of Religious Affairs was pressured to consider the idea for the first time. In late 1990 rumors of Jewish militants coming to set the temple's cornerstone next to the Dome on the Rock inspired some of the bloodiest rioting to date between Palestinians and Israelis at that sacred spot.

The tenth-century prediction was not fulfilled. Now the bets are on the twentieth. Most Christian seers of this closing millennium stake their wagers on the words of a document discovered in the sixteenth-century monastery of Maria Laach, which says: *The twentieth century will bring death and destruction, apostasy from the Church, discord in families, cities and governments...* Put in other words by the Abbot Genet, before 1798, *The twentieth century will not pass before the beginning of the Judgment.*

In the sleepy Indian state of Goa stands the 500-year-old Basilica of the Bom Jesus. One can escape the heat and glare of the tropical midday sun and find within the dark interior of a side chapel the cool-to-the-touch silver coffin of St Francis Xavier. The citizens of this former Portuguese colony will tell you that the body has remained uncorrupted by the tropical climate for five centuries.

THE MILLENNIUM —

1996	1998	1999	2000	2001
Nuclear disaster and/or terrorist incident — Nostradamus (1555-60)	Flooding of coasts begins — Edgar Cayce (1941)	Armageddon — Nostradamus (1557)	Old World dies — Various prophets	End of the world — Pyramid/Christian prophets

nium

The mummified saint is a desiccated device of prophecy. It is foretold that when Xavier's corpse begins to rot you can set your watch for the onslaught of the latterdays. All local claims to the contrary, one need only regard the current state of the Jesuit cadaver-under-glass to confirm that the **beginning of the end-time has begun.**

The Last Popes

St Malachy left Ireland on a pilgrimage to Rome in 1139. On first sighting the Eternal City stretched out below him and bathed in the warm light of a summer's eve, he immediately fell to the ground in an ecstatic trance. St Malachy began murmuring cryptic Latin phrases, which his servant recorded for posterity. Each of Malachy's 111 phrases signifies either the name, heraldic device or background of all the popes, from his contemporary, Celestinus II, until Judgment Day. His predictions were an accurate pointer to future pontiffs. Here are a few examples from our century: Benedict XV (1914-1922) is called *Religio Depopulata* or "religion depopulated." During his reign, the Christian flock lost thirty-seven million to the slaughter of World War I and the Spanish Influenza, plus 200 million Russian Christians who converted to the atheistic cult of Communism. John XXIII (1958-1963) is called *Pastor et Nauta* — "pastor and sailor." The former Patriarch of Venice (a city famous for its sailors) navigated his Catholic flock toward revolutionary reform. *Flos Florum* — flower of flowers — denotes the fleur-de-lis symbol seen on the family coat of arms of Paul VI (1963-1978). Malachy calls John Paul I *De Medietate Lunae* — "the middle moon," or "from the half-moon." His short reign ended in sudden death on 28 September 1978, roughly halfway through a lunar cycle. John Paul II is *De Labore Solis* — "from the Sun's labor." What are some of the sun's labors? Rising in the morning, eclipses. No one can objectively prove whether Malachy is stacking a lot of meaning in a few Latin words or his interpreters are trying to squeeze as much juice out of a phrase as they can. However the potential for interpretations of the phrase representing Pope John Paul II are rich indeed! J.R. Jochmans, author of the prophetic classic, *Rolling Thunder*, squeezes the meaning "Rising Sun" out of *De Labore Solis*, reminding us that John Paul II, like the sun, comes from the East. He is the first pontiff ever to come from Eastern Europe. Astrologer Doris Kay wrings one more drop of meaning from Malachy, interpreting the motto to read, "to enter from the eclipsing Sun." She reminds us that John Paul II was born on 18 May 1920 — the date of a total eclipse.

After John Paul II, Malachy's list is reduced to two. Given the average reign of Holy Fathers — less than ten years — this could bring us the coronation of the last Pontiff around 2000. After John Paul II comes *Gloria Olivarius* — "glory of the olive." Another prophet-monk from

2001
End of the world
– Berosus
(2nd century BC)

2002
Great spiritual king
anointed (recognized)
– Nostradamus (1557)

2012 —
End of the World
Mayan Calendar
runs out

eighteenth-century Padua believes this Pope will take Leo XIV for his name and that he will be an agent of peace between Israelis and Arabs. (The olive is also a symbol of Israel.) Regarding the final Pope, Malachy says:

During the last persecution of the Holy Roman Church, there shall sit Petrus Romanus [Peter of Rome], who shall feed the sheep amid great tribulations, and when these have passed, the City of the Seven Hills shall be utterly destroyed, and the awful Judge will judge the people.

The Wheel of the Dharma has stopped!

Entropy, the law of nature that says all things must lose momentum and stop, is not the monopoly of physics. The followers of Lord Buddha believe that even the evolution of truth — the Dharma — must wind down and die. Gautama Siddhartha, whose enlightenment sparked the creation of Buddhism, explained to his disciples that the quest for truth is like a wheel that requires a fresh push from a new Enlightened One every twenty-five centuries. Twenty-five centuries will have passed by the year 2000, and it appears that the wheel of Buddhist truth has already come to a complete standstill in materialist Red China, where monks and monasteries have become museum pieces. In Japan, the land which saw Buddhism's final and perhaps highest flowering through Zen, the dollar is becoming holier than the Dharma. And in the last stronghold of Buddhism, the hermit kingdom of Tibet, the holocaust foreseen as a terrible prelude to the next push of Dharma's wheel started right on schedule, in 1950, when Chinese soldiers began dynamiting the first of over 600 lamaseries. The systematic rape of Tibet continues to this day.

When wheels come into the country, peace goes out. **Ancient Tibetan prophecy BC**
(There was no wheeled transportation in Tibet until the British invaded in 1904.)

It may happen that here...in Tibet the religion and the secular administration may be attacked both from the outside and from the inside....The Dalai and Panchen Lamas...the holders of the faith, and the glorious rebirths, will be broken down and left without a name. As regards the monasteries and the priesthood [the lamas], their lands and other properties will be destroyed...[They] will find their lands seized and they themselves made to serve their enemies, or wander about the country as beggars do. All beings will be sunk in great hardship and in overpowering fear: The days and nights will drag slowly into suffering.
**Last testament of the thirteenth Dalai Lama (1932)
made eighteen years before the Chinese invaded Tibet**

When the iron bird flies and horses run on wheels, the Tibetan people will be scattered like ants across the face of the earth. **Padmasambhava, founder of Tibetan Buddhism (eighth century AD)**

The Kali Yuga

During the Kali age,
people indulge in...theft, falsehood,
deceit, vanity etc., and delusion,
hypocrisy and
vanity overshadow the people.

AD 2100 — AD 2150 — AD 2200 —

2100
Edgar Cayce reincarnates and
sees the world transformed by
20th & 21st-century cataclysms
– Edgar Cayce (1936)

And Dharma [religious seeking] *becomes very weak in the Kali age, and people commit sin in mind, speech and actions....Quarrels, plague, fatal diseases, famines, drought and calamities appear. Testimonies and proofs have no certainty. There is no criterion left when the Kali age settles down....People become poorer in vigor and luster. They are wicked, full of anger, sinful, false and avaricious. Bad ambitions, bad education, bad dealings, and bad earnings excite fear. The whole batch becomes greedy and untruthful....Many sudras [untouchables] will become kings, and many heretics will be seen. There will arise various sects; sannyasins wearing clothes colored red....Many profess to have supreme knowledge, because thereby they will easily earn their livelihood. In the Kali age...there will be many false religionists....The country [India] will become desolate by repeated calamities, short lives, and various kinds of diseases. Everyone will be miserable...owing to the dominance of vice and Tamoguna [quality of darkness], people will freely commit the sin of abortion, on account of which there will be a decline in the longevity and strength of the people. The people will live up to 100 years at most. In spite of all the Vedas [the Hindu Bible] being in existence, it would be as if there were no Vedas, and the performance of sacrifices would be stopped.*

From the Hindu Puranas (AD 330) Mat-P Ch 144: 29 F

Depending on one's interpretation of Hindu cycles of time, they can last anywhere from millions of years to a few millennia. If we side with the Russian mystic Helena Blavatsky, the Cosmic Year of Western Astrology roughly parallels the great clock of the Hindus, which consists of four 5,000-year cycles called yugas. Indian scriptures maintain that the entropy of human consciousness increases with each passing *yuga*. The process has been compared to a table losing its legs and therefore its stability. In the First Age, called the Sat Yuga (Age of Truth), spiritual understanding and awareness is upheld in every heart as securely as a table sits on four legs. During the Second Age, one leg is broken off. The table still stands but consciousness is weakened. Love is less secure. Two of the legs are missing in the Third Age, which sees humanity list sharply into unconsciousness and hatred. This brings us to our Fourth and darkest Age called the Kali Yuga — the Dark or Iron Age. Our table sways on one remaining leg of consciousness. The burden of all kinds of excess is about to send our awareness crashing to the floor.

The final age of the Hindu cycle is symbolized either by Kali, the god of sin, or by a fierce, black-skinned goddess of the same name, who wears only a bloodstained smile. This sword-touting, demoniacal deity is worshipped in India as the all-compassionate murderess, the butcher of our illusions. The accumulation of thousands of years of karmic excess may climax with Mother Kali banging at our door with the bill at the end of her Age. According to some modern Hindu astrologers, she started rattling our hinges in 1982. This could mean Kali will kick the door down between 2000-2012.

Modern India mirrors the worst nightmares of Vedic seers of the righteous past: Abortion is rampant (so is overpopulation — a by-product of Vedic tradition); life expectancy in India is around forty-five years — one of the world's lowest averages; there is widespread illness and disease. Many Hindu priests bewail what they view as a loss of true religious sincerity, indicated first by the rise of Buddhism, and most recently by the gaggle of gurus like the Maharishi, or "the Bhagwan," who seduced Westerners and dressed them up as red-robed sannyasin pilgrims. And so on.

Not all lost "virtues" may be worth crying over. The breakdown of the inhuman caste system which keeps a quarter of the Hindu population in slavery, or the decline of traditions like suttee (widows being burned alive on their husbands' funeral pyres) could be seen as a big improvement.

In the East, the ancient tug-of-war between good and evil is viewed more as a dance between intimate lover/enemies. Their dance is called *leela,* a play of the divine. It is hard for the occidental mind-set to comprehend the Eastern view that there is great good in evil and at times great evil in good. In a golden age, truth is taken for granted. That is why the table's legs fall. In this way, the darker the age the greater is the desire for light.

Before a new Hindu cycle can begin again with the next Age of Truth, all our illusions about civilization, God, time and reality will be ruthlessly destroyed by Kali's metaphorical sword. Her human garden needs weeding. To preserve a healthy Dharma, the old plants have to be uprooted whether they like it or not.

Purified by *Fire*

Variations on the theme of Noah's Flood run through the legends of nearly all ancient peoples. Equally common as the deluge myth is this additional forewarning: The next global house-cleaning will be by fire. The majority of ancient/future tales of catastrophe issue from the shamans and medicine men of the Earth's indigenous nations, categorized as the Fourth World.

The clearest warnings about the final conflagration come from the Hopi Indians of the American Southwest. "Hopi" means "peace," an appropriate name for a native people who share a profound love for the Earth. They see themselves as custodians of those secrets the Great Spirit gave man to help him establish a harmonious relationship with nature.

In 1948 the Hopi elders broke their long and silent witness of man's pathological treatment of the Earth and shared their prophecies with the outer world. The elders spoke of prior human epochs when man rose to great technological heights only to destroy himself. They believe it will happen again unless humans change.

Frank Waters was one of the first white men allowed permission to record Hopi secrets. He best describes the Hopi philosophy in the following extract from his classic, *The Book of the Hopi*: "Their existence always has been patterned upon the universal plan of world creation and maintenance, and their progress on the evolutionary Road of Life depends upon the unbroken observance of its laws....They re-assert a rhythm of life we have disastrously tried to ignore. They remind us we must attune ourselves to the need for inner change if we are to avert a cataclysmic rupture between our own minds and hearts. Now, if ever, is the time for them to talk, for us to listen."

2470
A new Messiah emerges
– Cheiro (1931) Cwp

The *Lost* White Brother

Old people told us how there were two brothers, the older white, the younger red. They were given a stone tablet with a sign of a circle, to help them remember the Great Spirit and to guide them. The tablet was broken in half. Each brother took half of the stone tablet. The older brother took his people to another land where he would develop the power of reason, to invent and create things. The younger brother would stay here (in America) where he would protect the land and develop the spiritual power.

The older (white) brother was to come back to his younger (red) brother and they would combine their material and spiritual powers to make a paradise. The younger brother would teach the older about religion, the older would teach the younger about technology.

But there was a warning: If the white brother returns having changed the sign from a circle to a cross, then beware!...Because the sign will mean that he has gone wrong.

Thomas Banyaca: A Hopi elder recounting the prophecy in 1985

Railroads and power lines

Before the time of the great Purification, they will make metal roads for iron horses and hang metal ropes in the air.

AD 2500 — AD 2750 — AD 3000 —

Mining on Holy Land

Then when you see the white man come into the Four Corners area (Hopi reservation land) and try to take it, then you will see a sign, the Danger Sign, the last stage before the Great Purification.

If we dig precious things from the land we will perish.

The US Congress passed the Indian Relocation Act of 1985 (H.R. 3011, calendar №318) to move the Hopi and Navajo tribes off the Four Corners area by July 1986. The Bureau of Indian Affairs gave many reasons for re-settlement, including the resolution of land disputes between the Hopi and their neighbors, the Navajo. The real reason may well be the Federal Government's long-standing interest in mining deep deposits of precious minerals beneath the Hopi's sacred Black Mesa. The mining of Hopi sacred lands continues.

The Axis Alliance & Communism

The three great forces of the Sun, the swastika and the Red will combine and come at once.

Interpreted as the pre-war alliances of Imperial Japan, Nazi Germany and Stalinist Russia.

The White Man's Atom Bomb

The white brother will bring the symbol of the Sun which makes a great explosion shaking the Earth...The Gourd of Ashes

The indigenous nations of the Fourth World feel World War III is already happening. All the testing of nuclear weapons since Hiroshima and Nagasaki has taken place exclusively on native lands. The Micronesians of Bikini atoll, the Aborigines of southwestern Australia and the Red Indians of Nevada and New Mexico, along with their tribal counterparts in Western China and Russian Siberia, had their lands and often their bodies irradiated by an estimated 1,900 surface and underground nuclear bombings between 1945 and 1990.

In 1953, the year the Great Pyramid prophecy marks as the beginning of the end of the Adamic Age, an extended family of Australian Aborigines beheld the flash of an English above-ground nuclear test. As a cloud of black ash descended, the people dug holes in the sand dunes for their children, the old cushioning the children with their bodies. Two days after the blast, as one survivor relates, "...everyone was vomiting and had diarrhea and people were laid out everywhere. Next day people had very sore eyes, red with tears, and I could not open my eyes. Some were partly blind and I lost the sight in my right eye....Five days after the black cloud came, the old people started dying."

THE THIRD MILLENNIUM

AD 3100 — AD 3250 — AD 3500 —

"Red" Tribe from the East

If these three don't come, [The Russians, Germans and the Japanese invading America during World War II] *then a great red power wearing a red cloak will come by a road in the air from the east to clean up the mess and they will be ruthless.*

In other passages of the Hopi prophecy the *great red power* comes from *the red cap and red cloak tribe.* The prophecy relates that this new tribe will first settle in and around Indian lands in the Western US. But their destiny is to disperse and slowly disappear from America and move from *west to east.* Within a short time *their tracks will become broken and vanish altogether.*

Some Hopi medicine men have cautiously admitted that the red-clothed followers of the late Indian mystic, Bhagwan Shree Rajneesh (who went by the name Osho before his death in 1990) have already fulfilled this prophecy. That is hard to prove; still, there are some interesting parallels between Rajneesh's invasion of America and this prophecy. During the first half of the 1980s, his red-clad followers flooded into America (by air from India and Europe — which are east) to celebrate and establish a commune city in the state of Oregon. Rajneesh's *ruthless* criticisms of American politicians angered the highest echelons of the Reagan Administration. After 1986, the Rajneeshee tribe dropped their distinctive clothing and dispersed out of sight after their guru was arrested and deported from America. Nevertheless, the fourteenth Dalai Lama recently made a courtesy call to the Hopi elders in the spring of 1991. The maroon-robed monks of Tibet flying from the East also fit the warning.

Space Station?

The Final Sign

First they will bring back pieces of the Moon which will upset the balance and unleash disastrous forces.

The Purification will begin shortly after humans build a great house in the sky. By then there will be fires everywhere and greedy, selfish, power-mad leaders, internal wars.

This is the last danger sign.

The US sent the Sky Lab space station aloft in the 1970s. The Soviets launched Mir in the mid-1980s. The US plans to build a new space station called Alpha, scheduled to be sent into permanent orbit sometime between 1995 and 2000.

AD 3600 — AD 3700 —

3755
Asteroids hit Earth
resultant fire storms
consume the surface
– Nostradamus (1557)

AD 3800 —

3797
Earth consumed
by expanding
Sun
– Nostradamus (1557)

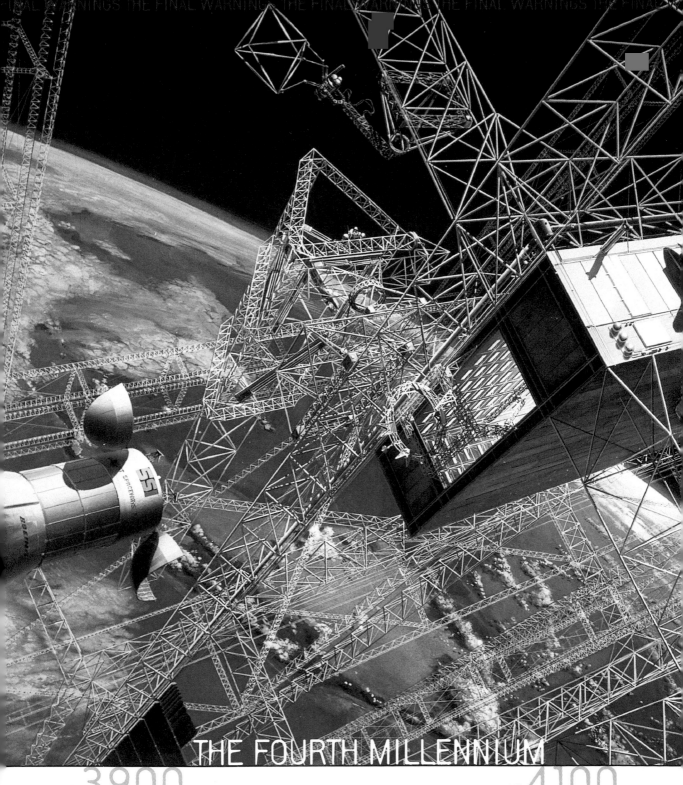

THE FOURTH MILLENNIUM

AD 3900 —   AD 4100 —

Signs in the Sky.

When a biblical or pre-Colombian prophet declares the end of the world will be heralded by *signs in the sky*, many of us might assume that to mean little green ETs making light shows with flying saucers. Actually the *signs* already exist. Man mastered flight less than ninety years ago and forever changed the firmament. The blinking lights of passenger jets running across star and moon, and the brush strokes of vapor they leave across blue skies, would adequately terrify any prophet living before this century.

I will show wonders in the heavens... **Joel (c. 600 BC) Jo 2:30**

Sign in the Sky
[in]
1990...
Fall of the Stars
[in]
1992.

Flowering Almond Tree Prophecy (19th century)

There will be signs in the sun, moon and stars....Men will faint from terror, apprehensive of what is coming on the world, for the heavenly bodies will be shaken.

Y'shua (AD 30-33) Lk 21:25, 26

Near the day of the Great Purification, there will be cobwebs spun back and forth in the sky. Hopi prophecy (pre-Colombian)

AD INFINITUM

AD4500 — AD4600 —

Part Two: Tomorrow of Fear

I watched as he opened the sixth seal.
There was a great earthquake. The sun turned black like sackcloth made of goat hair, the whole moon turned blood-red, and the stars in the sky fell to Earth as the late figs drop from a fig tree when shaken by a strong wind. The sky receded like a scroll rolling up, and every mountain and island was removed from its place. Then the kings of the Earth, the princes, the generals, the rich, the mighty, and every slave and every free man hid in caves and among the rocks of the mountains. They called upon the mountains and the rocks, "Fall on us and hide us from the face of him who sits on the throne and from the wrath of the Lamb. For the great day of their wrath has come, and who can stand?" **John of Patmos (AD 81-96) Rev 6:12-17**

I have been criticized for my lack of positive thinking. During a book-signing party in America for *Nostradamus and the Millennium,* I was reproached by a bright-eyed and dreamy fellow who zealously praised the virtues of projecting good thoughts and canceling all thoughts of things ugly or evil. This, he said, was the right way to bring about the New Age.

I replied, "Sir, you seem to harbor a deep-seated negativity toward negativity."

A popular New Age projection is that the year 2000 will magically bring peace and brother-hood to the world if we just think it so. We will live happily — and harmonically converged — ever after. Pollyanna never fantasized a better future hiding between the chambers of Pandora's box. To think positively represses the negative. In fact, doomsday may be coming solely because of our thoughts, whether they are positive dreams or negative nightmares.

Who is thinking these thoughts?

Understanding who we are is a way to have power over our thoughts and thereby gain mastery of our future. The first step to mastery requires that we strip off our denials and look with open eyes at our positive and negative thoughts-to-form and how they take us either towards a doomsday or a "bloomsday" (ie, a future wave of planetary death or a global flowering of consciousness and love).

I would like to propose here that before our "yes" to the future has any reality, we have to first encounter our "no." It is there, big and ugly, festering beneath all our goodwill and positive thinking. And fear is its root. We must first expose it before we can cut ourselves free from its manifest destiny of horror.

The forecasts concerning our survival into the next century presage two alternative futures. Part One of *The Millennium Book of Prophecy* will gaze through the magic mirror darkly at possible futures shaped by a long accumulation of human pathologies — taken to their logical conclusion. The following horrors are not presented to dishearten the reader, nor are they intended to feed a predilection for hopelessness many feel as a reaction to doomsday scenarios. I present the following account of prophetic nightmares because I am inspired by the old

From Four Horsemen of the Apocalypse

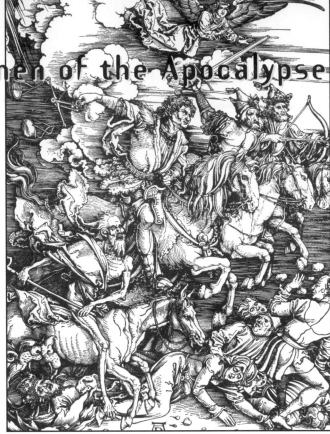

Eastern proverb which says that any journey into truth has the best chance for a sweet ending if you first have an honest encounter with the bitter beginning.

The root of doomsday is fear. Nostradamus, the famous healer and prophetic giant of the sixteenth century, had some unflattering words to say about tomorrow's cancerous tuber and how it can be pruned by each individual:

When people are desperate out of fear, then the doctor's job is to fight that fear and help them get strong. It alone is the cause of all damage. And fear comes foremost from unfulfilled desires. The one who tells people that life need have no cares and is nothing but "jolly" is worse than the prophet....Fear is the door. Through it comes all sickness. It creates war and all other activities. Fear makes plagues and illusions. Only fear. It is always so.

The one who is reasonable can learn from my prophecies how to find the right path to take as if he would have found footprints in the sand from someone who has gone before.

...People can only become more reasonable if they can lose their fear of each other and of themselves.

It has been my experience that the degree of becoming more reasonable comes in direct consequence to my deepening self-awareness. The more I become reasonably conscious, the more I recognize how I suffer from too much complacency with myself and too little willingness to examine how my hallowed sense of moralities, desires and the divisive traditions I blindly follow are about to ruin this beautiful planet and bring on a third world war, whether the Cold War is over or not.

Tomorrow of Fear is about exposing the festering wounds we hide beneath a thick blanket of civility and denial.

to the Four Hellriders of

Doomsday

I watched as the Lamb opened the first of the seven seals. Then I heard one of the four living creatures say in a voice like thunder, "Come!" I looked and there before me was a white horse! Its rider held a bow, and he was given a crown, and he rode out as a conqueror bent on conquest.

When the Lamb opened the second seal, I heard the second living creature say, "Come!" Then another horse came out, a fiery red one. Its rider was given power to take peace from the earth and to make men slay each other. To him was given a large sword.

When the Lamb opened the third seal, I heard the third living creature say, "Come!" I looked, and there before me was a black horse! Its rider was holding a pair of scales in his hand. Then I heard what sounded like a voice among the four living creatures, saying, "A quart of wheat for a day's wages, and three quarts of barley for a day's wages, and do not damage the oil and the wine!"

When the Lamb opened the fourth seal, I heard the voice of the fourth living creature say, "Come!" I looked, and there before me was a pale horse! Its rider was named Death, and Hades was following close behind him. They were given the power over a fourth of the earth to kill by sword, famine and plague, and by the wild beasts of the earth.

St John of Patmos (AD 81-96) Rev 6:1-8

Part Two of this book — Tomorrow of Fear — will examine the majority vote of history's greatest prophets — a terrifying apocalypse of war, plagues and ecological holocausts. I have placed their doom-ridden visions into four allegorical categories. These are presented as an updated version, if you will, of the Four Horsemen of the Apocalypse.

The First Hellrider of doomsday is a pregnant and starving woman holding an empty begging bowl. She is called **OVERPOPULATION**. She is the human breeding urge run amok and propagating a tomorrow of ecological holocaust. Through her, doomsday could be brought about by famine.

The Second Hellrider is a ravaged wiccan priestess, an archetype of Mother Nature, who is about to ride down her unseen attackers — namely you, me and six billion other eager breeders — with volcanic fire and lightning bolts. She is **EARTH TRAUMA**, the harbinger of doomsday through an ecological breakdown of the Earth's climate and food chains.

The Third Hellrider is a man with rodent features brandishing a syringe. He is called **THE LEMMING SYNDROME**, the harbinger of plagues. He is the stress of modern living, breaking down man's immune system and his will to live.

The Fourth Hellrider is the archetypal terrorist. He is hooded, and the green, glowing symbol for atomic energy hovers over his head like a halo. He shoulders a tactical nuclear missile bought on the black market after the collapse of the Soviet Union. He carries a sinister radar dish as a shield and proudly displays a happy-face button on his chest. The final Hellrider is called **THE THIRD WORLD'S WAR** — a future nuclear holocaust that may be more possible now because the Cold War has ended.

Fortunate is the man who knows how to read the signs of the times, for that man shall escape many misfortunes, or at least be prepared to understand the blow.

Hermes Trismegistus (c. first century AD)

18

The First Hellrider

OVERPOPULATION

The electric current in the surgical lamp at the Usha Nursing Home quivered ever so slightly, betraying the fact that this remarkably modern surgery room was situated somewhere in the energy-starved Third World. The twitching electrical glare displayed my fillet of testicle to the competent doctor. With the right apron string to biology and future children cut and the other about to go, the patient laying back on the operating table chose this moment to speak:

"Doctor?" I said with mock severity. "Doc!"

"Yes? Are you feeling any pain?"

"Doctor," I pressed, not answering his question and putting on my best tone of concern, "you've got to tell me the truth — will I ever be able to play the violin again?"

The doctor and his nurse chuckled as they stitched and stanched and cut me loose from fatherhood. For a few weeks my testicles would have lingering pains of some form of primal biological mourning as they got aquainted with life without the ability to inject others with the needed spice for a womb's brew of life.

I hobbled down the hospital hallway and stepped into the street.

A gritty, burned-out evening (typical of urban India) reeking of diesel exhaust, dung, and the spice of toasted banyan leaves, greeted me in the narrow, backed-up roads. My beloved Nadine held my hand as we brushed aside a gaggle of street urchins whining for *bakshish* (alms). We skirted through throngs of beggars at last reaching a cluster of rickshaws — those three-wheeled black and yellow beetles of the South Asian streets, nearly as numerous as that evening's mosquitoes. Nadine tucked me inside the revving and coughing metal carapace, which drove this bruised-balled though biologically liberated author back to his hotel room.

Life is hard in the land of exploding birthrates. I had made friends with an earlier generation of street urchins on my first visit to India, ten years before I was sterilized. To my question, "What do you want out of life?" I was surprised to hear them say they wanted to get married and have children. Nine years and nearly 200 million Indian babies later, I was seeing the effect of their pubescent desires as the rickshaw careened through an ocean of people trudging along under India's dim and flickering street lights.

I cupped my bruised jewels to protect them; too many potholes break the suspension springs of rickshaws weaving through too many crowds, who do their best to uphold a democracy which suffers too many crushing debts to too many affluent (and sparsely populated) Western nations.

I rode home, glad that in a world becoming ever more crowded with suffering children destined to multiply the suffering, no child will enter this misery of scarce clean water, little food, little education and a lot of disease through my chance biological injections. Though I respect an individual's choice to have children, I hold the conviction — and seal it with a surgeon's scalpel — that this time in history, there are already too many kids to love and too little love to give.

A famine of many dimensions exists. The majority of Earth's children are starving from lack of love at a time when there is no lack of wombs being impregnated. And the logical conclusion was anticipated over four centuries ago. The prophet Nostradamus forewarns us of the result of over-propagation:

The great famine which I sense approaching will often turn [up] in various areas then become worldwide. It will be so vast and long lasting that they will grab roots from the trees and children from the breast.

The Twenty-First Century:

*In the years 1986-1998 great famine will prevail not only in the United
States, but in France, Japan, India, and China as well.* Irene Hughes (1981)

*By the end of this century...50 percent of the population has to die simply of hunger. And just
think, if 50 percent of the people die, what will be the situation of the living ones? There will be
nobody even to carry their corpses to the graveyard; they will be rotting in your streets, in your
neighborhoods, even in your own house. The whole world will have become a vast graveyard,
stinking of death* Osho (1987)

This prophecy (bottom page 49), made in the mid-sixteenth century, was number 67 in the first
volume of his prophetic masterpiece, *The Centuries.* In my first book, *Nostradamus and
the Millennium,* I introduced a new theory that Nostradamus might have hidden some of his
future dates within the numerical indexing of his over 1,000 quatrains.

With this predilection to hide dates in the stanzas, the French seer might have intended
quatrain 67 of Century 1 as the year 1967 inaugurating a future global famine. According to
the Worldwatch Institute, the year 1967 did see grain production in Africa begin its current
and disastrous decline, as well as one million Africans starve to death in the Biafran Famine.
Since then the world has seen an upsurge of hunger in *various areas* of Africa and Asia, where
accelerating birthrates run mostly unchecked. Too many new consumers of food, fuel and
water devour steadily-decreasing harvests. The World Health Organization (WHO) declared in
1987 that with the birth of the five billionth child, we had already passed the point where
Earth's fragile ecosystem was stretched beyond the limit.

One can already hear the hoofbeats of Overpopulation, the First Hellrider of Doomsday.
She personifies our uncontrollable urge to multiply human want and hunger to the point of
disaster.

Three children are born every second, making a total of 250,000 new arrivals each day. The
momentum of our rapid growth will add another billion mouths to feed and throats to quench
between 1991 and 1998. That's the equivalent of adding an extra China in less than a decade.
Our birthrate bullet train is heading for a wall called unsustainable food production. This is
the point in our near future when an avalanche of new polluters exhaust our dwindling
farmland until we cannot sustain even the illusion of nutritional subsistence for half the
human race.

A few Third World governments who share the greatest burden of excessive propagation
have begun national family planning campaigns, but even the hopeful signs of a slowing
birthrate in countries like China and India may be little more than sparks flying off our brakes
as our acceleration headlong into a collision with agricultural collapse seems unstoppable.
The UN World Food Council in its 1988 report has all but admitted our defeat in the war
against hunger and malnutrition. America, the breadbasket of the world, holds the key to
sustainable food production and spreading the message of population awareness. The US led
the world in funding an international campaign for family planning until most financial support was withdrawn in 1987. If the program does not resume, many UN globe watchers think a
stabilization between the death rate and birth rate is not possible for the next 100 years.

Too little supply, too much demand

By overpopulating their range, human beings create more demand on a dwindling supply; the equation for a future apocalypse by famine.

[At a time when there is a] great nation across the ocean that will be inhabited by peoples of different tribes and descent [America]...many nations will be scourged by want and famine.
St Hildegard (c. 1141)

All public cult will be interrupted. A terrible and cruel famine will commence in the whole world and principally in the western regions, such as has never occurred since the world's beginning.
João de Vatiguerro (thirteenth century)

America has seen its global exports of grain and other food staples drop steadily into the red since the late 80s. If droughts continue to reduce the river of American grain to a trickle, the first decade of the next century could see the nightmare of Ethiopia played out across most of the nations of the developing world who depend on American exports. Food riots could be common in major cities like Cairo, Lagos, Caracas and even Tokyo and St Petersburg, since they rely almost exclusively on the farmers of America for their daily bread.

The Hellrider of Overpopulation is the undisputed trailblazer for a tomorrow that will be terrifying because mankind is afraid to change its gestalt from being a pack of competing nationals to a confederation of sharing inter-nationals. Following right behind Overpopulation's hoofs are the Hellriders of Earth Trauma, The Lemming Syndrome, and the Third World's War.

Man has put off facing the many various symptoms of global hypertension for so long that any one catastrophic incident foretold by prophecy, if it were fulfilled, could trigger a domino effect of cascading crises that could overwhelm all the good efforts and newfound awareness of the need for global maintenance arising in the final decade of the twentieth century. What would happen if Los Angeles and Tokyo were devastated by earthquakes, as most seismologists expect to happen sometime in the next thirty years? The loss of Tokyo or LA alone is enough to bring on a severe financial depression. All progress in paying off the global deficit or financing a worldwide crusade against overpopulation could be lost in a few seconds of seismic catharsis. Skyrocketing food export costs would climb out of reach of starving nations with little capital and a lot of debt. Famines would erupt throughout the Second and Third World, sending millions of refugees over sensitive borders. Regional and ethnic conflicts would increase, but with a new and frightening twist: Many of these wars will be fought by developing nations with a new-found chemical and nuclear weapons capability.

American grain not only sustains the developing world but also the Second World, or former Communist bloc. What if American grain reserves ran out and all wheat and corn exports to Russia ceased? The second Russian Revolution might fail if the new democrats or totalitarians to follow cannot forestall chronic crop failure and food shortages.

Rapid population growth is the chief source of food insecurity and social instability. The current lack of commitment by today's political leaders of the early 1990s to pool together and fight an all-out war against overpopulation could still bring on the Third World War by the mid-to-late 1990s, or later in the first decades of the twenty-first century.

How dreadful it will be in those days for pregnant women and nursing mothers
Y'shua (AD 30-33) Mt 24:19

The Second Hellrider

EARTH TRAUMA

We have to expect a day when the balance of nature will be lost.

Quetzalcoatl (AD 947)

They will no longer love this world around us, this incomparable work of God, this glorious structure which he has built, this sum of good made up of things of many diverse forms, this instrument whereby the will of God operates in that which he has made, ungrudgingly favoring man's welfare, this combination and accumulation of all the manifold things that can call forth the veneration, praise, and love of the beholder.

Hermes Trismegistus (AD 150-270) Asc III

The time has come...for destroying those who destroy the Earth.

St John of Patmos (AD 81-96) Rev 11:18

The first mother of life was not a blushing maid hiding behind a fig leaf in Eden. She was — and is — the primordial womb of minds, dreaming of Edens. Ancient man worshipped her body of soft mud and rocky flesh and made sacrifices to appease her quaking tantrums and molten rages. To pagans of every land, Mother Earth was a goddess.

Back in 1979, James Lovelock, a maverick scientist working out of a barn-turned-laboratory in Cornwall, England, stretched the limits of scientific vision by introducing a new theory: our planet is alive. Lovelock has synthesized the most recent findings in geology, geochemistry, evolutionary biology and climatology to make strange bedfellows out of pagans and scientists.

He proposes that our Earth, or Gaia as she was called by the ancient Greeks, is a vast organism sustaining her myriad expressions of evolution. She nurtures her children of leaf and limb in swaddling blankets of soil, meadow and forest, or tucks her creations beneath sheets of lake and ocean. And she keeps you and me and all the other creatures that "creepeth and crawleth" or vegetate upon her hide, safe from the cold radiation of space by enveloping all of us with a cozy quilt of invisible gases.

The scientifically inclined may find the note of pagan awe a bit hard to swallow. Still, whether one calls this rock and its envelope of life-sustaining gases a terrestrial planet — or just "Mom" — it can't be denied that Earth has provided the clay and climate which gave birth to life as we know it. Contrary to the Oracle of Delphi and other pantheists, James Lovelock believes our planet is neither a rational nor irrational goddess, but is inclined to view her as an unconscious organism maintaining the optimum conditions for life.

To better understand Gaia's unconscious mothering of life, one can find in the processes of our own bodies a smaller model of her mechanics for achieving homeostasis. We can feel thankful that a certain unconscious intelligence exists in our bodies to sustain life in spite of us. If we had to breathe or digest food by our own wits or knit our broken bones by ourselves we wouldn't last an hour. Muscles shudder automatically when it's cold; the body releases heat to sustain its temperature. If the body is sick it does its damnedest to soften the shock and bring us back into balance. In the same manner, Gaia has successfully provided a balanced temperature that has supported life in her seas, lands and skies, throughout 3.5 billion years of periodic catastrophes and cosmic shocks.

Before there was a "time" to "once" upon, our prehistoric

ancestors viewed Gaia as their adversary to conquer or be consumed by. After a few million years of misadventures and setbacks, man used his only advantages — namely his wits and his willie — to out-think and out-populate the other animals competing for kudos on Mother Earth's stage.

Gaia's evolution will go on by subconscious and sub-caring command, whether the current troupe of flora and fauna can sustain their act or are crowded off the stage by a new mutation.

In the United Nations' watershed report on civilization's sustainability entitled *Our Common Future*, an international panel of esteemed scientists and concerned world leaders concluded in 1987 that we have a grace period of less than two decades in which to transcend our Neanderthal view of ecology.

As Lovelock states in his book, *The Ages of Gaia*, "Gaia, as I see her, is no doting mother tolerant of misdemeanors, nor is she some fragile and delicate damsel in danger from brutal mankind. She is stern and tough, always keeping the world warm and comfortable for those who obey the rules, but ruthless in her destruction of those who transgress. Her unconscious goal is a planet fit for life. If humans stand in the way of this, we shall be eliminated with as little pity as would be shown by the micro-brain of an intercontinental ballistic nuclear missile in full flight to its target."

Intellectually speaking, man can see he must stop kicking the life out of his Mother Earth. He can celebrate his Earth Days, he can display his concern about all the trash to friends at cocktail parties, yet viscerally man's primal urge to dump on his mother remains.

I sense the stage manager's cane already casting a shadow on our act. A spate of predictions indicates that a number of human-induced disasters and Gaia-inspired natural responses are awaiting their fulfillment in the next few years. If we hold on to the illusion that we can muddle on without some very drastic encounters with our fear of change, well, we're not going to make it.

The longer we delay cleaning up our act, the sooner we will hear the hoofbeats of the Second Hellrider of doomsday. She's our ravaged and brutalized Mother Gaia in the guise of a goddess called Earth Trauma, the archetype of mindless and terrifying natural forces that exterminate meditators and madmen alike. She is the consequence of letting loose the First Hellrider, Overpopulation, on the terran range.

Earth Trauma is poised to ride down the only real ecological disaster on Earth: the biped who indiscriminately pollutes air and land, hacks down the forest and wantonly exterminates 100 species of his vegetable and animal neighbors a day, in what is becoming the greatest and perhaps the fastest mass extinction in the last four billion years.

More and more people are starting to discover that what you have created together is very fragile. And all that you are continuously producing and consuming is eating away the planet and beings on its surface. The rich countries are devouring the most to uphold their material standard. And the poor countries have the rich as their idols. This creates an evil circle. **Ambres: channeled by Sturé Johansson (1986)**

The Earth dries up and withers, the world languishes and withers, the exalted of the Earth languish. The Earth is defiled by its people; they have disobeyed the laws, violated the statutes and broken the everlasting covenant. Therefore a curse consumes the Earth; its people must bear their guilt. Therefore Earth's inhabitants are burned up, and very few are left.

Isaiah (783-687 BC)
Is 24:4,6

A popular interpretation of this Biblical passage points to nuclear war as the fire "burning up" humanity for its abuse of the Earth. But with the apparent end of the Cold War, that burning holocaust may be fulfilled in the next century by global warming.

Armageddon may yet arise from ecological rather than political, ethnic or religious tensions. The next century's hotter climate brings droughts to stifle food production, holes in the ozone layer to "wither" the human immune system with lethal radiation. Disease, famine and eco-disasters could undermine the efforts of statesmen to bring about a new world order of global peace because of global warming.

Heap of Trouble

In 1989, at the close of one of Europe's hottest and driest summers, hundreds of thousands of East Germans filtered through the first cracks in the Iron Curtain on a one-way summer vacation to freedom. It was as if the Biblical Rapture had come. In a twinkling of an eye, a sizable portion of the East German proletariat had been plucked from their houses, offices and grimy factories and catapulted into the castles in the clouds of a new paradisiacal dream.

To hundreds of thousands of East Germans pouring into the West every day throughout 1990, riding their global-warming Wartburgs or smog-belching Trabant cars through the breach in the Iron Curtain, freedom is spelled c-o-n-s-u-m-e-! They are only a part of 400 million Second Worlders eager to claim their inalienable right to tear away excess packaging, waste electricity and guzzle gas just like their First World counterparts.

Ever since the Cold War began, the Americans have been the world's role model for democracy, freedom, and apparently, for waste. Americans comprise 8 percent of the world's population and use one-quarter of the Earth's energy. Each citizen of the world's number one democracy discards an average of 3.5 to 4 pounds of trash every day. That creates an annual garbage pile thirty-three stories high covering 1,000 American football fields.

Chasing after the American Dream requires Americans to throw away 16 billion disposable diapers, 1.6 billion pens, 2 billion razor blades and 220 million tires annually, along with enough aluminum soda pop and beer cans to rebuild the entire US commercial airline fleet every three months. In the late 1940s, the New York City Government established Fresh Kills, a huge landfill in an empty valley on Staten Island, in sight of the Statue of Liberty.

The American symbol of hope and freedom still spreads the shadow of her backside on one of democracy's greatest dumps. God blessed America and shed his waste on thee, Fresh Kills — the nickname composed by the garbage men for the final resting place of so many new-murdered New Yorkers, transported from city dumpsters.

Fresh Kills has become the throwing-field of dreams. By century's end, it will become a ziggurat of refuse, as high as Lady Liberty and with as much volume as the Great Pyramid of Giza times twenty-five, if the good citizens of the Big (and disposable) Apple continue to throw out their pits, cores and crud at a rate of 24,000 tons a day.

In the village of Kishangarth outside New Delhi, Karan Singh, a sixty-six-year-old farmer, has found out that success has its price. His three children grew more demanding of consumer goods after he purchased a black and white television set, and the electronic ghost images of potato chips and toothpaste began dancing in their heads. Singh laments that his son, a TV repairman, spends too much money on cigarettes, clothes, and movies.

As world weather becomes more chaotic — a direct result of seven billion tons of carbon dioxide pollution dumped into the air annually — Mr Singh is thinking about giving up his traditional occupation of farming. In a country suffering a continued degradation of agricultural land, where five billion tons of topsoil are blown away each year, Mr Singh wants to black out his family's growing needs in a cloud of unregulated diesel exhaust:

"I would like to start a transport business," says Singh.

The farmer-soon-to-be-trucker of Kishangarth is but one drop in the tidal wave of what are called consumer boomers, India's rising middle class. He is representative of the coming wave of new markets in the developing world where four billion people dream of a standard of living as luxurious and as wasteful of Earth's finite resources as that of America's yuppies.

No true lover of democracy could deny a person's right to a better standard of living, better

[In the Kali Yuga] Earth will be venerated only for its mineral treasures...

The Hindu Puranas (c. AD 900) Vis-P IV 24: 26,27

food and more goods. But a standard of a waste-productive living equal to that of the average American and European, multiplied five to six billion times, is bound to usher in an apocalyptic nightmare by the middle of the next century.

Though the First World nations have some of the most stringent sanitation regulations for wastes and pollution, the Third World, in its race to share a slice of the consumer pie, does not have the capital to train technicians or contain its waste safely. Its industries are forced to use cheaper and dirtier fuels. People living in over twenty industrial urban centers in China suffer four to seven times more cases of lung cancer than people living in the countryside because most factories in the People's Republic use coal in outdated furnaces and boilers. The Hooghly estuary, which runs through the booming industrial parks of Calcutta, India, is choked with untreated industrial waste from more than 150 factories. India also sprays its rivers and lakes with 40,000 tons of DDT each year, a chemical banned by developed nations but manufactured by — or sold at bargain prices to — developing countries.

Less than half of urban dwellers in forty-six Third World nations have sanitation services. For example, of India's 3,119 towns and cities, the Worldwatch Institute estimates that only 209 have partial sewage systems and only eight have full sewage treatment facilities. The Ganges river is roiling with raw sewage, as is the River of Kings running through Bangkok in Thailand.

Not all the gunk and corruption in Asia's open-air garbage piles and rivers is home-grown. Richer nations often ship their garbage to the Third World. In 1988 the US and Europe exported three million tons of toxic wastes to ports in Africa and Eastern Europe.

By the time the last landfills of the developed nations top off, the window of disposal will rapidly close. Some frustrated captains of cargo ships have become the flying crud-Dutchmen of our times, forever cursed to roam the seven seas in search of someone to accept their deliveries. Without such redeeming Third World Sentas to take on such malodorous karmic burdens, those modern-day Vanderdeckens often dump their noxious cargoes out at sea. Their crimes eventually bob up — like a Fresh Kills corpse — on Third World beaches. Already some poor nations' lawmakers view such dumping in international waters as equivalent to an act of war.

It is hard to remain aware of, let alone interested in, the fate of the plastic shampoo container you just tossed in the trash can. The by-products of the things that define us and our culture are conveniently swept out of sight, and our attention easily becomes focused elsewhere.

Man's ultimate landfill is his denial.

Truly, wherever mankind goes he leaves behind him destruction and pollution: mountains and rivers ravaged, vegetation exterminated, the land laid waste, even the vast oceans defiled! To nature mankind [is] a malignant growth, spreading corruption. It is nature which has now begun to take the final reckoning of this grave situation by a movement toward restoring the balance. It is only to be expected that there should be natural calamities and disasters one after the other.

From the beginning, mankind is a part of the world of nature and always will be. But men have made the mistake of considering themselves separate from nature or even opposed to it, going so far as to subjugate nature and even, to a certain degree, to despise nature....In truth, mankind today, with very few exceptions, is suffering from nature's punishment...the more man despises nature the greater harm nature inflicts on him. The more speedily man tries to subjugate nature, the more speedily nature takes its revenge. **Tamo-san (1957) Mtb**

Gassed Planet

All nature will tremble because of the disorder and the misdeeds of men, which will rise to the very heavens. Prophecy of La-Salette (1846)

During the period of the hollow peace [the Post-Cold War era], *the seasons will change...* Prophecy of La-Salette (1846)

The Druids worshipped the great oak. They perceived wisdom in the tree's watchful silence on still summer nights and rejoiced in the poetry of branches dancing with gods of air in a winter gale. The oak represented the universe, which the Druids believed had likewise sprouted from some primordial seed. Its deep roots were cast in Hell's darkness so outstretched branches could grasp the unknown depths when stretching toward the bejeweled heavens.

We who live in a more scientific age might sneer at the ancient *Cultus Arborum*. By coincidence, or perhaps even by some intuitive insight which the modern world has forgotten, the Druids' belief that trees are holy and essential teachers of wisdom may not be incorrect after all. Before agriculture existed, the superstitious hunter-gatherer of 10,000 years ago roamed a world covered by a mantle of primeval forest stretching over an estimated 6.2 billion hectares. The air he breathed was refreshed by a vast arboreal atmosphere factory. By night, the forests of Gaia absorbed carbon dioxide released from man's smoldering campfires, farts, and snoring, and by day alchemically turned these waste gases into the breath of life. As man grew in numbers and self-importance, his reverence for life-giving trees was eclipsed by a growing need to clear woodlands, construct cities and plant crops.

The hunter-gatherer has become an consumer-exploiter of nature. The volume of cow needed to make each hamburger requires the destruction of fifty-five square feet of the planet's tropical rain forests, the sanctuary for 40 percent of all animal and plant species. The temperate forests are dying, the tropical air factories of the Amazon, the Congo and Indonesia are being burned and bulldozed at a staggering two acres a second — 120 acres a minute — at a time when the gas waste products these trees consume have risen above pre-industrial levels by 24 percent. The Worldwatch Institute estimates that of the over seven billion tons of carbon dioxide we dump into the atmosphere each year, 2.6 billion tons comes from burning trees.

A few centuries back, the temperate forests of the Northern Hemisphere began disappearing in man's forest of smokestacks. Pity the descendants of that Druid's oak; a 1986 survey shows that in Europe 22 percent of the forests have become sickened by the pollen of acids spewing from the mouths of man's brick trees.

The prophet Isaiah's threat that our wanton defiance of Earth's natural laws will see us *burned up* may not only stand for a nuclear holocaust. The heat is already on. Science calls it the greenhouse effect, which occurs when gases, such as carbon dioxide (CO_2) from the fossil fuels we use for industry, are dumped into the atmosphere faster than our dwindling tree cover can recycle. These undigested gasses are free to absorb some of the sun's heat, trapping it in the atmosphere rather than allowing excess heat to radiate back into space. Air pollutants therefore work like the glass planes of a greenhouse, heating up the planet.

Scientists cannot calculate exactly what damage we are doing to Earth's natural

With these swords [rockets] it will be possible to cut up the skies [the ozone

layer]... Pastor Bartholomaeus (1642)

*The weather will continue to change as it is already doing, and in the mid-

1990s there will be violent alterations in weather patterns...*

Spirit guides of Ruth Montgomery (1986) Hrd

constitution. They guess that global warming could mean a temperature rise of from 1.5 to 4.5 centigrade (2.7 to 8.1 degrees Fahrenheit) from the 1990s to the middle of the next century. At a time when mankind needs to cut CO_2 emissions by two billion tons a year to stabilize the atmospheric heat-up, all estimates show our emissions are on the rise.

The spread of industrial technology will soon bring the Second and Third Worlds up to par with the developed world. China possesses the largest reserve of the dirtiest greenhouse gas maker, coal; the People's Republic plans to double its coal production by the year 2000. The International Energy Agency projects a 32 percent increase in coal-fired generating capacity worldwide.

The much-publicized Earth Summit in Rio de Janiero in 1992 did much to bring the leaders and green activists of the world together to at least face the problem, but once again, the economic superpowers responsible for most of the damage did little to establish the draconian measures necessary to make a real difference in cutting down global warming before it goes out of control. In short, there were a few token motions to limit pollution, lots of talk about stronger measures — and in the end lots of hot air remains.

Between the lines of the final draft of the Earth Summit's resolutions hides the apocalypse which is spawned by our fear of taking change beyond talking. Like the preceding promises made in the international earth conference in the Netherlands, the Earth Summit charter acknowledges "the need to stabilize" emissions and notes that "many industrialized nations" agree that such a goal should be reached by the year 2000, but it postpones declaring what level of emissions it wants stabilized — let alone the means to achieve it — until a future conference. No doubt there will be more conferences and even a pledge or two of reductions. But this seemingly pre-programmed resistance to changing from exploiters to healers of Gaia may only begin to crumble too slowly and too late.

To postpone is human, to pass the buck into the future even more so. If one is young, and one's skin is still pliable and unblemished, the sun's warmth is especially blissful, a good tan is admired. One cannot see or feel the effect of one of the most life-threatening greenhouse gases, let alone pronounce it: Chlorofluorocarbons (CFCs). Each CFC sprayed out of a deodorant can or leaking from the sigh of an obsolete air conditioner is destined to eat away mother Gaia's atmospheric bedspread, the ozone layer.

The Earth's thin layer of ozone blocks lethal ultraviolet rays, protecting us against terminal radiation from space; each chlorine atom released by one CFC molecule can break up as many as 100,000 molecules of ozone and help you nurture a terminal tan for a century. Each CFC molecule is also 20,000 times as efficient in trapping heat as CO_2, as it opens a hole for radioactive sunburns, skin cancers, cataracts and a weakened resistance to disease.

The fourth angel poured his bowl on the sun and the sun was given power to scorch people with fire. They were seared by intense heat and they cursed the name of God.

St John of Patmos (AD 81-96) Rev 16:8,9

Fire will leap forth on the forests and meadows, wrapping all things there in a winding sheet of flame. Quetzalcoatl (AD 947)

The global body-corporate doesn't want the steam taken out of their engines or want the spunk out of their spray cans at a time when the thawing Cold War will bring hundreds of millions of new consumers into the burgeoning world economy. And can one blame them? Who wants to deal with a dirty problem, especially one we can't see clearly and can't make rational forecasts about?

I imagine the average, short-sighted, consumer-friendly politically correct, businessman trusts that consumerism will spread rather than slow down. Especially as the most strident predictions of ecological doom remain for the most part the property of fringe greenies, or find themselves in the pages of a book on collective prophecies.

Then the earth no longer stands unshaken...all voices of the gods will of necessity be silenced and dumb; the fruits of the earth will rot; the soil will turn barren, and the very air will rot; the soil will turn barren, and the very air will sicken in sullen stagnation. After this manner will old age come upon the world. **Hermes (AD 150-170) Asc III**

As pollution continues, pure water will become more valuable than oil, and

will be scarcer by far.

Spirit guides of Ruth Montgomery (1976) WbF

Because of drought there will also be famine in the early part of the next decade. This will not be confined to Africa or the Middle East. America will also be affected, and since it is the breadbasket for so much of the Third World, there will be few answers to calls for assistance.

Spirit guides of Ruth Montgomery (1986) Hrd

The tropical rain forests support the sky — cut down the trees and disaster will follow. **South American tribal legend**

Then shall the elements of all the world be desolate;

air, earth, sea, flaming fire, and the sky and night,

all days merge into one fire, and to one barren,

shapeless mass to come.

The Sibylline Oracles (second century BC)

62

The Great Drought

The waters of the [Nile] shall drain away, the river shall be parched and run dry; its channels shall stink, the streams of Egypt shall be parched and dry up. The reeds and rushes will wither, also the plants along the Nile, at the mouth of the river [the Delta]. Every sown field along the Nile will become parched, will blow away and be no more. The fishermen will groan and lament. Those who throw nets on the water will pine away. **Isaiah (783-687 BC) Is 19:5-8**

At the 48th degree of the climacteric, [at] the end of Cancer [late July], there is a very great drought. Fish in the sea, river and lake boiled hectic. Bearn and Bigorre [southwest France] in distress from fire in the sky. **Nostradamus (1555) C5 Q98**

(Note: The prophecy's indexing in Nostradamus' book, *The Centuries*, could give us a clue to which year: 1998. Other references pinpoint a catastrophe in July of 1999.)

No one can determine how much the greenhouse effect will change the shape of climates to come. The computer models and data presently collected are at best general overviews of Mother Nature's complex regulation of weather, water and earth.

There are variables still to be considered. For instance, currently no climatologist can conclude what effect a change in cloud cover would have in slowing the rise of global temperature. As the world heats up, more ocean water evaporates, creating more clouds. The increased cloud cover could reflect more of the sun's heat back into space. If government regulators around the world decide to follow America's lead and wait until computer technology can simulate all the twenty-five interactions of Gaia's cloud cover before they act, the greenhouse effect could get much worse.

The greenhouse effect will exert its greatest impact on agriculture and sea levels. Agriculture has evolved in response to a balanced climate that has changed little since the first hunter-gatherers began planting crops. Those who declare that the greenhouse effect will open as much new land for cultivation as is lost overlook the long period of climactic chaos we must endure before full-scale restriction of greenhouse gases brings the weather into a new balance.

Though the food burdens of countries like India may be relieved by wetter monsoons, the world's greatest source of staple grains, the North American heartland, will suffer decreased yields; the weather patterns needed to grow grain will continue to move a few hundred miles north, over the poorer soils of the sub-Arctic forests of Canada. And hotter skies, creating increased evaporation during the summer growing season, are likely to cause a decline in soil moisture in the greatest grain-growing areas of the northern hemisphere.

Scientists would rather stay mum about what life would be like in a global greenhouse, but the prophets in their subjective auguries describe in detail what it could be like. Nostradamus, in particular, threatens us with a future drought of Biblical proportions that will burn a swath across latitude 48 in the northern hemisphere. Drawing a line across a map at that latitude, we see nearly all the world's chief grain belts affected. Today's amber oceans of wheat stretching across North America and the Ukraine revert to prairies and inhospitable steppes in the next century.

Some scientists argue that warmer and wetter winters could produce greater harvests of winter wheat. This would be welcome news — as long as the freak greenhouse storms which are

Mars, Mercury, and the Moon in conjunction [which took place in 1987, '91, '92 and '93; and will again in April '94, December '95, March and June '96, March '98, July and August, 2000.], *toward the Midi* [South France and perhaps Africa as well] *there will be a great drought.*

Nostradamus (1555) C3 Q3

(Note: The early 1990s have seen a return of catastrophic droughts in Africa and a continuation of the long-term droughts of the Spanish and French Riviera regions.)

expected to double in intensity beyond today's wheat-flattening tornadoes don't blow them down. Add to this the corresponding depletion of the ozone layer by CFCs, and we can expect our crops to suffer an ever-increasing dose of UV rays, weakening stalks to the extent that even a mild windstorm will stamp out our food.

The prophecies of Earth Trauma follow in the wake of the Hellrider of Overpopulation. The one biological weapon that made us lords of this planet, our ability to remain sexually fertile year round, has now turned into the greatest threat to our survival.

The stresses to civilization from overpopulation are compounded by a string of greenhouse droughts across the world's grain belts at a time when the global grain reserve often drops as low as two months of bread on the table. If this Earth Traumatic pattern of drought settles in, there won't be much need for family planners and birth control in the twenty-first century.

Trashed-out forests will expose soil to the growing ferocity of greenhouse storms. The Worldwatch Institute reported in 1989 that annual sediment loads transported to the sea by major rivers in the early 80s totaled 6,363 million tons, much of it consisting of valuable topsoil. Nature takes two to ten centuries to produce one inch of topsoil. It is likely that in the next century a handful of topsoil will be literally valued in its weight in gold.

During America's endless summer of drought in 1987, the level of the Mississippi river dropped to record lows. America's greatest water highway, the passage for many US food and consumer products to the world, became too shallow for shipping. A string of killer summers taking place in the early twenty-first century might crack and bake most of the famous Mississippi mud and clog the world's greatest food-transporting water artery.

Imagine if a similar disaster befell Egypt's fifty-eight million people and their only lifeline through the African desert dried out, just as Jewish prophets of old have threatened. In fact, irrigating cropland and quenching the thirst of a population explosion along its banks is seriously depleting the Nile.

Coastal cities in the drier temperate zones of tomorrow may find their wells undrinkable. However, this could be of little concern to coastal city dwellers of the next century, who may wall up their shores against the greenhouse effect's second potential impact on the planet, the rising oceans.

Global Deluge

1996: Flood on Earth

Flowering Almond Tree prophecy (nineteenth century)

Scientists introduced a new theory during the 1980s which gives doomsday aficionados more fuel for interpreting prophetic flood warnings. Some climatologists predict that increasing global temperatures will precipitate a rise in sea levels of 1.4 to 2.2 meters (4.7 to more than 7 feet) by the end of the twenty-first century. The good news is that such a flood would come as steady lapping wavelets rather than a sudden drowning.

Picture this scenario: Thankful for the reprieve, the world's governments decide to drop their differences and combine their vast wealth and technology to save us from going under. First, to slow the global warming trend, they agree to drastically cut down prosperity along with industrial pollution, as well as severely restrain the coal production needed by developing nations to rise out of poverty.

Then, the wealthy nations bleed off hundreds of trillions of dollars to build sea walls and dikes (at one billion dollars a kilometer), not only for themselves, but also to save the tens of thousands of kilometers of coastline in the Third World. The Earth becomes a global Netherlands.

Now for the bad news.

We won't have the resources to build those dikes. Mother Nature's other attacks on man will have already overwhelmed our civilization through drought, ozone holes and famine.

The wavelets keep rolling in.

Forty years into the next century, the first nations will be drowned. Half a million environmental refugees from the island countries and homelands of Micronesia and Polynesia will join a few hundred thousand soggy Maldivians from a string of atolls in the Indian Ocean whose highest peaks are palm trees. And no one wants to consider what immense efforts will be needed to re-locate a hundred million drenched Bangaladeshis!

Dwellers in the river deltas will be next. The big dry-out of the Nile will cut off the supply of silt which shores up the Nile delta from wave action, clearing the way for the Mediterranean to chew off much of its rich cropland. Coastal cities of the developed nations, such as New York and New Orleans, are likely to build the dikes they need to survive. The resourceful New York cabby of 2040 might replace his yellow taxi with a yellow gondola, or the Mardigras in New Orleans might end up as a drunken boat parade. A half-dozen First World cities like Miami, Florida, are doomed either way you look at it, since they stand on porous ground that would let the ocean seep under the highest sea wall.

On the flat and congested coastlines of Asia, cities like Shanghai and Bombay will find themselves committed to the deep. Climatologists believe that long before the significant rise in sea level expected by the end of the next century, the warming atmosphere will generate hurricanes and storms 50 percent more destructive than Hurricane Andrew, which splintered and flattened South Florida in 1992. A cyclone like the one that devastated low-lying Bangladesh in 1970, killing 300,000 people, might recur in 2070, pumped up with winds and thunder from the future's hotter oceans. It will kill millions.

America's disaster relief fund was stressed almost to the limit by the back-to-back visitation of Hurricane Hugo and the San Francisco earthquake in 1989. Imagine, if you will, tomorrow's

Waters Will Overflow...

Madame Sylvia (1948)

financial and emotional drain on a superpower like America or the European Community if every storm in an average twenty-first-century hurricane season was 50 percent more destructive than hurricane Andrew, America's most costly natural disaster, which caused twenty billion dollars of damage.

On a cold November night in 1907, Swedish prophet Anton Johansson envisioned Northern Europe and America racked by tremendous hurricanes. Johansson's biographer, A. Gustafsson, tries to explain these phenomena as the prophet's misinterpreted metaphors for the fearful winds and destruction of a future nuclear war. Gustafsson wrote this educated guess before there was any awareness of global warming.

Johansson relates a scenario which could bankrupt a future American government through the violence of a single storm. He says that a hurricane will grow near Panama and then churn its way in a north-by-northeastern direction, smashing into the American gulf states and up the Mississippi valley, gaining extra clout as it passes over the Great Lakes, rattling and rolling some of New York's skyscrapers to the earth. He says America will not be able to restore what was lost.

Hurricane warning systems may be called for as far north as Oslo or Vladivostok. Long before the oceans permanently reclaim the planet's most arable river deltas, typhoons and tidal surges could leave most low-lying islands and vast tracts of coastal farmland sterilized with salt just a few years from now. Rice comprises 90 percent of Asia's staple diet, and most of it is grown at sea level. A string of greenhouse typhoons and saltwater floods might wipe out some of Asia's rice belts, creating famine for billions.

Some scientists worry that global warming could begin lifting the western Antarctic ice shelf off its continental moorings as early as the year 2040. The resulting meltdown would raise sea levels by sixteen to twenty feet! Most climatologists believe the rise of the sea level will accelerate after 2050. Author and futurist Dr Isaac Asimov has calculated there are eight million cubic miles of water locked in the ice shelves of Antarctica and Greenland. If we continue to flatulate greenhouse gases, this might result in a complete meltdown of these two trapped oceans of ice. Asimov believes this could cause a 300-foot rise in sea level, though the added gallons would push down the ocean floor, making the actual rise a mere 170 to 200 feet.

Professor Rhoades W. Fairbridge of Columbia University says the meltdown of all that ice could cause such a shifting of weight, the Earth might spin off its axis. And as we will see a little later, many prophets believe that is exactly what is going to happen.

The sea will heave itself beyond its bounds engulfing mighty cities. **Brigham Young (1860)**

And there will be signs in the sun, and the moon and stars; and on Earth the nations will be in anguish and perplexity and confusion at the roaring of the sea. **Y'shua (AD 30-33) Lk 21:25**

The balance of nature will be lost,

The Flooded World of the Future:

After a 200 Foot Rise in Sea Level

CITIES *Drowned* –

ANCHORAGE	RECIFE	OSLO	GENOA	ALEXANDRIA	COLOMBO	OSAKA
SEATTLE	RIO DE JANEIRO	HAMBURG	ROME	DAKAR	SINGAPORE	TOKYO
SAN FRANCISCO	VALPARAÍSO	COPENHAGEN	PALERMO	LAGOS	PERTH	VLADIVOSTOK
LOS ANGELES	MONTEVIDEO	LONDON	NAPOLI	CAPE TOWN	ADELAIDE	AUCKLAND
BALTIMORE	BUENOS AIRES	HULL	ATHENS	BASRA	SYDNEY	WELLINGTON
BOSTON	MURMANSK	DUBLIN	DUBROVNIK	KARACHI	BRISBANE	BANGKOK
ACAPULCO	ST PETERSBURG	ANTWERP	ISTANBUL	BOMBAY	DARWIN	
HAVANA	HELSINKI	LE HAVRE	LISBON	MADRAS	MANILA	
PANAMA CITY	REYKJAVIK	BORDEAUX	TRIPOLI	CALCUTTA	MELBOURNE	
BELÉM	STOCKHOLM	MARSEILLE	CAIRO	RANGOON	SHANGHAI	

[After the advent of] the great Comet [perhaps Halley's Comet in 1986 or 2062]...the great nation [clearly described as America in her predictions] will be devastated by earthquakes, storms, and great waves of water, causing much want and plagues. The ocean will also flood many other countries, so that all coastal cities will live in fear, with many destroyed. **St Hildegard (c. 1141)**

The earth will shake, seas will overflow their banks... **Emelda Scochy (1933)**

...and when the seas rise...every soul will know what it hath made ready [for the Judgment Day].

Mohammed (AD 620-30) Qur LXXXI, 12, 14

An unheard-of hurricane, raging over two continents....I was led in spirit to the great cities on England's east coast. I saw ships thrown on shore, many collapsed buildings, and much wreckage floating on water. At sea many ships were wrecked.
Then I was shown Holland, Belgium and the German coast of the North Sea, which all were heavily visited [by storm and flood]. Among the most afflicted cities I heard the names of Antwerp and Hamburg mentioned....Even Denmark's western and northern coast and Sweden's western coast had suffered. **Anton Johansson (1918)**

December 1994...till January 1996: Floods, typhoons, gales, hurricanes, a splitting apart of ships, submarines, aircraft, cars, locomotives. **Bejan Daruwalla (1989)**

From now on tidal waves and cyclones will cause enormous destruction. **Cheiro (1931) Cwp**

when the ocean tides shall obey no shore.

Quetzalcoatl (AD 947)

A Greenhouse or an Icehouse Effect?

"We're altering the environment far faster than we can possibly predict the consequences," says Stephen Schneider, a climate modeler at the National Center of Atmospheric Research in Boulder, Colorado. "This is bound to lead to some surprises."

Gaia usually shifts her global climates over tens of centuries, not tens of years. At present, the more popular scenario for the end-of-the-world weather forecast is a continued warming of the planet, which would be more suitable for swamps and dinosaurs than *Homo Sapiens*. On the other hand, a runaway global warming could realize Dante's hell on ice.

Mr Schneider, who in the early 1970s was one of the first climatologists to generate awareness about the greenhouse effect, is also one of the first to admit that no weather watcher can categorically predict what impact an increased evaporation of hotter seas will have on global cloud cover. The warm, wet blanket of clouds above our heads also displays a white, reflective wall to the sun, bouncing solar light back into space. So when all the scientific shouting is over, an increase in cloud cover might actually in the end slow down global warming and neutralize its effects.

Or, we could be in for a chilling surprise.

Schneider estimates that a 10 percent increase in cloud cover may be all that is needed to bring on another ice age.

The meltdown of the western Antarctic ice shelf could lower sea levels rather than lift them — so say Australian scientists monitoring the floating ice shelves on the fringes of the seventh continent. Glaciologist Dr Ian Allison, using data from satellites in polar orbit, recorded six large ruptures in the ice shelves in a twenty-four-month period between 1986 and 1988. The largest tabular glacier, designated B-9, broke off from the Ross Ice Shelf in a piece 160 kilometers long by fifty kilometers wide by 350 meters thick.

Most tabular icebergs exist for years, floating close to Antarctica, where they are eventually broken up by tides and winds. Ice has rarely found its way north to Tasmania and New Zealand in the past; nevertheless, a global warming might see the floating wall of Antarctic ice break up into sizable fragments which could be pushed northward by the expected increase in stormy weather and seas.

Since these fringe ice shelves are not land-locked but are already floating, their eventual melting has no net effect on sea levels; however, a slab the size of B-9 pushed by stronger seas could last until it was found floating off the coast of South Australia. A rain-bearing winter westerly blowing across it could bring a blizzard to the city of Adelaide. If the ice shelf continued calving monster-size bergs, the southern oceans could be littered with a mass of frigid flotsam which might cool winds and ocean currents and counteract global warming — and even bring on another ice age.

In the late 1980s, a number of researchers from the US Siple Coast Project sat together to examine their computer models of future ice flow over Antarctica. Their models predict melting will increase along with worldwide higher temperatures in all scenarios except one. That model shows climbing temperatures increasing evaporation over the ocean, which in turn will lead to heavier snowfalls on the ice sheets. In this one renegade greenhouse model the resulting ice buildup would more than offset any meltdown.

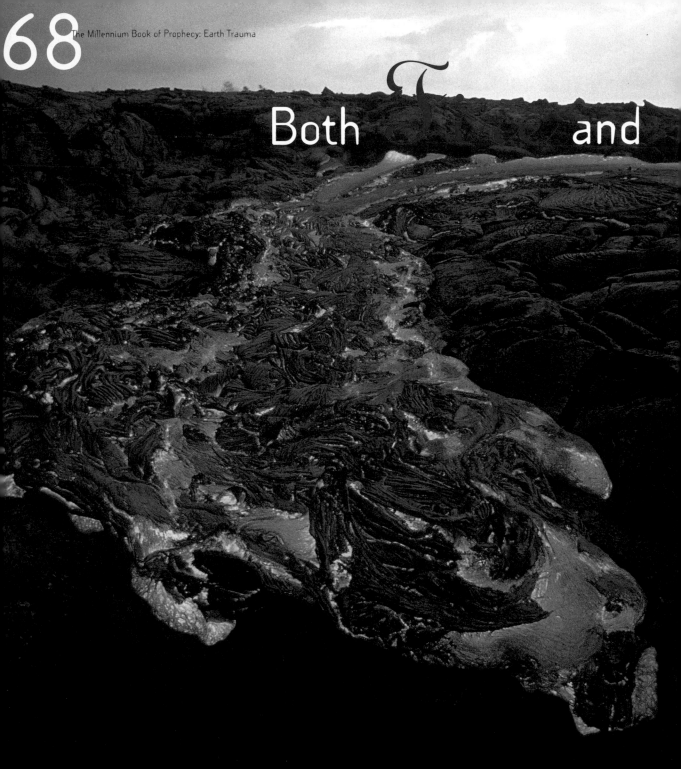

Both Fire and

ICE Spell FAMINE

These conditions [in America] *have not changed. For the hardships for this country have not begun yet, so far as the supply and demand for foods are concerned.* Edgar Cayce (1943) №257-254

Great afflictions will come....Nations will end in flames, and famine will annihilate millions.

Princess Billante of Savoy (early twentieth century)

In the previous ice age, so much ocean water was frozen that sea levels sank 300 feet. The nations of the twenty-first century may need to build new harbors instead of dikes, if the 70 percent of the population who live at or near sea level are left high and dry, rather than flooded out of house and home.

"It's not too soon to experiment with these models," says Ian Whillians, a glaciologist on the Siple Coast research team, "but it may be too soon to take them seriously. It will be five years at the earliest."

So concludes the cautious and rational scientific mind.

The prophets, trying to grasp the shape and temperatures of future weather, see our current pollution binge awarding us with two potential scenarios — either a greenhouse effect or an icehouse effect. Which destiny we follow — of fire or of ice — neither soothsayer or scientist can clearly predict. The prophet may catch fragmentary glimpses and make his own biased conclusions. Future time often appears to them in a subjective blender. Perhaps the vision of a warmer Europe augured by the Bavarian seer Irlmaier Von Freilassing is not the final result, as is intimated, but only a step toward a new ice age forewarned by Cheiro.

As far as objective evidence goes, we know that ice ages follow a cycle of roughly 100,000 years: 90,000 years of glaciation followed by a warm, interglacial period of 10,000 years. All man's weather tampering aside, we're due for a new 90,000-year cold spell any time now. New findings support the theory that ice ages are preceded by a sudden spate of global warming. Moreover, new evidence supports a frightening possibility that a shift of the Earth climatic axis from greenhouse to an ice age may take less than thirty years!

The end of the world is nigh — yet men are hard and cruel, and listen

Winds...Fimbul Winter now comes. All over the world, the heavens are

The sun is dimmed, it offers no gladness, while never-ending storms

...and the Glacial Age will by degrees be repeated in Northern Norway, Denmark, the north parts of Russia, Germany, France

This alteration will be compensated for by the development Africa, and Egypt, and in consequence a rapid increase of

The fact that neither prophets nor climatologists can confirm whether or not the twenty-first century will end with hell fire or hell-ice is of trivial importance, as the end result of either outcome will be the same. Whether we sweat or shiver, we will be hungry. Most of us will starve.

The human food chain is much more fragile than we like to believe. The weak link is North America, the breadbasket of the world. Canada and the United States suffer the same regional whims of climate. In the late 1980s, Worldwatch reported that global food output continued to decline 14 percent per person between 1984 and 1989. This is the result of soil over-farmed and degraded, or aquifers running out of water for irrigation.

The US Department of Agriculture recently abandoned 11 percent of the nation's croplands because they are too damaged to sustain continuous farming. That adds up to an estimated loss of fifty-seven million tons of grain output, one-sixth of the national total. If one subtracts this potential mountain of wheat and corn from the global output, farmers of the 1990s can say good-bye to the surpluses of the 1980s. This 11 percent loss puts global output below consumption, even before the big frost or fry makes much of its estimated impact.

In the 1950s, most nations were self-sufficient in grain production except for Europe, which relied on North American surplus grain. Since then, the population explosion and its resulting cropland stresses have forced over 100 countries to rely on North America for their life-sustaining food. Most of them are politically volatile nations in the Third World.

Whether the world's food resources are curried in the oven of a greenhouse atmosphere or buried in ice, whether the bread lines huddle near snow drifts or sand dunes, a climate damaged beyond repair and abused beyond human control could see us starved to near or complete extinction before the twenty-first century closes.

not to the doom that is coming. Now follows the Age of Northern

filled with falling snows, and the ground is covered with killing frost.

blow and devour the crops. From The Ragnarök: Ancient Norse prophecy

Europe; such countries as Ireland, Great Britain, Sweden,
and Spain will gradually become uninhabitable.

of a temperate climate affecting such countries as China, India,
civilization will be the result in all these countries.

Cheiro (1931) Cwp

Quakes, Shifts and

This planet is a living being. A high consciousness. The Earth is suffering. Waves of death spasms are passing through her body. Can't you hear her crying? Don't you see her situation? Can't you hear her shouting for help? She is beckoning her children to relent. But her children are turning their backs to her, and continue stumbling in the clouded labyrinth which they have created for themselves. This need for a farsighted vision has been set aside for shortsighted egoistic thinking. The human being has to wake up from her sleep. She must look around herself to see what is happening. She must act. Before it is too late. Before the Mother takes her children with her and disappears out of the flow of time.

Ambres (1986)

Shakes

But it is the nature of life that it exerts its power to the last moment. Now the Earth has come to the last moment and is exerting its final effort. If those people who understand the situation the Earth is in would spread [that understanding] all over the world, the Earth would immediately start to exert its healing power and heal itself. Some parts of the Earth's healing process are often referred to by us as natural disasters such as earthquakes, floods, etc. We then try to interfere with the Earth's own healing process rather than to cooperate with it. If we learn to cooperate with the power, the Earth itself will help us to clean up the unnecessary things that people have produced.

Tamo-san (1989) Trshr

In Swedish, the word for "human being" is feminine.

Whatever the source of contemporary channeler Sturé Johansson's spirit guidance, the message of the presence calling itself Ambres uses poetry to remind us that our modern-day society, with all its aggressiveness, has fallen out of touch with the feminine qualities of intuition and sensitivity. Can we sense Mother Gaia's call for help as we keep stuffing garbage into our only life-giving womb?

So far we've looked at only one side of the prophetic metaphor called Earth Trauma. However, the rampaging Goddess of Earth wields another weapon.

In the end, neither a greenhouse nor an ice age may happen. Many prophets sense a third dimension to the coming ecological disaster; the extremes of hot and cold, stormy and stagnant weather we are beginning to experience may be only a prelude to Gaia's nastiest surprise. An organism, whether conscious or not, will fight for its life. Our Mother may reach a reflex decision that it is high time for a crescendo of convulsions to break her fever and flush away the human virus. In this third ecological future, our numbers are drastically cut back, if not eradicated entirely, by an acceleration of natural disasters. These could cause a shift in the Earth's rotational axis as early as 1998.

The shifting of Mother Nature in her earthen sickbed has increased markedly in the first half of the twentieth century, and catastrophically in the latter half. Today, earthquake shares are definitely in a bull market. More volcanic eruptions and seismic activity shook the 1980s than in the prior eighty years. The final decade before the Second Millennium will see the seismic and volcanic activity only increasing. The eruption of Mt Pinatubo in the Philippines in 1991 was the greatest volcanic detonation in eighty years!

According to the late American prophet, Edgar Cayce, if you think something is loose and rattling beneath the Earth's crust, you're right. A recurring theme in Cayce's 14,256 trance readings declares that a shift in the poles will be the final climax of a crescendo of natural disasters. According to him the axis of the Earth had already began slipping its gravitational gears back in 1936, the year he believed triggered a shift of the Earth's magnetic core. He cautioned that this interior slide would take decades to build up stresses in the surrounding lithosphere, until the accelerating vibration reached the right pitch to fling the global mantle of rock over on its side.

Cayce warned us to watch out for a coming series of quakes so large that they could re-shape the continents in a twinkling of an eye.

Some of these superquakes can be expected within three months after Mt Vesuvius in Italy — famous for burying the Roman city of Pompeii in AD 71 — and Mt Pelée on the Caribbean island of Martinique blow their stacks in a violent eruption. If at that moment you happen to be vacationing in Los Angeles or trying your luck on one-armed bandits in Las Vegas, it'll be time to load up the pick-up, pack up your coins and leave as fast as you can; California and Southern Nevada are due to finally make that long-promised lurch into the Pacific ocean within three months of those eruptions.

When will Vesuvius and Pelée blow? Any moment now, according to the field's greatest forecaster of earth tremors. He clearly declares that the final surge of super shakes is just a prelude to the Earth's crust making a corresponding shift around the already dislodged magnetic core before 1998.

Where, then, does one move one's precious posterior? It could be said that Edgar Cayce influenced the real estate boom in Virginia Beach, Virginia, that began in 1945. Although this area of the American eastern seaboard is little more than a sand dune above sea level, Cayce firmly channeled that his final resting place would survive the continental floods and atomizing winds of a sudden tilt of Gaia. In 1941, not far from the shores of a placid Atlantic, the man who has inspired many visions of thousand-foot tidal waves raging over coastal cities at 1,000 miles an hour, said: ...[Virginia Beach] *will be among the safety lands as will be portions of what is now Ohio, Indiana, and Illinois and much of the southern portion of Canada, and the eastern portion of Canada; while the western land, much of that is to be disturbed — in this land* [western North America] *- as of course, much in other lands.* **(№1152-11)**

Cayce's successor in the Earth changes predictive tradition, Ruth Montgomery, a former Washington journalist-turned-spiritualist, has channeled a gaggle of spirit guides, one of them claiming to be the noted medium Arthur Ford. Some of their views on human history and the afterlife may suspend belief; in her book, *The World Before,* the guides report that man and dinosaur shared the same prehistoric turf!

Despite this psychic *faux pas,* Montgomery's guides — whether or not they are personifications of her subconscious — did foretell Nixon's re-election in 1972, his bout of phlebitis and his resignation. They foresaw the assassination of Anwar Sadat of Egypt, and the final outcome of the Vietnam War, the rise of Japan as an economic power and the Ethiopian famine.

The final verdict is still out on her forecasts of accelerating natural catastrophes. Her guides project a crescendo of natural disasters just before the turn of the century, climaxing in the ultimate shudder, a shift of the Earth's rotational axis. Since Montgomery began publishing their prognostications in 1971, these spirits have remained adamant that the poles will shift, even if the expected prelude of superquakes and volcanic eruptions hasn't tiptoed like Godzilla onto the stage of time in the early 1990s.

In 1986, Mrs Montgomery sat in a trance before her typewriter, fingers ready to do their walking through the akashic records. Her astral augurs guided her to type a gloomy message for beachcombers and surfers the world over: *Practically no coastal areas will be safe during the shift because of the tidal waves* **(Hrd)**. They suggest you tie down the surfboards and split for the inland slopes of your nearest coastal mountain range. Islands are a definite no-no unless those living in Hawaii have enough time to climb to the top of their dormant volcanoes and sit high and dry on the rim of a caldera (hopefully without the nasty surprise of an eruption). Montgomery's guides see Australia and New Zealand as safe areas that will greatly increase in size after the shift. Such insights into the future will no doubt create a headache for Aussie and Kiwi immigration officers in the late 1990s.

Lowlands of Europe are in a perilous situation, continue her Guides, *but large land masses away from the sea such as in Canada, Russia, Siberia, Africa, and China will be relatively safe.*

The shift will have its warnings, said Montgomery's para-imaginary friends in 1979. *The weather will become increasingly violent, with heavy snowfalls, strong gales and increased humidity* **(Amg)**. The 1990s have already witnessed some of the most violent weather on record. Europe suffered wide-ranging damage from hurricanes in 1990. There were record-breaking rashes of tornadoes in North America. And in 1991, Bangladesh suffered its worst cyclone disaster in twenty years. In 1992 the island of Guam was ravaged by five typhoons in one season, and Hurricane Andrew's rampage over Florida and the American gulf coast had scientists wondering aloud if the stronger greenhouse hurricanes were coming on earlier than expected.

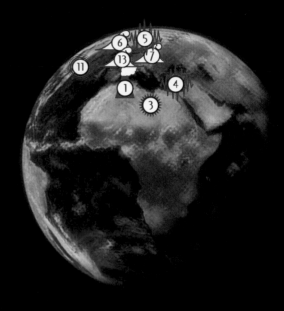

 If there is greater activities in the Vesuvius or Pelée [volcanoes]. **Edgar Cayce (1936) №270-35**

 ...Then the southern coast of California — and the areas between Salt Lake and southern portions of Nevada — may expect, within the three months following same inundation by the earthquakes.
But these are to be more in the Southern than the Northern Hemisphere.

Edgar Cayce (1936) №270-35

 Toward the south [perhaps meaning South France and Africa] *there will be a great drought. An earthquake will be reported from the bottom of Asia...Corinth* [Greece] *and Ephesus* [Asia Minor] *in a troubled state.* **Nostradamus (1555) C3 Q3**

 For several nights the earth will shake...Corinth and Ephesus will swim in two seas [be inundated by tidal waves?]. **Nostradamus (1555) C2 Q52**

 Trembling of the earth at Mortara, the tin islands of St George are half sunk [Southwestern England sinks]. **Nostradamus (1557) C9 Q31**

 Seven years before the last day, the sea shall submerge Eirin [Ireland] *in one inundation.*

St Columbcille (AD 522)

 The earth will be broken up... The upper portion of Europe will be changed as in the twinkling of an eye. **Edgar Cayce (1934) №3976-15**

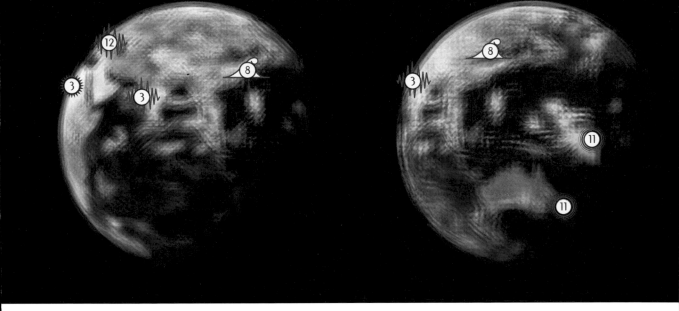

The greater portion of Japan must go into the sea. **Edgar Cayce (1934) №3976-15**

The weather will continue to change as it is already doing, and in the mid-1990s there will be violent alterations in weather patterns, with eruption of volcanoes in South America as well as North America and Hawaii. **Guides of Ruth Montgomery (1986) Hrd**

The earth will be broken up in the western portion of America. **Edgar Cayce (1934) №3976-15** The San Andreas Fault will begin to split within the next few years and will wreak havoc on some of the fine modern buildings erected on it. People knew better than to build there. It will begin to divide and parts of California will topple into the sea. Many lives will be lost...[It seems that San Francisco's Loma Pieta quake of 1989 is only a foretaste of what will come.]
Spirit Guides of Ruth Montgomery (1986) Hrd

In the next few years lands will appear in the Atlantic as well as in the Pacific.
Edgar Cayce (1941) №1152-11

In 1996 a quake will shake the whole world, and parts of Italy, Naples, Sicily, Portugal and Spain will disappear into the earth. **Prophecy of Warsaw (1790)**

Their great city [Paris?] will be greatly damaged by water. **Nostradamus (1555) C2 Q54** Very near the Tiber hurries the goddess of death; a short while before a great flood [a tidal wave?]. The captain of the ship [the Pope] taken and put in the bilges. The Castle [San Angelo] and palace [the Vatican] burnt down. **Nostradamus (1555) C2 Q93**

Just before the shift, the guides predict ferocious volcanic eruptions in the Mediterranean islands (perhaps Vesuvius?), South America and California, as well as continental-size quakes rocking Europe, Asia and South America. *These, then, will be the forerunners of the shift itself, they add, and for days and nights beforehand the Earth will seem to rock gently, as if soothing an infant in its trundle bed.*

The worst apocalyptic visions of Biblical prophets from Isaiah to St John of Revelation closely paraphrase the theoretical nightmares geologists and climatologists weave for a world suddenly sliding out of kilter between 10 and 50 degrees.

From Gaia's impersonal point of view, polar shifts are neither new nor catastrophic but an integral part of her natural mechanics. Spring house cleanings of the planet from a sudden flip of the Earth's dusty carpet of continents have taken place at least 100 times in the past billion years. The number is probably much higher, since geologists only collect evidence from land regions on what is predominantly an ocean planet.

Charles Hapgood, Professor of Science at Keene College, New Hampshire, and author of *Earth's Shifting Crust*, theorizes that Mother Nature has pulled the carpet out from under us three times in the past 1,000 centuries. The pole slid from its place over the Yukon Territory to a position off the northern coast of Norway, then pitched back to the Hudson Bay, Canada, 50,000 years ago and finally rolled to its present resting place under the polar star around 13,000 BC.

Hapgood theorizes that polar displacements could occur through changes in the tides of molten lava; these shifts stem from lateral rotation stresses, which he blames on the growth of the Arctic ice caps. Add to this the stresses of rising sea levels from a global warming and the weight of new water levels pushing down the ocean floor — or the opposite scenario of a sudden and uneven buildup of glaciers in a man-made ice age — and the Earth's crust could slide as much as 30 to 90 degrees over the magnetic core.

The handful of Bible bashers who survived the day the Earth shifts off its axis would bear witness to God's nightmare in the Old and New Testaments played perfectly to scripture. For once, the scientist and the fundamentalist preacher would see eye to eye on phenomena described thousands of years ago by Isaiah, Jeremiah and St John of Patmos: Stars appearing as if they are swinging out of their places, while in daylight areas the sun stops its motion entirely or even moves backward in the sky. This phenomenon is an optical illusion caused by the slide of the Earth off its poles. The Moon, Sun and stars turn blood-red from rising dust before they are buried in a shroud *as black as sackcloth*, made not from *goats hair*, but from water condensation resulting from atmospheric shock waves. Devil winds howling across oceans and continents at 1,000 miles an hour sandblast entire cities out of existence, while ocean swells of a 1,000 feet sweep and scour low-lying regions down to their bedrock bones. Volcanoes erupt in your back yard, Biblical hailstones ruin your picnic and pound your corporeal vehicle to a bloody pulp as heaven and earth move out of their places.

Is this God's retribution? One wonders what ran through a dinosaur's little brain when a renegade comet crashed into the Earth and brought the late Cretaceous Era to a rapid close. What sins do Tyrannasaurian ghosts fret about? What vengeful gods do they project?

Be that as it may, the whole cache of Montgomery's ectoplasmic pen pals are adamant that the shift will happen come ice hells or high warming. They see our sudden tilt into the new age occurring just prior to the year 2000. Nostradamus may have predicted the heavens slam-dunking us around *1999 and seven months* (C10 Q72). Another series of prophecies from Nostradamus keep referring to a global headstand sometime in the spring of a future unnamed year. Writing from the safe distance of 1557, the Provençal seer wrote to his King, Henry II of France, about an axis shift he calculated to take place at the end of his proscribed seventh millennium. That means the year 2000, he says:

There will be omens in the spring, and extraordinary changes thereafter, reversals of Nations and mighty earthquakes....And there shall be in the month of October a great movement of the Globe, and it will be such that one will think Earth has lost its natural gravitational movement and that it will be plunged into the abyss of perpetual darkness.

A great alignment of planets is expected in the year 2000 in the month of May (spring). Even some steadfastly objective astronomers admit that seismic activity could be high in the first spring of the new millennium. A few interpretations see the shift as either two sudden jolts between spring and autumn of 2000 or a less catastrophic slide spanning six months. The Chaldean astronomer Berosus calculated the end of the world to be October of the following year. And it must not be forgotten that the Pyramid prophet-architects say time will run into a dead end in September 2001.

The year 2000 could host the biggest spring cleaning since the sinking of the continent of Atlantis, estimated to have taken place around the time of the previous shift of the Earth's axis, 12,000 to 13,000 years ago.

Now, at the appointed time, the Midgard serpent [who encircles the Earth and seas in Norse lore] *is shaken with tremendous rage. It trembles and quakes on the Ocean's slimy floor, so violently that its motions cause waves to sweep across the...Earth, as high as the mountains....At the same time, the world's mountains shake and the rocks tremble....Mortal men...are killed in great numbers, and their shades crowd the path to Hel* [the Viking underworld]. *The sky begins to stretch, and finally breaks in half...*From The Ragnarök: Ancient Norse prophecy

The world is without support. The heart of the world is broken...The Earth breathes, whirls around in terrible catastrophes. Continents crumble and are washed away, but other continents and islands appear again. Madame Sylvia (1948)

The earth reels like a drunkard, it sways like a hut in the wind; so heavy upon it is the guilt of its rebellion that it falls — never to rise again. Isaiah (783-687 BC) Is 24:20

In the nighttime areas, the stars will seem to swing giddily in the heavens, and as dawn breaks the sun will seemingly rise from the wrong place on the horizon.
In daylight areas, the sun will seem to stand still overhead, and then race backward for the brief period while the Earth settles into its new position relative to the sun...

Spirit guides of Ruth Montgomery (1979) Amg

Then there came flashes of lightning, rumblings, peals of thunder and a severe earthquake.

St John of Patmos (AD 81-96) Rev 16:18

Those who are capable of reaching safety will see the Earth's surface tremble, shudder, and in some places become a sea of boiling water, as the oceans pour upon the land. Simultaneous explosions beneath the Earth's crust will bring new land above the surface of the waters, as other areas are swallowed by the sea.

Spirit guides of Ruth Montgomery (1979) Amg

No earthquake like it has ever occurred since man has been on Earth, so tremendous was the quake. The great city [Jerusalem] split into three parts, and the cities of the nations collapsed.

St John of Patmos (AD 81-96)
Rev 16:19

We ask that you picture a giant wave, higher than a ten-story building, racing toward shore. Impossible to escape it, so in that moment of terror it is well to put aside fear and think only of the good that is to come by passing into spirit.

Spirit guides of Ruth Montgomery (1979) Amg

Every island fled away and the mountains could not be found.

St John of Patmos (AD 81-96)
Rev 16:20

The Post-Shift World: South Becomes

Ruth Montgomery's delegation of discarnates goes as far as telling us where the new poles will rest: *It is not possible to designate the exact degree of the shift, but as we have already stated, one pole will be in the Pacific and the other somewhere in South America toward the southern tip.* (Hrd)

Using their guidance, one can draw a map that children of the Third Millennium will study in class. For the new South Pole to align itself close to the southern part of South America without the North Pole missing the Pacific completely, a shift of 40 degrees in a northeasterly direction is required. This slides the new South Pole from its current position to settle just north of Uruguay, next to the Brazilian city of Porto Alegre. That puts the North Pole several hundred miles east of Tokyo.

If Montgomery's guides have seen the future correctly, what is left of Japan after quakes and inundations will be enclosed in a tomb of ice. The Pacific shorelines of New Guinea, Indonesia, the Philippines and East Asia should experience weather similar to today's Arctic Alaskan and Siberian coastlines. The East China and South China Seas might remain locked in ice floes for centuries. Some of the most densely populated regions of Asia would quick-freeze in a sudden axis shift. Billions of Asians might share the same fate as herds of mammoths in the last big tilt; hundreds of thousands of years hence, archaeologists will find them in a final freeze-dried tableau of Earth Trauma's Apocalypse.

The same would be the fate of millions of South Americans living from São Paolo to Buenos Aires, stretching west to the snaggletoothed wall of the Andes. Balmy Rio de Janeiro would turn into a frigid Nome, Alaska, almost overnight. The turbulence and climatic chaos following an axis shift would dump a massive snowfall on the Andes, giving birth to a mile-high glacial wall. This would slide eastward from Patagonia in the south all the way to northern Peru, grinding and burying most of Argentina, Paraguay, Bolivia and half of Brazil under a blanket of mountainous ice. With time, what had not been destroyed of the Amazon rainforest would become Antarctic pine forests and tundra. The Amazon river might exchange its yellow-red flood of silt for a glacial gray run-off.

The former Arctic regions would undergo an equally drastic change for the hotter. Antarctica would emerge from its coat of ice as a large archipelago, tracing its former outline in chains of islands; most of its land mass will already have sunk beneath sea level because of the weight of its mile-high ice shelves. By the next millennium, the once-frigid and inaccessible continent would gather about itself coral reefs and sandy white beaches. What were sterile gray islands would find themselves wrapped in a sarong of palm trees and rainforests, rivaling the once-tropical (but now sub-Arctic) islands of Tahiti and Bora Bora. The icy graveyard of Scott's Antarctic expedition would become the next tropical paradise.

With time, another new tropical heaven would grow around the Hudson Bay. The Canadian Arctic outposts of Fort Reliant and Fort Churchill could become as sultry as present-day Singapore. The first week after a "Montgomerian" shift, the Eskimo nation of Greenland would see the island's ice shelf slush itself out of existence down new cataracts along the rocky and mountainous coastline. Nature would finally correct Viking explorer Erik the Red's famous misnomer: The future "green land" might become a tropical island outline of its former self, a vast atoll surrounding thousands of square miles of lagoon.

North and the Earth Turns Over.

From an Egyptian papyrus (BC)

One would find the Arabian desert transforming itself into a dense Amazonian jungle. Poland would look more like Paraguay. Central Europe and the western approaches of the Russia could end up covered by rainforest. The Rocky Mountains in former North (now Equatorial) America might resemble the present-day Andes mountains of a future (Antarctic) South America. The former east-facing slope of the Rockies would be covered with rainforests stretching southeast across what once was North America's greenhouse-dried fields of grain. New monsoon patterns would make the Mississippi rival the once-proud tropical flood of the Amazon. If Ruth Montgomery's spirits are right, the Australians who survive the ultimate eco-disaster will have to drop saying they come from "downunder" since the Australasian continent would find itself at the current latitude of the United States. Perth, Sydney and Melbourne exchange their cold and wet westerly storms coming off the southern seas at wintertime for an annual summer deluge — the gift of a newly-created monsoon pattern similar to the one that floods Bombay every June through September.

Central Africa becomes as temperate as Kansas. Senegal and Zaire welcome the English weather, while the entire eastern seaboard from Ethiopia to Durban, South Africa, becomes sub-tropical to tropical. Temperate Central Asia will be the next breadbasket of the world. The once inhospitable tundra fields and Arctic forests of Northern Canada and Siberia become mostly tropical, opening large areas of virgin land for man's future civilizations to build their resorts and get their sun tans on beaches overlooking the warm waters of the equatorial (Arctic) ocean.

The Earth will be like a vast cemetery. Corpses of the impious and the just will cover it. The Earth will tremble to its foundations, then great waves will agitate the sea and invade the continents.
Marie Julie (1880)

Many people will not survive this shift, but others will, because after a period of churning seas and frightful wind velocities the turbulence will cease, and those in the north will live in a tropical clime, and vice versa.

Before the year 2000 it will come to pass.

Ruth Montgomery channeling Arthur Ford (1971) Aby

When the Earth is shaken with her violent quaking, and the Earth brings forth her burdens, and man says: What has befallen her? On that day she shall tell her news, because your Lord had inspired her. On that day men shall come forth in sundry bodies that they may be shown their works. So, he who has done an atom's weight of good shall see it. And he who has done an atom's weight of evil shall see it.
Mohammed (AD 620-30) Qur XCIX

The Third Hellrider:

THE LEMMING
SYNDROME

You might say I once was something of a Hellrider of doomsday —

that is, if you were a fly living off compost piles too close to man's settlements, and liked to visit their kitchens uninvited. Or if your anthill happened to be in a human campsite and you enjoyed stinging vacationers' toes. Or if you were a member of any number of desert rodentia scampering about the dinner leftovers, scaring the wife and chewing holes in the Tupperware.

You see, I once was a part-time pest controller and ranch hand in the western United States.

There's a certain irony about a former pest controller becoming a scholar of doomsday scenarios. While observing the natural dynamics controlling animal populations, or while acting as holocaust agent when those natural checks and balances broke down, I became aware of a parallel between the excesses of lower life forms and the habits of man.

Certain prophetic consequences are waiting. We are accessing a destiny that will re-define the definer as nature's ultimate pest, ripe for eradication.

In the high desert region east of the Cascade Mountains in the northwestern United States, a few thousand humans had decided to install their mobile homes over a rodent habitat. Nature controlled the population of field mice and squirrel rats with scarce food and an extreme climate before the people invasion forever changed their lifestyle.

The prefab houses provided the hardy scruffy varmints with warm basements to hide from predators and shelter their litters from the hot summers and cold winters. There was food a-plenty in garbage cans, and if you needed a midnight nibble the human hoardings were just a short scurry upstairs in the kitchen cupboards.

The new homesteaders upset nature's balance. The mice populations exploded. Countless little runts that could never naturally reach breeding age were living full and fertile lives. The happy, horny rodents hadn't the consciousness to care about what this uncontrolled breeding and spreading of weaker immune systems into forthcoming generations would do to the future health of their race. Their uncontrolled growth added to a free and genetically easy life which would eventually expose them to a series of catastrophic plagues.

From his higher evolutionary standpoint, man thinks he's immune to the same fate. To paraphrase the biblical admonition, man can see the splinter, as it were, in the rodent's eye, but cannot see the beam in his own, for he is unaware of the effects of his blind defiance of nature's laws.

It took millions of years for the human population to reach one billion (around the year 1820). Without medicines and sanitation, only the hardiest lived long enough to pass their stout-hearted genes to the next generation. Then came the Industrial Revolution and a sudden jump in the living standard. Medical science blossomed. New vaccines and wonder drugs and an increase in nutrition lengthened life expectancy. The Green Revolution produced mountains of food.

We are clever mice who have built our own shelters and eased the hardships that kept our numbers under control. And now we enjoy a human population explosion of rodent proportions. From Bombay to Boston, the human warrens are overcrowded with people who might never have lived to age five in earlier times. They are set to propagate their weaker immunity into the twenty-first century and breed a crowd of seven billion spinners on the human hamster wheel by 2010.

We are not the hearty cavemen we used to be. Industrial and technological breakthroughs have produced pollution, toxic waste, urban blight and their corresponding social stresses to a degree never known before in human memory, nor to human immune systems. The man-rat race is chewing us down to size. The plague of drugs and booze consumed to deaden the stress and pain we suffer from technological gain might further compound our inability to resist modern man's new dimensions of "dis-ease."

The price of creature comforts is greenhouse gases like CFCs, which perforate the ozone layer, letting in ultraviolet light — a known agent for weakening the immunological defenses of crops, livestock and human beings. Like the rodents of overcrowded ranges, we suffer from higher levels of cancer than at any time in our existence. The toxic waste we bury beneath the earth seeps slowly into our water tables. The radiation from hundreds of atmospheric atomic tests dumped into the air as a rehearsal for World War III filters down through food and air into our bodies. Within the silent replication of a cancer cell and born from the carcinogens hidden in the junk food, there stalks a malevolent force. It is the death snuggle-smuggle of the AIDS virus to a lover. It is the loaded psychological gun hiding in the attic trunk of everyone's potential suicidal despair. One can see the approach of the Third Hellrider of Doomsday on a path made of stress and repressed desires to self-destruct. He is a half-rodent, half-man metaphor called The Lemming Syndrome. He is the final panic, a breakdown of society, riding the trail of pestilences that ecologists and disease-watchers are only just beginning to recognize.

The Seven **Final** Plagues

*I saw in heaven another great and marvelous sign: seven angels with the seven last plagues —
last, because with them God's wrath is completed...Out of the temple came the seven angels with
the seven plagues. They were dressed in clean, shining linen and wore golden sashes around
their chests. Then one of the four living creatures gave to the seven angels seven golden bowls
filled with the wrath of God, who lives for ever and ever. And the temple was filled with smoke
from the glory of God and from his power, and no one could enter the temple until the seven
plagues of the seven angels were completed.*

St John of Patmos (AD 81-96) Rev 15:1,6-8

Ecclesiastes III in the Old Testament tells us there is "a time for everything and a season for
every activity under heaven." The Biblical prophets pinpoint the final years before the Second
Millennium as the time we begin to see the seven pestilential scourges.

It could be argued that the Biblical prophets as harbingers of God's wrath were an institution
of ancient Israel, an old-time version of bad newsmongers. A party in Herod's palace wouldn't
get off the ground without the background din of John the Baptist echoing doom and
repentance off the stone walls of his cistern. Party animals from Solomon's court to King
David's entourage tolerated their share of holy gatecrashers. One had to lend a wine-saturated
ear to wailing Amoses or rancorous rabbis like Zechariah, and tradition commanded they take
note of a list of divine grievances and consider a future of hair powdered with funeral ash and a
party attire made of sackcloth.

Perhaps these denizens of the desert wilderness were indulged by their brethren because
Zion's corner in the geopolitical hotbed of the Middle East has all too often made her a target
for conquest in a hostile gentile world. Kosher doomsayers like Y'shua have the odds in their
favor when a touch of prophetic heartburn in AD 33 hits the mark in AD 69 and Jerusalem is
sacked and pulverized for the umpteenth time.

Modern men could attribute all the prophets' success to the good luck and clever guesswork
of a few eccentric stick-in-the-mud-slingers living in violent times. But the esoteric-at-heart
believe these misunderstood visionaries had their fingers on the pulse of their people's
predictability.

St John, the author of Revelation and the last and most heretical prophet in the Jewish
Biblical lineage, had discarded the menorah for the Christian cross and taken the hellfire and
brimstone tradition beyond the chosen few to the world of the gentiles. Today many Christians
learn to recite a litany of St John's visions that are bound to crash our late twentieth-century
party. A shouting from rooftops of a different kind reverberates from radio towers or TV aerials.
The message of God's wrath drones on about seven dreadful plagues scheduled to purge the
human race before the Second Coming of St John's personal choice for the Messiah.

Old St John, locked away in a cave by the Romans with only his parchment, pen and wild
imagination to play with, could not turn his spiritually sour grapes into party wine. The following
passages from Chapter 15 and 16 of his Book of Revelation describe seven dimensions of the
Third Hellrider, the rat-bag of pestilences called The Lemming Syndrome. John's jungle of
horrors is corroborated by non-Christian visionaries as well as contemporary Christian seers.

They point to stress and denial making a mouse — or worse — a lemming out of
modern man. And here are seven ways in which we can worry ourselves sick about it.

"Dis-Ease" ONE . . .

The first angel went and poured out his bowl on the land, and ugly and painful sores broke out on the people who had the mark of the beast and worshipped his image.

Revelation 16:2

Saturn joined with Scorpio [transiting] Sagittarius at its highest ascendant: Plague....The century as well as the age draws close to its renewal.

Nostradamus (1555-1557) C1 Q16

...in the meantime [there appears] so vast a plague that two-thirds of the world will fail and decay. So many die that no one will know the true owners of fields and houses, and there will be a complete desolation of the Clergy.

Epistle to Henry II

Swords [the occult symbol for the phallus] damp with blood from distant lands. A very great plague will come with a great scab. Relief near but the remedies far away.

Nostradamus (1555-1557) C3 Q75

Those at ease will be suddenly cast down...Hunger, fire, blood, plague and all evils doubled.

Nostradamus (1555-1557) C8 Q17

. . . Blood, Plague

Nostradamus's clues may indicate when the scourge we might call the Blood Death — a new version of the medieval Black Death — will take effect. The prophet warns that it will descend when the planet Saturn enters the constellation of Sagittarius. Since the event takes place at the end of a century, that narrows it down to November 1985, when doctors and the world press for the first time acknowledged AIDS as the most potentially hazardous pandemic in history.

Nostradamus, a distinguished plague doctor of the sixteenth century, not only weaves a hauntingly close description of one of the symptoms of AIDS, but also foresees the current frustrations in curing it. The black and purple lesions of Kaposi's sarcoma, a rare skin cancer that can afflict people with AIDS, could be the *great scab* Nostradamus is talking about.

Relief has indeed been *near*. Medical science continues to develop a plethora of symptom-retarding drugs like AZT, or ddI; however, the prophet stresses that the *remedy* or final cure for AIDS is still *far away* and perhaps even beyond our capability to find. Few doctors foresee an antidote in the near future. Luc Montagnier of the Institute Pasteur, one of the pioneers of AIDS research, believes we are less than a decade away from a cure (1999). Less optimistic scientists are hopeful about the year 2010. In 1990, Sir Donald Acheson, the British Government's chief medical officer, predicted a "Hundred Years' War against AIDS."

Initially, Nostradamus's claim that two-thirds of mankind would die from the "blood, plague" looks more like another example of a prophet's predilection to obscure his secret meaning with punctuation; the comma between *blood* and *plague* may be a deliberate attempt to challenge the insight of the reader. But in fact, AIDS remains a lethal sleeper. Our inability to change our attitudes about the cultural taboo of sex supports the prevalent head-in-the-sand attitude about AIDS, as well as its continued spread. An open encounter with the deeper causes of our sexual obsessions will most likely take place five to ten years too late for millions of AIDS sufferers who were infected five-to-ten years earlier.

The data collected in 1991 by the World Health Organization (WHO) place the current number of people infected by AIDS worldwide between five to ten million. In 1992, the Harvard School of Public Health released the new and shocking estimates that 110 million adults and ten million children will be infected by the year 2000. The reports adds that the first decade of the next century will see major and rapid breakouts of the disease in the Third World, primarily in Asia. India could be as severely overwhelmed by the plague as Central Africa. Worldwatch Institute projects that AIDS is destined to have an economic and social impact on the Third World far exceeding that in the West, where medical and financial resources are more plentiful. But if these interpretations of plague prophecies are not exaggerated, then scenes from Haiti and the sub-Saharan Africa of plague victims dying in hospital hallways will, with time, find their way into richer nations.

AIDS may be with us for a century. This would certainly make it one of man's worst killer plagues, especially if it keeps mutating beyond scientists' ability to make new vaccines. The two-thirds slice out of humanity foreseen by Nostradamus and confirmed by Osho could happen by 2100, not only as a reaper of the living but also as a harvester of the unborn. This disease is set to continue its current attrition of the expected growth curve of future generations. Rather than twelve billion souls on the planet by the twenty-second century, the number could decliine to three billion.

AIDS is only one of many plagues assailing our immunity, the first falling domino.

"Dis-Ease" TWO. . .

*The second angel poured out his bowl on the sea,
and it turned into blood like that of a dead man, and
every living thing in the sea died.*

Revelation 16:3

... The Waters of Death

These are the Signs that great destruction is coming....You will hear of the sea turning black, and many living things dying because of it.

White Feather of the Hopi Bear Clan:
recorded by Rev David Young (1958)

By December 10, Saturday, 1994...till January 3, Wednesday, 1996: Sea accidents of a terrible magnitude. Death and destruction of fish in the sea, birds in the air and an unprecedented, massive, pollution...acts of monstrosity and cruelty to human beings and animals, forest and sea life.

Bejan Daruwalla (1989)

The blood of a corpse oozes a thick, reddish black. It flows like oil from a ruptured supertanker. A few minutes past the witching hour on 24 March 1989, the sea otters and birds floating on the watery bed of Prince William Sound, Alaska, had no mindfulness of the bowl of wrath being poured into the sea. The hand guiding the wheel of the *Exxon Valdez* veered her off course, and the tanker ran aground, bleeding eleven million gallons of crude oil into the pristine waters. The otters and sea birds awoke to find themselves coated and suffocating in a sea of clotting petroleum.

In the shadow of oil derricks, seals of the North Sea search for dwindling schools of fish in some of the planet's most toxic waters. They were plentiful off the coasts of Northern Europe before 1988, when the first whiff of a human sent them bobbing and heaving into the waves. By the summer of 1988 you could get close enough to touch them — that is, if you had the stomach for it. That summer most of the seals one met were in various stages of decay.

A Dutch virologist, Albert Osterlaus, later announced that the great seal plague of 1988, which killed an estimated 70 percent of the seal populations in the North and Baltic Seas, was caused by a virus that produces distemper in dogs. Osterlaus believed that severe pollution off the coasts of Europe may have contributed to the seals' deaths by lowering their immunological defenses.

All practical evidence points to man himself as St John's angelic reaper pouring out his bowl of death on the seas. If our wastes keep stressing the immune systems of marine life, the frightening prediction published by oceanographer Jacques Cousteau in the early 1970s may side with Revelation 16:3. In short, Cousteau declared that pollution could trigger a mass extinction of marine life and even bring on the death of Earth's oceans. Without the living seas, we will die a slow, lingering death through suffocation because ocean plankton are the primary providers of oxygen for the planet.

"Dis-Ease" THREE . . .

The third angel poured out his bowl on the rivers and springs of water, and they became blood.

Revelation 16:4

By December 10, Saturday, 1994, Jupiter-Saturn, deadly square or malefic aspect [formation] starts, accompanied by the Moon's quarter in Pisces. It will last till January 3, Wednesday, 1996. Ganesha [the elephant-headed Hindu God — this seer's divine medium] says these will be the repercussions: a release of toxic gases, perhaps nuclear leakage.

Bejan Daruwalla (1989)

The third angel sounded his trumpet, and a great star, blazing like a torch, fell from the sky on a third of the rivers and on the springs of water — the name of the star is Wormwood. A third of the waters turned bitter, and many people died from the waters that had become bitter.

St John of Patmos (AD 81-96) Rev 8:10,11

In the Cyclades, in Perinthus and Larissa, in Sparta and all of the Peleponnesus [the southern Balkans and Greece]: a very great famine, plague through false dust. It will last nine months throughout the whole peninsula. Nostradamus (1555) C5 Q90

After a terrible defeat of Germany will follow the next great war [World War II]. Then there will be no bread for people any more and no fodder for animals. Poisonous clouds, manufactured by human hands, will sink down and exterminate everything. The human mind will be seized by insanity.

Prophecy of Maria Laach Monastery (sixteenth century)

Sometime in the early morning hours of 26 April 1986, the mysterious power of the stars exploded through a two-foot-thick roof of steel built over number four reactor at the Chernobyl power station. The smoldering wound bled more nuclear radiation into the atmosphere than all the atomic and hydrogen bombs exploded above ground since 1945. The Soviet nuclear disaster has set in motion a radiation plague, blowing across our crops, seeping into our drinking water and finding its cancerous way into our organs.

. . . Hidden Poisons

Some scientists estimate that future generations across a third of the world — primarily Europe — will see a rise in terminal cancer cases directly caused by the fallout from Chernobyl. It will be impossible to know how many lives will be cut short by cancers blown from death's radium dandelion in the Ukraine. Some doctors put the number as high as one million. Perhaps St John had foreseen this plague in Revelation 8:10,11 when he spoke of *Wormwood*. "Chernobyl" is Ukrainian for "wormwood."

Gonzalo Oritz, a leading Colombian environmentalist, once said, "We are fighting a nuclear war against our own planet. And the worst of it is, we are winning it!" For thirty years, until 1975, nations possessing the means to destroy the human race in a thermonuclear war have already weakened humanity's health. Several hundred atmospheric tests have injected the air we breathe with what Nostradamus calls a *plague of false dust*, greatly increasing our chances of contracting cancer.

While the denials go on, millions of gallons and tons of radioactive waste silently continue to weaken our immune systems.

No less dangerous are the cancer plagues awaiting us in toxic and chemical wastes. The same bowl of *God's wrath* poured on the seas around Prince William Sound also leaches out from our landfills in a slime of thousands of carcinogenic possibilities seeping into neighborhood water tables and out of your tap. And if your water arrives through lead pipes, like that of most people around the world, there is a good chance that heavy metal is seeping into your stressed gray matter this very moment.

The contamination of soil and water is difficult to measure on a global scale, but studies have shown that the chief sufferers of a Chernobyl plague also earn the right to endure some of the highest levels of toxic waste poisoning. Eastern Europe has the highest concentration of industrial waste in the world. One-quarter of the soil in Poland is unfit for crops and only one percent of its drinking water is untainted. Life expectancy for men between forty and sixty has fallen to 1952 levels. The World Health Organization says thirteen out of Poland's forty million can expect at least one environmentally-induced illness in the near future. The chance of acquiring respiratory disease, cancer, skin disease or a perforated central nervous system is only a little lower in the rest of Eastern Europe and the unmonitored industrial centers of the Third World.

And if that isn't enough Biblical "good news," the threat of more Chernobyl/Wormwoood accidents is expected to increase. Before the Ukrainian reactor sprinkled the world with rads, the US Nuclear Regulatory Commission liked to narrow our chances for a serious nuclear accident down to less than one in ten million. Now that Ukrainian farmers are seeing a 30 percent rise in cancer cases and livestock born without heads (or one too many), the NRC can't get away with such a pretension. Their new prediction is a "50/50 chance" for a serious nuclear accident occurring in the US during the 1990s.

This estimate comes from the country with one of the best safety records. Apply that probability factor of nuclear accidents to the 400 commercial reactors currently operating in the world, and we can see the odds are high for another Chernobyl-sized outbreak of the global radiation plague by the mid-to-late 1990s.

"Dis-Ease" FOUR . . .

The fourth angel poured out his bowl on the sun, and the sun was given power to scorch people with fire. They were seared by the intense heat and they cursed the name of God, who had control over these plagues, but they refused to repent and glorify him.

Revelation 16:8,9

The first blow of the sword of God, which will fall like lightning on humanity. The mountains and all nature will tremble because of the disorder and the misdeeds of men, which will rise to the very heavens. The Prophecy of La Salette (1846)

There will be poisonous clouds and rays which can burn more deeply than the equatorial sun. Prophecy of Warsaw (1790)

A great change will come to pass, such as no mortal man will have expected. Heaven and Hell will confront each other in this struggle. Old states will perish and light and darkness will be pitted against each other with swords, but it will be swords of a different fashion. With these swords it will be possible to cut up the skies and to split the Earth. A great lament will come over all mankind and only a small batch will survive the tempest, the pestilence and the horror. Pastor Bartholomaeus (1642)

There will be planes shaped like pencils that will take men into space and by so doing punch holes in the atmosphere, letting in lethal cosmic rays that will kill many millions.
Emma Kunz (1938)

At first will come several terrestrial scourges, as great wars, through which many millions will run into destruction. [World Wars I, II and perhaps III?] After that will come the celestial scourge in full severity, such as has never been. It will be short, but will cut off the greater part of mankind. Maria Taigi (1835)

. . . Plague from the Skies

A great famine through a pestilent wave will extend its rain over the length of the Arctic pole.

Nostradamus (1555) C6 Q5

Words can wander from their original meaning. The Hebraic root for the word "sin" is "to forget." And "repentance" simply means "to remember." This makes the original Biblical passages prescribing a formula for repentance sound more in harmony with a pagan like Socrates ("know thyself") or Buddha ("right remembering") than with preachers of hellfire and brimstone.

With this in mind, one might look past St John's prophetic biases and come up with a new interpretation of his God. From another, more agnostic, point of view, John's father figure is a personification of a natural force — perhaps conscious, perhaps a bio-relative machine like the Gaian model theorized by James Lovelock. Whatever Lord or "Lady" *it* is, we are suffering the consequences of sinning (forgetting) our part in the management of Earth.

St John's labels and opinions aside, the spirit, if not the letter, of this prophecy could still be accurate. It may be a warning that we will suffer a plague from the sky if we keep refusing to "repent" and rediscover our place in the natural process of our planet.

There are all kinds of pestilential avenues available to an uncalculating Gaia for the eradication of human lemmings. The sky's the limit. Even if the world's industries could shut down CFC production in the early 1990s, there may already be enough CFCs dining on the ozone layer to bombard your, my, and every animal's and plant's immune system with a terminal shower of ultraviolet rays throughout the twenty-first century. Like to be a mouse in a radiation experiment?

The recurring mention of swords in connection to plague stems from the medieval belief that pestilences descended from spectral armies of demons or angels who struck down their victims with invisible swords. The seventeenth-century German prophet, Bartholomaeus, may be describing the future through a traditional medieval expression when he speaks of *swords of a different fashion*. This could be his interpretation of a modern-day rocket.

Dr V. Filin, Deputy Chief Designer of the Russian Energia rocket, the world's most powerful space vehicle, published an article in *Krashnaya Zvezda* in 1989 confirming that during launch, rockets dump vast amounts of ozone-destroying chemicals. Every launch of the US Space Shuttle sprays some 200 metric tons of chlorine and chlorine-containing compounds into the atmosphere. Scientists have calculated that each shuttle launch will be responsible for the destruction of .03 percent of the overall atmospheric ozone over the next 100 years. There can be no more doubt that rocket exhaust is a vector of pestilence more noisome than the Black Death or AIDS.

Thus, if NASA plans a couple of hundred shuttle launches for the next few decades, they could significantly *cut up the skies* and bleed a plague of UV light upon us by the middle of the twenty-first century. We then are facing a future where plague swords of our own fashioning — or *pencil planes*, as Swiss seeress Emma Kunz called our rockets — are destined to indirectly strike us down and expose our livestock and crops to disease. Ultimately, these will bring Nostradamus's dreaded *famine through a pestilent wave* across the Northern Hemisphere.

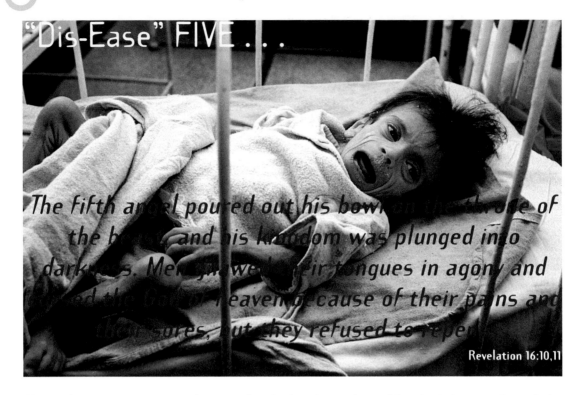

"Dis-Ease" FIVE . . .

The fifth angel poured out his bowl on the throne of the beast, and his kingdom was plunged into darkness. Men gnawed their tongues in agony and cursed the God of heaven because of their pains and their sores, but they refused to repent.

Revelation 16:10,11

Man is becoming mature and aware that he has been cheated by the false promises of the priests and politicians. Society has been feeding him on false hopes. The day he matures and realizes this, the desire to live falls apart. And the first thing wounded by it will be your sexuality. To me that is AIDS! AIDS has nothing to do either with homosexuality or heterosexuality; to me it means humanity is simply losing its will to live. Whenever a person loses the will to live, his resistance falls immediately, because the body follows the mind. The body is a very conservative servant of the mind. If the mind loses the will to live, it will be reflected in the body by the dropping of resistance against sickness, against death. And modern man has finally come to a point where he finds that the life he is living is meaningless. He suddenly feels that he's an existential orphan, and this feeling causes his will to live to disappear. **Osho (1985) DtoL**

I recall seeing a documentary about some American scientists who transformed a laboratory into a rodent city designed for the living and recreational needs of the average mouse. The scientists wished to use it as a model to better understand how overcrowding and stress cause a breakdown of society and health in human habitats.

At the onset of the experiment, there was ample food and shelter for the first furry dwellers. One had space to spare for a spin on a wheel. Water and food feeders everywhere! One could rub noses with one's mating partner at the local Rat Café and impress a litter or two out of her when she beheld the dark and cozy niche a typically macho mouse provided for pink progeny.

Life was good in the early days. Lots of housing and plenty of materials for nests. The pitter-patter of little paws soon increased.

The first minor annoyances began when one found one's favorite wheel already crowded with strangers. When there were three on a wheel, a push and a nip of another's ear was required if

...Depression, Hopelessness

one was to acquire that much-needed daily spin. Every day, the Rat Café became more crowded with new generations of cocky rodents. One used to drink and munch in peace at a feeder before the baby boom. Now it was claw your way over other mouse heads just for a basic meal. It was enough to make one chew one's fur out!

Things really took a downturn when an exploding number of new fathers competed for less nesting straw. A shagged and nervous dad received nagging nibbles from momma mouse because his straw caches were never adequate for her litter. And if that wasn't enough strain on a rodent's hyperdrive nervous system, the baby boom was forcing mother mice and their squeaking tots to share and writhe alike in niches comfortable for only one family. Still, those who had a nook were the lucky ones. These days, Mouse City was looking more like a furry and four-legged version of Calcutta. Growing mobs of destitute families with hungry litters tried making do in the streets, living without nests, sleeping in their own droppings and puddles of urine.

The new generations of Mouse City now huddled or surged in congested masses. One rarely saw a sparkle in a pair of black eyes. Their coats became dull and tattered, and the first ulcers of cancer began to appear.

Still, they struggled on somehow, so much like the humans they modeled, who live in inner city squalor or Third World shanty towns or First World slums. The rodents scratched, chewed and fought for their version of the American dream: some good eats, a little breeding and some spinning of their wheels.

Rodent crime was rampant. Wife-and-child-chewing became universal. The approaches to the wheels and feeders turned into a battleground of communal strife. At last the overcrowding precipitated a complete breakdown of mouse morality. The city was hit by an orgy of murder and cannibalism. Even mothers began eating their own children in despair. Finally the stress and strain of daily living brought on a plague of various diseases which nearly wiped them all out.

It seems that no animal — whatever the number of his brain lobes — likes to face his hopelessness or dash his dreams. Push on. Make do. Just let me eat, breed and pass pellets in peace and most important, don't burden me with warnings about impending disaster.

The Hopi prophets and many other native seers around the world believe that the majority of the human race will die out in the near future from a plague of fear and despair. They are convinced this will happen whether the nuclear missiles are unsheathed from their silos or thrown on a scrap heap, despite Communism losing the ideological battle to capitalism. (If the tribal peoples of Earth are guilty of prejudice against technology, it is certainly because they have been victims of its darker side.)

When all that we've held holy begins to tarnish and we are finally forced to encounter our empty feeders, overcrowded wheels, fouled and toxic nests and low resistance to plagues of all kinds, perhaps even then the human rats may go to any extreme to uphold their dreams and behave like their lemming counterparts in Scandinavia. When their warrens become hot-beds of disease and overcrowding, the Scandinavian lemmings will on occasion rush in one mass stampede into the ocean. It is theorized that lemmings possess some genetic aberration or habit that has them believe greener pastures exist across the Atlantic. In the end they drown in one last suicidal rush of hope.

The Hopi prophets warn that only those who can forget the past will have a future and live to see a new age. Those who cannot cope with the upcoming drastic changes may find themselves metaphorically drowning in their own fear of change.

"Dis-Ease" SIX . . .

The sixth angel poured out his bowl on the great river Euphrates, and its water was dried up to prepare the way for the kings from the East. Then I saw three unclean spirits that looked like frogs; they came out of the mouth of the dragon, out of the mouth of the beast and out of the mouth of the false prophet. They are spirits of demons performing miraculous signs, and they go out to the kings of the whole world, to gather them for the battle on the great day of God Almighty.

Revelation 16:12, 14

A short time before the king is murdered, Castor and Pollux [John Paul I] and the ship [a clue for the papacy]....A bearded star [Halley's Comet — 1986]. Public treasure emptied on land and sea... **Nostradamus (1555) C2 Q15**

Not from Spain but from ancient France will he be elected from the trembling ship [the Vatican]. He will make a promise to the enemy, who will cause great plague during his reign.

Nostradamus (1555):C5 Q49

Then the impurities and abominations will be brought to the surface and made manifest...towards the end of a change in reign [perhaps the end of the cycle of centuries in the year 2000?]. The leaders of the Church will be backwards in their love of God....Of the three sects the Catholic is thrown into decadence by the partisan differences of its worshipers. The Protestants will be entirely undone in all of Europe and part of Africa by the Islamics, by means of poor in spirit who, led by madmen "[terrorists]", shall through worldly luxury [oil, consumerism and drugs?] commit adultery....In the meantime there appears so vast a plague that two-thirds of the world will fail and decay. So many [die] that no one will know the true owners of fields and houses. The weeds in the city streets will rise higher than the knees, and there shall be a total desolation of the Clergy. **Nostradamus (1557) Epistle to Henry II**

... The Opiate of FalseProphets

The fulfillment of St John's sixth plague could surprise even him. A prophet can do little more than see the future through the rose-colored glasses of his own illusory hopes. Y'shua's caution to all "true" spokesmen and false prophets may have gone unheeded by two of Christianity's most influential post-crucifixion apostles, not only St John of Patmos but St Paul as well.

Many will say to me on that day [Judgment Day], *"Lord, Lord, did we not prophesy in your name, and in your name drive out demons and perform many miracles?" Then I will tell them plainly, "I never knew you. Away from me, you evildoers!"* **Matthew 7:22**

It could be said that St Paul gave shape to a psychological look and feel of Christianity that has gone astray from the master's vision. St John of Revelation writes in a turgid narrative style which bears no similarity to John the Apostle's writing, evidence enough that they are not the same intimate. Also, *The Book of Revelation* was written at least a half-century after the crucifixion. The prophet John's spiritual connection with the Christ, along with his view of the future, is a matter of faith, not fact. There's every possibility that his personal bias has become entrenched by twenty centuries of Biblical amen-sayers, leaving little chance of accuracy, despite the prophet's prescient powers.

If one takes this disquieting idea to its ultimate conclusion, then perhaps the priests of every religion who act as middlemen for their discarnate masters have as much credence as the current channelers of space aliens and dolphins?

If, for argument's sake, the church itself is St John's missed signal for *the beast*, Karl Marx's maxim that religions are "opiates for the masses" is closer to the oracular mark. In David Yallop's book, *In God's Name*, the author documents a conspiracy to murder Pope John Paul I. The Pope was discovered dead in his bed the morning he intended to expose the Papal Bank's extensive underworld dealings. The Vatican Bank is purported to be laundering Mafia heroin money at an annual rate of 600 million US dollars. Yallop's contacts in the Vatican believe the Pope was murdered by his own Curia to stop further investigation of the church's significant role in drug trafficking and other drug-related activities linking it to an ultra-right wing sect of Freemasons, the CIA, and the Italian Mafia.

When his successor, John Paul II, took office, he was presented with the same reports. Instead of dismissing Bishop Paul Marcinkus, the man in charge of the Vatican Bank — and therefore a prime suspect for masterminding the scandal — the Polish pontiff had him promoted to archbishop and kept him in firm control of the church's finances throughout the rest of the 1980s.

Nostradamus may imply that the Polish pontiff is an accessory to a global drug-laundering scheme when he speaks of a future pope *making promises to an enemy*. Karol Wojtyla was born near Kraków in southern Poland, which was once included in the frontiers of Charlemagne's ancient French Empire. The *promise* made by the pope of a future *trembling* theocratic state could be that of looking the other way as cash flows to feed the global plague of drug abuse. The evil tithe the church gives to drug money laundering in part sustains the worldwide flow of poison up the needles in many an addict's arm — what Nostradamus calls below the *pointed steel wounding all up the sleeve*.

O great Rome, your ruin draws near. Not of your walls but of your blood and substance: the harsh one of letters will make so horrid a notch, pointed steel all wounding up the sleeve.

Nostradamus (1557) C10 Q65

"Dis-Ease" SEVEN . . .

THIS WAY TO A NEW AGE

The seventh angel poured out his bowl into the air, and out of the temple came a loud voice from the throne, saying, "it is done!" Then there came flashes of lightning, rumblings, peals of thunder and a severe earthquake. No earthquake like it has ever occurred since man has been on Earth, so tremendous was the quake. The great city [Jerusalem] split into three parts, and the cities of nations collapsed. God remembered Babylon the Great and gave her the cup filled with the wine of the fury of his wrath. Every island fled away and the mountains could not be found. From the sky huge hailstones of about a hundred pounds each fell upon men. And they cursed God on account of the plague of hail, because the plague was so terrible. Revelation 16:17-21

...Do You Realize...

Because of the evil deeds of the land the ground is parched, no rain has fallen upon it...

Jeremiah (587 BC) Jer 14:4

There are those conditions that in the activity of individuals, in line of thought and endeavor, oft keep many a city and many a land intact, through their associations of the spiritual laws in their associations with individuals. Edgar Cayce (1932) №311-10

Hatred can kill the hated and the hater as well.

Nostradamus on "dis-ease" (1565)

The human being has abused all the holy connections and he has created total disharmony. If no change is happening, if his understanding about its meaning is not getting transformed from its roots, he will throw himself into the abyss of disaster. Nothing of what you see around you is contradicting this. Ambres (1986)

...You Are

Psychics tell us that thoughts are things. We can change them by changing our minds.

There are numerous reports of collections of housewives, executives, rationalists and New Agers cast in the infernal glow of a white-hot pathway of heated rocks. These coteries of conditioned labels and limits, once hypnotized, will discard the particular reality that fire burns the flesh and will tip-toe through the brimstone, emerging with little more than a smudge of charcoal on their feet.

There is also the story of a man under deep hypnosis who is told that the harmless coin in his palm has suddenly become white hot. A scream and spasmic throw of a coin later, the victim of his own thought projections will develop a blister where a cool and harmless coin once lay.

The power of our unconscious thoughts to affect the world within and around us is perhaps truly the final frontier man will explore. Preliminary experiments by Dr Jefferey Goodman, one of today's most controversial archaeologists and author of *Psychic Archaeology* and *We are the Earthquake Generation*, has shown evidence that we do affect the world around us with our conscious and unconscious mentations. Dr Goodman calls this phenomenon bio-relativity — an interaction of people with their physical environment via psychic or mind energy. A skeptic might scoff at such an idea, though a walk over hot stones while under hypnosis could make him a believer, like thousands of other skeptics who have risked it.

The germs of St John's seventh plague could be the product of billions of people weaving unconscious thoughts into collective psychic traumas.

The human lemming, like his four-legged Scandinavian counterpart, has unconsciously bred himself to a point where the weight of psychic and worldly pressures will trigger in him a mad urge to escape the world he has made. He and his kind might surge from their plague-ridden, polluted and crowded warrens in a mad dash to follow their respected lemming politicians and priests.

The rodents-in-charge must know of a greener pasture, a place beyond plagues of AIDS, and radiation weakening the body and spirit. These respected leaders of the pack must know of a Utopia across the ocean, beyond the torment of seven Biblical plagues. Or are they driving the whole human multitude into dangerous waters?

the Plague?

*Mankind will be decimated by epidemics, famine,
and poison...
Only few will be left to rebuild the world.
The future is approaching at a quick pace...*

Seeress Regina (prior to World War II)

*Merlin saith that in England shall be seen many strange things...great
hunger among the people, great oppression of blood.*

Merlin (Fifth century AD)

*This is the plague with which the Lord will strike all the
nations that fought against Jerusalem: Their flesh will rot
while they are still standing on their feet, their eyes will
rot in their sockets and their tongues will rot in
their mouths.* Zechariah (160 BC) Zec. 14:12

[The Biblical nightmares of Zechariah lurk behind the ambitions of space agencies. UV plagues from the skies might be behind Zechariah's prediction of *eyes rotting in their sockets* — in other words, pandemic cataracts. The Biblical plagues of "ulcers and sores" may be caused by a widespread skin cancer brought on by the loss of the ozone layer.]

*A horrible war which is being prepared in the West, the following year the
pestilence will come, so very horrible that young nor old, nor animal
[may survive]. Blood, fire, Mercury, Mars, Jupiter in France [September 1993].*

[The last line could target this date for September 1993. The war prepared could be the one the EC and USA may fight to restore peace in the Balkans. The pestilence could then come in several forms by September of 1994: a nuclear disaster, ozone depletion, or a new and rapid spread of AIDS .]

Nostradamus (1557) C9 Q 55

The Fourth Hellrider:

THIRD WORLD'S WAR

The *twentieth century* *will bring death and destruction,*
apostasy from the Church, discord in families, cities and governments; it
will be the century of three great wars with intervals of a few decades. They
will become ever more devastating and bloody and will lay in ruins not
only Germany, but finally all countries of East and West.

Prophecy of Maria Laach Monastery (sixteenth century)

It's the war eveyone's talked about and the subject of many nightmares. We have seen it immortalized in art and fiction and played out in lurid detail on our television and movie screens. We engage the enemy and face their infernal missile salvoes only in our imaginations. We win or lose a future conflict in yesterday's celluloid. Even the couples necking in the back row of every Bijou know how it will end.

Our movies and books describe chilling scenarios — soft and hard — of how you and I will find life in a post-nuclear catharsis.

Up until the 1990s we had met our future and projected it right where it wanted us. Then came Gorbachev, perestroika, and a democratic spring, blossoming after a long and Cold War. On one of his first visits to the United States, the Soviet President was having his socialist nose cordially rubbed into the capitalistic way of life by a host of millionaires. He took it in stride, politely remarking that he planned to take America's enemy away. It seems the Russians got tired of playing the bad guy. They had had enough of being blamed for the arms race after setting off their first atomic bomb in 1949 (when Uncle Sam already possessed 500).

Gorbachev overwhelmed our sense of tomorrow with new stimuli. A rapid geopolitical thaw set in, breaking all the rules of apocalyptic play. The Berlin Wall came tumbling down, a playwright became president in Czechoslovakia and the Ceaucescus of the Eastern bloc were rapidly felled like their Stalinist statues.

Someone's messing with the doomsday rule book.

World War III may go down in history as the greatest war man never fought. The superpowers have piled the Cold War furnace full of kindling, but there is yet hope that neither stoker will find the match.

Welcome to the whims of Uranus, the ruling planet and symbolic lord of the next great astrological Age of Aquarius. Whereas the futurologist errs in his logical extrapolation, the mystic poetry of astrology has long been warning tomorrow watchers that sudden changes and chaos are only just beginning. As we have examined in "The Crossroads at the End of Time," the world is set at the cusp between two astrological ages; the Piscean Age is losing influence on us each moment to the more unpredictable vibes of the Aquarian. Uranus, the archetypal magician, just loves to pull rabbits out of his hat. He is the alchemist of chaos. Out of his play of bedlam and his passion for disorganizing and destablizing the world order, he topples traditional base-metal ideologies and belief systems of the Piscean Age and creates the golden precepts of a new era.

The breakdown of Communism is but a foretaste of the confusion and excitement to come. We might soon feel nostalgic for the good old days of the Piscean Cold War. Pisces loves to dream of those better times when the Iron Curtain separated the righteously free from the politically evil. There was more security then. All the levels of national alert were color-coded and defined. Uncle Sam and the Russian Bear knew just what steps would obliterate their dance for world domination, so they never trod on each other's toes for too long.

Uranus will burn the rule book. And you can expect the chaos to increase before the 1990s are out. Russians and Americans alike might view each year of this decade as more nightmarish than the last. Even an arch-conservative relic from the McCarthy era of Communist witch hunts might look back with nostalgia at the days of Joseph Stalin. Yes, Uncle Joe was a murderer, and more successfully evil than Hitler; he managed to get away with terror and mass genocide, unlike his more theatrical Nazi soulmate. But still, the good uncle did keep the national and ethnic tensions of Eastern Europe and Transcaucasia under firm (though inhuman) control. A Soviet *union* for forty-five years, with only half of today's nukes, was enough to give the kiddies nightmares, yet a Soviet *disunion* could make nuclear disarmament as ticklish and seemingly impossible as convincing Arabs and Israelis to beat their weapons and ancient hatreds into plowshares and compassion.

In the end, the Cold War scenario of Americans and Soviets blowing up the world didn't hold much prophetic water. Now that the veil of Cold War fears has dropped away like the bricks off the Berlin Wall, we might examine the old images of Armageddon once again, with new awareness and care.

There is a dearth of Armageddon scenarios that ring potentially more true *without* the Cold War. The new and encouraging developments in the early 1990s about world peace are like cheerful sunlight dancing off the threads of a metaphorical spider's web woven over the open window to a millennium of peace. We may yet miss this opening and fly toward that which dazzles us — those flashes of reflected light that attract our attention off the path. One coruscating delusion is called "the Cold War has ended" and another is known as "nuclear disarmament." We are attracted by any deceptive glare that resembles our expectations, such as the word "democracy" being synonymous with "peace." The following dark auguries will reveal that which hides behind such hopeful lights so we might better avoid getting caught on the web that shivers and yet awakens Armageddon to slither down from her nest to feast upon our civilization.

Do not go gently into that new world order.

The fourth and final allegorical Hellrider is still setting his ambush. He is the Third World's War — the global conflict which can still sneak up on us if the means to feed, clothe and light our world break down from overpopulation, ecological disaster and epidemic "dis-ease."

The Will to Catharsis

While in theory there is nothing which is absolutely inevitable, in actuality there are things which are almost inevitable. People believe that wars happen in the future, whereas in reality they happen in the past; the fighting is only a consequence of many events which have already occurred. Viewed from this perspective, all the causes of the Third World War have already happened. There is therefore only a very remote possibility that the conflict itself will not take place. Osho (1982) Ltus

Armageddon, Ragnarök, the Great Purification...

There are many names for doomsday. Whether the prophet is a Biblical nightmare weaver, a killjoy Viking priest or a Hopi medicine man watching the US government mining uranium on sacred land; whether he is a moody Irish bishop from the Dark Ages or a profit-conscious soothsayer of the New Age, prophecies forewarning us of civilization disappearing in an ultimate war are among the most common. In the last 3,000 years the mask of humanity and civilized behavior has slipped 5,000 times and exposed the barbarous face of war.

But that's all passé, isn't it? We have a new world order. There are no Vikings burning churches nor hordes of Vandals or Visigoths sacking Roman cities these days (unless they're tourists hunting down a good bargain on a souvenir). No lions have fed on slave ribs or leg of Christian for our viewing entertainment lately — except with a few special effects from Hollywood. Let's face it, this is the twentieth century. We're civilized and advanced. This is the century of technological wonders, United Nations Organizations. We have our happy-face buttons. Modern man can proudly look down his nose and nasal spray atomizer and judge his ancestors as more barbarous and dark in their ages.

What the prophets see from the other end of memory lane isn't very flattering. Oracles of the past look back at us through their superstitions and have recorded their opinions of our century with abject horror. The prophetic consensus of the past is the consignment of twentieth-century man to hell's (thermonuclear) flames before, or shortly after, the century's end.

Michel Nostradamus spoke for nearly all prophets of the "barbarous" past when he said: *The ancient peoples have left behind witnesses of inner silence, radiance, benediction and beauty, and nations of the future will only pass on traces of plague and death. Every new generation develops weapons of destruction more horrible than before. This development you cannot stop because they have become slaves of their own fear.*

In our era of modern warfare, that began 200 years ago with the French Revolutionary and Napoleonic wars, all global conflicts have had their start on the battlefields of the Western world. The interludes of peace have nearly always lasted between forty and fifty years. The Napoleonic Wars ended in 1815. Forty years later, French and British forces joined those of Turkey to fight against Russia during the Crimean War, ushering in a new wave of international slaughter. A chain of conflicts raged throughout the 1860s and came to a gory close with the Franco-Prussian War in 1871. The battlefields of Europe remained fallow for roughly another forty years until the Balkan Wars in 1912 precipitated World War I; Eugen Weber, professor of history at UCLA, accurately lumps the two world wars together as "Germany's second Thirty Years War." In other words, the twenty-year interval between the World Wars was a rather long break between two rounds of unfinished business. After burying sixty-seven million dead with our prayers of "never again," we sift through new memories of techno-horror like Hiroshima and

And for the coming events of the twentieth century....A war will come, before which all previous wars will fade. Streams of fire will come from clouds, where there are no clouds (mushroom clouds?). And in the middle will be the great ocean. Big eagles will fly in the skies (intercontinental bombers?)....All capital cities on both sides of the ocean will be buried under rubble and ashes, and it will be cause for great wailing. The horrors of war will be also on and over the water, and the enemy will be smitten on the head with many casualties, and tears will flow and much blood, and then everything will be over...

From the Monastery of Marienthal (1749)

And after the second great struggle between the nations will come a third universal conflagration, which will determine everything. There will be entirely new weapons. In one day more men will die than in all previous wars combined. Battles will be fought with artificial guns (lasers, radar beams?). Gigantic catastrophes will occur. With open eyes will the nations of the Earth enter into these catastrophes. They shall not be aware of what is happening, and those who will know and tell, will be silenced. Everything will become different than before, and in many places the Earth will be a great cemetery. The third great war will be the end of many nations.

Stormberger (eighteenth century)

Nagasaki and promise our invisible gods that this really, honestly, will be the last time we do this to ourselves.

Until the next time the mask of civilization slips...

What can get you hung in times of peace will get you a medal in times of war. For example, General Earnest LeMay of the US Army Air Force is heavily decorated and revered to this day for perfecting the strategy of carpet bombing millions of German and Japanese civilians out of existence. The Nuremberg trials may select their war criminals from the losing side, but if this "hero" had murdered a single person during peacetime, he would most likely have landed in the electric chair.

We can maintain the appearance of being civilized for only so long. At a certain point, counting to ten doesn't stop our mass rage and *Homo Sapiens* reaches a cyclical boiling point. I would like to identify this as the "will to catharsis" since it is the Janus alternative to every man's desired and thwarted "will to power." People find the right excuse — any Nietzschean, Orwellian or Utopian excuse will do — to have a concerted vomiting of pent-up angers and frustrations in a state-sanctioned hecatomb. A nation-mob gets a collective buzz off high stakes which offer the chance to conquer or be conquered by those dehumanized objects of their group hate, the enemy.

When mob-national indignation is appeased, man welcomes the return of peace to fill the void left by his spent bile. The dust settles, the shed blood dries and the dead are buried. No prophet is needed to predict that a renewed buildup of collective angers and frustrations will lead to the next slaughter. You can count on it, no matter how many times you hear yourself and others — the victors and vanquished alike — sigh the collective prayer, "Never again."

Stormberger has exposed our denial of the inevitable in his prediction that each individual will surrender his intelligence to the dictates of political shepherds who lead national mobs to the slaughterhouse of war. He and other prophets warn that even after two global eruptions of the will to catharsis in this century there will be a third in which, *With open eyes will the nations of the Earth enter into these catastrophes.*

The next knee-jerk re-arming binge began almost as soon as we ushered in peace in 1945. Of course! we have to "protect the hard-won peace" by essentially the same program of alliances and large armies that made it so easy for our grandfathers to fight World War I rather than negotiate.

Our repetition of this ancient mistake has much more lethal consequences in a nuclear age. We might thank those ghost images of frozen timepieces and shadows of vaporized children photo-irradiated on Hiroshima's broken walls for serving to keep our will to catharsis suppressed longer than four decades. Maybe even five, or six. For all practical purposes, the real peace keepers don't sit in the world's parliaments but hibernate in missile silos.

As the Communist bloc crumbles, we replace the Communist nightmare with the nagging historical precedent: that world wars are more likely to be initiated by non-communist alliances. As much as Lenin and Stalin freaked the Westerners out, it was the monarchies and democracies that started World War I. And it was the capitalist giants (Germany and Japan), versus other capitalist giants (America, France, and Britain), who initiated World War II. The next pressure-cooker explosion of our will to catharsis is scheduled for the mid-1990s. There are disturbing signs that the next global conflict will — once again — begin in Europe, and in the Balkans.

And still we pray, "Never again."

It is only War in the end that will save humanity. It is only when the world will be satiated with blood, destruction and violence, that it will wake from its present nightmare of madness — and thus it is that the coming "War of Wars" fits into the design of things.

Cheiro (1925) Cwp

Disarming Dreams

In the late 1980s, the superpower leaders had a dream: a 50 percent reduction of the world's estimated 50,000 nuclear weapons; a demilitarized Central Europe; and NATO and the Warsaw Pact stripped down to a lean contingent of 195,000 Yankees and Ivans apiece. The superpowers wanted to deflate their forces, pumped up to doomsday levels for five decades, and release millions of troops back to the civilian sector. The Soviet and US pledges could take Isaiah's augured cliché halfway to reality if they beat their swords into *plowshares* and scrap 50 percent of their nuclear-tipped spears for *pruning hooks.*

Peace for Our Time?

Not so fast! For a moment, let's consider the weak links of superpower disarmament inherent in the Strategic Arms Reduction Treaties (START I & II). First of all, success relies on both the Soviet Union and the United States remaining as stable as they were during the Cold War. America appears socially and somewhat economically capable of fulfilling its disarming dream, but what about what was once the Soviet Union? A lot of history and a lot of hope rests on the political fortunes and survival of people like Boris Yeltsin. Can he or his political descendants succeed in re-structuring a crumbling military superpower or will the second largest armed force of destruction in the world splinter to wage the world's first nuclear and chemical civil wars? Will a collection of crippled post-socialist economies be able to stop the sale of nuclear and chemical war technology to rogue petro-states in the Middle East, or terrorist groups like Abu Nidal?

We have already explored some of the ecological and pestilential factors that could overwhelm the second Russian Revolution. The shock therapy being applied to kick-start a democratic government and a free market system may engender a great leap backward into neo-Czarism. Not a good atmosphere to verify the dismantling of weapons, especially if a terminal Russian Empire is run by a formidable military junta as stable as a banana (or should I say a borscht?) republic.

But let's just say the reduction of US and Soviet doomsday clout does move ahead despite the nasty surprises one can expect in a multipolar, Uranian-influenced, world. The superpowers beat the apocalyptic odds and in the next century actually reduce their nuclear arsenals by a whopping 75 percent by the year 2003 as already promised by START II. One need not consult the crystal ball to predict that neither China nor any nuclear Third World state of the Middle East will eagerly drop their Scuds — especially when the reduction of superpower nukes enhances the politics of numbers for the Third World nuclear club. Each Hindu, Pakistani, Kosher or Bedouin-banana-republican bomb becomes 100 percent more potent with the scrapping of every superpower nuke. If their leaders play their lies and empty promises right — if they openly dismantle their own efforts to build nuclear weapons while stockpiling a few dozen tactical nukes procured from the crumbling Soviet military industrial complex — then by the end of the century the arsenals of the developing nations will be closer to a parity with the superpowers.

Or there's another disarming nightmare. One that sees a thermonuclear war or two waged by the former Cold War adversaries despite an effective arms reduction and boycott of nuclear arms smuggling to the Third World. What it all may come down to is this: if by the first decades of the twenty-first century the road to goodwill and peace is washed out by rising oceans, or if the future global village dries up in droughts, there's still enough doomsday muscle left in the 75 percent reduction of US and Soviet arsenals to nuke all major US cities three times over. In retaliation, the US could still count on destroying the average Russian borough a meager 9.25 times.

We humans don't have nine lives, yet the cats in the Kremlin and White House seem satisfied to soften the overkill of each man, woman, tree, child, dog and cockroach from 800 times to a mere 200.

The START reduction numbers are only trimming the fat off Armageddon. Unless Ivan and Uncle Sam and all the other fondlers of nuclear phallic symbols start negotiating after they have mutually stripped down to a capability of killing you and me only once, there can be no real disarming dream. Peace on Earth may still turn out to be the peace of the cemetery.

Many people will want to come to terms with the great world leaders who will bring war upon them. The political leaders will not want to hear anything of their message.

Alas! If God does not send peace to the Earth. Nostradamus (1561) C8 Q4 dup

The false security of so-called disarmament will suddenly be broken by world war in 1999. Jeane Dixon (1979)

All manmade progress [in the twentieth century] will be enlisted for destruction. Manuscript from Montreal, Canada (1888)

The NewAge Weapons

Aquarius rules the element of air. The planet Uranus, the magician of sudden surprises, is its motive power. Uranus's magic is often manifested through the lower vibrations of Saturn, the Aquarian co-ruler of the structures and strictures of nations. Saturn will be either the wake-up call of the eleventh hour or the grim reaper of Uranus's invisible potentialities, by the medium of atmosphere, both of mood and air. A double line of electric waves symbolizes the sign of Aquarius and stands for serpents of secret and invisible powers. In the next astrological age, man's creativity, as well as his destructive potentials, will rise to the skies. Nuclear missiles and poison gases are only the first vulgar installment of the twenty Aquarian centuries to come. In future wars, man will think of using the sky, atmosphere, the air waves, all things invisible to the eye — even thought itself — as weapons.

The following is only a hypothetical nightmare. So far.

On a night in July 1999, the nuclear powers of the Middle East are poised for war. An Israeli convoy carrying a nuclear-tipped Shavit regional ballistic missile snakes through the Negev desert under cover of darkness. None of the security personnel can feel the electromagnetic crosshairs of a radio wave from another continent zeroing in on their cargo.

Deep in the Russian heartland, a special radar weapon seized by an ultra-right wing, anti-Semite faction of the splintering neo-Czarist empire receives the target signal within the weapon's phase-conjugation mirror.

Once the Shavit is locked in their beam, the radar gun crew uses an extremely large amplification of electromagnetic waves to deliver a radio signal of great destructive power at the Shavit rolling through the Negev. The signal penetrates right through the warhead to its radioactive fuse.

The unarmed missile detonates. The convoy and its security force disappear in a nuclear sunburst on the desert floor. Within minutes the surprise explosion pulls the nuclear hair-trigger of several Middle Eastern nations and the region is nerve gassed and nuked out of existence.

Evil spirits of air will call forth strange things

Retired US army Lt Col Thomas E. Beardon, a nuclear engineer and ex-war games analyst for the Pentagon, would have us believe that such a nightmare weapon is not only possible, but the Russians already have it. The former Soviet Union had already developed these new-age electromagnetic guns by applying the futuristic technology of Nikola Tesla (1857-1943), the Croatian-born pioneer in the field of electrical engineering and electromagnetism.

In his books, including *The Excalibur Briefing* and *Fer De Lance: Soviet Scalar Electromagnetic Weapons*, Col Beardon, a man with extensive knowledge of radar and advanced electromagnetic theory, claims the Soviets grabbed Hitler's best radar scientists after World War II. While the US was making advances in nuclear weapons, the Soviets were developing another weapon of mass destruction applying Phase-Conjugation and Time-Reversed (TR) wave technology. A prototype was ready by 1950.

A TR weapon can theoretically transform any radar into a powerful electromagnetic gun. Once a radar receives a return signal from a target even hundreds of thousands of miles away in space, an amplified time-reversed wave connection can send an extremely powerful TR pulse back on an unerring path to the target at the speed of light. Even a radar in receive-only mode can be plugged into a TR wave device and can focus the same directed energy on any target, as long as it emits signals picked up by radar. In short, the radar that can track jets, or even monitor the movements of individuals from space, can use the same scanning capability to destroy them.

There is one snag. And this may be one of the reasons why we don't see this weaponry used — yet. If the targeter does not use the utmost caution, he could inadvertently pulse his own nearby nuclear weapons or material with an electro-gravitationally triggered explosion. And this will happen whether the fissionable material is packed in the metal skull of a warhead or buried as nuclear waste.

Col. Beardon argues that Gorbachev's willingness to explore US President Reagan's Zero Option (a complete dismantling of the nuclear arsenals), may not have been motivated solely from a willingness to achieve nuclear disarmament. The former Soviet Strategic Command might simply be eager to introduce cleaner apocalyptic weapons.

In January 1960 the then Soviet premier Nikita Khrushchev announced that the Soviets were on the threshold of creating "fantastic weapons." Around that time, US Embassy personnel in Moscow began falling ill with unexplainable blood disorders. It was later discovered that the Soviets were bombarding the US Embassy with Scalar Electromagnetic (EM) waves carried on weak microwave beams. By using the Embassy employees as test mice, the former Soviet Union may have perfected a weapon that, if widely used, could be another cause of Nostradamus's forewarned *blood, plague*: a microwave radiation weapon that can induce large-scale epidemics in a future war of the new age.

Col Beardon has suggested that for decades, Extremely Low Frequency (ELF) transmitted on microwave broadcasts from the USSR have been continually beamed to the US, in what the CIA calls "woodpecker signals" because of the unique tapping sounds they make. Paul White, in his *Imagine* magazine article (Issue Two: 1988), encapsulates Beardon's technical explanations of the woodpecker signal and how it can be used as an invisible new age weapon: "...a normal electromagnetic wave and its phase conjugate are modulated (locked) together to produce an electro-gravitational (EG) wave. Interference with two of these energy beams in a target area

upon the Earth and will throw men into destruction.

Prophecy of La-Salette (1846)

allows EM effects to be produced and controlled at precise locations within the broad 'woodpecker signal transmission area.'" White says that the standing wave becomes a "gigantic capacitor or accumulator of infolded energy."

In other words, America sits in the radio gun sight of the woodpecker signal.

Not to be left behind in the new age arms race, America's military industrial complex expects to have a share of Uranian surprises for the wars of the twenty-first century. The invisible death rays from the Soviet Union will be met in the Aquarian skies by six armed American plasma cannons. The new US Stealth fighter and bomber technology may have a two-fold use: Escaping radar detection and radar attacks. The Biblical angel of the abyss, *Appoluon* (Greek for "Destroyer"), immortalized in the Book of Revelation, may already be set to fulfill St John's prophecy in the guise of America's new prototype weapon called Shiva Star. (Shiva is known in Hindu scriptures as "The Destroyer.")

It is reported that during a firing test at the US Air Force Weapons Lab in New Mexico, the technicians kicked Shiva's electrical capacitor banks into gear and their twenty-ton, five-meter high, six-armed god/angel of destruction generated a strong enough electromagnetic pulse to blow off the lab's roof.

A chief representative of the usually inscrutable Soviet top brass proffered a lightly veiled threat concerning the further development of SDI in an interview with the *Washington Times* on 26 August 1986. General Sergei Akhromeyev, the then Soviet Military Chief of Staff to President Gorbachev, warned, "If the United States deploys a shield in space, the Soviet Union will have several options, none of which Washington would wish....The Soviet Union will very quickly respond in a way which the United States has no inkling of as yet." In August 1991, Akhromeyev hanged himself after the coup of Communist hard-liners failed. The threat of a further electromagnetic arms race may wane if democracy survives in Russia. If...

Uranus loves surprises.

Russia is devising an electronic system that will be able to knock out US communications at the press of a button. Communication with orbiting satellites could then be lost, and the US thereby shut off from quick information and powerless to respond if a surprise attack should be launched at that time. Spirit guides of Ruth Montgomery (1985) Alns

Note that Ruth Montgomery's guides, Edgar Cayce, Cheiro and other seers noted for their high percentage of accuracy, do not use the term "Soviet Union" but "Russia." Before the remarkable events of 1991 interpreters might have excused this variance as a matter of semantics. Perhaps the best prophets have always foreseen that the Soviet Union had no future and now Russia has inherited the electromagnetic gun?

1st world

The Northern &

Gone is the Iron Curtain of East and West. However, prophecy describes the formation of a new curtain: A division of the world by

a Curtain of Hunger and Need.

One day the two great leaders will become friends: their great power will be seen to increase. The new land [America] will be at the height of its power.
Nostradamus (1555) C2 Q89

[This prophecy is numbered quatrain 89 of Century 2 in Nostradamus's book *The Centuries*, implying the year 1989 as the beginning of the end of the Cold War and the turn toward Russo-American friendship.]

Within fifty years there will be only three great nations [worlds]...Then, within fifty years there will be eighteen years of war and cataclysms...
Arghati prophecies (centuries ago)

[The First, Second and Third Worlds formed after the last World War. This may indicate that their collapse into chaos will begin just prior to 1995.]

There are prophetic indications that ecological catastrophe and its resulting human misery and desperation may unite several regions of the Southern bloc in a war of Armageddon with the North.

The stabilized populations of the industrial North — consisting of the former First and Second Worlds (the developed and Communist bloc nations) will find themselves increasingly alienated from the under-industrialized and overpopulated nations of the South — formerly the Third World.

third

When the Eastern War appears, know the end is near.
Joanna Southcott (c. 1815)

The peace among men which will set in after the great scourge [World War II] will be only an ostensible peace. During this period the Earth will shake because of manifold concussions and convulsions. Mankind will experience continuous wars, which finally will lead to the last great war. Prophecy of La-Salette (1846)

2nd world

Southern Blocs

Anyone who reads the papers or watches CNN already has become all too familiar with the new division of world tensions across Gaia's equatorial midriff. The social satire on the following page is a new slant on the growing nightmare of misunderstanding and unsettled scores between the North and the South. This is not done to trivialize the suffering and dangers ahead, but to use the disarming magic of a few absurd metaphors to clarify some of the steps we have already taken toward the end of the world.

The white men will battle against other peoples in other lands — with those who possessed the first light of wisdom. Terrible will be the result.
White Feather of the Hopi Bear Clan Recorded by Rev David Young (1958)

[The first known civilization was situated in Mesopotamia, in present-day Iraq.]

There will be perpetual warfare...
The crowns of kings will fall...
There will be a terrible war between the Earth's peoples...
Arghati prophecy

world

118

The First and Second Worlds could become one through economic necessity. Love of peace had nothing to do with the end of the arms race. Lack of consumer goods, not an American nuclear strike, finished the Communist threat. In the embryonic new order, the developed nations jump out of a clammy, Cold War frying pan into a Third World fire. The First World winners of the Cold War (America, Japan and Western Europe) will shower aid and attention upon their newly procured Second World, market-side mistress states.

Everyone knows what will happen when your average Northern sugar daddy is aroused by states that strip off their Communist clothes and brazenly display their dainty democrats before his eyes. He and his kind will come calling less and less on their Third World mistresses. They're busy with little Miss Perestroika or any half-dozen Eastern European democracies-in-distress. And all an industrial male giant's platitudes and sweet-nothings about aid and undying faithfulness to an old mistress aside, let's face it girls — his economic lust will continue to reveal tawdry realities in the coming decade. The First World sugar daddies are predominantly white creatures, who, when the chips are down and the Iron Curtain goes up, would rather ogle and woo their cool, Northern kind and stick it to you natives one more time.

Dare I say it? The fair and inflationary fat cats of the North may find a widening rift between themselves and the brown and black races of the South. One can only extend and extend, and over-extend promises and deficits on a limited number of mistresses. And when Northern dalliance and dollars fade, colonialism will return in a new guise. And if less tenderness and care from a former lover wasn't hard enough, you once-desired Southern "national bodies" will see the affectionate aid dwindle and messages of lightly-veiled racist imperialism returning in its place.

They will keep hitting you below the equator with cold messages, green with ecological righteousness. They will demand that every Southern state curtail her chance at economic prosperity.

Ultimatums will bellow from North to South: "There are not enough resources, and there's too much pollution to go around!"

What tensions and rumors of war will arise when the Northerners finally see the acid rain-tarnished forests for the dying trees! They abused the Earth beyond reason to obtain their riches and superiority over their Southern mistresses, and they will not take the rap. The assholes of the Arctic hemisphere will resolve to, in effect, order their former Southern mistresses to forego their slice of the consumer's pie. "The world needs ecological responsibility," they'll say.

The Southerners will see the same old colonial shaft in a new ensemble. The prophecies I have collected under the cape of the fourth and final Hellrider of fear's apocalypse indicate that whole regions of the Southern Hemisphere could go down fighting in a disastrous war for ecological-economic independence, sooner or a little later.

Or worse...

I'm at pains to remind you of that harem of Arab mistress states too hot to handle and too dangerous to abandon by their Northern masters. No true Northern state worth his industrial erections can do without them 'cause they "give good oil."

How to handle a harem? Keep 'em divided against themselves with their jealousies. And above all, don't let them ever become one organic, Pan-Islamic bitch of a well hole unless you've got them in your political pocket.

The Northern imperialist sheiks who seized the harem from the fallen Ottoman Empire after

World War I did their best to cut national garments and embroider political borders to clothe the ladies' naked Pan-Arabism. But the first of many tantrums of economic colonial war may have already happened on 3 August 1990, when Iraq's strongman, Saddam Hussein, stripped off Kuwait's nationalistic veil. At any moment, Northern geopolitical polygamy could find itself on the rocks. But so far so good. The last errant harem girl was put in her place during a Desert Storm.

Triumvirate of Terror

Four-and-a-half centuries ago, in his famous Epistle to King Henry II of France, Nostradamus displayed a chronicle of what appears to be tomorrow's World War III alliances: Sides will be drawn seven years before the end of the twentieth century. A triumvirate of *Eastern Kings* will secretly unite, using ambushes and anarchy as their main weapon against their chief nemesis, who the prophet calls the *Kings of the North*. Because Nostradamus usually defines all points beyond Greece as *Asia*, this Eastern alliance has every chance of being a Mid-Eastern and even North African Axis alliance.

I can only assume from continual references throughout the Bible and the auguring of Nostradamus, Cayce and Cheiro that the three most likely combinations for candidates for this triumvirate are *Libya, Syria and Iran, Egypt Syria and Iran* or even *Ethiopia, Libya and Iran*. There are also references to *Mesopotamia* — Iraq — playing a preliminary role in the greater war to come.

Whoever the Mid-Eastern triumvirate finally turn out to be, they will find support from some greater *Eastern King*, implying the leader of The People's Republic of China or North Korea. The desert triumvirate will be the cutting edge of what could be foreseen as the belligerent states of the Southern bloc of ecologically-stressed nations. They could become a desert sinkhole drawing the whole world to disaster over oil.

Christian revivalist scholars like Hal Lindsey, author of *The Late Great Planet Earth*, have long enjoyed interpreting the prophet Ezekiel's *Magog* hoards as Russians attacking Israel from the north in tandem with *Libya, Ethiopia and Syria*. He has proposed the Chinese — St John of Revelation's 200 million militiamen from the East — as the decisive ingredient in final battle.

Nostradamus, with his future eye positioned a little closer to the millennium, may see Earth's final battle with more down-to-earth "objectivity." His prophecies allude to China as the Mid-Eastern triumvirate's only second in a coming intercontinental duel. The geriatric generalissimos of the People's Republic will either survive or be replaced by more democratically inclined demagogues. They might continue to fuel their economy unto doomsday by being the chief weapons source for Syria, Iran and Libya.

Political analysts expect most of the Chinese old guard to die out between 1993 and 1999. A power struggle will ensue. US lawmakers who support the policy of giving China favored-nation economic status now and talking human rights abuses later, say a clampdown and boycott of China will do more to crush democracy and stimulate totalitarianism. As a political pariah, China will further expand its nuclear and conventional arms deals with other radical Third World states.

The seeds of Armageddon have already been planted. The technical know-how of the West and China used to build weapons of mass destruction has been shared with such cool-headed, peace-loving folk as Qaddafi of Libya, the Ayatollahs of Iran, Saddam Hussein, and America's newest ally on the desert dunes, the Syrians. A shift in political allegiances in the Middle East, brought on by religious, ethnic or even water disputes, could find both Iraq and the victorious Arab coalition against Saddam accepting shipments of Chinese missiles and know-how to help an unholy triad of future Middle-Eastern potentates. A nuclear war in the region could escalate into a wider conflict between an Arab triumvirate, their Chinese allies and the Northern bloc itself.

No one, at least no one living in the West, can believe that any alliance of Arab states could win a war against the full might of the Northerners. As we will examine later, the prophetic vote is heavy in favor of any triumvirate of terrorist nations being burned and bombed from the face of the Earth by Northern firepower; but the seers also warn us that the victorious will pay a price worse than defeat. The vanquished could take their revenge from beyond the nuclear grave.

Doomsday Alliances

Stage One: A gathering of Southern plotters

In 1986, peace will once again reign, yet it will last only a few years. **Prophecy of Warsaw (1790)**

Those at ease will suddenly be cast down. The world put into trouble by three brothers. Famine, fire, flood, plague, all evils doubled... **Nostradamus (1557) C8 Q17**

The hi-tech rout of one of the Third World's largest conventional armies during the Gulf War of 1991 may force politically radical states to switch to more covert tactics in the future. At present the Northern states appear to have terrorists and their supporters under control. However, future demagogues of the South may be waiting patiently for more advantageous times when there's an economic depression by the mid-1990s, or America becomes more isolationist. At that time we might see new tyranny arise from what Nostradamus calls "three brothers" or at other times he calls a "Triumvirate" of Eastern or Mid-Eastern kings.

Stage Two: The Axis Powers of the Middle East

Strifes will arise through the period. Watch for them near the Davis Strait in the attempts there for the keeping of the life line to land open. Watch for them in Libya and in Egypt, in Ankara [Turkey] and in Syria, through the straits about those areas above Australia; in the Indian Ocean and the Persian Gulf ... **Edgar Cayce (1941) №3976-26**

The period is the 1990s. The Davis straits are between Canada and Greenland. The land therefore is most likely Russia, to which aid is being shipped from America. By abandoning Communism, Russia is rapidly fulfilling collective prophecies that place it as America's ally in the coming Third World War to be fought mainly over Palestine. Cayce may be warning us to watch for terrorists or political adventurers based in Libya, Egypt and Syria who might be preparing for that war of Armageddon. Cayce clearly specifies the West's major oil shipping lanes and the Persian Gulf as vulnerable future targets.

Stage Three: The Invader from the North

'As foreshadowed in Ezekiel, Chapter 38, the great battle of Armageddon will be fought on the plains of Palestine. It is clearly set out for all those who may choose to read that this conflict will be a life and death struggle for the contending armies fighting in Palestine. It describes that the people of the North, by which Russia is evidently indicated...will descend into that country "with allies drawn from Persia [Iran], Ethiopia, Libya and many people."
Cheiro (1926) Cwp

Cheiro is rarely wrong about future players in wars. Still I wouldn't rule out a prophetic red herring when considering one of Semitic and Christian prophetic traditions' favorite doomsday scenarios: That Russia is the fearsome Northern invader of Israel. Why not Turkey? Or, three "brother" nations from a future alliance evolving from Turko-Islamic (and nuclear) states in Central Asia? Russia no longer supports its former Arab allies, Iran or Ethiopia. Either dooms-day missed its date or the great Northern invader of Israel is a Pan-Islamic alliance, not Marxist.

Stage Four: Armageddon's China Card

The United States will fight China, and Russia will be allied to the US. Europe will also be affected by war, several (EC) nations joining in alliance with the United States and Russia. China will dominate the entire East, and important battles will take place in the Middle East. Survey of the Future by Hans Holzer from The Prophets Speak (1971)

China has been the prime arms trader with some of the Triumvirate's most notorious candidates: Libya, Syria, and Iran. But how might China dominate Asia? Perhaps Japan may be eclipsed by economic or natural disaster? Unfortunately a large number of prophecies implicate China as the next "Evil Empire", supporting terrorist nations during Armageddon.

Nuclear Bush Wars

Mabus will soon die, and then will come a horrible destruction of people and animals. C2 Q62

Nostradamus's fearsome Mabus is an enigmatic name popularly interpreted to be that of his third and final Antichrist. His career of mayhem is short-lived, like a match, but he sets off the flames of Armageddon, the final ultimate battle of mankind. Mabus could be a missile rather than a man.

The International Atomic Energy Agency (IAEA) reports that there are twenty-six countries that could become nuclear powers in the next century. The current acknowledged members of the nuclear club are the United States, Russia, the United Kingdom, France, and China. The newest kids on the atomic block are Ukraine, Kazakhstan, Belarus (if they keep their slices of the former Soviet nuclear arsenal), Israel, Pakistan, India, and South Africa. By the late 1990s, Armageddon's nightclub could be frequented by Libya, Iran, Iraq, Syria, Algeria, North Korea, South Korea, Taiwan, Argentina and Brazil.

Israel, the linchpin of Middle East tensions, initiated the region's nuclear and chemical arms and missile race. The successful test of their Jericho IIB missile in 1987 gave their nuclear warheads a reach of 900 miles. In response, Iraq developed several models, one of them called the Al Abbas (Mabus?) IRBM (intermediate-range ballistic missile), with which Saddam Hussein could threaten to hurtle a chemical warhead at Tel Aviv and gas tens of thousands of its citizens. The world squeaked by the threat of chemical-tipped Al Abbas with Iraq's recent rout in Gulf War II. Saddam Hussein pledges to adhere to the UN resolutions and dismantle his remaining IRBMs and ambitious nuclear program. However, the leader of the UN monitoring team stated his belief that Iraq already possesses at least one nuclear device.

If the interpretation is correct that the Abbas missile or any IRBM system stockpiled in the Middle East is Nostradamus's *Mabus*, Quatrain 62 of Century 2 is given a new and terrible meaning: Mabus becomes the Antichrist launched in a surprise attack and soon dies in the flames of its own successful explosion after its supersonic journey. (The speed of such a weapon is five times faster than a jet fighter.)

The last Gulf War has clearly shown how perfectly designed for surprise IRBMs are in the compact theater of the Middle East. An Arab or Israeli leader would have to detect a launch, figure out where it's heading, alert the target and direct the people who are to knock out the launchers — all in seven to twenty minutes. Defending the Holy Land's air space was hard enough when Iraq's missiles were armed with conventional weapons. Saddam's quixotic mother of all battles has proved once and for all that even a stupid missile can find a city and drop its nuclear payload.

The chemical or nuclear extermination of just one of the region's capitals would result — as Nostradamus implies — in the *sudden* exposure of the Holy Land's ancient vengeances in a region-wide orgy, or as the prophet calls it, *a horrible destruction of people and animals.* World War III in miniature erases the land were Y'shua walked and Mohammed drove his camels.

Iraq may scrap its selection of hell's new missiles, the Bible's best "rods of iron" that can smite targets within a range of 170 to 900 miles. But that doesn't mean the victorious Arab Coalition rehearsing Armageddon in Kuwait, or the Israelis, Iranians and Libyans watching in the wings, will stop upgrading their arsenals of IRBMs for the real thing later on. In time, with smarter bombs and the shortening memory spans of modern men, even Iraq might find its missile stocks replenished by an Eastern source.

As I mentioned earlier, Christian and Semitic prophetic traditions point to the Middle East as the final battlefield and allude to China playing a pivotal role. It is doubtful whether St John's vision of 200 million Asians climbing over the dried riverbed of the Euphrates to get their hands on the Jews will ever be any more than a wild exaggeration. The People's Republic of China may never directly fight in the Biblical or Nostradamian version of Armageddon. But if the unthinkable did occur and a regional nuclear bush war in the Third World spread to the superpowers, it would happen because the Chinese supplied most of the missiles and missile technology to the Arab combatants. They have sold to Libya's Muammar Qaddafi their most advanced IRBM, the "East Wind," which has a 1,500 to 2,200-mile range. This will give Libya enough ballistic reach to threaten Israel, Rome, or even Paris with a chemical, biological or even a nuclear warhead by the century's end.

The end of the Cold War has brought about new opportunities for Third World nuclear powers. For nearly five decades since the last World War the Western world shuddered at the thought of the "Commies with the Bomb." Now "Commies" are transforming into respectable "commonwealth citizens." And even that other doomsday favorite, China, may have to step aside as the next Antichrist's arms merchant. If the new nations rising out of the rubble of the Soviet Union can't jump-start their economies, and if the developing world becomes too hard-pressed by its own economic strains to adequately aid the new Second World democratic revolution, there will be a very real chance that one of collective prophecy's most talked about nightmares will come to pass: A proliferation of hundreds, if not thousands of former Soviet tactical nuclear and chemical weapons being smuggled into the Southern Hemisphere. Just where do all the Russian nuclear scientists in the bread lines go? Just how do the hundreds of thousands of soldiers forced-marched out of the splintering Warsaw Pact into tent cities on the steppes feed their families? It can be expected that most will be good model-suffering-citizens. But it would be a bit too naive to think that there isn't a handful of desperate, hungry and unethical people in the new Second World democratic dictatorships who might be dreaming of Libyan or Iranian petro-dollars and the luxuries and material security they would bring. One might argue that to be a genius in the service of nuclear and chemical destruction is unethical to begin with. There isn't therefore much farther down to go when a wealthy terrorist state-cum-former ally holds out the ego-empowering petro-bucks for a trade in knowledge and even some of the nearly 30,000 nuclear weapons laying around inside the late, great Soviet Empire. As *Komsomolskaya Pravda*, the Russian youth daily, warned, "Emigration can be attractive to a person capable only of making atom bombs who feels he is no longer needed by his own country."

Indeed, the trade in doomsday materials is already happening. In late 1991, Italian undercover agents seized a sample of twenty-two pounds of black market plutonium-239, which physicists have identified as of Soviet origin. As one of the chief investigators, Romano Dolce, concluded, he had no doubts that this "proletarian-quality" material was the "battle horse of the Soviet nuclear program." Moreover, it was obviously destined for countries with appropriate Soviet technology to "get as much out of the stuff as the Russians do." Iraq, Libya, and even Syria, and Egypt—the prophetic candidates for a future Middle East triumvirate — could be the present and future buyers.

And then there's the greater nightmare, the post-Soviet brain drain.

US intelligence reports estimate that 900,000 people were once employed in the Soviet nuclear-weapons program. Of these, around 2,000 have the technical know-how to design atom bombs. Between 3,000 to 5,000 technicians have the experience in enriching uranium and manufacturing plutonium. Even if we were outrageously optimistic and said that only one in 1,000 of these people successfully emigrate to assist some Third World potentate's nuclear program, that still sees two unethical nuclear scientists successfully giving one or two Southern dictators the secret to launch the Fourth Hellrider of Doomsday. As few as three to five nuclear mercenaries may be successful in training one or two terrorist nations how to enrich uranium or manufacture plutonium. And there will be at least 850 people with enough tech-support know-how to help said terrorist nations improve their missile technology to deliver those weapons in a few years, rather than decades, from now.

Ironically, the end of the Cold War has seen an end to a certain balance of power and restraint which took decades to evolve. If not the doomsday weapons then certainly the doomsday-laden genius will arm the desperate and the insane of the Southern Hemisphere. If in the final seven years of this century no enlightened solution is found to dismantle the new division developing between Northern and Southern Earth — if with the fall of the Iron Curtain we overlook the new Curtain of Hunger and Need — then nuclear detonations are certain before the millennium.

Biblical prophecy describes lurid accounts of tomorrow's most likely installment of nuclear bush warfare. Both the Old and New Testaments promise that the final battle of mankind will be fought by the Israelis against an Arab coalition allied to mighty Northern powers called "Gog" and "Magog." God's prophets-with-*chutzpah* promise victory for Israel. The invaders will *become like fine dust* after a great fire from the skies descends upon their armies.

It is popular in Christian circles to implicate Russia as the Northern invader siding with *Iran, Ethiopia and Libya* against Israel. One new interpretation for Ezekiel's fearsome Gog and Magog hits below the American Bible Belt. Gog and Magog may already be maneuvering for position within the Middle East for the final battle. American Christian revivalists propagate the idea that Russia is God's bad guy (or bad Gog) in the coming war. Who then is the other, the fearsome Magog? Christ forbid, could it be America?

Oh my Gog!

Gog and Magog may also turn up in Nostradamus's magic mirror as the superpower brothers of the North *who are not yet brothers*. My apologies to all of you who treasure the bias that America, the country of the Puritans, the nation the Bible built, may turn out to be a future enemy of God's Chosen People. (Get thee behind me, Uranus, with your nasty surprises!)

When the latter-day Indian Mystic, Osho, was asked to characterize the final decade of the twentieth century, he declared it *The Nightmarish Nineties*. And so they may be. They begin with America drawn deeper into the political labyrinth of the Middle East, first over Kuwait, and later over its attempt to untangle the Gordian knot of ancient hatreds between Arab and Jew over the Arab territories occupied by Israel.

Where could it all lead to? It appears that America's leaders will continue to indulge their moth-like attraction to the fires of burning oilfields for the rest of the decade. In the worst-case scenario, America's petroleum flow could become more important than its alliance with Israel. It was America, not the Babtists' favorite bad guy, the Soviet Union, that united the Arab world like never before to defeat Iraq in Operation Desert Storm. Out of the coalition of 1991 could come the Triumvirate of Terror of 1993 through 2000. They might act as America's tight-fisted pusher, using her addiction to oil as a political weapon to neutralize America's support of Israel and therefore become, tacitly at least, the Northern power, "Amer" — or should I say — Amer-*magog*-ica, the country Gog and the Bible built.

With this disturbing interpretation in mind, let's return now to the passage taken from Nostradamus's Epistle to King Henry II, which describes the balance of Southern powers assembling to wage war with the Northern giants (Gog/Russia and Magog/America):

What a great oppression shall be made upon the princes and governors of kingdoms and...especially those that shall live eastward and near the sea. Their language intermixed with all nations. The language of the Latin nations [southern Europe] mixed with Arabic and North African communication...

Israel, Syria, Lebanon, Egypt — all tagged by prophetic consensus as prime movers in the march toward doomsday — are *eastward* of Nostradamus's homeland, France. Language *intermixed with all nations* places this prophecy in modern times. Note the North African allusion to Tunisia, the headquarters of the PLO. Libya's close ties with France and Italy through oil are also implied. Next we see the Arab triumvirate and its eastern ally, China, suffer the mother of all massacres through the overwhelming firepower of the great Northern powers as early as sometime during the final seven years of this century:

All the Eastern Kings shall be driven away, beaten and brought to nothing, not only because of the strength of the Northern Kings just before the new age [2000], but also by means [or by the fault] of three secretly united [Iran, Libya and Syria?], seeking for death by ambushes [terrorism?] one against the other. The renewing of the Triumvirate shall last seven years [1993-1999]...

The Middle East is *Eastern* to the sixteenth-century Western mind. If Nostradamus wants to specify China or India he often uses the word "Asia." The present-day maneuvers of supra-national blocks against the Middle East begin to reveal new interpretations behind the grammatical punk haircut of this cryptic Epistle. The theme of *renewing* Arab power can often be found in Nostradamus's writings. It may be more than a coincidence when the two wings of the Baathist party ruling Iraq and Syria are dedicated to *renewing* the lost glories of the first Arab Reich. The word "Baath" implies renaissance — renewing.

By as early as 1993 the Baathists of Syria may have learned how to avoid repeating the mistakes and blunders made by the Baathist Saddam Hussein in 1991. The next time the Western allies dust off their Desert Shield, they may not have so long to rattle their sabers and prepare their attack. For two decades the United States has stockpiled a vast conventional weapons stash for use in defending the Saudi kings in a Gulf oil crisis. The armaments, network of bases and airfields possess the most sophisticated weapons in the US arsenal. The speed of the American buildup to fight Saddam Hussein is a testament to the extent of supplies and military infrastructure paid for in trillions of dollars by the Saudi kings. It all sounds too similar to another American investment to protect a friendly Middle Eastern king controlling a volcano of potential Islamic fundamentalism in his country. The Shah of Iran was the previous recipient of American military buildup and support. The potential for the Saudi monarchy to fall to Islamic pressure is higher than the US government would like us to know. The Saudis possess all of America's best techno-weapons. They also buy the best that China can offer. In doing so they have exhausted their financial reserves in 1993. An economic collapse by the mid-90s could see a fall of the House of Saud far more disastrous to world peace than the fall of the Shah of Iran!

The destruction of a major Third World army by the Northern-dominated coalition of Operation Desert Storm has sent a message to the radicals and aggressors of the South. As we will examine a little later, there are prophecies hinting of a lesson the Northern powers never wanted the Southerners to learn. If a conventional war with the North is doomed, this will only encourage Third World nations to go nuclear and will see China, Libya, Syria, Iran, North Korea and even the new countries splitting free from the former Soviet Union, improve their IRBM technology, as Iraq's Scud missiles seemed to be the only Third World weapon to show some promise. US intelligence reports in 1993 admit that North Korea (which will become a nuclear power by the time this book is released) is experiencing a booming business selling long-range missile technology to anyone who wishes to buy. Iran, Syria and Libya are the current top buyers. A more clever Baathist like Syria's Hafez Assad will bide his time, preparing for tomorrow's war either with the American weapons they've earned for being an ally in Gulf War II, or by smuggling American hi-tech electronic gear and smart bomb technology.

Many visions of total war followed by vast plagues abound in prophetic literature. The *false dust,* or *yellow vapor* threatened by seers need not be caused by radiation alone. The yellowish vapors seen by survivors after the Hiroshima blast may be witnessed by survivors of a small nuclear attack on Wall Street. Tourists with blistered skin and lungs from a chemical attack on the Vatican will also observe something similar. Once released in the atmosphere, mustard and nerve gas, and biological powders like anthrax and botulism, take on the appearance of a "false dust" of a yellow hue.

The forewarned destruction of a future triumvirate of Middle Eastern nations may not bring an end but only a beginning to the killing. Once faced with defeat, the triumvirate's terrorist vassals may release biological plagues across the Northern Hemisphere, as is implied by Nostradamus in C9 Q55. The citizens of cities like Rome, Paris, or New York may not even take notice of an inconspicuous civilian plane flying over boulevards and public squares, spreading a few pounds of biological agents or plutonium dust over them. The Saudi oil fields the North's industries so dearly depend on may still remain mostly intact after a future war. But who will work there if the valves and control panels that draw the oil are covered in sand laced with anthrax?

At the onset of the last crisis in the Persian Gulf, American Indian medicine men were deeply concerned that former US President George Bush might launch air attacks on Iraqi munitions plants. Their spokesman, James Fry, director of the Elders Survival Fund, an adjunct to the Teton Treaty Council in Pine Ridge, South Dakota, sent a world communiqué about the prophetic nightmare Native Americans on the Council collectively foresee. They envisioned US jets bombing factories in Iraq in an air attack which would *release clouds of death that will circle and devastate the entire planet.* Fry added that these clouds would consist of *chemical or biological weapons that the US doesn't know anything about.*

Fortunately, their prophecy has proved partially inaccurate so far. The obliteration of Iraq's atomic plant and chemical warfare industries did not release a plague of global proportions; nevertheless, by 1993 hundreds of American veterans of Gulf War II were showing symptoms of being gassed or at least exposed to the detritus of destroyed chemical and BW weapons strewn on the desert sands. Environmentalists have already called the great cloud of flaming Kuwati oil rigs the worst regional ecological disaster since Chernobyl. If there is a Gulf War III, the American Indians may still see their cloud of botulism, anthrax and nerve gas agents spread over the Earth.

The ongoing subsection will examine the prophetic warnings concerning how best to avoid getting caught in a trap even now as peace seems so close at hand.

The Armageddon Web

Mainstream prophetic thinking has generally painted a picture of World War III being a show-down between the superpowers over political ideology and Mid-Eastern oil. However, this scenario is less plausible with the collapse of the Soviet Union.

While the window to world peace truly is opening, rather than relax our awareness of potential doomsday, a second hard look at prophecy is needed, and without the grimy illusion of Godless Communism as Armageddon's initiator to obscure our view.

Upon closer examination one might recognize the signs of Armageddon's potential fulfillment coming from tripping over the subtle threads of a spider's web. Get caught on just one of her threads (right) and all might shake Armageddon into action. She might slither out for her doomsday feast on humanity.

drought

FAMINE

ethnic

TERRORISM

?FAIL SAFE?

SuperSystem

On that day men will be stricken by the Lord with great panic. Each man will seize the hand of another, and they will attack each other.

Zechariah (160 BC): Zek 14:21

Armageddon

2. Both Israel and Jordan use their known water reserves 15 percent faster every year. Forty percent of Israel's water supply comes from underground aquifers beneath the occupied West Bank. Amman is pessimistic about the outcome of negotiations with Jerusalem over the Jordan river. A Western diplomat in the region says, "Water is like a gun to the Israelis' heads, and this particular problem may be unsolvable."

1. Libya's Muammar Qaddafi has begun a twenty-four-billion-dollar project of man-made rivers to pump deep ground water beneath the Sahara desert for his desiccating croplands on the Mediterranean. This water resource is unreplenishable and will most likely run out shortly after the project is finished early in the twenty-first century.

LIBYA

JORDAN

EGYPT

3. Ethiopia is studying ways to harness the headwaters of the Blue Nile. Egyptian politicians break out in a cold sweat about it. Already, Ethiopia and the Sudan are demanding greater volume from the only life-giving river that irrigates the crops and quenches the thirst of nearly sixty million Egyptians. Egypt nearly shut down the Aswan High Dam in the late 1980s because of low water levels. If the Nile is tapped, the Ethiopians will draw 20 percent of Egypt's water supply. "Egypt will go to war to protect its Nile waters, if it has to. There's absolutely no doubt about it," declares a Western diplomat in Cairo.

WHEN THE EUPHRATES RUNS DRY

TURKEY

IRAQ

IA

IRAN

4. Turkey's ambitious Ataturk dam project might greatly diminish water flow down the Euphrates. Syrian cotton farmers could see their ration cut by 40 percent, and the rice, wheat and fruit crops of Iraq could experience a cut of 80 to 90 percent. In 1990 a Syrian farmer standing before a string of stagnant pools — all that remained of the Euphrates — said, "[the Turks] have told us the water will come back. But maybe it won't. We are desperate and angry."

"Before the twenty-first century, the struggle over limited and threatened water resources could sunder already fragile ties among regional states and lead to unprecedented upheaval within the [Middle East]." So says a report written in 1988 by the Washington-based Center for Strategic and International Studies. In a projected greenhouse future, the Nile, Euphrates and Jordan rivers may dry up. Water disputes in the Middle East are as old as the Pyramids, but the population explosion and the strain of ambitious agricultural and industrial projects are not. Neither is the growing nuclear and chemical weapons capability of Israel and its Arab neighbors.

American Professor Tom Naff, head of a recent study of Middle East river basins, believes Israel is using its might as "the local superpower" to draw "water as it needs and from wherever it can get it." Naff discovered that Israeli settlers in the occupied West Bank use four times as much water as the Palestinians. He warns that unless these well-armed and dangerous nations of a fragile desert ecosystem "act fairly quickly and get some [water] agreements in place, conflict will be the result. Crisis is [already] here."

In his *State of the World 1989* report on enhancing global security, Michael Renner, a senior researcher for the Worldwatch Institute, said that current disputes over water resources are "rapidly becoming a prominent source of international tension."

According to Renner, 40 percent of the world's 5.5 billion people depend on 214 major river systems shared by two or more countries for irrigation, hydropower, or just a life-sustaining drink.

"The next war in our region will be over the waters of the Nile, not politics," warned Butros Butros-Ghali (the current Secretary General of the United Nations) in 1985 when he was Egypt's Foreign Minister.

In nearly a dozen river regions of the Earth, nations disputing water diversion or reduced water flow, or suffering the salination of streams and industrial pollution by their neighbors, could go to war. The most sensitive of these regions being the political and religious tinderbox of the Middle East.

The sixth angel poured out his bowl on the great river Euphrates, and its water was dried up to prepare the way for the kings from the East [those destined to fight Israel in the battle of Armageddon]. St John of Patmos (AD 81-96)
Rev 16:12

Mars, Mercury and the Moon in conjunction
[taking place again in 1990, 92 and 93].
Toward the South [the Southern bloc?], there will be
great drought....Both Corinth [Greece]
and Ephesus [Turkey] will then be
in a troubled state. C3 Q3

In the year Saturn and Mars are
equally fiery [1996 or 1998], the air is very dry,
a long meteor [missile?]. From hidden fires
a great place burns with heat. Little rain,
hot wind, wars and raids. Nostradamus (1555) C4 Q67

"Release the four angels who are
bound at the great river Euphrates." And
the four angels who had been kept
ready for this very hour and day and
month and year were released to kill a
third of mankind. St John of Patmos (AD 81-96)
Rev 9:14-15

Armageddon

In the late 1970s, Anne Ehrlich, a senior researcher at Stanford University and wife of Dr Paul Ehrlich, the founder of Zero Population Growth, had this to say about the future we are about to enter (1993 to 2030): "Population growth will slow, but the occurrence of large-scale famines is virtually certain during this time. Death rates may temporarily rise high enough to cancel out or even reverse growth. Maintaining food production will be even more difficult; many regions may lose ground in the quantity and quality of food supplies. These problems will be reinforced by environmental deterioration, which limits agricultural production, either by bringing on deleterious climate changes or through land and soil depletion. Resource problems will become severer; competition might lead to a nuclear war."

Adding prophetic insult to objective injury...

The time is the late early twenty-first century. The North American grain belts are blowing away in dust devils. The grain harvesting equipment, barns and empty grain elevators of America and Canada are hosts for gathering sand dunes. America's grain reserves have run out. The former food superpower is forced to cut off all exports. One hundred countries begin to starve.

Since the turn of the century, 100 governments began watching their social machinery break down. Eastern European nations begin the twenty-first century as they did the preceding century, by fighting yet another Balkan War. The world holds its breath as Russia, with 3,500 nuclear weapons remaining after START, disintegrates into a pack of military dictatorships fighting over what's left of the food.

Azerbaijan has cut off grain imports to Armenia, and rumor has it that a group of Armenians, former officers and non-coms in the Soviet missile command have seized a tactical nuclear device on the black market. Outside the high Kremlin walls, tanks patrol Red Square, ready to grease their treads with the hungry mobs. Inside the Presidium, a new military junta is frantically trying to re-establish communication with the Armenian junta. Satellite photos have just detected an atomic flash over the Azeri capital of Baku and no one in Moscow knows if it came from America or Armenia!

> *After a great misery for mankind an even greater approaches when the great cycle of the centuries is renewed [AD 2000]. It will rain blood...famine, war...*
>
> **Nostradamus (1555) C2 Q46**

> *Famine will spread over the nations, and nation will rise against nation, kingdom against kingdom, and states against states, in our own country [America] and in foreign lands; and they will destroy each other, caring not for the blood and lives of their neighbors, of their families, or of their own lives.* **Brigham Young (1860)**

> *Suddenly vengeance will be revealed coming from a hundred hands [nations?].*
> *In the sky will be seen a fire dragging a trail of sparks [a missile?]*
> *Hunger, plague, war...*
>
> **Nostradamus (1555-1557) C2 Q: 62, 46 & C7 Q6**

WHEN THE FOOD RUNS OUT

The battles of the past will be only skirmishes compared to the battles that will take place....Famine and pestilence will join the war.

St Odile (AD 720)

Armageddin'

Nation will rise against nation

History is heating up an old Slavic dish that gave the world political heartburn and killed seventeen million in the century's first global slaughter. The post-Cold War world is cultivating a new spring garden. Within it are weeds of ethnic and religious strife among the budding flowers of Eastern European democracy. The weeds come from the same seeds born during an earlier spring of resurgent national identity.

Old issues leap out of the yellowed journals of the early 1900s and reappear on the covers of *Newsweek* and *Time* to bedevil us in the 1990s: The German question, Balkanization, Serbian nationalism. Prior to World War I, the decaying Austro-Hungarian Empire — the flash point of the conflict — was nicknamed the "sick old man of Europe." Today we have the "sick old man of Eurasia" — a crumbling Soviet Empire.

Of today's 168 post-Cold War states, only 5 percent are made up of one ethnic group. A nation, that is, a people with a common language, ancestry, customs and territory, is often divided by the invisible borders of political states. A state can be defined as a centralized political system, not ethnic but bureaucratic and military. This state, or any other state of mind, is often imposed upon ethnic groups and indigenous peoples in places like Eastern Europe, the Soviet Union and the developing nations, with complete disregard for any pre-existing claim these people have to land and resources.

Some observers of the world's 5,000 indigenous nations claim the Third World War already started at the close of World War II, when the white man finally dropped his burden and handed back his colonies with their arbitrary borders to a new generation of black and brown colonialists. The end of the colonial era in the Third World precipitated five decades of continuous wars, pitting state governments against guerrilla insurgencies. Indigenous nations are often fighting for their very existence rather than to defend their ideology. It is a global conflict raging in the jungles, deserts and plains of every continent except Antarctica.

The fighting has already claimed nearly twenty million lives since the "peace" of 1945. The battlefield is largely centered in the Southern bloc. The 1990s began with 120 conflicts, of which 98 percent are in the Third World and 75 percent are between Third World states and a Fourth World of unrecognized indigenous nations.

The loss of the Cold War's bi-polar balance of security through terror could see the spread of long-suppressed ethnic spot fires in the Northern Hemisphere into a general conflagration. Eastern European Slavs, Balts, Ukrainians and a plethora of hot-blooded post-Soviet Islamics could not only strike out for freedom in the coming democratic decade, but strike out at their nearest and dearest enemy as well.

This future trend is right on course with a common prophetic theme: The catastrophe of world war will be the result of a plague of small regional conflicts increasing in number until they infect our entire civilization.

ETHNIC

and kingdom against kingdom. Y'shua (AD 30-33) Mt 24:7

Russia in three years will have new leaders who will declare for détente with the Western world, loosen the iron grip on its satellites, and hold out an olive branch to China. These leaders will willingly negotiate some strategic power plays with the United States, in the hope of keeping China off their doorstep, but they are to be watched, as they are nationalists who will be secretly upgrading Russian warheads and missiles.

Spirit guides of Ruth Montgomery (1976) WbF

Gorbachev's period of ordeal by fire, as we Indians say, starts from February 7, 1991, when Saturn enters Aquarius...Saturn enters Pisces...January 29, 1994 and remains there till April 7, 1996. I hope I do go wrong, but this span will be tough and rough for Gorbachev.

Bejan Daruwalla (1989)

[From the Gulf War onwards, 1991 was a disastrous year for Gorbachev. Montgomery's prophecy seems to be off by ten years but could turn out to be no less insightful in the near-future.]

TheGermanshatethePoleshatetheCzechshatetheSlovakshate...shate...shatetheCroatshatetheHungaria...shatetheRom...Russianshatethe Muslimsha...shatetheDhruzhatetheMaroniteChristi...

There will be perpetual warfare . . . . There will

be a terrible war between the Earth's peoples.

Arghati prophecy (centuries ago)

Armageddon

Since the early 1970s, Western intelligence agencies have grown increasingly concerned about the efforts of radical terrorist groups to enter the arena of hi-tech weapons of mass destruction. The spread of nuclear technology over the world only increases the chance that some day, soon, warheads will be stolen, civilian reactors will be seized and we will awaken to the day when the whole world may be held hostage by a handful of fanatics.

Even the tightest security measures of the First World cannot guarantee our safety. For instance, NATO stockpiles of atomic and chemical weapons have been successfully infiltrated in staged tests. America has some of the most stringent restrictions and safeguards for the military and civilian transport or export of fissionable fuels, yet the US government admitted losing over 9,000 pounds of the hot stuff during the 1970s. A single US atomic weapons plant located in Savanna, Georgia, cannot account for the disappearance of enough plutonium to make a dozen bombs the size of those dropped on Hiroshima and Nagasaki.

And then there's the greed factor. In the late 1980s, a Belgian nuclear plant illegally identified plutonium as low-grade waste, allowing it to be re-sold and shipped to a second party. The customers were Libya and Pakistan. For a few francs more, some Belgian nuclear technicians sold enough "low-risk" plutonium to Muammar Qaddafi, the patron saint of terrorism, and the Pakistani nuclear weapons project to manufacture seventy Hiroshima-size bombs!

A home-made nuke three times more powerful than the Hiroshima blast requires as little as 4.4 pounds of high-grade plutonium. A crude device small enough to fit in a suitcase could be smuggled to its target. Once positioned, a terrorist group of a few hundred members (the size of Abu Nidal) could blackmail an entire continent to obtain military or political concessions.

There are prophetic indications that the citizens of New York, Paris and the Vatican, places far from the desert battlefields of World War III, could become front-line casualties. For example, prophecy C6 Q97 of Nostradamus says: *The sky will burn at forty-five degrees* [near the latitude of New York City, but exactly on the latitude of "New Belgrade" the city district next to the Serbian capital]. *Fire approaches the great new City. In an instant a huge scattered flame leaps up...* The prophet could be hiding the date for this disaster by numbering the quatrain "97" for 1997.

Finally, one doesn't even need to use an atomic bomb to be a nuclear terrorist. There's a scenario giving intelligence agents hypertension: A zealous terrorist band seizes one of hundreds of lightly-guarded civilian reactors and threatens to trigger a reactor meltdown with only a few cases of well-placed dynamite. The cloud issuing from the cauldron of a fully-exposed meltdown could send a pall of radiation over most of North America or Europe 100 times more poisonous than Chernobyl.

There shall come the Son of Man, having a fierce beast in his arms, whose kingdom lies in the Land of the Moon [The Crescent of Islam in the Middle East & North Africa], *which is dreadful throughout the whole world.* **Mother Shipton (c. 1561)**

THE WAR OF INTERNATIONAL TERRORISM

I [Allah] will cast terror into the hearts of those who disbelieve.
Therefore strike off their heads and strike off every fingertip of them. Mohammed
(seventh century AD)
Qur-VIII 12

In the Southern Balkans and all of Greece, a very great famine and plague through false dust [fallout?]. *It will last nine months through the whole peninsula* [Italy] *as of Peleponnesus* [Greece]. Nostradamus (1557) C5 Q90

Prophet scholars like J.R. Jochmans, author of *Rolling Thunder*, theorize that Nostradamus foresaw a nuclear disaster taking place on the southern European coast of Italy between 1994 and 1996. The cause may be accidental, but my own research indicates that a disturbing number of his quatrains point to an Arab terrorist attack as the possible cause. The prevailing wind patterns of the Mediterranean during a reactor meltdown would form a radioactive cloud of dust extending over the regions mentioned above. It would be wise for Italy to continue its moratorium on the construction of nuclear plants, as well as continue to keep their two existing reactors closed — forever.

140

FAIL SAFE

October 1973: Israeli armored units have successfully crossed

the Suez Canal and are penetrating deep into Egypt. Zion's dusty and sunburned warriors have broken the back of the Egyptian surprise offensive unleashed upon them on the Jewish holiday of Yom Kippur. Their blood is up. The Israelis can see victory within their grasp after facing defeat a few weeks before. The Soviet Union, Egypt's allies, can also see that America is unable to keep the Israelis on their side of the negotiated cease-fire line. Soviet airborne divisions begin taxiing down a half-a-dozen Russian airfields. Leonid Brezhnev informs American President Richard Nixon that Russian paratroopers are on their way to Egypt's rescue...

For the next nine hours, the Cold War came its closest to a sudden thermonuclear thaw since the Cuban Missile Crisis of 1962. Nixon managed to pull the Israelis back to the proposed cease-fire line. Later on, the world found out that Nixon, the only man other than John Kennedy whose finger was poised over the nuclear button, was suffering a severe depression at the time over recent revelations about the Watergate scandal, which later forced him out of office.

In Bob Woodward and Carl Bernstein's book *The Final Days*, Nixon's Secretary of State, Henry Kissinger, a key player in the Egyptian-Israeli cease-fire arrangement, is reported to have expressed deep anxiety over the state of the President's sanity. During the closing weeks of the war he said, "Sometimes I get worried. The President is like a madman." The President's son-in-law, Ed Cox, stated that when faced with resignation during the following summer, Nixon walked through the halls of the White House one night talking to pictures of former presidents. Cox said he was "giving speeches."

The "**crazy factor**" which can trigger Armageddon is not only the territory of crackpot potentates of the Third World rattling their newly-procured nuclear sabers.

The United States alone entrusts roughly 100,000 people with guarding and maintaining its nuclear arsenal. Five thousand are removed every year because of mental disorders and drug abuse. Perestroika and the end of the Cold War aside, could time and the odds be running out on psychiatrists trying to nab lunatics before they uncap the nuclear trigger?

Which brings me to a mid-to-late 1990s doomsday scenario: Russian troops are fighting the armies of the pan-Islamic nuclear Alliance consisting of the Soviet Union's former Central Asian republics, Iran, Turkey and Pakistan. Israel is surprised by a second Yom Kippur-style sortie — the result of a water rights dispute with the new Republic of Palestine. The Arab alliance that America built and re-armed in the early 1990s has turned on Israel. The new Islamic republic of Saudi Arabia joins the anti-Israeli alliance, bringing along all their American hi-tech arsenal. This time the combatants have tipped their regional ballistic missiles with nuclear warheads. The Middle East is poised to go atomic any second.

Picture President Dan Quayle (just kidding) receiving a call from the head of the Russia's newest military junta, the third in five weeks. Tomorrow's Czar-apparent will not send paratroopers to Egypt; they are already committed to re-take Ukraine's grain fields. Quayle gets an ultimatum from the new Russian dictator: If the US Government doesn't immediately resume

Armageddon

grain imports to the starving Russian Democratic Republic, there will be war. The American President cannot even be sure if the desperate man on the phone is in fact the real boss over there.

Meanwhile, we leave the President pressing his ear against a tense and expectant silence as he formulates his reply, and we take you a few hundred miles above the White House, where a spy satellite monitoring Russian missile sites is hit by a micro-meteor causing a malfunction.

Another phone rings in the Oval Office. It is a call from SAC headquarters in Colorado. They have just received a garbled report of an incoming Russian nuclear attack.

Nuclear warriors have added a new phrase — "fail safe" — to the family of immortal embarrassments such as "peace for our time" and "the *Titanic* is unsinkable." This term is used by the top brass to promise you, me and the kiddies that technological or human errors can never cause a nuclear war. Governments of the superpowers have made great efforts to ensure their nuclear warriors are "safe and sane" and to guarantee their weapons — newly re-vamped and ever quicker to the trigger — won't glitch the world back into the Stone Age. Developing nations can't afford half the sophisticated safety measures used in the West. Muammar Qaddafi watched his chemical weapons plant go up in smoke in 1990. Can an investigative board of Iranian Ayatollahs adequately ensure their nuclear weapons systems are maintained by cool heads and redundant safety systems? Psychiatrists are rare in an Islamic republic. So are spare parts for tanks, let alone the computers and software needed to sustain hi-tech weapons systems in economically and politically isolated states. Malfunctions can trigger at least a regional if not a global nuclear war.

All good intentions aside, one of the qualities of being human is being a human in error. Officers on both sides of the nuclear hair-trigger succumb to personal problems, temper tantrums, too much nagging from the wife, and a few have drunk, toked and sometimes flipped out on the job.

During the closing stages of the Iran-Iraq war a highly-trained sailor on the US missile cruiser *Vincennes* misread his computer and shot down an Iranian civilian airliner. Iran's Ayatollahs and Qaddafi threatened retribution. The bombing of Pan Am Flight 301.

Let's move a decade into the future, to an American missile cruiser involved in a similar "accident," this time with Iran as a nuclear power. If the sailor had the opportunity to misread an even faster computer spitting out a blur of data into his brain, our pac-Navy-man might once again mistake civilian for military jets. This time, Iran's response might be more immediate and devastating.

Nostradamus describes a fleet destined to *founder in the Arabian* (Persian) *Gulf...* It is not likely he is talking about Saddam Hussein's little flotilla in the Iraqi marshes. The US will continue to keep a strong naval presence in the Gulf. Human error in Gulf War III (any time in the final few years of the twentieth century) may cause a US carrier task force to melt down to the sea in radiation from an Iranian submarine attack.

Armageddin' ECOLOGICAL

World War III started tomorrow because the postman didn't ring twice. Didn't ring at all. The ICBMs came down like rain around the year 1999 because the toilets backed up, the phone didn't work, and your bank went on a vacation — forever.

Sound ludicrous? This is only the tip of the iceberg. How ironic it would be if Armageddon came because the electricity was cut off. What if all the prophetic threats of nuclear terrorism and every warning of doomsday proved to be full of hot air — and still World War III happened because the grain trucks never came into town?

By delivering a fatal blow to a Middle Eastern triumvirate, the US and Soviet blocs of the Northern Hemisphere could receive a mortal wound in return. Peace on Earth would be celebrated with the firework fountains of burning oil fields. The millennial peace dividend will be an apocalyptic energy conservation program that locks industry's precious oil reserves beneath a pall of biological plague dust and radiation.

But even if the oil fields were free of plague and left intact. Even if by the dawning of the new millennium the Arab lion lay down with the Israeli lamb in peace, ecological stresses being put on this planet by too many breeding peace-loving polluters may sabotage all efforts for a new age. According to prophetic astrology the world might slip past a threat of Armageddon at the turn of this century, solve its political and religious division and still fight Armageddon between 2024 through 2037 because the rainforests had been cut down, and the crops wouldn't grow.

In his book, *The Coming Dark Age*, futurist Roberto Vacca's posits that our

WHEN THE SUPERSYSTEMS BREAK DOWN

modern civilization's survival depends on what he calls supersystems — super-organizations sustained by machines and single energy sources. Any collapse of one of these interdependent global systems — such as information retrieval, telecommunications, medicine, transportation, global agricultural production or distribution — could have a domino effect on all the other systems.

For instance, if oil ceased to flow, the plastics industry would go down, no more new computers, telephone lines, nylon clothing or winter heating oil. Then the tractors harvesting food would stop running. The trains and trucks shipping wheat to the cities would dwindle. Next the supersystem of law enforcement would be overwhelmed by food riots, even in America. Without fuel, world commerce would grind to a standstill. No jets would fly, no ships would carry their cargoes. Finally, governments collapse, revolutions and dictators abound. Nostradamus, the Biblical prophets and others forewarn of a close relationship between the coming final war and global famine.

Add to this the expected climatic chaos if global warming is not forestalled in time. At present levels of consumption and pollution, most scientists generally expect we have only twenty more years to avert ecological disaster before nature goes out of our control. That projection coincides with the astrological view, that numerous wars are possible over the planet during the next transit of the planet Neptune through the constellation of Aries (2024-2038).

If by that time ozone holes devastate North America's breadbasket, and the people of that continent stockpile their food rather than export grain to sustain hundreds of nations, hunger will speak louder than logic, survival will overrule any treaty. The world will go to war to fight over what meager natural resources are left.

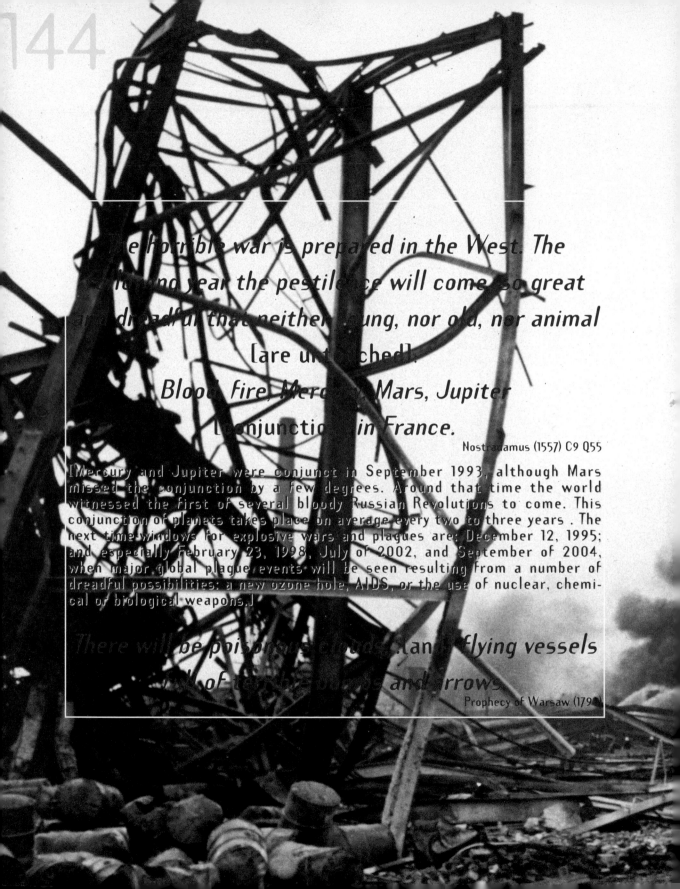

The horrible war is prepared in the West. The
following year the pestilence will come so great
and dreadful that neither young, nor old, nor animal
[are untouched].
Blood, fire, Mercury, Mars, Jupiter
[conjunction] in France.

Nostradamus (1557) C9 Q55

[Mercury and Jupiter were conjunct in September 1993, although Mars
missed the conjunction by a few degrees. Around that time the world
witnessed the first of several bloody Russian Revolutions to come. This
conjunction of planets takes place on average every two to three years. The
next time windows for explosive wars and plagues are: December 12, 1995;
and especially February 23, 1998; July of 2002, and September of 2004,
when major global plague events will be seen resulting from a number of
dreadful possibilities: a new ozone hole, AIDS, or the use of nuclear, chemical or biological weapons.]

There will be poisonous clouds [and] flying vessels
full of terrible bullets and arrows.

Prophecy of Warsaw (1790)

Poisonous clouds, made by human hands, will strike down and exterminate everything. The human mind will be seized by insanity...

I see Yellow Warriors and Black warriors advancing against the rest of the world [implying a Sino/Arab alliance?]. Europe will be completely covered with a yellow fog that will kill the cattle in the fields. Those nations which began the war...will perish by terrible fire...May the Lord grant my grandchildren the grace of perseverance in the coming hard times...

—Francesca de Billante of Savoy (early 1900s)

For a long time there will be disharmony in the MidEast, until at last Israel faces up to the terrible truth that it is not always right and others always wrong. They have been termed the Chosen People, but are they more chosen than those who themselves choose God?....It would be ridiculous to say that the MidEast crisis will pass until the hearts of men are uplifted. The smoldering fire remains until man himself alters his consciousness and overcomes hatred and greed. **Spirit guides of Ruth Montgomery (1971) Aby**

The word of the Lord came to me: "...In that day, when my people Israel are living in safety...you [Gog of the land of Magog] will come from your place in the far north, you and many nations with you..."

[Perhaps this means that any apparent resolution of the Palestinian homeland questions is a precursor to Armageddon. Gog and Magog sound like the return of the allied coalition against Saddam or Assad or someone of their ilk.]

On that day I will give Gog a burial place in Israel, in the valley of those who travel toward the Sea. It will block the way of travelers because Gog and all his hordes will be buried there. So it will be called the Valley of Hamon Gog. **Ezekiel (593-571 BC) Ez 38 & 39**

[Here's a Biblical link to Nostradamus: according to him Baal *Hamon* is the Antichrist's God. He is worshipped in the regions of presentday Syria, Libya and Iraq, implying the source of Israel's enemies. In his destructive mood, Baal Hammon is known as the terrible lord of the skies. Nostradamus, in C10 Q72 of his book *The Centuries*, predicts that a *King of Terror* will descend from the skies in July of 1999. This terror could be a thermonuclear war escalating from a war in the Middle East at that time.]

At the same time when Gog shall come against the land of Israel...there shall be a great shaking in the land...and all the men that are upon the face of the Earth shall shake at my presence...and every wall shall fall to the ground... **Ezekiel (593-571 BC) Ez 38:18,20**

At the time of the end the king of the South [bloc?] will engage him [the Antichrist] in battle, and the king of the North [bloc?] will storm out against him....He will invade [and]...extend his power over many countries; Egypt will not escape....The Libyans and Nubians [Sudan] in submission....He will set out in a great rage to destroy and annihilate many....Yet he will come to his end and no one will help him [international boycott?]....There will be a time of distress such as has not happened from the beginning of nations until then. But at that time your people [Israel]...will be delivered. **Daniel (sixth to fourth century BC) Dn from Ch 11 & 12**

On that day men will be stricken by the Lord with great panic. Each man will seize the hand of another, and they will attack each other. **Zechariah (160 BC) Zek 14:13**

But your many enemies will become like fine dust, the ruthless hordes like blown chaff. Suddenly, in an instant, the Lord Almighty will come with thunder and earthquake and great noise, with windstorm and tempest and flames of a devouring fire. Then all the hordes of all the nations that fight against Ariel [situated in the currently disputed West Bank], that attack her and her fortress and besiege her, will be as it is with a dream....As when a thirsty man dreams that he is drinking, but he awakens faint, with thirst unquenched [an allusion to water running out in the MidEast?] So will it be with all the hordes of all the nations that fight against Mount Zion. **Isaiah (783-637 BC) Is 29: 5-8**

The Second Holocaust

Alas, how we will see a great nation [Israel?] sorely troubled and the holy law in utter ruin. Christianity governed throughout by other laws, when a new source of gold and silver is discovered [oil?]. **C1 Q53**

Six days the assault is made in front of the city [Six-Day War of 1967; battle for Jerusalem]. Freedom attained in a strong and bitter fight: Three will hand it over [Egypt, Syria, and Jordan], and to them pardon and slashing... [new borders cut to make the occupied territories?] **C3 Q22**

A new law will occupy a new land around Syria, Judea and Palestine: The great empire of the [Arab] barbarian will crumble before the Century of the Sun is finished. **C3 Q97**

[The twentieth century is implied here as it is the century which saw the Sun of nuclear power harnessed. Also, the number 97 could stand for the year 1997.] **Nostradamus (1555)**

The Israeli atomic weapons program produces an estimated ninety pounds of plutonium a year, enough for 100 Hiroshima-sized warheads! Because of Israel's size, her potential Arab adversaries need not be so ambitious. Only five nuclear bombs detonated over major Israeli cities would be enough to immediately kill 60 percent of the population; most of those remaining would be exterminated by fallout. The Jewish nation, finding itself placed in a new atomic oven, will not go submissively into that second Holocaust. She will fly her own nuclear bombers like a miniature superpower. The Jews will face another threat of the Holocaust with their own regional version of the Third World's War.

The Middle East, albeit the hottest and most politically unstable region, may not be the first to go up in thermonuclear flames. Conservative estimates at Pentagon think tanks give Pakistan and India a three to one chance of fighting a nuclear war before the new millennium. Bejan Daruwalla, one of India's most respected contemporary astrologers, warns us that India's and Pakistan's most "crucial period" in their tense relationship is to come between 10 December 1994 and 3 January 1996.

Now that Pakistan has nuclear capability, India's atomic weapons race may have resumed. Both countries deny they are building bombs. Western intelligence agencies estimate that by mid-decade, Pakistan, along with Libya, will be capable of manufacturing six Hiroshima-size bombs per year. Experts believe that India has already stockpiled 300 kilograms (660 pounds) of weapons-grade material. Current intelligence estimates put her nuclear arsenal at twenty bombs. And if a future Chinese regime should threaten another invasion of India's Himalayan provinces, the Indians are capable of transforming their current stockpile of plutonium into an arsenal larger than the entire Chinese arsenal to date.

If global economic tensions dim the first faint hope of renunciation of the Koreas, a second (and perhaps even atomic) Korean War is still possible. In 1991, during an interview with CNN's Bernard Shaw, former US president Richard Nixon said he considered North Korea the most likely Third World power to use nuclear weapons in a war. A breakdown in the food supply or a financial collapse might bring on a nuclear confrontation even in South America. Argentina and Brazil could become nuclear powers in the next century. Chile may initiate its own nuclear program to forestall any future concessions with Argentina in their age-old dispute over Tierra del Fuego.

WORLD WAR III?

THE PRELUDE: THE WAR OF THE ANTICHRIST (1973-1999)

A period of peace will follow [Second World War is implied], but only for the space of twenty five years [1945 to 1970]. The forerunner of the Antichrist will assemble an army of men drawn from many nations united under his banner [Islam?]. He will lead them in a bloody war against those still faithful to the living God.

The Prophecy of La-Salette.

One year before the foretold moon walk that sees the beginning of the end of Islam (1969), 1970 is just three years off Nostradamus's dated beginning for the war of the Antichrist in 1973. Tomorrow's Hitler wages war by sabotage and terrorism:

The Antichrist very soon annihilates the three. Twenty-seven years his war will last [1973-1999]...

Nostradamus (1557) C8 Q77

It is not clear whether *the three* refers to the First, Second and Third Worlds, or the triumvirate of terrorist nations.

WAR IN EASTERN MEDITERRANEAN REGION THROUGH TERRORISM

When those of the northern pole are united together, in the East there will be a great fear and dread. A new man elected....Both Rhodes [Greece] and Byzantium [Turkey] will be stained by barbarian [anagram for "Arab" or "Libyan"] blood. **Nostradamus (1555) C6 Q21**

My interpretations of the prophet logged in articles and television interviews since 1984 concerning US Presidential elections of 1992 were correct: George Bush did not politically survive the American military adventure in the Middle East. This prophecy of Nostradamus could also pertain to the election of Boris Yeltsin as President of the new Russian Republic in the early 1990s and presage his political debacle through a Middle Eastern or North African source.

PHASE ONE: THE BATTLES OF WORLD WAR III

...important battles will take place in the Middle East. Europe will also be affected by war....Nuclear weapons and germ weapons will be used, though only to a limited degree. New York, Chicago and the West Coast are possible targets for destruction. China will eventually lose the war, but only after the United States and her allies will have suffered great loss.

Survey of the Future by Hans Holzer from *The Prophets Speak* (1971)

PHASE TWO: WORLD WAR III IS FOUGHT OVER PALESTINE IN 1995?

The populated lands will become uninhabitable. Great disagreement in order to obtain lands [the Palestinian question?]. Kingdoms given to men incapable of prudence. Then for the great brothers [US & Russia] death and dissension. **Nostradamus (1555) C2 Q95**

The prophecy's indexing could imply the year 1995.

BREAKDOWN OF US-RUSSIAN FRIENDSHIP BY 1995?

The rule will be left to two [superpowers?]. They will hold it for a very short time. Three years and seven months having passed, they will go to war. **Nostradamus (1555) C4 Q95 [1995?]**

The difficulty here is to ascertain when one starts the countdown. With the Soviet Union vanishing and the unprecedented openness arising between Russia and the US, the countdown of a new friendship dissolving to a future war may have already begun. Since he has dated the terrifying end of the Antichrist's war in other prophecies as 7/99 we could begin the countdown to breakdown of this friendship in January of 1996 — when Russia elects a new president.

A POLITICAL AXIS SHIFT, A SECOND COLD WAR?

1998 to 2000 is a treacherous wicket, as Saturn, Jupiter, Neptune shift signs, as we change car gears. And when they do so shift, it does mean tensions, trials, tiffs, tribulations, tests, and the long, winding trail of blood, gore and devastation and "resultation" of death, debris and decay. **Bejan Daruwalla (1989)**

World War "FREE"-FOR-ALL!

WAR (or revenge) OF THE ANTICHRIST

A horrible warrior will unleash it, and his enemies will call him Antichrist. All nations of the Earth will fight each other in this war. The fighters will rise up in the heavens to take the stars and will throw them on cities, to set ablaze the buildings and cause immense devastations....The nations will cry "peace, peace," but there will be no peace. **Prophecy of St Odile (AD 720)**

CIVIL WARS ERUPT, SUPERSYSTEMS BEGIN TO BREAK DOWN

What then will be the condition of that people when this great and terrible [civil] war shall come? It will be very different from the war between the North and South [in America]...It will be a war of neighborhood against neighborhood, city against city, town against town, country against country, state against state, and they will go forth destroying, and being destroyed and manufacturing will, in great measure, cease, for a time, among the American nation.

...Their cities will be left desolate. The time is coming when the great and populous city of New York...will be left without inhabitants. **Orson Pratt, Mormon leader (1879)**

ECONOMIC DISASTERS, COMPLETE SUPERSYSTEM BREAKDOWN...

...financial disasters and ruin of property will cause many tears to fall....Almost the whole world will be turned upside down. Men will be without sanity and without piety. There shall be poisonous clouds, and rays which can burn more deeply than the equatorial sun, armies on the march encased in iron, flying ships full of terrible bombs and arrows, and flying stars [future SDI space weapons?] with sulfuric fire which destroy whole cities in an instant. **Prophecy of Warsaw (1790)**

...THE PRELUDE OF A NUCLEAR EXCHANGE BETWEEN EAST AND WEST

Moles will be the models for soldiers under the earth to the depth of 300 feet. **Marienthal prophecy (1749)**

[US officers can monitor and fire their missiles in bunkers several hundred feet deep.]

A THERMONUCLEAR JUDGMENT DAY?

There will come in the year 2000 the day of the Lord, who will judge both the living and the dead. Stars and comets [missiles?] will fall from above, the Earth will be set ablaze with lightning [nuclear flashes or laser beams], and the old Earth will pass away. **Prophecy of Warsaw (1790)**

THE DEATH OF MANKIND?

A single day will see the burial of mankind, all that the long forbearance of fortune has produced, all that has been raised to eminence, all that is famous and all that is beautiful; great thrones, great nations — all will descend into one abyss, all will be overthrown in one hour. **The Sibylline Oracles (second century BC)**

THE END OF THE WORLD?

At sunrise a great fire will be seen. Noise and light extending toward the North...

It is a well known fact among doomsday warriors of both sides that the first thermonuclear detonations will start with southern US and Russian targets and move northward. Finally this prophecy of Nostradamus adds this chilling coda:

...Within the world death and cries are heard, death awaiting them through weapons, fire and famine.
Nostradamus (1555) C2 Q91

One can only hope he meant "1991" and was wrong.

From Cold War—

Frenzy, folly and madness....Two corpses by the roadside, two fallen colossi [US and USSR?]; terrible struggle, lament, wreck, ruin and smoke. Where is the sun? Where is day? Where is God and his help? Everything is dark on Earth. Hell has opened its gates. **Madame Sylvia (1948)**

...heavy snows are driven and fall from the world's four corners. The murdering frost prevails. The Sun darkened at noon. It sheds no gladness. Devouring tempests bellow and never end. Men wait for the coming of summer in vain. Twice winter follows winter over the world which is snow-smitten, frost-fettered and chained in ice.

[Fimbul Winter, the holocaust of ice forewarned by Viking prophets, could take place after the battle of Ragnarök, the Norse version of Armageddon.]

From *The Ragnarök*: Ancient Norse prophecy (pre-AD 1000)

Immediately after the suffering of those days the sun will be darkened and the moon will not give its light and the stars will fall from the sky
[stars: atomic warheads?] *and the power of the universe will be shaken* [atomic detonations?].
Y'shua (AD 30-33) Mt 24:29

A winter will come, darkness for three days, lightning, thunder and cleft in the earth....
A poisonous breath will fill the night with dust. Black pestilence, the worst human battle...

Prophecy of Passau, Germany (nineteenth century)

The whole country [Scotland] will become so utterly desolated and depopulated that the crow of a cock shall not be heard, deer and other wild animals shall be exterminated by horrid black rain. **Brahan Seer (1665)**

A powerful wind will rise in the North, carrying heavy fog and the densest dust, and it will fill their throats and eyes so that they will cease their butchery and be stricken with a great fear. **St Hildegard (c. 1141)**

Add a few more phrases to the family of eternal idiocies: The Pentagonisms "limited" or "protracted but controlled nuclear war." It assumes that the American President, safely aloft in Air Force One, can command his nuclear warriors while the American skies are filled with Russian or Chinese ICBMs, heat blasts and lethal clouds of radiation. It also assumes that enough safe and sane politicians and military commanders will survive being priority targets to carry on a gentlemanly nuclear response, rather than become intoxicated by the mayhem and shoot off every ICBM they have.

...the heretics are dead, captives exiled; blood-soaked human bodies, water, and a reddened, icy rain covering the entire Earth. Nostradamus (1557) C8 Q77

If the human race can't learn to understand and transcend its Will to Catharsis, Stormberger's and the Sibylline seeresses' chilling threat will come true, and the next war will kill more people in one day than all wars through history. Even with disarmament agreements moving forward, any sudden change in the political fortunes of a growing Russo-American friendship could see the strategic missile commands of the two move back to full alert status within weeks. People want to believe that a signed agreement is tantamount to the weapons already being destroyed. This is a dangerous delusion. The START treaties destroy the missiles, not the warheads. The bombs can be — and are being — stockpiled for a future day. Within months or a few years a country can rebuild its missiles. In fact even the work to destroy the missiles has scarcely begun. The 1990s are still young and already the political changes are moving much faster than politicians (and prophetic interpreters) can handle. The forces of the Aquarian age which can overthrow a Russian superpower this year can overthrow a Russian Commonwealth in the next. Astrological and prophetic indications point to 1994 through 1996 and 1999 as the high-water marks for Armageddon in this century. The next period to look out for is 2009 through 2012 and the 2020s. If disarmament schedules continue undisturbed by the immense changes and stresses going on in civilization, the danger of human extinction through nuclear weapons certainly will become less as each cosmic window for Armageddon passes. In a way, as we move foreword to disarmament we are also moving backwards into the levels of nuclear terror stockpiled during the tensest years of the Cold War. If by the year 2003, we dismantle the worldwide estimated nuclear arsenal of fifty to 60,000 weapons by 75 percent, we will still have far more potential nuclear terror lying around than had existed when Russia and America nearly waged Armageddon over the Cuban Missile Crisis of 1962. There will be thousands more missiles! And they will be placed on mobile launchers beneath the near-impenetrable seas. There is a strong collective vision in prophecy that Armageddon's fires falling from the skies will be launched by nuclear submarines.

With the high danger of a START disarmament slowdown, the death toll of a thermonuclear war in the mid-to-late 1990s will be roughly equivalent to the estimated destructive force and casualties of a nuclear war waged during the 1980s.

Within ninety minutes of a full superpower exchange, of 1.4 billion people in the Northern bloc, an estimated 750 million will be killed immediately from the blast effects and 350 million will be injured. Most of the seriously wounded will soon die. The 300 million northerners still left standing can look forward to radiation plagues and infectious diseases. If our nuclear clout is "fail-safe" only 200 million northerners will survive to celebrate the new millennium of "peace."

What the worst scenarios of the greenhouse effect and pollution might unleash in four decades would happen in one year's time. The northern breadbasket, which feeds most of the world, would disappear in flames. Blast effects and radiation would kill one billion people, the majority within ninety days of a full apocalyptic exchange. But the highest number of casualties will come from areas not directly in the wake of ICBMs; around 2.5 billion people will die of starvation the following year.

152

— To Nuclear Winter

Many ancient seers give a frighteningly close description of what will happen after thousands of cities disappear under nuclear fireballs. The resulting smoke and debris is hurled into the upper atmosphere and blocks the sun's light for six months to a year. The Norse seers warn us of **"Fimbul Winter,"** an unremitting cold and dark future that follows Ragnarök, the Norseman's version of Armageddon. Contemporary scientists call it nuclear winter.

Its effects are devastating.

The supersystem of agriculture will be totally disrupted. Even a regional nuclear war could be enough to undermine civilization. The smoke plume from a regional Armageddon in South Asia or the Middle East, or even a small nuking of the Koreas could effect enough changes in rainfall patterns to disrupt the Asian rice crop or America's grain belt, causing a breakdown of food systems.

Even a small superpower exchange in a "surgical nuclear war," which targets only military installations and fuel storage, could be all that is needed to unleash enough smoke to cause widespread freezing and destroy the world's crops for a whole year.

Hell hath no ozone holes like those created by the electromagnetic pulse of many nuclear detonations. A nuclear bush war or a little superpower nuclear tiff could find whole regions waking up to lethal ozone holes, making the land uninhabitable and sterile for centuries.

A nuclear winter will disrupt the normal air flows which keep the Northern and Southern Hemispheres' weather systems separate. A substantial amount of the Northern bloc's funeral shroud will then cover the Southern Hemisphere.

According to Nostradamus, rather than radioactive snows, a milder nuclear winter – or even a nuclear autumn of icy "rad"-dusted red rains – will poison the planet.

The aftermath of nuclear winter will perhaps bring the extinction of Earth's remaining life forms, if enough atomic detonations have decimated the upper atmosphere's layer of ozone. The prophecies of Emma Kunz concerning rockets making holes in the atmosphere may also apply to a rush of hundreds — if not thousands — of ICBMs.

And then comes nuclear spring. After the clouds have dissipated, the survivors may find cataracts blocking their sight of newly-sprouting crops. Their immune systems, and that of the plants they so desperately nurture for their survival, may collapse from a lingering, ultraviolet death.

and the Horse They All Ride:

Terror and the pit and snare await you, O people of the Earth. Whoever flees at the sound of terror will fall into a pit; whoever climbs out of the pit will be caught in the snare.

Isaiah (783-637 BC)
Is 24:17,18

And the time is not far away, because the sleeping humanity has suffered much and is going to suffer more, and as the suffering grows deeper...it is a blessing in disguise. Man can tolerate only a certain quantity of suffering and then he wakes up. And man has suffered enough.

Osho (1985) DtoL

A NIGHTMARE UNCONSCIOUS

I follow my course with the calculation and security of a sleepwalker.

Said by Adolf Hitler in 1939 when asked to define the secret behind his near-miraculous political and military successes prior to World War II.

# of POPES and the POPULATION EXPLOSIONS

In the mid-1980s, Pope John Paul II visited a squalid barrio in Tumaco, Colombia. He was dressed to the holy hilt in his finest white vestments. The cap, solid gold cross and Pontiff ducked through a hole cut into tin sheets and plastic and entered a shack that was the home of an unemployed peasant farmer, his pregnant wife and a half-dozen emaciated kids. The lean-to structure and the family of hopelessness within were typical of the crowded barrios he had seen on his tour, which was little more than a cesspool of poverty and violence, a dump site of shattered dreams. No doubt the Pope was a seasoned observer of the sight of many countless children in slums with their stick limbs and swelling bellies, playing in the open sewers. While in the hut, he tried to speak soft words of comfort over a cacophony of babies crying for want of food, as they sucked at breasts run dry from overwork and overbreeding.

The stench of dysentery shriveled the papal nostrils. The hollow and awestruck gaze of the farmer and his tattered tots made him weep. He re-emerged from the shack, displaying tears like shining medals to the tropical sun and the relentless flashing eyes of cameras. He declared with a moving voice, to the press and the world at large, "I bless the people in this home." As he left the area a papal aide was seen slipping $300 into the Columbian farmer's hand.

Upon the Pope's return from the South American crusade he stressed with even more righteous certainty than ever before that all birth control and contraceptive methods are a sin.

I am in favor of complete birth control for at least twenty years, so that the population of the world can be reduced to one-fourth. But the great servants of the people will not allow it to happen because if there are no poor people, no orphans, no starving nations, what will happen to these people like the Polack pope, Mother Theresa, et cetera? Just for their glory they need the world to remain in poverty.

Osho (1985) LTst

The people here now don't care about Mother Earth, because when they die, they're going to heaven. They're going to get a harp, a pair of wings, and a halo, and they're going to be playing all the time. It is very unattractive to me. I don't even know how to play a harp.

Grandfather Semu Huarte: American Indian, Chumash Nation (1983)

Four Dimensions of NIGHTMARE

The EARTH Day After

Monday morning comes whether Sunday's prayers or debaucheries were average or unique. Such was the case with one Sunday in April 1990, when global awareness of the dire condition of Mother Gaia was stirred as it had never been before. The first Earth Day of the 1990s was truly a global festival of environmental activism that captured the world's imagination. Millions of people from all our polluted continents took a few moments, a few hours — and for a few zealous individuals, a whole day — to ponder and pick up the trash and pay tribute to their only fouled nest in space.

Tributes, like hands, reached across barriers of light and sound of nation and religion. For one day the kings of garbage-making in the industrialized North and the kings of baby-making in the open sewers and denuded forest lands of the South reached out and touched Utopia. For a single day one and all could feel the grip of others, feel the *response-ability* humanity must cultivate if there's going to be a twenty-first century worth living in.

Gestures of solidarity followed the sun's long swing over ozone-perforated skies. There were effigies of ecological death in Washington DC, and some Kenyans planted a handful of the few billion trees desperately needed to keep ahead of the billions of trees being cut down in the rainforests. Rock concerts around the world seduced people into listening to a good word for the Earth between their favorite songs.

In Oregon, USA, one could feel the drumbeat of awareness when the sun reached the CO_2-laced heights of the noonday sky. Native Americans and other Oregonians thumped their drums to abandon to remind the earth spirits that mankind had not forgotten its soil-and-water womb. The noontime rhythms were also a reminder for polluters to think about improving the planet's condition.

Some of the gestures approached the poetic with their heartfelt efforts to awaken a lasting concern for our only source of life in this universe. In Tours, France, 3,000 kites were fashioned by school children and tied together to make a flying bridge across the river Cher. In Toulouse, Friends of the Earth activists unveiled a garbage sculpture 2.5-meters (eight feet) high called *Monument to the Unknown Refuse*. In Rome, nature lovers put their bodies on the line for the planet and lay down on the hot tarmac of Rome's central boulevards, bringing the cars and the pollution to a standstill — at least for a day. In Solano, California, children released 300,000 ladybugs — a natural pest controller. Kids in the Main Square of Munich, Germany, released 10,000 balloons carrying cards with pro-environmental maxims heavenward on the unnaturally acidic winds of Western Europe, hoping they would eventually glide down upon the sooty and highly polluted industrial boroughs of Czechoslovakia.

Then Monday came...

It always comes, with some degree of a hangover. Some film of weekend joys goes stale in the mouth of Monday. One must battle the traffic and smog and go back to the office. Where greenies had lain in the central thoroughfares of Rome, there was the usual screech of traffic and a few invisible tons of CO_2 exhaust. In Oregon, the pounding of drums had long been silenced and time clocks were punched by sore fingers at woodmills from Medford to Albany.

By Monday, most of the kites of the Tours children, the papier-mâché animal masks of endangered species and the countless tons of pamphlets and signs advertising Earth Day were in the trash. Monday saw 10,000 wilting balloons tangled in trees and bushes across Czechoslovakia, hanging like withering fruit beneath coal-tainted morning skies.

By the close of that Monday work shift, most people would probably have been too tired to care about the words of Luis Manuel Guerra, a Mexican environmentalist: "For twenty years now, people all over the world have talked, published books, formed organizations. But the truth is that the Earth continues to suffer more each day."

We need to save what's left on this Earth. Because the prophecies say that when the coyote and the crow and the Indian perish from this Earth, everybody, including all races, will die.

Grandfather Semu Huarte: American Indian (1983)

Most people don't know they have overeaten until they have had a bellyache....
Wake up, America!

Good Horse Nation, Visayan Medicine Man (1982)

PLEASURES AND PLAGUES

Hunched in his cage, the mouse blinks at the levers in surprise. If he pushes the one of the left side, the little electrode hat sewn into his brain by his human masters gives him the best sex he's ever had. It makes one's whiskers into curlicues, that!

Pumping the lever on the right releases a jackpot of food pellets. But who can think of food at a time of orgasmic joy? And who cares about something as mundane as feeding when a pulse of ecstasy that could father a thousand litters has disappeared as quickly as it came leaving despair in its wake? Mousy fingers press the left lever for just one more hit before a meal. Then again. And again. "Just one more hit and I'll feed," instincts the mouse.

Pink paws push the lever again.

The days add up and the mouse thins down. The lever on the right is hardly touched anymore; it is forgotten in a rhythm of momentary highs that mask the depressing reality of being a lab mouse in the control of people far beyond his understanding. Push the left lever and forget!

For brief moments, the mouse can imagine he is the greatest stud of litters. He possesses the *Shivalingam* of rodents! His electronically-scrambled instincts ignore messages for food, or warnings of sickness. Tufts of fur fall out in clawfuls. The scientists will soon find him slumped over the lever with an ecstatic expression of death (at least for a mouse). The cause: Immune system collapse, exposing the electronically-addicted critter to one of a number of rodent plagues.

Fear is inherent in your condition. You can put illusions in the way and desensitize yourself to it temporarily but to identify with bodily existence is to be afraid. **Da Avabhasa (1979) Sci**

The CHANGELING WARRIORS of DOOMSDAY: A FAIRY TALE

Once upon a time, two empty, open, no-thing-nesses parents later labeled "baby boys," were born on the future battlefield of World War III, in a hospital in the Israeli-occupied West Bank. One was named Abdul, the other Moshe.

Both children had scarcely entered life through the stretched vaginal curtains of their suffering mothers when fate switched their identities. While both tots gurgled in the maternity ward, there was a terrorist explosion. In the resulting confusion, the newborns were somehow mixed up. Baby Moshe was safely carried out of the flaming hospital by little Abdul's parents to a refugee camp, and Abdul found himself driven away in a land rover to the nearest kibbutz.

Within the worlds of a kibbutz and of a Palestinian refugee camp, two sets of well-meaning parents tried to fill the empty pages of two tender souls with the signatures of their way of life. The Jewish tike became a good Muslim, and learned to hate Israelis and to address God as "Allah." The Arab child followed the Ten Commandments, prayed to "Yahweh," learned his Hebrew well and aped his parent's fear and hatred for Palestinians.

By the 1990s, Moshe the "Arab" had willingly performed his duty as a soldier in the Israeli Army. How else could it be? His parents had trained him to regard all Arabs as his enemies.

Abdul's mom and dad were also right about the Jews. These occupiers of Palestine treated "his" people like dogs, they said. That's why a childhood of stone throwing and rubber bullets made the "Jewish" Abdul itch to join the "freedom fighters" of Abu Nidal.

The nightmarish nineties begin with Abdul, the kosher Palestinian, dreaming of the day he can string his body with explosives and blow up the Zionist enemy or help set off a chemical warhead to kill tens of thousands of his true blood. And if such a horror were dared by the Arabs, Moshe "the Arab" knows just what to do in retaliation. Let the Palestinians and their Arab neighbors be gassed and irradiated back to the brimstones.

One needs intelligence to produce a materialistic world and the worst of all, destructive machines of war, when there is no more love. One needs love and intelligence to understand that the reality is, we don't possess anything. For example, when we die, we leave this world without any possessions, only with our experiences. I hope that people will wake up before they destroy the future of our great-grandchildren.

Tim Sikyea, Yellowknife Tribe (1988)

What Makes PREDICTION

The four metaphorical Hellriders of Doomsday prefer riding only one breed of horseflesh. **They ride our night "mares" — our unconsciousness.** Without them they will never fulfill their potential destinies. We must grab the nightmares by the muzzle and turn the Hellriders away.

I cannot do it for anyone but myself. When I reach inside the dark meadows of my mind where nightmares graze, I catch hold of my particular horse's muzzle — the tendency to take another's criticism personally. I will chew and chew on a slight, an injustice, or any mis-understanding. Before I started practicing a technique of observing the nightmares browsing in fields of my expectations, I would hold on to my hurt feelings for years.

When I look inward at the mechanics of hurt, I discover that the pain has a voice. If I breathe deeper into it, I can even identify whose voice it is. By stripping off layer upon layer of logic, by discarding those justifications for feeling hurt by what someone has done or said, I can grab the mane and stroke the flanks of a nightmare — the essential root of my pain. And almost always, the shadow of this animal is a childhood memory.

The nightmare responds. She speaks with the voice of my mother. I remember how I learned to imitate her way of indulging hurts and slights. By touching the nightmare consciously, carefully, so that it does not start and run behind my awareness, I can study and understand this breed of unconsciousness that imitates my mother's suffering and calls it my own.

If I delve still deeper into that dark meadow, I come across another nightmare: my mother's voice of misery was her mother's way of gnawing on misery and slights. **Standing deep in the meadow of the subconscious, I can examine the pedigrees of unconsciousness passed from hell horse to dreaded horse.**

$\mathcal{SO}$ PREDICTABLE?

The horses are legion. They graze in everyone's dark meadow of unconscious motivations.

No doubt a number of my readers would profess to a patriotic feeling for their country, and would watch with pride as *their* Olympic athlete climbed on the platform to receive his or her gold medal. Of course many of you (as I used to) would automatically feel your breast swell with patriotism, and some of you might even shed tears when *your* national anthem played and the cameras displayed *your* national flag hoisted high over the head of *your* athlete.

Just for one moment can we step out of our habitual identities and ask ourselves why? Just who is this stranger with the gold medal we are feeling so proud about? Few of us would ever come to know the athlete, or, if we are honest, ever care to meet the athlete outside the context of flags and medals.

When I was a child, I remember seeing some old newsreel footage showing a group of Japanese soldiers during World War II gleefully stepping on an American flag. When their jackboots stomped on the stars and stripes, I felt as if they were stepping on my stomach. Later, during Vietnam War demonstrations, I saw hippies wearing vests made out of American flags and felt the same indignant rage.

Why?

Let me show you. There are other nightmares grazing in the meadow. Awareness reaches out and touches the flank of another dark horse:

Looking inside myself I discovered that my patriotic rage was a breed of unconsciousness that spoke with my father's voice. Digging deeper, I remembered the first time I was spanked by him, when I was only five or six years old. My childhood need to be loved compelled me to be good, dutiful and as phony as I could be. I thought if I eagerly agreed with whatever my daddy said about our flag, he would love me.

All nightmares hate being watched. Once I had

consciously encountered the source of any robopathic habit, it became more difficult to continue the behavior without some annoying tug of awareness. When I risked venturing into the unconscious mind to find out why a certain feeling was hurt, I found the shadow of a repressed and forgotten incident. When replaying that incident in my memory, I discovered that I bought my concept of hurt from mom, dad, country and priest. And I realized then why I bought into these hurts. It was because I was trained never to question authority and ascertain the truth for myself. The risk and the freedom in looking inward is discovering that it is not that someone hurts my feelings — I am hurting because I purchased and hold on to that hurt feeling.

Those who do not learn from the mistakes of the past are condemned to repeat them. This maxim has fueled my fascination with history since childhood. I devoured everything I could about the past and its patterns, in an attempt to understand why the empires that arose never acknowledged the warning signs of their fall. Why were new inventions and insights always reviled? Why do geniuses like Van Gogh die mad and penniless, yet their paintings sell for tens of millions of dollars a century later? Why does Charles XII of Sweden read about the disastrous invasion of Russia by the Teutonic Knights and repeat the same bloody gaffe?

Napoleon reads the history of Charles XII to better understand why the Swedish King was defeated and commits the same tactical errors during his disastrous invasion of Russia. Not only does the successful "sleepwalker" Adolf Hitler brush aside these warnings, he even invades Russia on the same date as Napoleon — 129 years later. Like Napoleon, Charles XII, and the Teutonic Knights, Hitler ignores the weather. He allows his armies to push deep into Russia and they suffer the same fate.

When I became satiated with my study of history's repetition of follies, I proceeded to wolf down every book I could find concerning "future history" — namely prophecy. There again I saw the same mistakes repeated in glimpses of tomorrow. In the past, leaders spoke of new world orders and built up massive armies and better arsenals of destruction to preserve peace. Peace-keeping forces and guns have always been used, and prophetic signs show no change in the history of the future.

In the prophetic scriptures of every culture, I saw the shadows of unconsciousness galloping into tomorrow's events, such as the habit that makes us postpone a problem until it becomes a disaster. I read the forecasts of plagues that were the outgrowth of denial, helplessness and impossible dreams. Historically, people have tenaciously held on to their outmoded traditions when their repressed intelligence ached for change. They are doing it still. They will probably do it tomorrow.

It seems that the past and the future are two halves of an endless race track of habits spinning around the present.

When I was a baby I didn't feel insulted if someone called me names. I just

gurgled. The words "Christian" or "American" or "atheist" or "Commie"— what were they to me? What were they to you when you were in your crib? How is it that we can follow a certain mechanical progression of conditioning and find ourselves on a battlefield slaughtering each other because of our borrowed identities, national tribes and superstitiously-based religions?

I have my own answer. It comes from exploring forbidden meadows of the id and reading the pulse of ancient and future repetitions of history. My answer is quite simple: Each generation billets a particular breed of misery and mayhem into the tender meadows of each new generation.

As far as the world of man is concerned, I don't think there is much chance of converting the masses against their own past. They are creations of the past, and their past will come to its crescendo in the coming crisis. The masses will be drowned in that crisis. I feel sad about it, but the truth has to be said.

Only a few people in the world will be able to survive after this global suicide, and those will be the people who are deeply rooted in consciousness: alert, aware, loving, and ready to disconnect themselves with the past completely and unconditionally, and ready to begin **the New Man and the new humanity with the freshness of a child.**

I have been enjoying the fact that there are many people in the world who are capable of going deep into themselves.

Their only hope is a self-realized being.

It is too late to do anything to prevent the immense destruction that is going to happen. **If we can protect only a few genuine human beings, that will be enough, more than enough.** The past of humanity has been completely accidental; they have been doing things without knowing the consequences. Now we are suffering the consequences, and there is no way to change those consequences.

Osho (1988) Hari

The Doomsday BODY COUNT

Now I lay me down to sleep
I pray the Lord my soul to keep
If I should die before I wake
I pray the Lord my soul to take

If only one-third of humanity will survive it is better!

Meishu-Sama (1955)

*Only one-third of humanity will survive crossing the
great mountain pass of time*

Deguchi Nao (c. 1896) Omo

*A third of mankind was killed by the three plagues of
fire, smoke and sulfur...*

St John of Patmos (AD 81-96) Rev 9:18

The blind leadeth the blind into a
ditch.

Y'shua (AD 30-33)

After the stampede of unconsciousness

The human's incredible fear of life and death is sharpening her judgments into weapons. She cuts the world into pieces, she creates territories, she builds walls and draws limits. She creates a false security for herself within her own family, the tribe, the group, the town, the country — although in reality there exists nothing separating one human being from the other or one group from the other, other than all the divine differences, the wonderful nuances and individualities. Ambres (1987) Amb

Many of the dreams or visions don't necessarily mean the end, they could also indicate a change. Our people say that people who are not spiritually in tune can't adapt to this change. They won't have the necessary physical, mental and spiritual strength to change themselves.
It is being said that humanity will become mad.
There will be an energy or something similar that will influence the atmosphere (radiation from ozone holes?). As a consequence, the pressure in our brain will increase by 35 percent. But people who have become spiritually clear and accept these approaching energies of the cosmos will be able to adapt to them and use them positively for themselves. They will find protected areas where they will be secure from this "human cleansing process."
Seventy to 80 percent of humanity are not spiritually but materialistically oriented. That's why they won't be able to endure this transformation; they will go mad. They will kill themselves and destroy everything around them. It will be like a madhouse. Probably somebody will then push the famous button because of this. Tim Sikyea: Yellowknife Tribe (1988)

Mankind will be decimated by epidemics, famines and poison. After the catastrophe they will emerge from their caves and assemble, and only a few will have been left to build the new world. The future is approaching at a quick pace. The world will be destroyed in many quarters and will never be the same as before. Seeress Regina (early twentieth century)

...water and fire will purify the Earth, and the period of true peace will begin.
prophecy of La-Salette (1846)

Through intense tribulation shall man be brought nearer to perfection and more fitted to enjoy the wonders of the new Aquarian Age, that, born in the blood and sacrifice, will in the end fulfill the meaning of its symbol "the Water Bearer," whose pouring out of water on the earth is the emblem of unselfishness — the negation of Self — arrived at through suffering. Cheiro (1926) Cwp

Times of disaster make you aware of the reality as it is. It is always fragile; everybody is always in danger. You just go on dreaming, imagining beautiful things for the coming days, for the future. But in moments when danger is imminent, suddenly you become aware that there may be no future, no tomorrow, that this is the only moment you have.
So times of disaster are very revealing. They don't bring anything new into the world; they simply make you aware of the world as it is — they wake you up. If you don't understand this, you can understand this, you can become awakened. Osho (1986) Myst

A house with a light never attracts thieves.
Lord Buddha (c. 500 BC)

164

PART THREE: TOMORROW

# of BLESSINGS

The Heart of the World Is Broken, Yet it Rises Anew

—— I Cannot Understand It...

Madame Sylvia (1948)

Apocalypse!

The word conjures visions of **divine revenge** and the Earth splitting open, welcoming sinners to **Satan's reception.** It threatens the final moment when destiny's back is against the wall and history's excuses have run out. It is a spiritual foreclosure. A time to pull a mantle of mountains over one's head and hide from **St John's acid trip of angels** with swords for tongues, who hang on every bleat and low of a lamb with seven eyes. **And why?** Because Captain Karma (AKA God Almighty) is looking in the Book of Life and *your* name isn't there. **The Judgment Day has come!**

Apocalypse?

Words by themselves have no life except that which we invest in them. They pass down the centuries, taking on new psychological charges like stories whispered down a queue. The Greeks never intended this word to be a noun of doom. Apocalypse literally means "to uncover" or "to expose" the truth. There is a naked truth here, hiding beneath the changing fashions of syntax. However, the price of truth revealed may be a degree of change one is not ready to risk. Why else, then, do we react with such hopelessness and fear to a word that signifies the real hiding behind the false? Can we see only catastrophe in the revelation of truth?

In my mid-twenties, I experimented with a variety of mediumistic techniques to gain direct experience of the prescience and politics of forecasting. I wanted a taste of the word "apocalypse" as it was originally understood. For a time I gave tarot card readings. I learned that one way to be a good psychic was to let my own expectations and fears take a break, and allow insights — my own inner oracle, if you will — to take over. The cards had to speak for themselves. I wasn't going to "read" them. If nothing came, then even nothing was an answer. There was no rule but one: remain a judgeless presence and completely trust whatever I — *IT* — did or said. And this oracular "rule" almost always moved the client's energy toward the same "gap" I experienced while breathing and waiting. Whether I or my client judged the reading right, wrong or rude was apparently none of my inner oracle's concern.

Waiting... waiting... Breathing each moment in and out. Mouth speaks on its own, hands whirl cards and thoughts weave themselves out of subjective silks. I presume this gap is the very essence of what the ancient Greeks meant by the word "apocalypse." It is a state of naked unknowing where all etiquette and social politics, all presumptions of knowledge and self-identity are discarded. Sometimes my hands, flying on their own, pulled out a few nasty surprises. They often exposed a fear or two and enticed a tear of regret hiding behind the mask of a client's smugness. Answers came that perplexed the reader and the read. My "oracle" almost always replied to questions the poor client had, but never asked.

Case in point: I once was a guest reader at a psychic center in California (where else?). A woman entered — better to say squeezed — through the door into the reading room. It soon became clear that my "oracle" sensed that this woman was unconsciously flaunting her obesity, daring anyone to confront her about it. And confront her the oracle did, using John's big mouth. It told the woman that she had felt robbed of something around the age of five and that she had been trying to fill the gap ever since.

"I had my thyroid glands taken out when I was five," she said, stunned. "That's why I...look like this," she confessed, gesturing to her elephantine folds.

This only egged my oracle on. It said the woman was intellectually bloated with borrowed knowledge in esoteric matters and this obesity of learning was smothering any hope of a direct experience of the mysteries she had sought for so long. That statement hit her like a brick. She admitted to being a psychic reader herself and told me she was checking me out because I was what you might call a new kid on the metaphysical block.

The accuracy of these sudden and unexpected surgical slices at her most private psychological parts caught her completely by surprise. I saw the vulnerability and tears of a five-year-old girl who couldn't love herself anymore because she was a prisoner of other people's ideas of beauty. Caught by the sudden exposure, she confessed to be a believer of the Eastern theory that the body has seven centers of energy called chakras. These are invisibly present in each of us in the subtle bodies we possess beyond our physical form. She felt the communication chakra corresponding to her throat was in some way missing or not functioning because she could rarely feel it. To this the oracle blurted out that she was seeing it backwards. It wasn't her chakras she was feeling, but the blocks made by all her book knowledge on the subject. If anything, her throat chakra was open and the others were closed.

The last thing I wanted to do was be brutal and make her cry. During my readings, I often find my own limitations and sense of morality trying to block and condemn the oracle's words. However, with every new breath, something swept aside any tendency to comfort this woman with goody-goody falsehoods. The trance was sustained. My mouth waited for the oracle to move tongue, click consonants and pour vowels together into whatever it wished to say. This time there was only silence coming from the oracle's uncomfortably frank emptiness.

She cried.

I sat, waiting, watching the breath. Her sobs were the hurricane rotating around the silent eye of the oracle's apocalypse. There was a sudden gap in the sobbing. I heard my voice speak gently to her gap of silence: "That is the place beyond your borrowed knowledge." I didn't know what the hell that meant, but it nurtured both of us, and I felt our hearts and bodies relax into what I can only call a *presence*.

The moment was floating
clouds heavy
a falling

of a silent rain that drenched my spine with wholeness and caressed random thoughts and feelings away from the mind. It reflected John, the fear, the elation, the crying woman, and the more these things were clearly observed, the more the oracle was untouched — free of them all.

After the tarot session, my client exuded a beauty that I can only say was beyond the body and all the judgments we use to insulate ourselves from our spiritual nakedness. She had undergone an apocalypse. The childhood wound that had hid and festered for thirty years was exposed to the air of truth. And acceptance of it brought freedom.

She left the reading a thankful, though fragile, client.

An hour later I experienced the other mainstream reaction to the word "apocalypse" acquired through centuries of reading St John of Revelation. The phone rang. The psychic of the once freed-of-fat-feelings was on the line and very angry. She condemned me, wrapping away the little girl wound in judgments and posturing so it could fester again.

I sighed from weariness at the diatribe. I knew "too" well this same conditioned knee-jerk habit of ego, for it was my own. I too have my own hurts to hide, my own denial of the naked, and sometimes heartbreaking truth. And, it is that acquired fear of the truth about ourselves which buries all uncomfortable revelations.

This is the motive force ensuring endless tomorrows of fear. If we insist on keeping our egos glued together, we will never muster enough courage to acknowledge, let alone discard, an outdated mind-set or morality; the truth will always remain hidden from us. We will continue to suffer.

One day Mrs O., who ran the center, made me aware of what psychic influence was being used to have me thrown out. Apparently this madame of the corpulent chakras was a major esoteric in the Southern California psychic church circuit. As far as new age politics goes, I was in deep chakra. There were no thank-yous for my sharing!

Mrs O. also told me that a number of my clients had felt their egos ruffled. I had no defense. It was often true. Rather than telling them they'd been Nefertiti or a personal friend of Jesus Christ (it seems that no one in California lived a past life as a janitor), my naughty oracle would undiplomatically point out how in a past life as an imaginary emperor they wore "new clothes" just as illusory as those in the famous fairytale. Instead of whispering a revelation about a future soul mate, my ornery oracle would expose the block or bullshit that made their current soul mate their cellmate.

I told Mrs O. that no compromise was possible. If people came to me with their ballooning dreams, my oracle was bound to act like a bed of needles. I was willing to encounter the apocalyptic consequences and would resign rather than pretend-read for my clients. Mrs O. didn't fire me, but soon afterward I dropped my experimental career as a psychic card player to become a gardener.

The taste and smell of fear experienced around the phenomenon of apocalypse originated with St John of Patmos. In his essay, *Apocalypse* D.H. Lawrence attributes the Bible's final prophet with a "second-rate mind" that dirtied the meaning of apocalypse enough to make it the war cry for overzealous members of Christ's flock. These hysterics forgive poor sinners today, secretly hoping they'll get their own in spades on Judgment Day.

Despite St John's fear-mongering, he might be right in another sense. Perhaps there is a real catastrophe waiting for those unprepared to understand this word's essential meaning. No one likes it when reality overturns one's cup of dreams. No one can honestly say they'd gladly flash a revelatory torch inside the dark closet of their unconscious: Before revelation's light can dispel the darkness of unwanted fear and evil, it must first reveal the illusory stuff our dreams are made of.

Perhaps the greatest dream is believing we are securely in control of our lives. And perhaps the revelation we fear most is discovering that security is a fairy tale.

St John's Sunday school nightmares aside, you don't need to consult the prophecies of Part Two to get my future drift. The Judgment Day doesn't need a God/Father figure or one more prophetic interpreter's projection. It only needs a few too many CFCs sprayed in the armpit, or just enough people to stand by and believe reductions of nuclear overkill can be called nuclear disarmament.

Judgment Day can be a secular phenomenon. It comes with just the right critical mass of denial to assure disasters have their day, whether God, the promise of heaven, or the nightmare of hell exist or not.

There is a prophetic train of thought that says we can't get to the future from a present ruled by the motivations of the past 10,000 years. The next great age will only come for those who are ready to change, to drop those traditions of the dying Adamic Age which no longer work to keep the human race growing in consciousness. Tomorrow of Blessings — the second half of this book — takes a look at the minority future view. These prophecies indicate that in the eleventh hour an *Apocalypse of Consciousness* will preclude a global death.

So far, our prophets have shown us what's wrong with us. In Part Three, some of them will step down from pure forecasting to suggest how we can forestall some of their doom-laden predictions. The first half of the book was a warning. The second will use collected prophetic vision as a means to break through our fears and surmount our ancient resistance to change before we flow out of time.

All man-made progress will be enlisted for destruction. However, the great fate will raise her hand in warning and will command to stop. If men will listen to the judicious ones among them and stop, it will be to their advantage; if not, it will be their misfortune, and a great calamity will follow. Prophecy of Montreal (1888)

Everything will be decided by how we travel over this precipitous passage [in time]. If we survive the trail, carefully traversing it without falling, then everything will be recovered and health will return. But if we miss one step we will fail; the world will remain unhealthy. Man will grievously suffer from the effects or die altogether.

Attributed to Deguchi Nao (c. 1896)

Yes, all the predictions of the ancient seers, like Nostradamus, that the world is going to end by the end of this century, are true in a very different sense than it has been understood....The old [humanity] has to disappear to give place to a new man with fresh values: with one Earth undivided into nations, with one humanity undivided by religion....Changes have been happening. They will come to a peak by the end of this century, when the moment of ultimate decision will have to be faced by humanity. Transform yourself totally: drop all that is old, don't look backwards. Start creating new values, look forward — because the past is past and to visit the graveyard too much is dangerous....It is the future that should be your concern. It is the future and the faraway stars that will become your challenges.

Osho (1987) GrCh

is there a bridge to

the Golden Age

Then I saw a new Heaven and a new Earth, for the first heaven and the first Earth had passed away....I saw the Holy City, the new Jerusalem, coming down out of heaven from God, prepared as a bride beautifully dressed for her husband. And I heard a loud voice from the throne saying, "Now the dwelling of God is with men, and he will live with them. They will be his people, and God himself will be with them and be their God. He will wipe every tear from their eyes. There will be no more death or mourning or crying or pain, for the old order of things has passed away..."

I am making everything new!"

St John of Patmos (AD 81-96) Rev 21:1-5

UTOPIA

comes from the Greek words *Ou topos* — no place. This is the root word for the dreams of social and political perfection without addresses. This is the non-existent hat rack one hangs one's thinking cap on when a shower of ideals has made it soggy. It is that window of possibility from which all pies-in-the-sky are thrown. It is that illusory isle of paradise immortalized by Sir Thomas More and Bloody Mary. It is Rogers and Hammerstein's "Bali Hai" sung to the lyrics of Lyndon Baines Johnson's "Great Society." Utopia is danced to the tune of Jack Kennedy's Camelot. It is the rap song of world unity, peace on Earth, and weapons beaten into crop cutters and grandma's knitting needles; Utopia is the tango danced in the halls of the United Nations to the rhythm of Khrushchev's shoe.

How do we get to Utopia from here?

It is said there will come a time when man will know not the miseries of hunger, death or war; when man will be one family, without the scars of borders and the schizophrenia of diverse religions; nations will stop fighting, lying, and competing for the last polluted scraps of Gaia's earth, water and air. But, alas, the glories of "peace for millennia" come with a common karmic bill. There's a price for Utopia: CHANGE. We can't have today's cake and eat it tomorrow. The 7,000-year feast in civilization has reached the final course.

But wait. Something just dawned on me. I'm cooking up the wrong metaphor for this section. What we have here is an engineering problem.

As Part Two has shown, the hazards now threatening man's survival are more plentiful and severe than at any time in Earth's history. We may not make it through the dark waters of the next few decades. Even the finest prophetic surveyors cannot design a bridge for us to cross to the other shore. They can only give hints about how we get to a golden age from our neurotic present.

What follows are five plans of prophetic engineering. These prototype bridges to Utopia are called: Invention, Meritocracy, Russia is the Hope of the World, Commune Earth, and The Humanitary-Industrial Complex.

Each prophetic drawing begins with the trellis of the few authentic prophecies concerning the building of that bridge. This is followed by a conceptual sketch consisting of possible remedies offered by compassionate prophets who would love to see their predictions of doom proven wrong. Some of their future designs are ingenious; others are radical.

BRIDGE ONE:

THE *New* WOMAN

The "Aquarian" or "New Age" has also been set down as the period when woman in the order of upheaval, revolution, and change, would appear on the world's stage in a completely new role.

...women have to come to the front in all matters of public life, I have no hesitation in saying that there is no body of men who will be able for long to resist the tide of thought that for either good or evil is bringing women into power. Cheiro (1926) Cwp

MYSTERY MEETS OBJECTIVITY:
A QUANTUM LEAP IN SCIENCE

Materialistic science will receive a deathblow...one by one, facts and processes in Nature's workshops are permitted to find their way into the exact sciences, while mysterious help is given to rare individuals in unraveling its arcana.

Madame Blavatsky (c. 1888-1897)

CANCER CURED

Many new chemicals, helpful in healing cancerous diseases, were being discussed at great length in this year of 1993.

Irene F. Hughes (c. 1979)

FIFTY BILLION WILL BE FED AND CLOTHED

Soil will be stimulated into maximum productivity, and the entire range of plants formerly considered weeds will be utilized for food or for clothing. These breakthroughs will enable the Earth to support comfortably fifty billion people.

David Goodman Croly (1888) Glmp

NEW ENERGY SOURCES: ANTIGRAVITY

...by a machine three fingers high and wide and of less size a man could free himself and his friends from all danger of prison and rise and descend.

Roger Bacon (1220-1292) Epsc

NEW LIFESTYLES

People will work no more than six hours at a time, and this will be in staggered shifts. A whole range of goods and services will be available during the nighttime hours...People will live beneath domes which will provide temperature-controlled environments and will filter harmful substances out of the air. David Goodman Croly (1888) Glmp

Pestilences extinguished, the world becomes small. For a long time the lands will be inhabited in peace. People will travel safely by air [over] land seas and wave...

Nostradamus (1555) C1 Q63

INVENTION

Aquarrius THE AGE OF SCIENCE

The future belongs to the scientist, not to the politician...[they] will fade away on their own accord. They have been exploiting scientists for their own purposes, and to [exploit] anybody is not an act of dignity. Osho (1987) GrCh

AN END TO CRIME THROUGH EUGENICS?

Legal measures will be instituted to prevent the criminal, the insane, and the diseased from bearing children.

David Goodman Croly (1888) Glmp

GENETIC ENGINEERING LENGTHENS LIFE?

Never again will there be in it [New Jerusalem] an infant that lives but a few days, or an old man who does not live out his years; he who dies at a hundred will be thought a mere youth; he who fails to reach a hundred will be considered accursed.

"Third" Isaiah (c. 500 BC) Is 65:20

THERE WILL BE NO DEATH

He will wipe every tear from their eyes. There will be no more death or mourning, or crying of pain, for the old order of things has passed away.

St John of Patmos (AD 81-96) Rev 21:4

A MATERIAL (as well as Spiritual) HEAVEN ON EARTH

These improvements and discoveries will refresh the soul, give it leisure and prepare it for a natural voyage to post-mundane climes. A glorious period is before mankind. It will be a kind of material heaven — a preparation for the Spiritual Harmonium...Fall in love with the new dispensation....Have intelligent confidence in the advancement of the material world.

Andrew Jackson Davis (1856) Pen

The incoming energy of the Aquarian Age will turn our attention to a future influenced and dominated by the **inventions of science**. The Piscean Age's mode of controlling life through limitation will begin losing its control of human imagination. Rebellious curiosity, knowing rather than blindly trusting, will be the way. Science means "**to know**," and that discipline of knowing will touch all dimensions of life. Sudden and drastic changes will take place throughout society.

The ruling class of the future will be the intelligentsia. Aquarius will bring to the human mind a synthesis of science and mysticism. Uranus is the ultimate alchemist, the near-mad genius of rebellious insight. Uranus dares to think like a lotus opens, spreading itself in all directions. He is at home with the paradoxical and can pierce the veil of the irrational. To put it simply, the scientist, artist, or visionary of the Aquarian Age will feel at home in the gap between constantly shifting gestalts. Uranus, archetypal ruler of the Aquarius, turns base knowables into unknown gold.

The late J. Krishnamurti spoke and thought in a fluent Aquarian stream of consciousness, giving form to future man's contradictions-in-harmony. One of the things Krishnamurti will be remembered for is his many dialogues with David Bohm, the scientist currently pushing the limits of our understanding of quantum physics, reality and time. A mystic in dialogue with a scientist, the subjective dancing with the objective, is the way of tomorrow. Krishnamurti stressed again and again that for one to explore the subjective-spiritual realms, one must live in complete material and economic comfort. As the late Indian mystic Osho (Rajneesh) once observed, "I can meditate better in a Rolls-Royce than in a bullock cart."

The Aquarian Age will not live on Uranian archetypes alone. Viewing the future from Aquarius's more down-to-earth and lower vibratory ruler, the planet/archetype Saturn, the forces of structure and limitation will try to organize Uranian future chaos. By understanding Saturn's vibe, a bridge can be built to Utopia called "Invention."

There are other Uranian surprises. The discovery of a new and unlimited energy source could erase overnight many of the world's ecologically-induced political and industrial tensions. Roger Bacon's medieval reference to antigravity may have foreseen the success of current experiments with electromagnetic propulsion systems. The Japanese are making promising advances in superconductivity that could see the chief producer of greenhouse gases — the internal combustion engine — go the way of the mammoth.

In the inland sea near the city of Osaka, the Japanese are applying to ocean transportation the same technology used to levitate trains. In Kobe, a magnetically-powered ship is being manufactured at the docks of Mitsubishi Heavy Industries; the maiden voyage of Yamato No. 1 could rival in significance Robert Fulton's first steam-powered ship. She is propelled by a magnetic drive that pumps the ocean waters through an electromagnetic vacuum to glide silently through the waves. In the mid-twenty-first century, ocean commerce may skim with a whisper across waters that will never again suffer the footprints of man's oil spills.

There is a rebellious tinkerer living in the Australian bush, named Sandy Kidd, who claims to have invented the reactionless engines that will make man's flying saucers slip and slide through the folds of space. He says his gyro propulsion unit is the genuine antigravity machine which laughs the Laws of Newton off the map. (Uranus loves laughter.) Professor Eric Laithwaite, a world expert on gyroscopes, calls Kidd "ingenious."

Kidd's prototype gyro is around the same height as the "device" foreseen by Roger Bacon in the Middle Ages: *three fingers high and wide and of less size.* The device is forty-five centimeters high with a gyro at each end of a cross arm. During its first public demonstration at the Imperial College, London, in early 1985, Kidd's gyro did just what Bacon visualized over 700 years ago. It *freed itself* from the gravitational *prison* of a counterweight, to *rise and descend.*

After the demonstration, Laithwaite declared, "What we have here is a potential space drive. Properly developed, this would take you to the outer universe on a spoonful of uranium."

If his assumption is correct, we can expect Star Trek and a galactic federation to move beyond television and into reality 300 years earlier than expected. Kidd puts it in his own brash Aussie tones, which float on a Highland accent as thick and rich as Scottish whiskey: "Scientists will simply have to accept that I am right and physics is wrong. Only then can we open up the universe and take man to Mars in just a few hours longer than the present flying time between London and Sydney."

If someday a scientific eccentric like Kidd makes good his claim, he will fulfill the vision of nineteenth-century techno-prophet Andrew Jackson Davis. Davis believed that a transportation revolution would usher in a *universal brotherhood of familiarity,* creating a paradise on Earth. The Jet Age and the invention of the satellite have already broken the barriers of separation and made the world, as Nostradamus foresaw it, *a small place.*

The price we will pay for living and thinking globally is the loss of many of our traditions which were sustained by isolation, such as excluding half the human race from participation in the creation of the world by keeping them "barefoot and pregnant." Look out! The harem has a television. They see how other women live.

David Goodman Croly had his feet stuck deep in the mire of Piscean moralities — the Victorian Age of the nineteenth century. In 1888, his far-reaching vision of women's lib corresponded to that of another Victorian contemporary, Count Louis Hamon (Cheiro), when he declared: *Women throughout the world will enjoy increased opportunities and privileges. Along with this new freedom will come social tolerance of sexual conduct formerly condoned only in men. In addition, because of the greater availability of jobs, more women will choose not to have children* (Glmps).

Many of our traditions will go softly into the Piscean twilight when we achieve a universally high standard of living that only a Utopia bridged by inventiveness can bring. During the late 1980s, the Worldwatch Institute reported a significant rise in the number of mothers in the Third World who want fewer children. Inventions that lower ecological stresses and raise the standard of living around the world may buy enough time for a gradual decrease in birth rates in areas that have been politically and ecologically volatile, such as the Southern Hemisphere.

For instance, most poor people in Asia feel the need to propagate as many cash-making sons and caretaking daughters as possible for security in their old age. In contrast, many countries with a high standard of living, like Germany, Italy and Greece, have an annual birthrate in the minus. Tomorrow will see inexpensive and readily available birth control devices sold to Third World women. A Norplant stick of hormones, implanted in a billion women of childbearing age, smothers the fuse of the overpopulation bomb for five years at a stretch.

While we're on the subject, let's look at the future of Utopia's hormones. The bridge called Invention might also be genetically engineered. A metaphorical trellis that sustains a crossing to a technologically advanced Utopia could be woven out of a double helix of human DNA. We stand at the threshold of becoming gods of our own creation. We will soon be capable of genetically removing criminal impulses from the human brain, and disease and deformity from the body. We will be able to breed a world of geniuses.

I can hear the past crying, "Heresy!"

The future shrugs and says, "It is **unavoidable.**"

Every new discovery is fraught with potential evil. The greatest resistance to genetic engineering will come from those whose belief systems have conditioned them to seek and project imaginary father figures as their creators. Loathed be anyone rebellious enough to snub God's game of gene roulette, which leaves each newborn accidentally brilliant or flawed by the luck of the draw. From church and synagogue, mosque and temple, the religious bureaucracies of all faiths will yell, "Foul!"

The Vatican tried to keep Galileo's discovery that the Earth rotated around the Sun under wraps for centuries. The co-dependent religions of the Piscean Age may delay the coming of a genetically-engineered human. In the end, though, man will create himself. And perhaps he will only be what he has always been, his own god-devil-divine self-creator.

Whether the technology that makes every child a healthy, long-lived genius can counter the darker potentials of genetic mind control is a social and moral issue we cannot postpone grappling with for long. Now is the time to morally prepare ourselves for a new genetic dispensation which could make us monsters or supermen.

The Age of Aquarius will be, for better or worse, the age of mystical sciences and invention. *Man is not for science, science is for man*, declared Osho in 1988. *Science can be of tremendous help if all the scientists of the world who are creating destructive power are removed. They want to move, but they have no place to move to. We have to create a place for them.*

He posed that the future of man depends on the formation of a United Nations of scientists. It would be dedicated to finding global solutions to the world's problems and coordinating scientific research in all fields, without the interference of religious and political control. He called this forum the World Academy of Creative Science, Arts, and Consciousness.

No small dream, I must say. However, history's past lessons indicate its potential success. In the early 1980s, Lech Walesa's Solidarity Movement was deemed utopian. Now with Communism overthrown in Poland and Walesa ruling as Poland's freely elected head of state, democracy in Poland is no longer a utopian dream.

In the same way a labor movement toppled a Communist monolith, a movement of scientists at the leading edge of the age of discovery could undercut the politicians. There is no language barrier to speak of because English is the universal language of science. The inventors of the world are but a modem away from communicating with their fellows across the globe.

As the greenhouse gases thicken and the supersystems of civilization begin cracking, it is time for each scientist to put his ethics under the microscope and see how far he is ready to risk his children's future to help the politically minded to control and destroy human beings. If enough scientists reviewed their activities and dropped out of military or other destructive research, the politicians would lose their brain trust. I doubt any of our respected leaders knows how to build B-1 bombers and electromagnetic pulse weapons.

A change of scientific thinking will force politicians and businessmen, even in the coming global market economy, to steer industry away from products destructive to Earth and toward man-nurturing inventions and technologies.

The above scenario is indeed utopian. Nevertheless, predictive astrology indicates that the higher potentials of the coming new age will help us solve our woes through grassroots revolutions such as those toppling Marxism around the world during the early 1990s.

BRIDGE TWO:
COMMON MARKETS AND THE *Rumor* OF COMMON MARKETS

Europe will become a unity of one nation, not many nations anymore. There will be different people and different souls, but not nations. I see one banner — white. In the middle of Europe — a tower. The map of Europe white, not bloody any more.

Madame Sylvia (1948)

The US will absorb Canada, Mexico, Central America and the West Indies.

David Goodman Crowly (1888) Glmp

REVOLUTIONS IN COMMUNICATION & TRAVEL help bring about the FIRST INTERNATIONAL CONSTITUTIONAL CONGRESS

[In the early twenty-first century:] And as if by instinct all will wish to have the same kind of representative government, so that each area will choose delegates to a world body that will oversee the Earth. Thus it will be one government and one world, and the new currency to be introduced will be usable anywhere. By that time a new kind of communication will have been established, with travel by spaceships throughout the globe, and magnetic and solar energies replacing fossil fuels. Spirit guides of Ruth Montgomery (1979) Amg

AMERICA DISSOLVES INTO THE WORLD STATE BY 2026

A body of censors will be created who will be responsible for policing the US legislature at all levels. David Goodman Crowly (1888) Glmp

In the year 2026, the constitution of the United States will be no more. In its place will be an entirely different document, and an entirely new way of governmental rule. I predict that man will live in greater trust and love of his fellow man at that time.

Irene F. Hughes (1974)

NATIONAL BORDERS DISAPPEAR — MAN'S PERSPECTIVE GOES AQUARIAN: HUMANITY SETS ITS SIGHTS TO THE Skies

The "religion of the heavens" is still the only religion by which God "talks with man" today as He did in the days of old. In the light of such knowledge, all mysteries will be made plain, God's message written across the heavens will in the end become correctly interpreted; the language of stars, planets, and suns will translate "the Book" into words "understandable by the people." Nations will so realize their zodiacal affinities that they will group themselves together, and the unnatural frontiers of the present day will be swept away. Under such conditions war will become impossible and the "promise of peace" will at last be fulfilled. Cheiro commenting on Isaiah (1931) Cwp

MERITOCRACY

CULTURAL/SEXUAL/RACIAL BOUNDARIES
DISAPPEAR IN A BROTHER/SISTERHOOD OF *Man*

Even in such old civilizations as China and Japan, in spite of the most rock-bound laws of dynasties and religions, women have everywhere thrown off their shackles.

Cheiro (1926) Cwp

Color lines will be eradicated, because since the human soul is without color, skin tone has no meaning here. Government will be of one type, with all sending delegations to occasional world parleys, and as the population increases [after the disastrous shift of the Earth's axis] there will be smaller units to handle local matters, but these will scarcely be needed because of the harmony among the people. National barriers will be nonexistent, as each strives for the good of all. Spirit guides of Ruth Montgomery (1979) Amg

Soon will the present-day order be rolled up, and a new one spread out in its stead.

Bahá'u'lláh (1863) Aqd

In the times of those kings, the God of heaven will set up a kingdom that will never be destroyed, nor will it be left to another people. It will crush all those kingdoms and bring them to an end, but it will itself endure forever.

Daniel (6th-4th centuries BC) Dn 2:44

For I dipt into the future, far as human eye could see,
Saw the vision of the world, and all the wonder that would be;

Saw the heavens fill with commerce, argosies of magic sails,
Pilots of the purple twilight, dropping down with costly bales;

Heard the heavens fill with shouting, and there rain'd a ghastly dew,
From the nation's airy navies grappling in the central blue;

Far long the world-wide whisper of the south-wind rushing warm,
With the standards of the peoples plunging thro' the thunderstorm;

Till the war-drum throbb'd no longer, and the battle flags were furl'd
In the Parliament of man, the Federation of the world.

There the common sense of most shall hold a fretful realm in awe,
And the kindly earth shall slumber, lapt in universal law.

Alfred, Lord Tennyson (1842)
From the poem "Locksley Hall": lines 120-130

THE BRIDGE TO POLITICAL UTOPIA:

As designed by 'Abdu'l-Bahá. Excerpts from:

THE LEAGUE OF NATIONS AND THE UNO FORESEEN

True civilization will unfurl its banner in the midmost heart of the world whenever a certain number of its distinguished and high-minded sovereigns — the shining exemplars of devotion and determination — shall, for the good and happiness of all mankind, arise, with firm resolve and clear vision, to establish the Cause of Universal Peace.

THE UNO

They must make the Cause of Peace the object of general consultation, and seek by every means in their power to establish a Union of nations of the world. They must conclude a binding treaty and establish a covenant, the provisions of which shall be sound, inviolable and definite.

AFTER THE UNO? A WORLD GOVERNMENT WITH TEETH

They must proclaim it to all the world and obtain for it the sanction of all the human race. This supreme and noble undertaking — the real source of peace and well-being of all the world — should be regarded as sacred by all that dwell on earth. All the forces of humanity must be mobilized to ensure the stability and permanence of this Most Great Covenant.

A UNO THAT IS NOT A RUBBER STAMP OF THE STRONGEST

In this all-embracing Pact the limits and frontiers of each and every nation should be clearly fixed, the principles underlying the relations of governments toward one another definitely laid down, and all the international agreements and obligations ascertained. In like manner, the size of the armaments of every government should be strictly limited, for if the preparations for war and military forces of any nation should be allowed to increase, they will arouse the suspicion of others. The fundamental principle underlying this solemn Pact should be so fixed that if any government later violate any one of its provisions, all the governments on earth should arise to reduce it to utter submission, nay the human race as a whole should resolve, with every power at its disposal, to destroy that government.

GLOBAL RULE BY MODERATION

Should this greatest of all remedies be applied to the sick body of the world, it will assuredly recover from its ills and will remain eternally safe and secure.

Global politics throughout the last twenty centuries has been dominated by a *Piscean* golden rule:

"Do unto others as you would have them do unto you."

The downtrodden have experienced the darker side of this rule:

"Do unto others as they undo you."

There's an even darker version of the golden rule whispered by those who believe the United Nations is only a rubber stamp for US policy:

"Those who have the gold, rule."

THE FIRST SKETCH

The Secret of Divine Civilization (1875)

The year 2000 will bring the first strong implementation (or abuse) of the *Aquarian* version of the golden rule:

"Do whatever you like as long as you don't hurt others by doing it."

Aquarius will challenge each of us to expand our vision from the limits of nation to the wide-open potentials of a united family of humanity. National boundaries currently imprison many people in regions where they don't have sufficient export or economic potential to adequately sustain themselves. Famine, disease, and ultimately, war are the results. Only a global system with worldwide political and military support can forestall catastrophe by regulating resources, food, land, and wealth in service of a citizenry of the Earth.

'Abdu'l-Bahá, son of nineteenth-century Persian prophet Bahá'u'lláh, and first to succeed him as spiritual leader of the Bahá'í Faith, wrote these words forty-four years before the creation of the League of Nations, seventy-one years before the inception of the United Nations and 115 years before the UN's greatest test to date, the Gulf War of 1990-91. His statements are prophecies in process.

The former US and Soviet Presidents George Bush and Michail Gorbachev were the first superpower leaders since the 1950s to rely heavily on UN consensus when they sought confirmation for every political move (and almost every military move) against Iraq. Perhaps Bush stepped into line with the Bahá'í prophet's vision when he threatened to gather *the human race as a whole* resolving to destroy *that government* (Saddam Hussein's Baath party) if they didn't kowtow to international vital interests in the Gulf.

It is a refreshing sign of change that the UN body is commanding some respect for its resolutions. In the past, its condemnations of aggression were continually viewed with contempt by the perpetrators of war in places like Indochina, Grenada, Afghanistan, Lebanon and the West Bank. Less than a year before the Gulf Crisis, the UN's call to international moderation was all but ignored when Panama (a UN member) was attacked by a regional neighbor (also a UN member pledged to abide by international law).

In a few cases even diplomatic immunity of embassies was completely ignored. The invading soldiers stormed through the diplomatic compound of Cuba in Panama City. In the same city, the Papal Legate's embassy was encircled by armed troops, who put pressure on the priests to release Panama's head of state into their custody for trial in America. The invaders subjected the embassy to a psychological bombardment of round-the-clock heavy metal music. When UN lawmakers condemned such inhuman behavior, hardly a grunt came from the soldiers' commander-in-chief, the ruler of the invading country. The invasion of Panama was a dark time for global law. How good it is to see such a drastic change in the political climate a year later.

Iraq's posting of soldiers around Western embassies in Kuwait City was enough to elicit full-fledged sanctions by the UN Security Council. Does the UN at last have bite behind its ballot?

It seems that Gorbachev, the protégé of the late KGB chief and former Soviet Premier, Alexi Andropov, and Bush, the former CIA chief, had got 'Abdu'l-Bahá's vision right where they want it.

The prophetic judgment is still out on the new American and Russian Presidents. Perhaps Bill Clinton and the successor of Boris Yeltsin will nurture the resurgent UNO and will make its policies a law above that of national interests and finally get 'Abdu'l-Bahá's vision right where he wanted it.

POLITICAL UTOPIA:
As designed by Edgar Cayce Trance reading excerpts

THE NECESSITY OF ONE NATION "UNDER EARTH"

There has arisen, and there is arising in the affairs and experiences of man everywhere, the necessity of there being not only so much consideration of a land as of all lands as a unit. For mankind is his brother, and thou art thy brother's keeper. **(1936) №3976-16**

With the present conditions then that exist — these have all come to that place in the development of the human family where there must be a reckoning, a point upon which all may agree, that out of all this turmoil that has arisen from the social life, racial differences, the outlook upon the relationships of man to the Creative forces or his God and his relationships one with another, must come to some COMMON basis upon which all MAY agree. **(1932) №3976-8**

AMERICA: FOR OR AGAINST GLOBAL UNITY?

Not that all would be had in common as in the communistic idea, save as to keep that balance, to keep that oneness, to keep that association of ideas, or activity, or the influences throughout the experiences of all. These are to be kept in those attunements in which there may be the land itself defining what freedom is; in that each soul is by his OWN activity to be given the opportunity of expression, of labor, or producing.
All individuals are not to be told where or what; but are to seek through their own ability, their activity to give of themselves... **(1938) №3976-19**

AMERICAN DREAM OR AMERICAN "HYPOCRISY"?

...all groups must have their representation and their privileges that they, too, may have the opportunity. Unless we begin within ourselves and our own household [America], we are false to ourselves and to the principles that we attempt to declare. By setting classes or masses against other groups, this is not brotherly love. **(1943) №3976-28**

Know that right, justice, mercy, patience...is the basis upon which the new world order MUST eventually be established before there is peace. Then, innately, mentally and manifestly in self prepare self for cooperative measures in all phases of human relations. **№416-17**

SKETCH TWO

On the eve of the US-led war between a UN coalition and Iraq, the UN Secretary-General, Javier Peres de Quellar, had a last-minute meeting with Iraq's dictator, Saddam Hussein. After the war began, the Iraqi government leaked a transcript of the meeting. The Secretary-General was caught praising the Iraqi dictator for bringing the Palestinian dispute with Israel to the world's attention. Now it was time, he said, for Hussein to avoid war by pulling out of Kuwait. He assured Hussein that there was a better chance for peace in the region than ever before. (A prophet, de Quellar is not.)

Saddam Hussein replied that we are living in "the age of America" — the United States calls the shots. He accused the United Nations of being a rubber stamp for US foreign policy. The UN chief executive readily agreed, never imagining that the landlords of the UN building would hear about it. He admitted to Hussein that he just had to make do with the situation as it was.

America's greatest prophet, Edgar Cayce, often

admonished his fellow countrymen not to reduce the vision of their founding fathers into shadowy clichés. Americans could miss playing a positive role on the stage of manifest (Aquarian) destiny. America screams bloody murder and sends out the troops when international laws supporting their foreign policy are breached — for example, when Iraq invaded Kuwait. But she justifies herself when the whole world screams bloody murder for American's invasion of Indochina, Grenada and Panama. In America's book, the PLO are terrorists but the Contras are freedom fighters.

America cries "freedom!" and sees itself as the champion of democracy, while employing a Panamanian drug-dealing dictator as a CIA spy. During the 1980s, America pumps up Saddam Hussein as its ally against the Iranians; in the 1990s they pop his balloon and label him the Arab Hitler. But there's still hope that America will let freedom ring throughout the world. There's Hafez Assad, America's new Arab dictator-darling....And so it goes.

Edgar Cayce believed that America's definition of herself and how she applies her ideals in world events is crucial to the flow the future will take. With this in mind 1993 has already seen a dramatic change in America's political course with the new pro-UN Clinton presidency just as the world begins its final seven year countdown to the new millennium. America is redefining itself beyond the Reagan/Bush Cold War mind-set.

POLITICAL UTOPIA:

As designed by Osho. Excerpts from:

Step One: A DEMOCRACY IS A "MOBOCRACY" IS A "HYPOCRACY"

Either there will be an ultimate war — which means death to all and everything — or a total change of the whole structure in the human society. I am calling that change "meritocracy."

Choosing the government should be a very skillful, intelligent job. Just being twenty-one you may be able to reproduce children — it needs no skill, no education; biology sends you well prepared. But to choose the government, to choose people who are going to have all the powers over you and everybody, and who are going to decide the destiny of the country and the world, just to be twenty-one is certainly not enough.

Step Two: INTELLIGENTSIA OF THE WORLD, UNITE!

I would like all the universities — within each state — to call a convention of all the chancellors and the eminent professors; of the eminent intelligentsia who may not be part of the university; painters, artists, poets, writers, novelists, dancers, actors, musicians. It would include all dimensions of talents, all kinds of people who have shown their caliber — excluding politicians completely.

All Nobel Prize winners should be invited — excluding the politicians again....So from each state a delegation should be chosen for the national convention, which goes into details of how the Meritocracy can work.

From the national candidates there should be an international convention of all the universities of the world and the intelligentsia. This would be the first of its kind because never has the whole intelligentsia of the world come together to decide the fate of humanity.

They should write the first constitution of the world. It will not be American, it will not be Indian, it will not be Chinese — it is going to be simply the constitution of the whole humanity.

...And a world constitution will be a declaration that nations are no longer significant. They can exist as functional units but they are no longer independent powers. And if the whole intelligentsia of the world is behind this convention it will not be very difficult to convince the generals of the world to move away from the politicians.

And what power do politicians have? All the power that they have we have given to them. We can take it back.

The vision of Indian mystic, Osho, is pure spiritual punk. He is pure Uranus.
Osho supports a golden rule of governing expressed in Socratic terms:

"Those who know, should rule."

There is vast historical evidence that human misery is primarily caused by people surrendering their power to those who are the least emotionally and spiritually qualified to wield it.

Osho advises the intelligentsia to initiate a variation of the meritocratic revolution described in Aquarian-born Ayn Rand's book, *Atlas Shrugged*. In her story, all the gifted inventors, artists and businessmen — those holders of human genius who make the world work and evolve — get fed up with the envy and obstructions hurled at them by the common folk.

They decide to abandon civilization to the mediocre mob and, one by one, mysteriously slip

SKETCH THREE
The Greatest Challenge: The Golden Future (1987)

The members of the World Government will choose the world president. But the world president will be chosen not from members of the World Government, but from outside. And one thing should be absolutely certain about him — that he is not a politician. He can be a poet, a painter, a mystic, a dancer, but not a politician.

Step Three: AND FROM NOW ON, PREPARE PEOPLE FOR POWER

...for thousands of years you have never prepared anybody [for power]. If somebody is going to be a boxer you don't just push him into the ring and say, "Start!" ...You don't just give a guitar to somebody who has never seen the instrument before and expect him to be an Amadeus Mozart or a Ravi Shankar. Now this is your fault.

These people who are in power, have you trained them? Has anybody ever thought that the people who will be holding so much power need certain qualities so that they don't misuse power? This is not their fault.

So I propose two institutes in every university. One institute is for deprogramming. Anybody who gets a graduation certificate will first have to get a clearance certificate from the deprogramming institute — which means it has deprogrammed you as a Christian, as a Hindu, as a German, as an American, as a Communist, as a Mohammedan, as a Jew, or whatever trademarks you had. It [the institute] has taken out all the rubbish, because this [conditioning] has been our trouble.

So while you are being educated you are in a very silent and subtle way being prepared to be in power, in such a way that power cannot corrupt you, that you cannot misuse it.

I am not asking much, just an eight-year preparation parallel to your [collegiate, graduate and doctoral] studies. And if the whole government is meditative, deprogrammed, unprejudiced — just visualize it — then bureaucracy disappears, hierarchy disappears...

Once we move the power from the mob into the hands of intelligent people, people who know what they are doing, we can create something beautiful.

away to a commune known as Galt's Gulch, named after the guru of the revolution, John Galt. The masses run amok and nearly destroy civilization. The book ends with the meritorious few happily waiting to be called back to society from their hideaway. But they will emerge from their Shangri-la only on one condition: The world must be run only by the merit of genius.

The intelligentsia in Osho's version of *Atlas Shrugged* quietly withdraw their influence from politicians and establish a branch of "Galt's Gulches" in every university and college on Earth. What could the power freaks do about it? Who would write their speeches and cover their Dan Quayle-isms? Can the leaders of any country launch a missile or scam out a bogus treaty without the help of brilliant intellectuals and scientists? An old and befuddled actor in the role of president needs to surround himself with a brain trust just as Frank Sinatra masks a voice past its prime with a good orchestra.

"Who *will* be John Galt?"

BRIDGE THREE:

The day will come when Russian waste of blood — the blood he has and will yet pour out like water — will make "a new heaven and a new Earth..."

...the mysterious Aquarian Age has commenced its dawn across the world, and already its first rays have revolutionized Russia...

Cheiro (1926) Cwp

The communal law will be made in opposition. The old orders will hold strong, then [are] *removed from the scene. Then* [the old order of] *Communism put far behind.*

Nostradamus (1555) C4 Q32

[In Russia] *a new understanding has come and will come to a troubled people...when there is freedom of speech, the right to worship according to the dictates of the conscience — until these come about, still turmoils will be within.*

Edgar Cayce (1938) №3976-19

Russia, however, having for its zodiacal ruler the sign of Aquarius...and Uranus, will recover more quickly from revolutions or disaster and will advance more rapidly towards the achievement of its purpose than will Mexico or India.

Cheiro (1931) Cwp

On Russia's religious development will come the greater hope of the world. Then that one or group that is the closer in its relationship [with Russia: ie, the United States or possibly the European Community] *may fare the better in gradual changes and final settlement of conditions as to the rule of the world.*

Edgar Cayce (1932) №3976-10

I predict that Gorbachev is going to succeed in bringing the second and greater revolution to Russia; and his revolution in the Soviet Union is going to affect everything in the whole world.

Osho (1986) Rebl

Russia
IS THE HOPE OF THE WORLD

A new idea of government will little by little spread from [Russia], which will completely revolutionize Europe, Asia, the Far East; and Russia will become the most powerful nation in the history of modern civilization.

Cheiro (1926) Cwp

The success of a meritocracy requires at least one of the Cold War superpowers to sacrifice its national egomania and dedicate itself to the birth of true international law. So far neither the late Soviet Union nor the United States has done this. As host nation, America regularly denies passports to United Nations emissaries whose agendas are contrary to US policy. In the past twenty years, nearly two-thirds of the United Nations Security Council's vetoes have been American. More than half the others have come from the British. France is third. And the Soviets? In the past twenty years, Soviet vetoes were a distant fourth.

In 1944, before there was even a Cold War brewing, Edgar Cayce forewarned his countrymen of the future to take stock of themselves. The hope of the world would depend on it:

> What is the spirit of America? Most individuals proudly boast "freedom." Freedom of what? When ye bind men's hearts and minds through various ways and manners, does it give them freedom of speech? Freedom of worship? Freedom from want? Not unless these basic principles are applicable... for God meant man to be free...
>
> ...What then of nations? In Russia there comes the hope of the world, not as that sometimes termed of the Communistic, OR Bolshevik, no; but freedom, freedom! That each man will live for his fellow man! The principle has been born. It will take years for it to be crystallized, but out of Russia comes again the hope of the world. **(1944) №3976-29**

When I first read this trance reading I thought Edgar Cayce might be a Communist.

Actually, Cayce envisioned a future that might shock both Capitalist and Marxist power freaks. Cheiro and Nostradamus support Cayce's claim that ultimately Russia will be the catalyst for world peace and brotherhood. They were certainly not Communists; the first was the capitalistic Count Louis Hamon, and Nostradamus was a God-and-king-fearing royalist and wealthy physician.

This is not the first time I've been confounded by an extremely utopian prophecy. Being born and raised an American, I find this collective vision particularly hard to swallow. But I've seen too many fulfilled predictions cut through my outrage and assert their truth.

Nostradamus's sixteenth-century contemporaries thought him a bit of a loon for predicting the quick fade-out of Portugal as the maritime superpower. Adding insult to injury, he proclaimed that tiny, insignificant England would fill the superpower void for 300 years.

He was correct.

I stretched my biases to the breaking point trying to contradict the Nostradamian forecasts that date the beginning of a US-Soviet friendship around the year 1989.

This interpretation at least seems to be correct.

When I shed my nationalistic righteousness for a moment, I understood that it is lethal for our future if we believe our world must be run "American-style" or "Soviet style" — or according to any other national ideology. History is the witness to this; the Pax Romana, the Pax Britannia and now too, the Pax Sovietica — are all extinct. Hopefully, the UNO will not become the fading rubber stamp for the Pax Americana.

But the Uranian jack-in-the-box factor may pop up at any moment and expose victory's deeper insights first to the superpower defeated by the Cold War. Perhaps losing twenty million to World War II and ten million to Stalin's purges has taught the Russians a lesson about war that America has yet to learn — restraint. Would Americans have been so eager to Rambo their way into Iraq if they had lost twenty million people in World War II? History does not forget that America is the only nation to use nuclear weapons prior to Armageddon, and rumors of Armageddon.

Cayce closes his famous declaration about Russia's destiny by offering a challenge and a dose of compassionate criticism to Americans:

It will take years for it to be crystallized, but out of Russia comes the hope of the world. Guided by what? That friendship with the nation that hath even set on its present monetary unit "In God We Trust." (Do ye [America] use that in thine own heart when you pay your just debts? Do ye use that in thy prayer when ye send thy missionaries to other lands? "I give it, for in god we trust"? Not for the other fifty cents, either!)
In the application of these principles, in those forms and manners in which the nations of the Earth have and do measure to those in their activities, yea, to be sure, America may boast; but rather is that principle being forgotten when such is the case, and that is the sin of America.
№3976-29

Apparently to Cayce, if Russia is tomorrow's great hope, America will nurture her transformation. An economic marriage between US technology and Russian natural resources was foreseen by Edgar Cayce in 1932 during the Great Depression: *Many conditions should be considered, were this to be answered correctly,* cautioned the prophet to a businessman. *You could say yes and no, and both be right, with the present attitude of both peoples as a nation, and both be wrong, for there IS to come, there WILL come, an entire change in the attitude of both nations as powers in the financial and economical world. As for those raw resources, Russia surpasses all other nations. As for abilities for development of same, those in the US are the farthest ahead. Then these UNITED or upon an equitable basis, would become or COULD become — powers; but there are many interferences. [These]...will take years to settle.* №3976-10

The prophecy reminds me of an interview of Boris Yeltsin by "60 Minutes" reporter Ed Bradley in the mid-1980s. At the time, the current president of Russia was party boss of Moscow. At one point in the interview, Bradley asked Yeltsin, "All right, what can we teach you and what can you teach us?" Yeltsin replied that the Americans could help the Russians by teaching them more efficient business practices and sharing their technological know-how. In return, the Russians could teach the Americans how to live a less stressful life beyond the neurosis of uncontrolled competitiveness. Indeed, Boris Yeltsin or his successors may be expressing the practical outcome of Edgar Cayce's prediction on future US-Russian relations and may be the one most likely to implement it. The cross-pollination of the two ideologies could change the political/social structure of twenty-first-century civilization.

If the Cold War has a karmic bill for America to pay, her people will not suffer the same magnitude of shattered dreams as the Russian people have from the scandal called Soviet Marxism. Then again, the deeper the repentance, the greater, perhaps, the potential for wisdom.

Remember what now I say, begin in Russia, finish in Russia

G.I. Gurdjieff (1949)

[The twentieth-century mystic made this prediction to his disciples a few weeks before his death. Russia was where he launched his spiritual movement for the "conscious evolution" of mankind. This admonishment points to the future completion of his great work through a renaissance of his primarily Eastern teachings in the former Soviet Union.]

BROTHERS' KEEPERS, LOSERS WEEPERS

It is also understood, comprehended by some that a new order of conditions is to arise, there must be a purging in high places as well as low: and that there must be the greater consideration of the individual, so that each soul being his brother's keeper. Then certain circumstances will come about in the political, the economic, and whole relationships in which a leveling will occur...or a greater comprehension of the need for it.

Edgar Cayce (1938) №3976-18

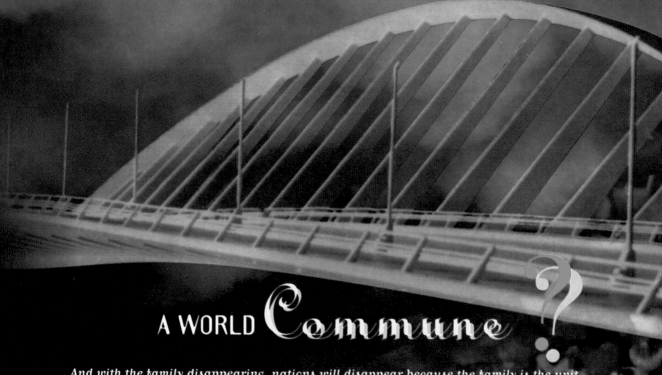

A WORLD *Commune* ?

And with the family disappearing, nations will disappear because the family is the unit of the nation.

...The whole world should be one humanity, only divided by small communes on a practical basis. No fanaticism, no racism, no nationalism — then, for the first time, we can drop the idea of wars. We can make life with honesty, worth living, worth enjoying — playful, meditative, creative — and give every man and every woman equal opportunity to grow and bring their potential to flowering.

Osho (1987) GrCh

COMMUNE
EARTH

GLOBAL FRIENDSHIP

No more will treacherous gold and silver be
Nor earthly wealth, nor toilsome servitude,
But one fast friendship and one mode of life
Will be with the glad people, and all things
Will common be, and equal light of life.

The Sibylline Oracles (second century BC)

Spiritual COMMUNISM

...for changes are coming, this may be sure — an evolution, or
revolution in the ideas of religious thought. The BASIS of it for
the world will eventually come out of Russia; not Communism,
no! But rather that which is the basis of the same, as the Christ
taught — His kind of communism!

Edgar Cayce (c. 1930) №452-6

Once the *Piscean* moral load is off our imagination, the future society of the new *Aquarian* dispensation will be Christian.

Or, in other words:
The future is communist.
What!? Did I really say that — with the Berlin Wall of a Stalinist Jericho tumbling down at the blast of capitalist Joshua's horn?

Yes, it must be said, because it will be the case. Aquarian Age concepts will be expressed through a more communal form of society. Marxism, like nationalism, is a hybrid social phenomenon of the cusp period of mixed Piscean and Aquarian Age influences. In his article "From Pisces to Aquarius" (*The Great Bear Presents: Planet Earth, 1989*), astrologer Dan Oldenburg reminds us that even Marx expected his theories "to be applied to America and Germany first."

"Russia and China, in his opinion, were simply not ripe for them. We are seeing the reality of this now!" Oldenburg observes.

The Communist bloc is crumbling because the baby was born premature. It lacked an essential dimension — that of the spirit.

"Marx, Engels, and Lenin had no understanding of higher consciousness," Oldenburg writes. "...Deep, mystical experiences beyond the mind had no place in their theories. This is a problem of Communism because the authentic spiritual quest of the individual must be the foundation of any truly comprehensive approach to life."

After long study of the issue, using the archetypal language of astrology, Oldenburg believes new communistic experiments are unavoidable in a coming age. Man will feel compelled to experiment with new forms of civilization.

Even Cayce scholar, Lytle Robinson, finds his vision of a spiritually communist America a bit difficult to fathom. In his book, *Edgar Cayce's Story of the Origin and Destiny of Man*, Robinson concludes that Americans of today are not spiritually prepared to be communist "in any form".

But Robinson is too insightful a Cayce watcher to leave it at that. He, like Oldenberg, interprets Cayce's version of communism to mean a fraternity of the spirit, motivating a closer union of individuals in a group. He believes humans have a basic "cooperative impulse" which is greater than their competitive one. "Competition has its place, but in survival it is brutal, impoverishing and out of place," Robinson adds.

Is it accurate for Cayce to peg Christ as a communist?

Listen to this:

"All the believers were together and had everything in common. Selling their possessions and goods, they gave to anyone as he had need....They broke bread in their homes and ate together with glad and sincere hearts...No one claimed that any of his possessions was his own, but they shared everything they had." These are not Marxists described here, but members of the early Christian communes chronicled in the New Testament (Acts 2:44, 4:32).

The essential Christian community is *commune*-istic.

Christ's communism is quite close to the Marxist model. Indeed, some commentators posit that the Communist precept of sharing wealth equally — namely, its dictatorship of the proletariat — is the culmination of 2,000 years of a Christian propaganda campaign initiated back in AD thirty-something.

Blessed are the poor from the New Testament to Das Kapital.

Early in my study of the future, I tried to find a prophetic model of society that would have the best chance of survival in the Aquarian Age. I decided therefore to study and at times live in communal settings.

One can live in any era, today. Just walk into a Quaker town and see the nineteenth-century living in this present moment. On the other hand, some societies live in their present *ahead* of our time.

Aquarius rules the eleventh house. This means that the play of Saturnian and Uranian energies is expressed in the physical world through interactions on a mass, impersonal level. The small family expands its vistas and becomes a greater family.

Because of the Piscean love of romance, the sense we have of the word "impersonal" feels dry, distant, withholding. But like it or not, Aquarius will destroy many of our dreams and expectations about relationship. There will be a science of love that will enable us to experience love *as it is* — not as we think it should be.

After recognizing this principle of apocalyptic love, and researching several economically and socially viable communal systems, I came to the conclusion that the most progressive and Aquarian model was that of the Indian mystic Osho (Rajneesh).

I began my prophetic investigation of his spiritual and social experiments in 1980. I spent the greater part of four years living in Rajneeshee communal households, and even participated in the building of this century's largest and most controversial experiment in alternative living, Osho's commune city in the eastern Oregon desert called Rancho Rajneesh or Rajneeshpuram.

I intend to write more than one study on Osho and his followers in the future. But this is not the place or the time to untangle controversy from myth or pass judgment. I will only say that Osho has earned a place in this book because his prophecies fit my criterion for past accuracy and because his projections of the future offer sound possibilities to consider. With this said, I'd like to share with you a brief account of communal lifestyle that may stand as a prototype for a future society beyond the nuclear family.

Between 1981 and 1985, the Ranch, as it was called by its citizens, grew from a few dozen pioneers to a permanent population of 5,000 people, increasing to about 15,000 during the peak summer months. Rajneeshpuram, the incorporated city within the ranch property, was a microcosm of the world. Osho's followers (called sannyasins) came there from every corner of the globe.

Demographic and psychological studies were made of the citizens of Rajneeshpuram in 1983 by Professors Carl A. Latkin, Richard A. Hagan, Richard A. Littman and Norman D. Sundberg of the University of Oregon's Department of Psychology. Their study showed that the majority of sannyasins were college graduates, a population with a higher than normal ratio of MAs and PhDs. They were, for the most part, the upper crust in education and financial success.

The new pioneers brought to the experiment the willingness to undergo hardships and the determination to surmount them. They were already aware that one of the biggest obstacles to their success would be each person's unconscious national and religious prejudices. In short, their utopian community could be sabotaged by their conditioning from the past. The experiment would succeed or fail depending on whether or not people of every national bias could pull together and transcend those habits. They said yes to change, and tried to make a city thrive in spiritual and ecological harmony. They put into practice the utopia of a global citizenry living in harmony.

Their communism-out-of-abundance experiment had no shortage of cash. With the financial help of 300,000 other sannyasins, and sannyasin-run businesses worldwide, an estimated

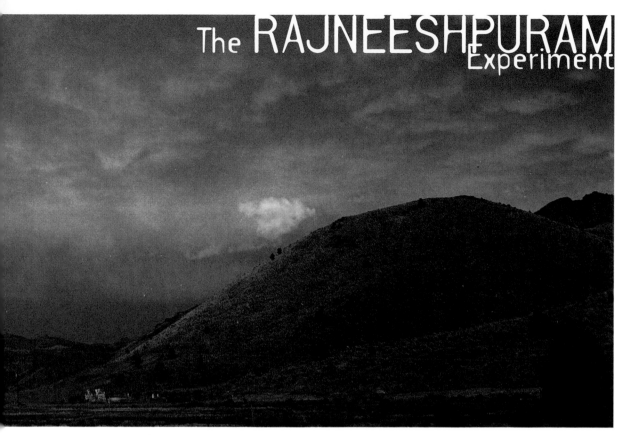

The RAJNEESHPURAM Experiment

eighty-five million US dollars was invested in Rajneeshpuram's development.

They proved that communing with financial and intellectual abundance can get a lot done in very little time. During the first year, with less than 1,000 residents, the sannyasins cleared and planted 1,400 acres of crop land, cleared an additional 700 acres for planting, built irrigation lines to serve 135 acres of fields and planted fifty acres of vegetables. They built a Class A dairy barn for a new herd of Holstein cows, set up fifty-four double-wide mobile homes, drilled twenty-four wells for domestic water and built more than 20,000 linear feet of drain fields. They installed twelve miles of three-phase high tension electric power lines, built 6.5 miles of roads and substantially improved twenty-five miles of country and private roads. They established six small greenhouses and started construction of an 88,000-square-foot greenhouse which was later converted to a meeting hall with a seating capacity of 25,000. The hall was used during their international summer festivals.

In one year, the old pioneer ethic of helping your neighbors build their homes raised a 10,000-square-foot cafeteria and bakery, a 4,000-square-foot vehicle maintenance barn, a 10,000-square-foot administration building and a rock-crushing facility which pulverized 75,000 yards worth of gravel for roads, leach fields, drain fields, surfacing and concrete. By the end of 1982, these cheerful people in their distinctive red clothes created a 4.5-mile potable water system of eight-inch and ten-inch mainlines and a 3.9-million gallon reservoir that made officers of the Army Corps of Engineers green with envy in as many shades as their camouflage uniforms.

The location of the commune city was perfect for testing the ecological viability of the social model. The sannyasins set up their homestead in an area of Eastern Oregon state that had a long legacy of the white man's abuse of the land. For decades, the former Big Muddy ranch had remained 64,000 acres of overgrazed and near-useless range land.

Their recycling of all waste products earned the praise of many visiting ecologists. The sannyasins constructed a 125,000 gallon sewage lagoon with a lift station to pump effluent to the lagoon. The treated effluent was piped down to the valley to water the grazing land for their eighty-head dairy cattle herd.

The community cafeteria was a greenie's paradise of energy conservation and food recycling. Dishes were washed by a solar hot water system. Much of the waste food went to feed the chicken farm and most of the organic matter was sent to a special composting area and turned into acres of natural fertilizer. In a few years, this open-air manure factory provided enough organic matter to turn the valley floors and hills into a green oasis. Nearly all pest control was organic and non-toxic. The farmers made extensive use of natural insect predators.

The communards planned their city zoning so that no arable land was wasted. Residential and industrial areas were mostly built on the sides of the valleys, keeping the valley floors free for farming. Buildings were painted in earth colors to create visual harmony with the austerely beautiful desert hills.

The river systems had suffered extensive erosion owing to topsoil loss from overgrazing. The resulting flash floods washed the river systems down to sterile bedrock. A highly successful program of check dams and riprapping reclaimed tens of miles of eroded river banks. This, along with the new lake, helped catch the topsoil and raise the water table. Within three years, the river systems made a remarkable recovery. Species of bird and animal life returned to the levels of the previous century.

Rajneeshpuram was not a Marxist commune. Abundance rather than poverty was for the most part shared equally. Theirs was a high, though simple, standard of living. Their abundance had many forms. When I remember my life at Rajneeshpuram, the first thing I recall is the wealth of laughter and playfulness of its people. Residents who had been professors, corporate executives, artists, doctors and lawyers happily got their hands dirty digging, planting, and building their little oasis. The commune's concept of work as play distinguished them from billions all over the world who found work a dreadful but unavoidable necessity for survival.

Tension and crime among the citizens was all but absent. You could forget your backpack full of valuables on a Main Street bench and find it the next morning (as I did several times). No one locked houses or car doors. If crime or theft happened, it was usually committed by people from the outside world driving along the county road that ran through the commune.

I would say the Rajneeshees had near-bottomless sources of energy because their collective vision wasted little energy in divisiveness and competition. If properly managed and motivated, this is one of the strongest advantages of a communal system. And it is one of the reasons Rajneeshpuram could heal the ecosystem.

Their city was the home of the largest extended family of the 1980s. Imagine your family being 5,000 to 15,000 people sharing chores and handling survival issues. After a day's work I'd find my room clean and my clothes washed, ironed and put away. I'd go to the commune cafeteria and find a delicious dinner waiting for me. When I did my job, I made the life of those cooks and cleaners easier as well; whatever one did at Rajneeshpuram, everyone profited by it. Even the burden of keeping track of expenses and taxes was removed; the commune had a department to take care of that.

If things started sliding, everyone was affected, so they got fixed quickly. The degree of responsibility generally felt for the city far exceeded any level of community involvement I have

There was always the feedback and support of other adults, who encouraged the kids to nurture the growth of their innate intelligence and creativity, rather than become dully obedient and inauthentic just to please their folks.

observed in the outside world.

Modern psychologists agree that most of our conditioning and its corresponding neuroses come from being dependent on limited parental role models during our formative years. Daughters marry men who are just like their daddies, and even the most macho men unconsciously try to turn their newly-wedded into "mom." Of course, there's the usual disastrous result — marital misery.

The adults living at the commune were aware of this neurosis and set about breaking this pattern. Simply put, all children belonged to the whole commune rather than to small, sequestered nuclear families. In a nuclear family, children depend on mom and dad alone for their essential ration of love and material survival. Using the spoken or unspoken threat of withdrawing their love, adults have the power to force children to be "good girls and boys," ie, fit with ideas passed down from generation to generation. This keeps us repeating history and therefore sustains a prophet's ability to predict our future.

This mold is easier to break in the extended family of a commune. Since their source of survival and adult love was expanded from two parents to thousands of "aunts" and "uncles," the development of the Ranch children was not limited by one or two adults' pre-conditioned neuroses.

There was always the feedback and support of other adults, who encouraged the kids to nurture the growth of their innate intelligence and creativity, rather than become dully obedient and inauthentic just to please their folks.

In turn, the parents, now freed from the burden of being sole support and role model for their kids, developed a genuine closeness to them that had been difficult to achieve before coming to the Ranch. The kids slept in a communal house but could visit their parents or stay with other adults whenever they chose. Early freedom brought its natural complement of responsibility. By living together, the children quickly learned to work things out and pool their creativity to improve the lot of the group. The kids often submitted propositions to the adults about ways to improve life on the Ranch. When the suggestions were good, they were implemented. The kids were not just living in their parents' world, they were co-creators of a new way of life. This model may be just what humanity needs as an alternative to the estrangement and abuse of individuals (especially apparent in America) within the traditional family.

At first I wondered if so many role models would make Ranch kids totally confused. Not so. Of the eighty children living at Rajneeshpuram in 1983, the Latkin, Littman psychological study reported that seventeen older children had practical learning experiences and responsibilities in adult work settings; fifty attended school; the remaining thirteen or so were infants. The school children were given age-appropriate forms of the Harter Perceived Competence and Social Acceptance Scales. The study revealed that sannyasin children's overall self-worth in a communal family unit was at or above the national norms of children reared in the accepted nuclear family.

At the time of this experiment, there was a moratorium on childbearing, which is why the population of children was so low. As I understand it, the sannyasins felt they could not serve as a true model of an ideal future society if they contributed to the increasing overpopulation of the planet. Still, there were plans to drop the moratorium once the commune city was self-sufficient. It is unfortunate that the commune had to disband before this futuristic experiment of child rearing could see itself through a generation or two.

I occasionally run into some of these kids in my travels around the world. It is my observation that many who grew up in the commune have matured into self-assured, intelligent and physically attractive young adults who lack most of the neuroses of young people from nuclear families. They haven't lost a healthy dimension of rebelliousness. They doubt and experiment before they believe. They are on their way to being adults who will take responsibility for the world they live in, rather than blame on the sins of their parents.

There was an unwritten law concerning relationships in the commune: a man and woman were free to stay together as long as love remained fresh. Whether that was a night or a lifetime depended solely on love and not on marriage contracts and expectations.

The preachers and the press liked to condemn Rajneeshpuram as the commune of free sex. Unlike the press, I feel I can speak on the "free sex" issue with some authority because I explored relationships in the commune firsthand. I was loved and returned love many times. I am grateful to my sannyasin lovers for playfully calling me on my Piscean Age prudishness. Gradually, I came to agree with sannyasins that many of the tensions we feel in our past-oriented society come from being "faithful" to one spouse after love has turned into hate. They taught me that true commitment does not necessarily mean keeping a formal contract of togetherness. It is the ability to remain committed to the truth of one's feelings, expressed with love. These people successfully lived the pattern of the coming Aquarian dispensation: joy and fulfillment this very moment — every moment, while being sensitive to the hearts of others.

A freer sexual lifestyle certainly needs an infrastructure like that of the extended family of a commune in order to work. The old excuses that kept unhappy adults together, like child support and education, don't pan out in a communal society that shares the burdens and joys of child-rearing. Adults sharing family responsibilities can experience many others and gain a rich education in love. In those three years, I learned more about women and myself than in my prior thirty years of relationships in the traditional world. If this kind of loving is the future, the belief barrier called monogamy will find the coming age hard to weather.

The Littman/Latkin study tested a cross-section of citizens at Rajneeshpuram for perceived stress, social support, depression and self-esteem. The Rajneeshee mean on the Perceived Stress Scale was a very low 15.22. The normative mean of American nuclear family units is 23.34. The maximum score in the standard Interpersonal Support Evaluation List (ISEL) is forty; their mean score for social support was 37.91. The Rajneeshee mean for depression on the Center of Epidemiological Studies Depression (CES-D) Scale was 5.86. A study by Radloff (1977) reports a normal depression mean ranging between 7.94 to 9.25 for average white Americans at the time. And finally the general self-esteem of communards, based on the Rosenberg Self-Esteem Scale was very high, 35.71, as opposed to the usual normal average of around thirty points.

The usual sex role stereotypes which modern societies are working so hard to erase were virtually non-existent at the Ranch. At first I was surprised to see quite beautiful and delicate-looking women running heavy earth-moving equipment such as backhoes and D-8s. Likewise, there were men who delighted in sitting at sewing machines all day. It was the rule rather than the exception for residents to have many jobs throughout their stay at the commune. This gave everyone a better understanding of how the place worked and expanded the skill pool of the commune. During my time on the Ranch I was a pest controller, hotel desk clerk, security watchman, brush-fire fighter, cook, carpenter (not a very good one), ditch digger, heavy equipment spotter, a bull-prodder and cow-milker, and just a good old general ranch hand. A good friend of mine was at different times a bus driver, a waitress, a sign maker, a hostess for the Rajneesh Airlines, and the head of the tool shop. The fact that you'd never known how to do these things before was irrelevant; everyone became both teacher and taught, and people ended up with highly developed and specialized skills which they later applied successfully in the world.

At Rajneeshpuram there was no time for fear of the unknown. And no need to fear it, either.

When people work together to mutually enhance their lives, not only is there less psychological stress, there is also much less of a strain on the ecology. People living communally require fewer consumer items than the nuclear family, and require considerably less energy output. Centralized food production creates less waste and pollution. Trash, like anything else, becomes a family affair. Some government-employed stranger isn't going to come along and pick it up.

The glut of automobiles and their exhaust you would find in an equivalent population base was markedly absent in Rajneeshpuram. The city provided its citizens with the second largest rapid transit system in the state, using recycled school buses. There were free commune taxis as well, so the use of cars by individuals was minimal.

Who made all of this run so smoothly?

In theory, there's less chance to divide people into the hierarchy and the masses if the whole community is an extended family. The commune system gives incentive for commune members to meet and decide what is needed for the community as a whole. This doesn't always pan out in reality. In fact, a hierarchy did arise and did abuse its power and victimize the citizens of the commune. Their crimes gave the prodigious number of anti-Rajneesh supporters with political power the means to arrest and deport the sannyasins' religious master, freeze the commune's assets, and thereby force its citizens out of their homes by 1986. Prior to the political controversies that destroyed their experiment, the Rajneeshees were in the process of building a bridge of their kind of utopian commune-ism to the world at large. Initially there was a parasitic relationship between the main commune in Oregon and the world at large. This dependency ran counter to the Rajneeshees' desire to create a life-affirmative economic system rather than one that is based on competition and greed.

Recognizing this, they attempted to correct it. The first step was to establish a multi-skilled and mobile labor force. Ranch residents volunteered to spend six months to a year in smaller communes around the world. There they shared their creativity and skills with others, which enriched both groups. Moving around the world, the communards were able to experience diverse national atmospheres and cultures, business concepts and artistic dimensions, further enhancing and expanding the commune family.

In the Rajneeshee vision, the commune family would expand from 5,000 people living just in Oregon to 300,000 and more living in communes around the world. They were beginning to establish a large commune in each country that would help establish smaller ones in their region. This would snowball into a network of communes that would ultimately stand as a real alternative to a society based on the nuclear family. They felt that eventually observers might recognize that their formula for crossing the bridge to Utopia worked better than the traditional social model.

If political and religious prejudices had not destroyed it, there is every possibility that, with the developing and maturing of this model over a few centuries, humanity might have seen a shift from a tight-fisted, grab-what-you-can-get society to a truly communing and sharing society.

Perhaps Rajneeshpuram can still serve as one of several possible blueprints for deprogramming and transforming man's Piscean society to the Aquarian — from that of a nuclear family to an extended family of the planet Earth.

BRIDGE FIVE:

FROM ARMS RACE TO ALMS RACE

The Soviet Union becoming an open society will take away all the power that America has accumulated because of creating fear in the world against the Soviet Union. If that fear disappears, the power of America will disappear with it....Just by [Russia] bringing freedom to their own people they will take the mask off America — its so-called pseudo-democracy. For this new kind of war...[The question in an alms race will be]...Who is more free? Who is more independent? Who respects the individual? Who respects individuals' differences, their freedom of expression, their freedom of creativity? Now this is going to be the real war. ...For the first time, a totally new kind of war has come into existence...

Osho (1987) GFutr

NATO DISBANDS

The aimless army will depart from Europe and join up close to the submerged island. The Arton [anagram for "NATO"] fleet folds up its standard: the navel of the world substituted by a greater voice.

Nostradamus (1555) C2 Q22

Humanitary-INDUSTRIAL COMPLEX

GIVE *Peace* AND PERESTROIKA A CHANCE?

I hasten to tell the other world leaders, hurry, give your best to world peace, make use of Gorbachev's goodwill and grace, support him, hug him to your heart, and give your best shot to goodwill on Earth. "Peace hath her victories no less renowned than war" should be the slogan of the 90s.
Bejan Daruwalla (1989)

These...ruinous wars shall pass away and the "Most Great Peace" shall come. Bahá'u'lláh (1890) Gpb

WAR DISAPPEARS

They shall beat their swords into plowshares, and their spears into pruning hooks: nation shall not lift up sword against nation, neither shall they learn war any more. Isaiah of Jerusalem (738-687 BC) Is-2:4

Prepare yourself for the final war of the future:

The armies of the nations are moving into position. The jets are taxiing on airfields, ready to take off. Fifty million soldiers advance into the battle-field-and-stream, forests and mountains. The allied nations of the entire Earth are poised to spend 1.5 million dollars a minute and are prepared to suffer hardships at home to ensure victory for all.

But this war is not to be nuclear. It will not see civilization extinguished in thirty minutes. In fact, this war could go on for a few centuries.

We can call it World War *Green*: The war to end all wars. This war pits our armies, with their logistical powers and sophisticated "weaponry," against the causes of planetary destruction. The vast amounts of genius and wealth which have been stockpiled for bloodshed are finally being used for healing and enriching the Earth.

Rather than starving our human enemies, we starve all potential for violence by using our resources to sustain the flow of food and clothing to the needier nations. Rather than dig trenches, the armies scoop out furrows for the planting of wheat. Tanks become tractors. A Maginot Line of dams captures water in parched lands and fires their salvoes of water into lines of irrigation ditches. Soldiers search for land mines without explosives — a treasure trove of untapped wells — and helicopter gunships drop organic pesticides on the swelling Third World armies of locusts. Millions of villages are defended from ignorance with forts of education.

We have yet to explore the potential good in our will to catharsis.

Consider the last catharsis: World War II. Tremendous amounts of energy and creativity were used to destroy fifty million fellow humans and maim and displace several hundred million more. What would an equivalent six-year outpouring do if it were focused on healing the planet?

Consider how the British and the Germans sustained their war efforts while their cities and industries were being bombed day and night. German railways were bombed into moonscapes one day and rebuilt the next. On the Russian front, Hitler and his generals did not take into account the burst of creativity that propels human beings in danger to manufacture miracles. A people without adequate food or shelter moved entire factories into Siberia almost overnight and re-armed and drafted armies ten times the size of those in peacetime in a few months. During World War II, the dockyard workers at Pearl Harbor took less than seventy-two hours to patch up the aircraft carrier *Yorktown* and send her back to sea. The *Yorktown* was perforated by several bombs and had much more serious damage done to her than the *Exxon Valdez* suffered from an Alaskan reef. Yet it took peacetime dockyard workers a year to repair that tanker's puncture.

In less than four years of World War II, the American worker produced 296,429 aircraft, 102,351 tanks and self-propelled guns, 372,431 artillery pieces, forty-seven million tons of artillery ammunition, 87,620 warships, forty-four billion rounds of small-arms ammunition — worth 183 billion mid-twentieth-century dollars. Workers at one factory produced one four-engine bomber every sixty-seven seconds. America sent more tanks, planes and weapons to Russia during the first six months of the Nazi invasion than existed in the invading army itself! If Americans can apply themselves to help stop Hitler's invasion of the Soviet Union in 1941, what could they do to stop the invasion of the Sahara Desert in the Sahel right now?

That innate spirit of urgency still remains in us. All that is needed is for the world's people to recognize the danger and view each of our ecological problems, such as the gas oven of the greenhouse effect, with as much moral indignation as the gas chambers of the Nazis.

The frenetic pooling of brain power that went into the building of atomic bombs can happen again in a new Manhattan Project to eliminate the cause of global warming. By committing ourselves to finding a new Earth-friendly power that can light the world, we can bring universally high standards of living to all rather than the threat of universal radioactive fallout.

To bring our "forces" to bear upon the real enemy will require the world's network of military-industrial complexes to re-channel resources from martial destruction to the enhancement of human life. A will to catharsis *can* be changed into a will to create.

WE WON THE COLD WAR, LET'S WIN THE MILLENNIAL PEACE

The following financial trade-offs from bloodshed to beatitudes were collected from various sources by Michael Renner of the Worldwatch Institute, in his article "Enhancing Global Security," published in Lester E. Brown's *State of the World 1989*.

Trident II submarine and F-18 jet fighter programs	$100 Billion	Estimated cost of cleaning up the 10,000 most hazardous waste dumps in the US
Stealth bomber program	$68 Billion	Two-thirds of estimated cost to meet US clean water goals by the year 2000
Requested SDI funding, fiscal years 1988-1992	$38 Billion	Disposal of highly radioactive waste in the United States
2 weeks of world military expenditure	$30 Billion	Annual cost of the proposed UN Water and Sanitation Decade
German outlays for military procurement and R&D, fiscal year 1985	$10.75 Billion	Estimated cost to clean up German sector of the North Sea
3 days of global military spending	$6.5 Billion	Annual cost to cut sulfur dioxide emissions by 8-12 million tons/year in the US, to combat acid rain
2 days of global military spending	$4.8 Billion	Annual cost of proposed UN Action Plan to halt Third World desertification over 20 years
6 months of US outlays for nuclear warheads, fiscal year 1986	$4 Billion	US government spending on energy efficiency, fiscal years 1980-87
SDI research, fiscal year 1987	$3.7 Billion	Enough funds to build a solar power system serving a city of 200,000
10 days of European Economic Community military spending	$2 Billion	Annual cost to clean up hazardous wastes sites in 10 EC countries by the year 2000
1 Trident submarine	$1.4 Billion	Global 5-year child immunization program against 6 deadly diseases, preventing 1 million deaths a year
3 B-1B bombers	$680 Million	US government spending on renewable energy, fiscal year 1983-85
2 months of Ethiopian military spending	$50 Million	Annual cost of proposed UN Anti-desertification Plan for Ethiopia
1 nuclear weapon test	$12 Million	Installation of 80,000 hand pumps to Third World villages, access to safe water
1-hour operating cost, B-1B bomber	$12,000	Community-based maternal health care in 10 African villages to reduce maternal deaths by half in one decade

WARNING!!

It is time to get positive about negativity.

There is very little written in the New Age genre about the darker potentials of the Aquarian Age. I experience this omission as a blend of Piscean and Aquarian denial: The Piscean escapes into dreams rather than face reality — in this case, the subconscious manipulation of our minds. The Aquarian is a blind idealist, optimistic about the future — at all costs. The adherents of New Age thinking glibly encourage this misplaced idealism in others: "Don't give the negative any energy and it won't happen."

Their definition of "apocalypse" is as dark as their fear of sweet dreams evaporating in the presence of sobering, sometimes frightening realities.

Phenomena like Adolf Hitler, Joseph Stalin, terrorism and mind control are not going to die with the Piscean age. These are the more ominous aspects of the dawning Aquarian epoch which mankind must dodge and parry for the next 2,000 years. Dictatorial Piscean father figures will certainly die out in the coming centuries, but unless we remain aware of *all* the potentials shaping man's behavior in the coming age, we may not recognize the return of Hitler and Stalin archetypes in less vulgar and more palatable forms.

Aquarius rules the urge to impersonalize. This might herald a more tolerant mankind that takes and perceives slights less personally. Used unconsciously, however, the same potential for impersonalization can see a man lose his soul to a dictatorship of the computer. Dictators of the Piscean Age control the human flock through manipulating the emotions of hope, demanding sacrifices and worshipping divine superstitions. Future tyrants won't use the threat of the sword or promises of bread and paradise to conscript believers, they will instead fashion psycho-weapons out of the Aquarian element of atmosphere and mood. And you may not even feel the repression.

In fact, you will feel as if you are happy, as if you are a citizen living in the harmonious New Age. You will be seduced into believing it. In fact, in the darker realm of the future, the more people will be programmed not to think for themselves at all. One can already see signs of a more shadowy Aquarian dispensation in the seemingly innocent words of a cable TV ad from a Tele-Communication Inc. (TCI) broadcast in the early 1990s. It ends with the words: "...as we head into the future, maybe the secret lies not so much in knowing what tomorrow will bring, just in making sure we know someone who does."

Big Brother knows.

What Fukuyama is saying [in his "End of History" theory] is absolutely baseless. History moves in waves — there will again be something like Fascism arising in the world. Man cannot find any meaning in life, so he becomes a victim of a utopian life in the future, and by taking away his future you are turning him into a robot....What Fukuyama is saying is more dangerous to humanity than anything [said] by Stalin or Mussolini, or Hitler!

Osho (1989)

Never before in world history has there been such potential for a few wrong-minded people to control the masses.

There is real danger of a few evil people slipping into these positions [of power] in order to disrupt important work and governmental economies, or to control universal thought and action.

Spirit guides of
Ruth Montgomery (1985) Alns

A machine can easily be made by which one man can draw a thousand to himself by violence against their wills and attract other things in like manner.

Roger Bacon (1268) Epsc

The business world will be in the hands of a few great firms which will control the wealth of many nations.

David Goodman Croly (1888)

Glmp

There is a DARK SIDE to *Aquarius*

In a certain way television has introduced a new kind of primitiveness....Right now you have memories; soon you won't have. Everybody will be carrying his own computer...carried in the pocket and which can contain all the knowledge contained in the libraries of the world — you just have to know how to make it function. Man will fall tremendously as far as intelligence is concerned, memory is concerned. Everything that comes into existence brings changes so silently you don't see them. Osho (1987) Omph

Since 1984, puritanical Communism has been disintegrating along with the Cold War, and one can hope that the negative Utopia portrayed in George Orwell's book is no longer a possibility. Big Brother, the Stalinist, is replaced by Max Headroom, the computer-manufactured TV host. He's funny, he's witty, he has no soul. He even admits it, and invites you to have no soul as well. Having no soul is cool. Orwell's Ministry of Culture has long ago been replaced by a brighter and more entertaining propaganda organ called Madison Avenue with its computer-morphed ads made in Hollywood.

Before the Stalinists went the way of the dinosaurs, they taught power freaks a valuable lesson in perpetuating a dismal new age: Take free thinking away from the individual. Program people to think the way you want them to. And this is precisely what the darker side of Aquarius is skilled in.

In 1990 consumer activist Ralph Nader addressed the *Utne Reader* Early Warning Environmental Conference about a clear and present danger. He warned, "Corporations are more important in raising children than parents."

"Let's start with infant formula — a destructive and costly displacement of the best food infants could ever consume," said Nader. "Let's go to war toys. Let's go to over-medication to tranquilize the super-active kiddies. Let's move to seven and eight-year-old-girls being taught cosmetics by the cosmetic industry so they can learn to be proper objects and subjects later in life. Let's move to music. However much we may like it, it's designed to blot out the mind walking down the street with the Walkman, never allowing a true reflection that might take the place of sonic assault....Who's raising the kids? Kindercare is raising them. McDonald's is feeding them. HBO and Disneyland are entertaining them. They are spending more time with corporate products and services and entertainment and addictions than they do with adults. Now that's got to have an effect on them. It's got to twist and distort their values and rupture their sense of history."

The New Age is already making us robopaths of product.

Many prophets in the past 10,000 years foresaw something akin to a one-world government. A common projection of the New Age movement is living "happily ever after" the millennium. But those who covet power won't just disappear by the wave of some plastic magic wand bought from a New Age bookstore. Nor will a weekend spent chanting in some high-powered energy spot on some auspicious date in the Mayan Calendar sing away the Will to Power Blues for the next twenty centuries.

The future, like energy, is neutral. We make the best or worst out of its potentials, they don't make us.

A flowering global society that celebrates the uniqueness of everyone is possible. In the end, wars and ecological disasters might bring the world together. Those who survive get on with rebuilding their lives in a new age. But no prophet is needed to predict that there will still be power mongers afoot doing all they can to establish their dominance even within a new world order.

If World War III is averted and we weather the greenhouse effect, watch out for the worldwide corporate police-state-with-a-smile. George Orwell's puritanical and brute quality of Utopia foreseen in *1984* is less and less possible in the age of science and communication by light wave. But paradise on Earth could still become a paradise lost.

Don't worry, be happy. There is hope that a negative world Utopia will not become an international Stalinist Third World state-in-crumbling. The police state of tomorrow will be clean

Wait just a minute. **Mute** the volume! **Listen:** Have you forgotten your childhood? Has the wisdom of innocence and simplicity become an abstract? Do the three or four dozen murders — *real or fictional* — you see on a daily dose of television move you less than the car ads? If the answer is yes to all the above you might be suffering from *brain fade.*

and corporate, and you *will* be happy. You can't help it because your genes were altered at birth. And whatever bad moods or anti-social behavior that cannot be altered by gene splicing, can be dulled by drugs or distracted by an entertainment fix. Tomorrow's negative Utopia will be more like Aldous Huxley's *Brave New World* and the neo-yuppie police state of Ray Bradbury's *Fahrenheit 451.*

The first steps toward Huxley's social nightmare are already upon us. The speed and accessibility of information are not enlightening mankind as much as overburdening us with knowledge and entertainment stimuli. Ultimately we are running the danger of suffering what Ted Mooney, author of the novel, *Easy Travel to Other Planets,* calls "brain fade" — a kind of information pestilence.

Ma-Ma-Max Headroom, the "future shock" personality-without-a-soul, becomes the conscience of the future brain-dead and sensorially overloaded society. This Cyberpunk TV show about a hopeless though vastly entertained future humanity rapidly faded in the ratings. The show cut too close to the truth of the future. The boob-tubers of the 1990s still harbor a Piscean penchant to dream in Aldous *Huxtable* heaven. Neither Max Headroom's synthetic wit nor Orwell's gibberish-cum-morality called "doublethink" will be the means for our fall in Aquarian darkness. The fall will come from our current lulling brain virus of "telethink."

"The commercial has deeper waves, deeper emanations. But we have reversed the relative significance of these things," Mooney explained. "This is why people's eyes, ears, brains and nervous systems have grown weary. It's a simple case of misuse."

Extrapolating from the 1990s to the 2090s, you find the misuse of Aquarian energy creating the nightmare vision of Ray Bradbury's negative Utopia: Firemen will not fight fires, but set them. Books are outlawed and burned. The technologically advanced society gives neo-yuppies all the creature comforts they desire. The earshell radios and four-walled 3D televisions supply all the "human" contact people are programmed to desire. And being rebellious has become a fad. Rebellion, and even anti-social behavior, can be expressed at your neighborhood Fun Park. There you can break windows, shoot, and even run down people, just for kicks. In Bradbury's future you can act just like your own ninja turtle toys.

Your typical Aquarian Ager is a born rebel. If during his development that innate activism is repressed, astrology tells us that it might erupt in minor eccentric gestures such as the man in a conservative business suit who wears a loud bow tie. If the repression runs deeper, the straight-laced rebel resorts to absurd or gutless acts, such as those of drunken male collegians cruising Palm Springs, California, and stripping young women waiting at red lights in their convertibles.

Or, the Aquarian natural tendency for rebellion can be debauched by empty and often harmless gestures. Rather than risking a real rebellion against their parents' hypocrisies, some kids put their hairdos in a blender and wear black as if they are mourning the loss of their future.

The future shift will be from Orwell's mindless terror to Huxley's and Bradbury's terror of blissed-out mindlessness. Freedom of thought can be packaged and supplied with the ease of a home video store. Tomorrow's rebel-gelding will walk into a hologram device and "become" Arnold Schwarzenegger.

In his book, *Amusing Ourselves to Death*, Neil Postman reminds us that social visionaries like Huxley believed man was "in a race between education and disaster." We must be ever alert to the pivotal role played by "the politics and epistemology of media."

"For in the end," Postman writes, "[Huxley] was trying to tell us that what afflicted the people in *Brave New World* was not that they were laughing instead of thinking, but that they did not know what they were laughing about and why they had stopped thinking."

But if we continue to evolve into a race of spectators (ie, *Homo recumbere rädix*, AKA Couch Potatoes) preferring to watch actors make love rather than make love ourselves, there's a new generation of power-mongers set to rule us by means of a darker Aquarian maxim. No Hitler or Stalin, but something witty and inhuman like Mr Headroom, the computer byte-spliced Johnny Carson of tomorrow, will shock/treat you with the

Cyberpunk manifesto:

Everyone is mentally, physically, and genetically programmed to serve the World State. It exists to control the mind and feelings of the individual and impart an artificial sense of achieving his full potential.

If we remain alert enough to think and feel for ourselves, the future shape of things Aquarian will have us live by this axiom:

Everyone is equally unique and the World State exists to nurture an individual's **uniqueness** to its full potential.

Nothing will be holy anymore. Everything will be upset. The great clearance will commence. All states will be pitted against each other. The free life and thought will be imprisoned and banished. Severe masters will rule and will try to get everything under their discipline. It will be a terrible time. **Stormberger (eighteenth century)**

I'm SORRY, DAVE. . . .

Tendencies in the hearts and souls of men are such that these may be bought about. For, as indicated through these channels oft, it is not the world, the earth, the environs about it nor the planetary influences, nor the associations or activities, that RULE man. RATHER does man by HIS COMPLIANCE with divine law — bring ORDER out of chaos; or, by his DISREGARD of the associations and laws of the divine influence, bring chaos and DESTRUCTIVE forces into his experiance. **Edgar Cayce (1935) №416-7**

Evil ones will not go away just because you wish them to. They are firmly entrenched there and eager to seize power. **Spirit guides of Ruth Montgomery (1986) Hrd**

Never before in world history has there been such potential for a few wrong-minded people to control the masses; yet never has there been so much potential for good if right-thinking, peace-loving people are there to direct the machines that will be "read" daily by many millions in schools, offices and homes. Lives will be saved, time conserved, and a new life style emerge as people take their informational readouts from computers.
Spirit guides of Ruth Montgomery (1985) Alns

DEATH of the

By their fruit you will recognize them....A good tree cannot bear bad fruit, and a bad tree cannot bear good fruit. Every tree that does not bear good fruit is cut down and thrown into the fire. Thus, by their fruit you will recognize them. Y'shua (c. AD 33) Mt 7:16-20

Furthermore, not only have these sacrilegious beings gradually distorted for their egoistic and political aims the teachings of the Divine Teacher, but they have now begun to destroy the memory of it. G.I. Gurdjieff (1924-27) Beelz

Even if the whole world disappears [nations and organized religions] politicians will be prepared to accept that, but they will not be ready to surrender all of their arms, all of their armies to a world organization. Osho (1987) GrCh

...religious, racial, national, and political bias: all these prejudices strike at the very root of human life; one and all they beget bloodshed, and the ruination of the world. So long as these prejudices survive, there will be continuous and fearsome wars.
'Abdul'-Bahá (c. 1920) Slc

For then there will be great distress, unequaled from the beginning of the world until now — and never equaled again. If those days had not been cut short, no one would survive, but for the sake of the elect those days will be shortened.
Y'shua (c. AD 33) Mt 24:21.22

If we are going to solve the problems of the future and dissolve them, then we have to look for their roots in the past.

...We have to take a quantum leap and teach the new generation not to live the way we have lived. Only then can the future be changed. Osho (1987) GrC

Past.

At the Restaurant at the End of the World, **the waiter skips forward with the menu of karmic confectionery.** Before you order dessert, it might be wise to heed those prophets who have already seen the writing in the menu. They are all too familiar with the waiter's recitation:

"**Tonight, at the end of the eleventh hour of the Adamic Age,** we will be serving you overpopulation hors d'oeuvres, and as an entrée, your choice of Earth Trauma pies with toxic sauce, or AIDS crêpes. Then, if you have room to spare, please consider something from our 'just-deserts' menu...

"Perhaps you'd care for an after-dinner round of **Armageddon cocktails,** such as White and Black Russian **ethnic wars,** or any number of chemical-biological bomb brandies. And, I must say, our selection of cold and bracing plutonium winter mint liqueurs is the best. I do hope you'll enjoy your meal. We'll do our very best to satisfy **your taste for suffering.**"

Sound appetizing? Do you think we should pass on dessert tonight? Or perhaps it's time to drastically change our eating habits.

There is a Chinese proverb: "If we don't change direction we are going to wind up where we are going."

Those who hope that new scientific inventions alone will build a bridge to Utopia overlook the fact that the traditional mind-set will not support the journey. In the 1960s, the American oil monopolies blocked the development of the Chrysler gas-turbine car. If they hadn't, the world of the 1990s might have been relieved of much of its smog and noise pollution. But the car's success would have undermined the power of the oil barons and the Detroit gas-guzzler moguls. When running cars on fuel-efficient engines is more profitable — or when ecological pollution becomes so noisome to make such a change impossible to delay — then and only then will Detroit wrap itself in the new clothes of an ecologically responsible institution.

Change usually happens out of dire necessity, or because someone stands to profit from it financially; rarely does it come out of true understanding.

"Death of the Past" takes a prophetic look at the great icons of social programming, which are dead-set against the construction of any bridge to Utopia. Our past traditions act like rigid building codes. If we don't go beyond them, we will never rise to fashion a new social and religious architecture that can bridge these dangerous times to the golden future foretold.

As "A Crossroads at the End of Time" pointed out, the Adamic cycle of centuries may reach its Judgment Day in our lifetime. And since the forces of Pisces symbolically stand for completion, it is a sure bet of augury to predict that between now and the next few centuries, most of our connections with the past will be severed. The runaway history of the early 1990s is already leaving us breathless. The past is losing its grasp on tomorrow. And seen through the eyes of our familiar values and traditions, the future looks like a chaos. To the punks and skinheads it looks like there's no future at all. After 10,000 years, our fixer-upper called Morality still has drafts and structural flaws that endanger all who dwell within it.

In a way we have already come to a Judgment Day. Whether one believes in a divine father figure or not, the proverbial camel's back can only suffer so many straws before it breaks. It might be called a miracle or just a natural law, but water can only sustain its placid appearance until the heat reaches 100 degrees Fahrenheit. And paper stubbornly retains its reality until hell fires burn at Fahrenheit 451. Our four most hallowed icons are also flammable. They are: God, The Nuclear Family, The Rat Race, Nationalism and the root icon — the traditional syndrome of dividing individuals against themselves. Within the next few decades, all of society's holiest values may go up in smoke.

In the end, the forewarned shift of the Earth's axis between 1998 and the spring of 2000 may be more metaphorical than literal: a shift from an orientation to the past to an orientation to the future.

The most important need of humanity today is to be made aware that its past has betrayed it; that there is no point in continuing the past — it will be suicidal — and that a new humanity is absolutely and urgently needed. Osho (1987) GrCh

Until we all Awaken to the Situation and purpose of human existence, we will create no lasting peace or order, and each day will bring the world closer to the finite chaos of War and Bewilderment. But if the Wisdom of the true Spiritual Adepts is "heard" in the human world, then the true revolution can begin, and all dreadful destiny that now lies before us can be dissolved in the Heart of God.

Da Avabhasa (1979) Sci

The Kabala does say that the twentieth century, vibrating to the number twenty, evidently means, The Trumpet and Judgment Day.

Bejan Daruwalla (1989)

The "old" is about to give birth to the "new." In all lands, in all peoples, the "travail pains" are becoming more and more intense. The last War [World War I] was but "the turning in the womb" of Nature; the real birth has yet to come.
Alack and alas, to those who must cling to the "old"; to the traditions of the past, to the habits of their forebears; — their day has already passed forever.
The Clock of Time has struck the "Midnight Hour"; the blackest darkness lies before the greatest dawn.
The cry; "O Lord, how long — how long?" will break from many hearts before the light of the new civilization will chase away the shadows of the night.

Cheiro (1926) Cwp

GOING, GOING,

O Egypt, Egypt, of thy religion nothing will remain but an empty tale, which thine own children in time to come will not believe; nothing will be left but graven words, and only the stones will tell of thy piety. **Hermes (AD 150-270) Asc-III**

At that time many will turn away from the faith and will betray and hate each other, and many false prophets will appear and deceive many people. Because of the increase of wickedness, the love of most will grow cold, but he who stands firm to the end will be saved. And this gospel of the kingdom will be preached in the whole world as a testimony to all nations, and then the end will come.

Y'shua (c. AD 33) Mt 24:10-14

I already see in my mind's eye that before many of their years have passed, there will be on the spot where the planetary body of the Divine Jesus was buried, a place for parking contemporary cars, that is, a parking place for those machines which for contemporary beings were just the marvel needed to drive them crazy.

G.I. Gurdjieff (1924-27) Beelzb

Priests and servants of the church will be reduced to misery, the youth led by atheism, and republics will be established in the whole world. And everything will be destroyed by wars. **Pastor Bartholomaeus (1642)**

If religion becomes a cause of enmity and hatred, it is evident the abolition of religion is preferable to its promulgation; for a religion is a remedy for human ills. If a remedy should be productive of disease, it is certainly advisable to abandon it.
'Abdu'l-Bahá (1912) Prm

...God?

My chiropractor, a devout Christian, once held a class for his patients on creating better posture habits. This sincere man was trying to help folks like me (with a writer's aching neck) learn how to be more caring to our "mortal vehicle." The miracle of the human body was enough proof to him that God had created it. Certainly Heaven and Earth are filled with miraculous mysteries, one of them being the enigma of God putting the human pleasure centers so close to the exhaust pipes.

Another religious mystery is the much-touted infallibility of God's word in scripture. If the scriptures say Noah can cram 12,000 of all the Earth's known species of reptiles, amphibians and mammals plus the vast majority of 9,040 known species of birds into an Ark 450 feet long, seventy-five feet wide and forty-five feet high — for God's sake, we must believe it is possible.

The *Book of Genesis* and God don't mention the specific fauna and fodder requirements for Noah's Ark. For that I had to consult the secular and scientific "scriptures" of the Worldwatch Institute. I collected those statistics from Edward C. Wolf's article, "Avoiding a Mass Extinction of Species" (*State of the World 1988: Worldwatch*). Since there must have been a lot more species around 6,000 years ago, you can be sure the number of creatures pairing up in the shadow of thunderheads massing for the deluge were much higher than Wolf's estimate of today's 21,000 known land-loving and fresh water species times two. Actually, the Bible records that poor Noah had to pick seven pairs from those species God deemed kosher, not just two.

Add that to the other pairs and you get a menagerie of at least fifty to 60,000 landlubbing critters. The salt water fishes were fine where they were, but did Noah have tanks in the bilge for the thousands of freshwater fish? A close reading of Genesis, chapters 6 and 7, shows that our divine creator forgot that salt water is poison to freshwater critters. And what about all the non-soluble insects that number an estimated 10,000 to 30,000 species?

No matter. The Lord doesn't ask his pundits to record how Noah fed and cleaned the cages of his maritime zoo for forty days — should we care? God just gave the order to supply them with food and creature comforts, whether or not it could sink a 450-foot boat.

Nor is there any mention in God's Bible of a round Earth that orbits the sun. Just an Earth with "four corners" (ie, as flat as unleavened bread). Loathed be you or any other gay Galileo offering evidence to the contrary. But lest I be judged as too hard on the Christians, the same unwavering faith is demanded from their followers by other Piscean Age theocracies. Like Samson, the Sikhs believe in hair power and do not cut one splitting end for the harm it might do to their faith, whereas many monks and nuns of orthodox Buddhist, Jain, and Hindu orders believe bald is divine. Too bad there's no *sutra* on the virtues of hair remover. The Jain scriptures order their monks to practice a complete ban on all machinery, down to the razor. Each year the Jain believers gather to watch their naked monks pluck out every hair one by one, from pate to pubes. Life is a little easier for the Gopis, the wives of Krishna the Hindu Avatar. Still, I wonder how he kept his health so "blushing." Servicing the affections of 12,000 wives would turn anyone blue, and apparently not just in the you-know-what.

HERE LIES JUDAISM
BEFORE 8,000 BC–AD 2000

Calamity upon calamity will come, and rumor upon rumor. They will try to get a vision from the prophet; the teaching of the law by the priest will be lost, as will the counsel of the elders. Ezekiel (c. 593-571 BC) Ez 7:26

The religion founded on the teaching of Saint Moses, although it existed for a long time and is still maintained after a fashion by its followers, yet, owing to the organic hatred formed in the beings of other communities toward the beings who follow their religion, due only to that "maleficent" idea called "policy," infallibly sooner or later they will doubtlessly "croak it" as well and also "with a crash."

G.I. Gurdjieff (1924-27) Beelzb

FAVORITE LAST PROMISE:
Only they are the "Chosen People" and only their faith will survive the holocaust. Jerusalem will be the religious capital of the world.

Here Lies Islam
AD622-1969?

Islam will fall when a man walks on the lamp of the night [the Moon].

Saying attributed to Mohammed

Men will increasingly neglect their souls....The greatest corruption will reign on Earth. Men will become like bloodthirsty animals, thirsting for the blood of their brothers. The crescent [Islam] *will become obscured and its followers will descend into lies and perpetual warfare.*

Arghati prophecy (hundreds of years ago)

Of course, by the destruction in Turkey of this "dervishism" [the Sufis] *those last dying sparks will also be entirely extinguished there which, preserved as it were in the ashes, might sometime rekindle the hearth of those possibilities upon which Saint Mohammed counted and which he had hoped.* G.I. Gurdjieff (1924-27) Beelzb

FAVORITE LAST PROMISE:
The Twelfth Imam, or Mahdi, ie, Messiah, will come and see all other faiths put to the sword. Only Islam will survive. Jerusalem will be returned to the faithful, and Mecca will be the capital of the Earth.

Here Lies Hinduism
Before 8000 BC– AD 2000

Whenever there is noticed an increase [in the number] *of heretics, then...should the full swing of Kali* [the darkest, most apocalyptic age] *be estimated by the wise. When the people do not show respect to the sayings of the Vedas but are inclined towards the heretics, then...the augmented influence of the Kali age should be inferred.*

Vishnu Purana: VI, 1, 44-47 (circa 500 AD)

FAVORITE LAST PROMISE: When Krishna returns it won't be too late.

Here Lies Buddhism
483 BC?–AD 2000

The holders of the faith, the glorious rebirths, will be broken down and left without a name. As regards the monasteries and the priesthood, their lands and other properties will be destroyed. The thirteenth Dalai Lama of Tibet: final declaration (1932)

Most probably I am the last [Dalai Lama]. *Nothing wrong. When there is no longer any benefit, then naturally the Dalai Lama ceases to be.* The fourteenth Dalai Lama of Tibet (c. 1980)

FAVORITE LAST PROMISE: A new Buddhist Messiah called Maitreya ("the Friend") will incarnate and bring all the world's people back to the Dharma — the path of (Buddhist) truth.

Here Lies Sikhism
(c.1521-2000)

Spiritual people [Sikhs] *and Gurus will be harassed, so therefore the calamities will come.*

Guru Nanak (c. 1521)

FAVORITE LAST PROMISE: Only Sikhs will survive the holocaust. I guess Jerusalem will move to Amritsar, Punjab.

Here Lies the Family of Shamanist and Animist Faiths
Before 8000 BC?-AD 2012

When holy metals are dug out of Mt Isa the end is near. Ancient Aboriginal prophecy

(White Australians currently mine uranium from M. Isa, Queensland.)

If we dig precious things from the land we will perish. Hopi Indians of North America.

(Uranium mining on Hopi lands continues unabated.)

The tropical rain forests support the sky — cut down the trees and disaster will follow.

Amazonian Indians of South America

FAVORITE LAST PROMISE: Non-aboriginal peoples can wake up before they destroy the planet; however, if they do not reconnect with the Earth they will perish, and only the native peoples will survive to build a new world.

Here Lies the
Roman Catholic Church
c. AD 400-2000

*The church will suffer great ills; a torrent of evil will open a breach
on her, but the first attack will be against her fortune and her riches.
[Vatican Bank scandal?]*

Ravignan: a Jesuit priest (1847)

*The profession which will be topmost in this business of AIDS will be the priests, the nuns,
the monks...because they have been practicing perverted sex longer than anybody else.*

Osho (1984) RajB IV

*I had a horrible vision. Was it of me or one of my successors? I saw the Pope leaving Rome
and, to get out of the Vatican, he had to step over the corpses of his priests.*

Pope Pius X (1909)

FAVORITE LAST PROMISE:
After the Apocalypse, the world will live in a papist earthly paradise under a papist Christ in
papist New Jerusalem.

Here Lies
the Family of Christian sects
1517-2000

*Christianity forsook the teachings of "the gentle Christ" for the domination of the
Church. For the sake of power, it allied itself with Kings and Emperors; with their fall
"the Church" of all religions must also fall.*

Cheiro -(1931) Cwp

FAVORITE LAST PROMISE:
After the Apocalypse, the world will live in a non-papist, earthly paradise under Christ in a
non-papist New Jerusalem.

According to the most up-to-date revelation on the historic Y'shua, reported in books like Michael Baigent's *Messianic Legacy*, they'll have to hire God a better researcher. Nazareth never existed during the time of Christ; it came into existence around the third century AD. On second thought, get God a new film editor too. Those scenes in Bible movies of Jesus bumbling around in Nazareth as a poor carpenter's son have all gotta go! With Baigent's and other scholars' findings in mind, the tabloids of the twenty-first century could read:

JESUS AND JUDAS WERE BROTHERS

Judas did his brother's bidding, and on Christ's orders betrayed him to manipulate Old Testament prophecy in his favor.

ST PAUL WAS A HERETIC GURU!

New findings show that St James filled in for his crucified twin brother as Messianic Priest-King and officially condemned Paul in a post-crucifixion ideological struggle. The Roman agent-turned-Church-leader skillfully changed the focus of Christian thought away from Christ's original plan.

CHRIST BUMPED BY CONSTANTINE!

The Roman Emperor who ruled between AD 312 and 337 exerted major influence upon Christianity's ascent as today's most powerful global faith. He legalized and institutionalized the cult and spread it throughout the Roman world.

Constantine established and presided over the Council of Nicæa in AD 325, which brought discipline to the chaos of divergent Christian beliefs and marshaled it into an orthodox form by establishing its' priesthood. Through his influence, much of what is known of the historic Jesus was censored. The degree of divinity of the Galilean was established by ballot.

Constantine endeavored to blur the distinction between Christian and other Pagan rites and celebrations. After his successful publicity blitz, future generations were conditioned to celebrate Christ's birth on the Pagan Yuletide celebration day around the winter solstice. Constantine saw himself as more successful than Jesus in fulfilling Bible prophecy. As long as he lived the church all but ignored Jesus and revered Constantine as the Second Coming.

It's enough to make a dogma drop dead!

Pisces, thy name is escapism, thy hideout is the monastery of the distant hill or of the closed-minded. And with the passage of just a few more decades, Old Man Pisces, the Neptunian ruler, lies on his deathbed, ready to meet his Kingdom that is not of this Earth.

Someone is tugging on his life-support tubes. It is Uranus. He's been poking and pulling for over three centuries now, pestering belief-mongers with his iconoclasm.

Actually he's not being so mean. Uranus's efforts only cut off our life-support systems to dogma. The rising volume of fundamentalism injected into the IV drip is just a last-ditch effort to stop the nervous breakdown of belief and forestall an outdated morality's heart failure.

The last successful tug of the tube may be terrifying, but Uranus gives us the opportunity to experience a limitless, miraculous universe in return.

There are hard times ahead for priesthoods of every faith. The holy givens are becoming gones. The television, computer — and soon, variants of these stitched into the brain — will instantly call up facts that have remained hidden in foreign libraries and cultures, safely out of traditional view.

For instance, on the question of Christ's special place in gynecology, it turns out that Quetzalcoatl, one of the Native American prophets cited in this book, is just one example of many messiahs claiming birth from a virgin. And are Christians aware that 500 years before Christ, Buddha declared, "Do unto others as you would have them do unto you?"

It goes both ways. The information revolution has punched holes in the Eastern belief barriers too. For instance, Gautama Buddha's image, replicated in millions of statues spread all over Asia, does not physically resemble the founder of Buddhism. All subsequent versions of the idol of ultimate contemplation come from a design modeled after Alexander the Great — neither a meditative nor peace-loving man. The Aquarian Age will only drive this fact home to billions of Buddhists. And will it ever disturb their mantras!

The greatest crime against humanity has been committed by the religions: they have made humanity schizophrenic; they have given everybody a split personality. It has been done in a very clever and cunning way.

First, man has been told, "You are not the body," and second, "The body is your enemy." And this was the logical conclusion: that you are not part of the world, and the world is nothing but your punishment; you are here to be punished. Your life is not, and cannot be, a rejoicing; it can only be a mourning...a tragedy. Suffering is going to be your lot on Earth. Osho (1987) Womn

Buddha attained enlightenment two thousand and five hundred years ago and warned that the Earth would become hell if the things continued as they were. Hell is not somewhere beyond, but wherever there is fire that can never be quenched, it can be hell.

People do not go to hell after death. The designers and builders of hell are human beings. The designs and buildings are almost completed. It is becoming difficult to add more to hell. Maybe the materials to be burned have become scarce on the Earth? Tamo-san (1989) Trshr

The day humanity is completely finished with these exploiters in the name of religion, this very Earth can become a paradise. There is no need to wait for death. What has death to do with paradise? Paradise is the way you live. Paradise has something to do with life, not with death.
Osho (1985) FtoT

Write to your brothers throughout the world, telling them that it is necessary to bring about a reform of both customs and people themselves. If that is not achieved, the bread of the Divine word will not be broken among the people. St John Bosco (1874)

Even "the Church" will have revolution within itself. Strange creeds will be preached from all pulpits.

For a time Religion will save herself from catastrophe by abolishing her Bishops' "palaces," her gilded ceremonials, and her alliance with Monarchs. State and Church will separate and will cease backing up one another. Under the guise of humanity, Religion will creep back to her cradle of poverty and persecution, and in the next hundred years there will be as many religious sects in the World as there are pieces of supposed "true Cross" in existence at the present time. Cheiro (1926) Cwp

So you will see how absurd is the whole structure that you have built, looking for external help, depending on others for your comfort for your happiness, for your strength. These can only be found within yourselves. J. Krishnamurti (1929)

The Church has had much to do with this situation [souls regretting leaving their physical bodies for a better spirit life], with its dire preachings of hell-fire and damnation, and so have the old wives' tales of sleeping in the cold earth until Judgment Day, or of frightening apparitions that allegedly wander in the night. All are so false as to be degrading even to contemplate.
Spirit guides of Ruth Montgomery (1979) Amg

If religiousness spreads all over the world, the religions will fade away. It will be a tremendous blessing to humanity when man is simply man, neither Christian, nor Mohammedan, nor Hindu....Only then will there be a peace that passeth all mis-understanding. Osho (1987) GrCh

Just WHO's Calling WHO an

Whether the prophecies are Sikh or Seventh Day Adventist, whether their divine source is Mohammed, Free Masonry or Methodism, each of today's established cults of God or Godliness condition their forecasting brethren to declare the members of their faith and their messiah to be the only victors (or stunned survivors) of Armageddon.

Flip the coin of religious bias. Call divine heads! There is a 50/50 chance you'll get the devil's tails. The personification of our collective evil has been labeled "the Antichrist" for the last 2,000 years of the Christian-dominated Piscean Age.

Matthew 7:22 (right) could stand the whole religion on its head if Y'shua meant it to implicate a future priesthood as a Curia of the false. To those who will protest "Did we not prophesy in your name?" Y'shua may complain, "Jesus Christ, it wasn't even my name!" Y'shua was a Jew and never heard the words "Jesus," "Christian," or "Christ" in his lifetime. In fact, even Greco-Latin grammatical collisions like the word "Antichrist" might be seen by him as the gibberish of "evildoers."

The appropriate term for "the Antichrist" in other religions depends on which god they pray to. Now, if you've been taught to see all Arabs as servants of the Antichrist, as are most prophets under the influence of Christianity, then this *forerunner* (quoted above) has to be someone like, if not actually, Saddam Hussein. Certainly no non-Christians can be *faithful to the living god*, can they? But if you grew up having your reality shaped a different way and were programmed to think that God was "Allah" and had only one prophet worth remembering, "Mohammed," the *forerunner* to the Antichrist might be President Bush instead. And if you are an Iraqi, the *army of men drawn from many nations under his banner* must be those under the UN banner in Operation Desert Storm.

Then there's Nostradamus, always ready to catch one's projections in the flypaper of his obscurity. C8 Q70 could adequately describe the ascent of Saddam Hussein, and perhaps refers to the subsequent alliance of some Arab states with America in Operation Desert Storm: *He will enter, wicked, unpleasant, infamous, tyrannizing over Mesopotamia [Iraq]. All friends made by the adulterous Lady: the land dreaded and evil in aspect.*

Nostradamus often used symbols for countries. Christian-programmed interpreters might figure this *adulterous Lady* to be the modern-day Babylon of Baghdad. An Iraqi interpreter of Nostradamus might think she represents America's hypocritical "Statue of Liberty." An Islamic interpreter would perhaps say Nostradamus is implicating the "great Satan" America as modern-day Babylon. Moreover, pro-American Arab leaders are her evil *friends*. If your childhood was spent in a Palestinian concentration (excuse me) refugee camp, it is quite clear who the wicked, unpleasant, infamous, tyrannizing fellow *entering* Mesopotamia was. American coalition forces *entered* Iraq with an air and land offensive after 17 January 1991, so the prediction could also stand for a past or future American President. Prophecy doesn't care about the West's identification with being the good guys.

(References to Bush as Islamic Antichrist were composed in September of 1990, four months before Operation Desert Storm.)

AntiCHRIST?

[After 1970:] *The forerunner of the Antichrist will assemble an army of men drawn from many nations, united under his banner [Islam/Christian?]. He will lead them in a bloody war against those still faithful to the living God.* **Prophecy of La-Salette (1846)**

Not everyone who says to me, "Lord, Lord," will enter the kingdom of heaven, but only he who does the will of my Father who is in heaven. Many will say to me on that day [Judgment Day], "Lord, Lord, did we not prophesy in your name, and in your name drive out demons and perform many miracles?" Then I will tell them plainly, "I never knew you. Away from me, you evildoers!" **Y'shua (AD 30-33) Mt 7:21, 22**

The end of time is not far off, and the Antichrist will not delay his coming. We shall not see him and not even the nuns who will follow him, but those who will come later will fall under his domination. When he comes, nothing will be changed, in the nunnery everyone will be dressed as usual; the religious exercises and the services will go on as usual...when the sisters will realize that the Antichrist is in charge. **Bertine Bouquillon (1850)**

Shortly the kingdom of Christ will be founded on this Earth, but in the meantime, the prince of this world has been permitted to found a kingdom of his own, which will be only an empty mold of the undivided kingdom of Christ. Many members of the church will not see the difference, because even they seek the temporal, and they will be deceived by the prince of this world [the Antichrist]. **Emelda Scochy (1933)**

The one who will pretend to be the Christ [has] already been born in [America]...he presently resides in a Maryland suburb of Washington, DC. A schoolboy now, he is handsome, gregarious, and well liked by his friends. His parents are attractive, well-bred people, and his father is a lawyer. Spirit guides of Ruth Montgomery (1979) Amg

[Hmm...I wonder if his name is Damien? This could {did} make a great horror movie!]

NUCLEAR FAMILY, NUCLEAR WAR

THREE STEPS TO COOKING A FAMILY DISH

1

STEP ONE:
Prepare the fixings for a happy family.

2

STEP TWO:
Allow a few decades in the oven of expectations.

3

STEP THREE:
Remove and serve with ample karmic seasoning.

WARNING!

Do not whitewash with extra hope and sugar. Overcooking may result.

There are two stones that stand in the tidal pools of Ikema, an island off Okinawa. They are called the Miotozee, or "husband and wife" stones. For centuries, the dwellers of this Western Pacific island gauged the strength of the institution of marriage in the world by the fortunes of these stones. As long as they stood apart, the legend goes, the institution of marriage would be sustained throughout the world, *but when the Husband and Wife stones meet there will be fighting and great discord everywhere between friends, family and relations.*

In the early 1980s, heavy equipment from a construction project reclaiming land from the ocean inadvertently jammed the two stones together. Okinawans believe this is a sign that the misuse of technology is the evil agent dividing man from wife, children from parents, and ultimately, every human being from the world around him.

The icon of the family is the sacred cow of civilization. Even the iconoclastic Communists of the early Bolshevik Revolution, who first considered abolishing marriage, quickly changed their minds. They discovered that without the unit of the family with its co-lieutenants "mother" and "father" and its platoons of kids, the leaders lost the means to perpetuate their control of the masses. Without the dictatorship of the wedding ring and the family, there could be no dictatorship of the proletariat, no fatherland or motherland.

Past-dominated society is sustained by a moral chain of command. We start with God the father. Then comes the fatherland, which is usually guided by a paternal head of state. Next, the

$5.00 Overestimates the Taste of the Canadian Public: $6.50

FUTURE RECIPE FOR FAMILY HAPPINESS?

STEP ONE:
Take 1 cup of the Biblical prophet Micah.

The godly have been swept from the land. Not one upright man remains. All men lie in wait to shed blood; each hunts his brother with a net. Both hands are skilled in doing evil: the ruler demands gifts, the judge accepts bribes, the powerful dictate what they desire; they all conspire together. The best of them is like a brier, the most upright worse than a thorn hedge. The day of your watchmen has come, the day God visits you. Now is the time of their confusion....Do not trust a neighbor; put no confidence in a friend. Even with her who lies in your embrace be careful of your words. For a son dishonors his father, a daughter rises up against her mother, a daughter-in-law against her mother-in-law. A man's enemies are the members of his own household. But as for me, I watch in hope of the Lord. **(After 721 BC) Mic 7:2-7**

STEP TWO:
Take one trusting heart of woman — any woman. Marry her and beat her vigorously. Then add one ounce of ancient South Asian prophetic spice.

Wealth will be the only source of devotion; passion will be the sole bond of union between the sexes;
falsehood will be the only means of success in litigation; and women will be objects merely of sensual gratification. **The Hindu Puranas (c. 900 AD) Vis-P IV**

father of our nation dictates to the father figures in the Cabinet, Senate, and so on down the ladder of power, to the father commanders of armies and CEOs of corporations. At the bottom, the "king" of each household must also have his family subjects to rule. Break this chain of moral command at the lowest level, and the whole power trip suffers from athlete's clay feet.

Prophets collectively speak of a time when the basic foundation of power in civilization — the family — will be shaken. That may turn out not to be as bad as it sounds. We've profited from losing the world we have known in the past. Perhaps the plantation owners in the nineteenth-century American South believed the end of their world was nigh when the slaves were emancipated. But the termination of a social icon like the white man's right to enslave blacks proved to be a great beginning.

STEP THREE:

Mix this food-for-thought with pumpkin-punk sauce and cover from sight. Bake for twenty minutes and serve. However, don't overdo the Indian spices, or your family dish will be too hot to chew.

The punks and the skinheads are simply reminders that you have failed. The Western civilization has come to its end. Naturally it is always the youth who are most vulnerable to what is coming...that all Western scientists, Western politicians, Western churches are preparing a big graveyard for the whole of humanity....Those people [the punks] are not strange phenomena: you [the parents] are a strange phenomenon....They are simply revolting against you, and it will be good to listen to them....I am all in sympathy for those people; I would like to meet them. I will have immediate rapport with them because I can understand their misery, their anguish. They may prove your saviors. Don't laugh at them, laugh at yourself. They are your children, you have produced them — you must take the responsibility...a tree is known by its fruits....You are the tree — and those insane-looking young people are the fruits. Somewhere you are responsible. They are a question mark on you. Think about them sympathetically...

Unless you understand that the West is in urgent need of a new way of life, more and more outrageous reactions will be there around you, and you will be responsible for it.
Osho (1986) Soc

WARNING!

In case of prophetic indigestion use some bitter herb of Gurdjieff.

The difference [between the destruction of America and that of monarchic Russia] will only be in the process of the destruction itself. The process of destruction of the large community "monarchic Russia" proceeded in consequence of the abnormalities, so to say, the Reason of the power-possessing beings there, whereas the process of destruction of this community America will proceed in consequence of organic abnormalities. In other words, the "death" of the first community came, as they say, from the "mind," whereas the death of the second community will come from the "stomach and sex" of its beings. **G.I. Gurdjieff (1924-27) Beelzb**

Let us take revelation's flashlight and rifle through the dark closet of the American family dream at the end of the millennium:

My flashlight has found something hidden in mommy's honeymoon trunk. There I see, concealed behind her moth-eaten wedding dress and daddy's dusty tux
— are they timeless love letters?

The corners of the paper are crumbling with tradition and the ink is fading like a fashion long past its prime, but I can just make out the writing. Here are all the unanswered and repressed questions of any-mom and any-dad of America, penned in a rigid, frightened hand:

Darling...

...If our religions are teaching us "to love and cherish, honor and obey," why are two to four million women beaten by their husbands and boyfriends each year? Why are one out of eight American women destined to be rape victims — making 700,000 raped each year?

If we have as our ideal honoring our mother and father, why are more and more children beating up or murdering one or both parents?

And if the sanctity of the home is preached from every pulpit in the nation, why do 70 percent of all murders take place between family members?

If we are told to be moral and upright models for our children, why do one in four girls and one in six boys learn about fornication from a family member or friend before the age of eighteen?

If we are taught to love and cherish those whom we have brought into the world, why have nearly thirty-eigtht million adults been subjected to abuse as children?

A man and woman can find true happiness in wedlock? Then why do roughly half of all marriages end in divorce?

Our kids have a great future beyond the Cold War. The 1990s started with one out of three households including someone who toasts the American family too much. Forty-four out of every 100 young adults face the happy prospect of family life as full-fledged alcoholics. Why are one in 200 Americans snorting coke? What are they numbing themselves from? Don't they look forward to fatherhood and motherhood?

Your loving husband-to-be...
John "Doe"gue

The most popular tune to tip-toe down the aisle with on your way to wedded bliss is Wagner's "Wedding March" from Act Three of *Lohengrin*. (Just what the subconscious meaning is of calling it a march I've yet to divine.) Are man and wife marching to war? And what luck matrimony when you place sweaty finger to shaking hand to receive a wedding ring to a tune written by a man legendary for his adulteries? Yes, "Here Comes the Bride..." is a beautiful piece of music. Maybe Wagner tried to capture in music his own failed ideal of marriage. Still, I would ask those tens of millions of newlyweds stepping down the aisle to the strains of the "Wedding March" to examine what happens next in the opera. Lohengrin expects the impossible and his bride, Elsa, breaks all her vows, a man is murdered in their honeymoon suite and the newlyweds divorce — all within twenty minutes of the bridal march. Nothing more was consummated than a few incomparable arias. In other words, their marriage ended in an all-too-brief harmonic exchange of hot air and decibels.

In that way, theirs was a typical marriage.

RAW

UMBER EIGHT

$7.95

Birth of the Bomb:
**THE BEGINNING
OF THE END**
by Paul Boyer

JIMBO
by Gary Panter

The RAT RACE:

Man's answer to everything has been POWER — *power of money, power of position, power of wealth, power of this, that, of the other. This has* NEVER *been God's way, will never be* GOD'S *way.*

Edgar Cayce (1932) №3976-8

Wealth and piety will decrease day by day, until the world will be wholly depraved. Then property alone will confer rank; wealth will be the only source of devotion.

The Hindu Puranas (c. 900 AD) Vis-P IV:24

And so the gods will depart from mankind — a grievous thing! — and only evil angels will remain, who will mingle with men, and drive the poor wretches by main force into all manner of reckless crime, into wars, and robberies, and frauds, and all things hostile to the nature of the soul....Darkness will be preferred to light, and death will be thought more profitable than life...the pious will be deemed insane, and the impious wise; the madman will be thought a brave man, and the wicked will be esteemed as good.

Hermes (AD 150-270) Asc III

A Society of Homo "HAMSTER" Sapiens

*Of course, such a "record" will only lead to this, that the already sufficiently trifling
size of their ill-fated planet will become, even in their bobtailed being-picturings of reality, completely trifling....Whatever speed they may obtain with this "machine" of theirs
[the car] all the same, if they remain as they are not only they themselves but even their
thought will never go any farther than their atmosphere.*

G.I. Gurdjieff (1924-27) Beelzb

*In that day men will throw away to the rodents and bats
their idols of silver and idols of gold which they made to
worship.*

Isaiah of Jerusalem (c. 783-687 BC) Is 2:20, 21

*Soon the Earth will shake and will tumble down and people will say, "Oh
my God! Oh my God!" But the Great Spirit will say, "They're not praying to
me, they're saying, 'All my Gold! All my Gold!'" This is how it will be.*

Wallace Black Elk (1985)

*Those who are not embroiled, mere spectators — good men
as well as bad, wise men as well as fools, rich and poor,
old and young — all are fish panting in the stream of
poisoned waters.*

Tamo-san (1960) Look

Our Holiest Mother, our lady the bitch goddess of competition, is one of today's most worshipped icons.

In our times, a person's worth is often defined by how much money he makes and how much power he wields over others. We deem successful those parents who are best able to control their children and guide them toward accepted social or religious behavior. And from tit to tithe to tomb, the pressure is on to look, think and be extraordinary. Success requires many a loser's chest to stand on.

The same holds true if one strives for success through passivity. Even saints go to extraordinary lengths to be humble. One might call their rise to the top a sort of competition for *unachievement*. People in Christendom walking up holy mountains on their knees are not immediately thought of as competitors, or extraordinary. They are acknowledged as the *most* humble believers in God. Who can do the longest prayer vigils, the most punishing austerities, the most arduous fasts, which Jain monk can pluck out his pubes the quickest — these feats are the gauge of religiousness!

If you can't be best, then strive to be the most pitiable. Is it not said by Constantine's Christ that the poor are the "children of God" and the meek "shall inherit the Earth"? If we take this virtue to its final conclusion, nuclear war and its wintry aftermath will make the survivors of all lands the poorest and therefore closest to God.

The price paid for all this clawing to the top is stress, division and wars. There's a pyramid of disappointment, envy and greed supporting every pinnacle of success.

Many of the things we consider our greatest attributes as human beings — our competitiveness, our territorial urge and the willingness to fight for it, our ability to perpetuate our bloodlines — are throwbacks to our animal past. The yuppie with the most expensive four-wheeled erection is man's answer to the most impressive rack of antlers on a stag. Human hinds flock around the biggest corporate stag. The leader of the herd and the CEO share similar stress at the top; the only difference is that one brandishes his antlers and the other a cellular phone. To exalt in the survival of the fittest in the rutting room of the Executive Board or the Oval Office or the secret chambers of the Vatican Curia is more animal than human.

I have had my own experience of the "bitch" in worshipping the goddess of success.

My teachers, conductors and other colleagues foresaw a promising career in opera for me. I was the protégé of a prominent baritone from the New York City Opera and was being groomed for a career in the European opera houses. Some of them may still not forgive my retreat from the rutting grounds. I couldn't explain to them that this broken buck could not turn his joy of singing into a vehicle of commerce and survival.

The world is set up in such a way that human heartfulness is all but repressed. One sure way to repeat history unto doomsday is to accept as gospel that competition and struggle *are* our reality.

Competition seeps into all dimensions of life. One competes for affection, spiritual attainment or to manipulate others with the power of knowledge. In the Kali Yuga, all human virtues become mere animal currency.

Of this prime directive of a dark age, psychologist R.D. Laing said, "We are a dangerous species, the only species we know of that is in immediate danger of its own survival."

NATIONALISM:

...Yea, to be sure, **America** may boast, but rather is that principle (of freedom) being forgotten...that is the sin of America.

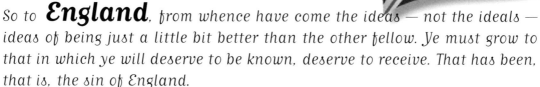

So to *England*, from whence have come the ideas — not the ideals — ideas of being just a little bit better than the other fellow. Ye must grow to that in which ye will deserve to be known, deserve to receive. That has been, that is, the sin of England.

As in **France**, to which this principle (of being superior to others) first appealed, to which then came that which was the gratifying of the desires of the body — that is the sin of France.

The Global **PENITENTIARY** System

In that nation which was first **Rome...** what were they that caused the fall? The same as at Babel. The dissentions, the activities that would enforce upon these, in this or that sphere, servitude, that a few might just agree, that a few even might declare their oneness with the Higher forces. For theirs was the way that seemeth right to a man but the end is death. That is the sin of Italy.

The sin of **China**? Yea, there is the quietude that will not be turned aside, saving itself by the slow growth. There has been a growth, a stream through the land in ages which asks to be left alone to be just satisfied with that within itself.

Just as in **India**, the cradle of knowledge not applied, except within self. What is the sin of India? Self, and left the "ish" off — just self!

Edgar Cayce(1944) №3976-29

"*Those countries which you now think of as closed will soon be open. And those*

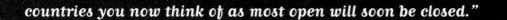

countries you now think of as most open will soon be closed."

"The inherited fear since millennia — suspicion from the beginning of time, combined with fear of losing possessions and properties — has created a greedy, intolerant and directly suicidal human being. Progress is measured in coins and commodities, and those who have made collecting and owning their goal, in the richest and most materialistic countries, are guarding their possessions. Armies are patrolling boundaries and walls. Watchtowers and customs agents make sure the borders are not trespassed; passports and visas give some people permission to temporarily visit and travel in parts of the planet which belongs to you all.
"Don't you see how ridiculous all this is? Don't you respond to the causes and laws which have created this life-negative way of living?
"Start questioning what's happening around you, and go into your own depth and ask what you would like to change."

Ambres (1987) Amb

Raise not democracy nor any other name above the brotherhood of man, the Fatherhood of God! Edgar Cayce (1939) №3976-24

You are ready now. You can trigger it [global suicide]...so that you don't waste the tremendous accumulations of your money and toil or don't betray the great producers of all these prepara- tions, whom you have supported, admired and thanked so much. You have elected to leadership of your governments and all other walks of life those people who you thought were most stead- fast in making these preparations with persistent efficiency and boldness, to take advantage of any and all resources of entire nations. They are by no means to blame. They have been chosen by you to accomplish the showdown of your subconscious wills.
They are therefore your godchildren.

Tamo-san (1957) Moor

These are signs of a decadent society, a society which has come to a suicidal point — a society which itself does not have any reason to live, and feels: Why should anybody else have any reason to live?...The whole thing depends on America because America is in a hurry to go into a third world war....The danger is from the White House in Washington. That is the most dangerous place on the Earth today....There is still time for the people of America to prevent the catastro- phe from happening. If the people of America cannot do anything, then these politicians are going to drag the whole of life on this Earth to the graveyard.

Osho (1986) Trns

Politicians have brought this great challenge to the whole of humanity. In a way we should be thankful to these fools.

Osho (1987)

Man Divided AGAINST the SELF

One person takes his or her own life every eighty seconds. Over 1,000 people kill themselves every day, and 300,000 commit suicide every year. We hold on to dreams while Colombian drug cartels ease the pain. A man divided against the Self — his Inner Being — is consoled into believing that blissfulness and fulfillment every moment is not a realistic goal. He is fearful for his survival most of his waking and dreaming hours yet denies this is so. One who is not divided against the Self acknowledges fear and accepts that it is inevitable, but is not fear's prisoner. One who is whole sees anger in the world but is not a prisoner of anger.

An undivided human knows something is missing the mark in society's definitions of good and evil. I have met such people, and their words and actions challenge my concept of morality. From them I have learned this: Before we have a chance to discern truth for ourselves, we are indoctrinated into a system of morality which distorts our perceptions and behavior for our whole lives. This conditioned mind is the Antichrist.

Isn't the legacy of human misery and war enough proof that our values impede rather than nurture a humanity undivided by fear?

GOING...GOING...GOD?

The holy Icon: Religion
"God made me do it."

The global suicide is the ultimate outcome of all our cultures, all our philosophies, all our religions. They have all contributed to it in strange ways — because nobody ever thought of (the needs of) the whole....Hell is your fear projected. Heaven is your greed projected. **Osho (1986)**

One is divided against the Self by belief in God. Many drugs can be used to dull intelligence along with misery. One of man's longest addictions may be the God-habit. A man will not rebel at injustice and poverty if he is convinced by the God-pusher of his particular religion that justice is not here, but always "there" — in the never never lands of heaven and hell. In the name of omnipresent and divine opiates, fear becomes "love of God," and being "on a mission from God" makes murder, torture, rape and pillage a sacrament — as long as the victims are unbelievers. It is as true for Operation Desert Storm as for the Holy Crusades. The opium of faith has been responsible for more war crimes than any other "moral" concept.

NUCLEAR FAMILY, NUCLEAR WAR

The Icon of micro-tribalism: The family
"We do it for the children."

Marriage will no longer be considered a religious rite. It will be a civil contract which will allow a change of partners whenever the contracting couple mutually agrees to separate.
David Goodman Croly (1888) Glmp

I'm not saying that all families will disappear. Only spiritual families will remain; non-spiritual families will disappear....Life will be more liquid, more trusting. There will be more trust in the mysteries of life than in the clarities of the law...the court, the police, the priests of the Church.
Osho (1977)

One is divided against the Self if culture dictates that one should remain monogamous, when behaviorists and psychologists again and again publish findings that man and woman are polygamous creatures. I have friends who are physical therapists. They report to me that around 90 percent of their clients are unhappily married men who pester them for more than a rub-down. They persist even when a "no" has been clearly stated. Sometimes I wonder. Maybe the best way to end prostitution is to end marriage. At least disband the institution of marriage that presumes "love, honor and cherishing" another human being can be promised by signing the dotted line.

Can true relating thrive in the confines of contracts? There is a subtle violence in treaties drawn over the heart. Lovers in the Aquarian Age will no longer demand such things from their beloveds. It will be viewed as unloving.

Brothers kill brothers, and even children spill one another's blood. Everyone steals and hoards great wealth, and sensual sin prevails. The end of the world is nigh — yet men are hard and cruel, and listen not to the doom that is coming....No one heeds the cries of his neighbor, or lifts a hand to save.
From *The Ragnarök*: Ancient Norse prophecy

One is divided against the Self by a multitude of well-meaning but spurious role models thrust in our faces. Competition brings success to a few and loneliness to all.

In an age of truth, people no longer bear the stress of having to prove themselves; they are aware of their own unique miracle of existence. They don't waste their lives begging for acknowledgment from others, or fighting for power positions so others can beg for their approval. Their energy is freed up so they can grow and develop in ways that nurture themselves and their world.

It may be that the revolutions and upheavals we see around us on all sides may for the time being bring about the fall of Empires, the destruction of Thrones, the death of the "old" and the birth of the "new."
Cheiro (1926)

Soon will the present-day order be rolled up, and a new one spread out in its stead... **Bahá'u'lláh (1863)**

One is divided against the Self when it becomes second nature to deny the innate humanity of all people. At birth one is simply human; then one is taught that one is Iraqi or Christian or Moslem. National tribalism makes a child labeled "American" grow up to be the commander of Operation Desert Storm, who can publicly shed a tear for the loss of a few Americans, but crack jokes about the daily slaughter of thousands of Iraqis.

It seems only the victors call the moral shots. Nazi atrocities are rightly condemned, their perpetrators punished. But what of Allied war crimes? Who brings the fire bombers of Tokyo, Dresden and Hiroshima to justice? As long as morality is defined according to the survival of the fittest, a word like "humanity" will only remain a fine idea.

Human society is not harmonious because each individual is divided inside, and his divisions are projected onto society. **Osho (1989)**

THE RAT RACE

The Icon of the Golden Rule:
"Those who have the gold, rule."

NATIONALISM
THE GLOBAL PENITENTIARY SYSTEM

The Icon of macro-tribalism:
Nationalism
"My country right or wrong."

Every limit placed on what we call the universe is eventually broken. We say man will never break the sound barrier or live in space, and not long afterward the barrier is blasted and astronauts dance in zero gravity. We are also told that no one can soar beyond the barrier of accepted moralities. This, too, will be transcended in time – if there are

The Book of

One may imagine the sight of billions of ants on board a driftwood, floating on a fast-running stream. The ants are apparently unaware that their driftwood is nearing a cataract. They seem to be even ignorant of the fact that they are on a driftwood. If they were aware, how could they afford to hate one another, scheme against one another, and be occupied with greed and hostility?

The moment when their driftwood falls down the cataract, what would anything mean to one or another ant, friend or foe?

This pathetic sight is nothing but an epitome of today's mankind.

Tamo-san (1957) Moor

If the people would change their minds and really be spiritual, there would be no need for arms and fighting. Everything could be settled by speaking the truth. But now, people wouldn't know the truth if you spoke it. It only upsets them. It hurts their ego. And then you are their enemy. Grandfather Semu Huarte (1983)

According to the Sacred Hoop and the prophecies, it is time to share this ancient wisdom....It is time for the Great Purification. We are at a point of no return. The two-legged are about to bring destruction to life on Earth. It's happened before and it's about to happen again. The Sacred Hoop shows how all things go in a circle. The old becomes new, the new becomes old. Everything repeats. White people have no culture. Culture is having roots in the earth. People without culture don't exist very long, because Nature is God. Without a connection to Nature, the people drift, grow negative, destroy themselves. In the beginning we had one mind, and it was positive, a thing of beauty, seeing beauty everywhere.

The Earth People [indigenous natives] never wrote anything down, had no written language. They knew that if they wrote anything down it would be disastrous. If you write something down you don't have to remember it. And mind goes off into unconsciousness. It becomes negative, or unconscious force.

Brave Buffalo, Brule Sioux Nation (1985)

enough future moments left for man to live.

The belief barrier stands to break us and all our tomorrows.

Here is a small cross-section of the prophetic pressure exerted down through the ages for us to drop old ideas and outmoded moral standpoints before they drop us into a catastrophe.

We are no longer alert. We continuously lie to our children and teach them to be liars. Easter bunnies, Santa Claus, denying what their senses tell them, these are all lies....If you're well educated you'll work to hurt people, you'll do the work of big institutions. You'll work to make alcohol, drugs, TV, schools, religion, things to put people's minds to sleep. Grace Spotted Eagle Inuit Native American (1985)

As long as we remain passive, we shall have in the course of our further existence to submit slavishly to every caprice of all sorts of blind events, and as a result inevitably shall serve solely as means for Nature's "involuntary and evolutionary constructions." G.I. Gurdjieff (1930) Lfe

The prime cause for all these happenings is racial, national, religious, and political prejudice, and the root of all this prejudice lies in outworn and deep-seated traditions, be they religious, racial, national, or political. So long as these traditions remain, the foundation of human edifice is insecure, and mankind itself is exposed to continuous peril. 'Abdul'-Bahá (1920)

The pacifist theories, the conventional ethical codes of the world, and the international goodwill movements are all but void in coping with the ultimate catastrophe that mankind as a whole is now facing. So are Communism, Democracy and whatnot. The history of man has witnessed great statesmen, great thinkers, great inventors and great scientists who have accomplished so many great works. And mankind has worked day and night so hard to disseminate education, to imbue people with numerous ideologies, thoughts, systems and all the nice things.

To our regret, all these efforts have not proven rewarding. On the contrary, human conscience has kept on disrupting, social turmoils accelerating, and accidents and natural calamities adding their frequency and scale. This is owing to the grave illusion underlying man's life outlook itself. The error was so fatal at its source that the entailing outcomes have formed a huge stream of incongruities during a long passage of time. Thus it is obvious that any deliberations or efforts, so long as the human behaviors — economic, political, educational, etc. — remain to be derived from the keynote of that root illusion, will work against their intentions as they have done in the past. **Tamo-san (1957) Moor**

What do you expect? People are machines. Machines have to be blind and unconscious; they cannot be otherwise, and all their actions have to correspond to their nature. Everything happens. No one does anything. "Progress" and "civilization," in the real meaning of these words, can appear only as a result of conscious efforts. They cannot appear as a result of unconscious mechanical actions. And what conscious effort can there be in machines? And if one machine is unconscious, then a hundred machines are unconscious, and so are a thousand machines, or a hundred thousand, or a million. And the unconscious activity of a million machines must necessarily result in destruction and extermination. It is precisely in unconscious involuntary manifestations that all evil lies. You do not yet understand and cannot imagine all the results of this evil. But the time will come when you will understand. **G.I. Gurdjieff (1916) Mira**

We have done enough stupidities. We have done enough harm to nature, to ourselves. We have been a nuisance on the Earth. Our whole history is a history of crimes — man against man, man against nature. What have we been doing here? Why should we be bothered to survive?...What have you done in the thousands of years that you have been here? Can you justify that your being here on the Earth has been a creative addition to existence? Has it made it more blissful, more peaceful, more loving? Has it changed nature for something better?

What have you done in thousands of years except killing, murdering, butchering, slaughtering? — and in beautiful, good names: in the name of God, in the name of truth, in the name of religion. It seems you want to kill and destroy, and any excuse is enough.

Perhaps it is better that this world does not survive. But I am saying "perhaps" — remember that. Again perhaps.

...The whole humanity perhaps may not be able to survive, but the few, a chosen few, can be saved. And that's enough. Osho (1984) RajB IV

It may be that the revolutions and upheavals we see around us on all sides may for the time being bring about the fall of Empires, the destruction of Thrones, the death of the "old" and the birth of the "new." It may be that times of great tribulations lie in store for humanity — I am, however, such a believer in the ultimate perfection of Divine Design that I see in the symbol of the Aquarian Age the promise of "the Water Bearer" pouring out water on the earth, that in the end seeds may have more richness, flowers more fullness and all sections of humanity more love for one another. Cheiro (1926) Cwp

There are two systems of power: one creative and one destructive. If the human being is using only the destructive power, then it will become suicidal. For a start it can look as though it is creative, but very soon it will show itself to be destructive. And the more technology is involved in it, the stronger it will accelerate so that at the end the creative power cannot balance the destructive.

The human being has to awaken the force of love in the long run, whereas the negative force is short-sighted and hard. It can live longer in its aggressivity and build stronger and stronger momentum so that it can even kill the power of love.

Sometimes the human being says god is evil, god creates war. How can god condone destructive weapons; how can god condone starvation? Cannot the human being see that she is the one who has created the wars out of her fear generated by negative force? Can she not see that she has created the starvation, that she has created the different cultures and traditions which allow starvation?

She has created the different religions which fight with each other and kill each other. In war human beings are standing against each other and shouting, "It is a holy war, god is with us." Do you think god is fighting with himself or that there are different gods? No, the human being is fighting because of her fear. She has pushed away her paradise and she closed her eyes to paradise. And she doesn't see that she is really right in the middle of it. **Ambres (1985)**

Look at the world. Though people have been trying to do even a hundred good deeds, the world has been going worse and worse. But why? It is because that which people have been trying to do is minor goodness, and that they have forgotten the existence of major goodness.

The Earth has come to the verge of destruction. Its survival depends on our actions at this very moment. But dear friends, we are in the Dark Age and it is impossible to make right actions in the darkness. Thus it is of vital importance to bring Wisdom Light. When the Wisdom Light appears in the world, the darkness will disappear. And we will become able to see clearly and understand truly what is right to do and what is wrong to do. Then the Dark Age will transform into the New Age. When the nature of Wisdom Light is recognized in the world immediately, the New Age begins. **Tamo-san (1989) Trshr**

When I look, I find that there is no more dreadful a disease than fear. What else is there in life to be feared more than fear itself? Fear paralyzes the very being of a person. Fear destroys the whole capacity for rebellion. Fear makes any change impossible. Fear binds one to the known, and the journey to the unknown is completely stopped — although whatever is worth knowing and achieving in life is all unknown.

God is unknown. Truth is unknown. Beauty is unknown. Love is unknown. But the fearful mind always clings to the known. It does not go beyond the drawn line. It walks on the beaten track. The fearful person becomes mechanical, and he is no different than the drudge. Religions teach fear: fear of hell, fear of sins and fear of punishment. Society teaches fear — fear of dishonor. Education teaches fear — fear of failure.

Simultaneously there is greed attached — greed for heaven, greed for the fruits of virtue; greed for respect, position, reputation, success and rewards. All greed is the other side of the coin of fear. This way the consciousness of a person becomes full of fear and greed. The fire of jealousy and competition is aroused. The fever of ambition is created. There is no wonder if, in all these circular patterns, life is wasted.

Such education is dangerous. Such religions are dangerous. Education is that which teaches fearlessness, stabilizes one in non-greed, gives energy to rebel, gives courage to accept the challenge of the unknown. Education should not teach jealousy and competition, but love; it should not encourage the insane speed of ambition, but natural and self-inspired growth. But this can happen only if we accept the uniqueness of everyone's individuality. **Osho (1966)**

Behold,

I will create new

heavens and a new Earth.

The former things will not be

remembered, nor will they

come to mind.

Third Isaiah
(fourth century BC) Is-65:17

Spiritual

REBELLION

All reforms, however extensive and seemingly lasting, are in themselves merely productive of further confusion and further need for reformation. Without understanding the whole complex being of man, mere reformation will bring about only the confusing demand for further reforms. There is no end to reform and there is no fundamental solution along these lines. Political, economic or social revolutions are not the answer either, for they have produced appalling tyrannies, or the mere transfer of power and authority into the hands of a different group. Such revolutions are not at any time the way out of our confusion and conflict.

J. Krishnamurti (1963) Liah

There comes a moment where reason fails, where the absurd, the irrational, the mystical, the miraculous, raises its head. The coming 100 years are going to be more and more irrational. I do not ordinarily make prophecies, but about this I am absolutely prophetic: the coming 100 years are going to be more and more irrational, and more and more mystical. Osho (1986) RajUp

The next twenty years [1979-1999] are crucial to the unfolding of a soul's spiritual being, for unless mankind uses these years to smooth out past karma and prepare for the spirit state, the opportunities may not come again for thousands of years, inasmuch as the human population will be decimated and opportunities for entering physical bodies will be slim. Those who strive now to complete their rehabilitation will advance more rapidly in spirit, to compensate for the lost opportunities in the Earth life.

Spirit guides of Ruth Montgomery (1979) Amg

Adaptation becomes a frog's worst enemy when the amphibian is placed in a jar of water undergoing a slow boil. He adapts to the ever hotter temperature rather than jumping out. Perhaps he's praying to the only begotten pollywog of his froggy god for a better tomorrow. Otherwise, how could he endure temperatures beyond his tolerance and without complaint until he's boiled alive?

Man is on a boil of another kind. A mind boil. The shaman seers of the Fourth World generally agree that those who tenaciously cling to the past will fall into mass insanity. The serpent power of the Aquarian Age is upon us. The Kundalini of Gaia is about to awaken. No one can avoid being affected. Most human beings may go out of their minds; others will go beyond mind.

The global rave has already started, according to Hopi prophets. They targeted 19 January 1991 as the beginning of *the days of Purification*. The world as we have known it is now beginning its death and renewal. We might not finish the critical passage from breakdown to human breakthrough until 2012, the year the Mayan calendar marks as the end of time.

Madness has its good side. Astrologer Linda Goodman has said that more mad people (and their therapists) are born under the sign of Aquarius than any other. Madness from Uranian chaos, tied to the grounding vibes of Saturnian forces, will make the next age more mad-friendly, so to speak.

Many native seers share the Eastern view that identification with pain — be it physical or psychic — creates more agony than the pain itself. If people can create a little distance from their attachments and expectations, they may find themselves entering the new millennium free of the burden of identification with their mind's prejudices and programs. In other words, they may be able to drop attachment to the mind instead of going insane.

Mystical prophets, primarily from the East, contend that man's consciousness is more than a product of his biological computer, the brain. It is beyond thoughts, emotions and the body. Some mystics would say the human Being is even beyond the soul. The Eastern mystics tell us we are not the personality, which is merely a web of thoughts and desires; we are rather an awareness imprisoned by the personality. This mental-emotional periphery that we think we are moves around an inner world of consciousness that does not judge for or against, that is untouched by all that bodes good fortune or bad. The Being described by the adjective "human" is neither good nor evil. Consciousness is not a darling of dialectics. However, the mystics indicate that this "it"-ness is at the very core of an Apocalypse of Truth.

The rediscovery of this Being will be the greatest of Tomorrow's revelations.

If a power surge in Gaia's spiritual amplitude between now and 2012 is going to pump up the volume of thoughts to a level of mass insanity, the only people who may be capable of surviving the coming Apocalypse of Madhouse Earth are the spiritually rebellious.

Rebellion is a word we're programmed to absorb in the negative, just like apocalypse. Yet rebellion is the nickname of Uranus the deprogrammer, the higher potential of the coming age of Aquarius. Rebellion is part and parcel of the New Age.

Throughout history, the orthodox, the past-oriented, have feared any degree of spiritual rebellion. Not a single founder of any of today's socially acceptable religions has come from an established priesthood or hierarchy.

Two thousand years ago, the Sanhedrin, the council that defined Hebraic law, was not too happy with a cultist rebel from Galilee who was contradicting the laws of Moses. Moses himself rebelled against his adopted Egyptian society to become what Pharaoh viewed as a cult leader of the Jews. Mohammed rebelled against the pantheistic faiths of fellow Arabs. And then there's Gautama Siddhartha, the Hindu heretic and spiritual hippie. He tuned in to a Dharma of a different and non-Brahmin vein, turned on to Nirvana and dropped out of Hindu society to hang out by the Bodhi trees in Bihar province.

As far as the history of human enlightenment is concerned, rebellion, as part of the spiritual evolution of man, is a necessary shock to the status quo of dogma.

A rebellion in spiritual matters may be akin to catastrophism in geological evolution. During long periods of rock-solid dogma, the crust of the Earth hardly changes. Then, abruptly, a great upheaval, a release of age-old tradition, caused by great tension between two plates of earth, brings on a sudden quake. A new dispensation of valleys and hills appears. Streams change their course, and may run through new territories for eons without changing again.

The life of a great mystic is like a sudden volcanic eruption. For a short time, the earth is white-hot with change. A magma of rebellion shocks, shakes and burns the countryside. Then, the flames die down nearly as suddenly as they appeared. The rocks cool. In time, grass conceals every fluid word of fire. All is peaceful and safe. For centuries, nothing is disturbed.

We are conditioned to view catastrophe, whether geological or spiritual, as a terrible thing to be avoided at all costs. When Mount Saint Helens erupted in 1980, most observers could only bemoan the devastation of one of North America's most beautiful mountain lake resorts. They forgot that a series of geological "rebellions" in earlier ages had shaped St Helens' pristine beauty in the first place.

Destruction is the first part of the equation of creation. Strange that we only fear and curse the sudden violence of earthquakes that form the abiding mountains, bays and valleys that watch over our insecure history. The peaks and valleys of spiritual truths follow a similar law of sudden catastrophe after a long stasis. We are equally terrified of those brief and violent eruptions and earthquakes that suddenly disturb ages of thought and spiritual stasis.

When a Messiah erupts, deep down we yearn for his words of fiery lava to settle down into dormant dogma. Few risk approaching the catastrophe of living and fire-breathing spiritual masters while they blast, bubble and shake the Earth. Truth-sayers disturb the static world. Most people fear being burned by a master's living presence and will retreat away from his path, returning only after his flame has burned out. Many worship a master when the spiritual presence has become cold stone and it is again safe to walk on the new rocks of faith. Peters, Popes and pundits sustain uniformity until a new eruption of truth-saying is at hand.

If you are a thrill-seeker of truth, if you like risking your life hiking around the lip of Dharma's caldera, if you question your society's programming job, if you are a misfit-at-heart, trying unsuccessfully to fit into your society's constraints, you might count yourself fortunate that you are living in the nightmarish nineties. If you are a spiritual geologist of the catastrophe school, you are best positioned to see one of spiritual evolution's biggest Krakatoan blow-ups. Running parallel to the prophetic schools of end-time are the forecasts in this section.

Most will find it disagreeable to see the crust of their own dogmas crack and bleed. And they might find ways to seal them up before newly-formed truths have a chance to take shape in their being.

But be assured: if it gets too hot, the eruption of a global spiritual rebellion is short. You can miss it and hold onto your dogmas for another eon.

The time is very short....So much destructive force is accumulating that unless a few individuals gather courage and revolt against all that is past...I am not telling you to choose, to choose that which is good and to leave that which is bad. They are all together; you cannot do that. The past has to be simply erased, as if we are for the first time on the Earth and there has been no history. That is the only possibility to create a beautiful world full of love, full of fragrance, with deep respect for everybody. The past has lived centered on hate. The future can live only if it is centered on love. The past has been unconscious. The future can only be conscious....We can either die with the past or be reborn with the future.

Osho (1987) Omph

Religionless Religion

Once you have tasted your own immortality, you start spreading an invisible fire...people will be immensely touched by your very presence, by your aroma, by your fragrance, by your love. We need in the world more love to balance war. Osho (1987) NewD

But there is a revolution which is entirely different and which must take place if we are to emerge from the endless series of anxieties, conflicts and frustrations in which we are caught. This revolution has to begin, not in theory and ideation, which eventually prove worthless, but with a radical transformation in the mind itself. Such a transformation can be brought about only through right education and the total development of the human being. It is a revolution that must take place in the whole of the mind and not merely in thought. J. Krishnamurti (1963) Liah

Forget doing, grow into your being. And the growth of your being is contagious; it will help many people to light their unlit torches from your life fire....Politicians will be left alone without any support from their armies, from their scientists, from their intelligentsia, from mystics, from poets. And against all this intelligence, all their nuclear weapons will become impotent. They can create war only if unconsciously we are ready to commit suicide, if in some way we are supportive to them. It is our support that has given them power. If we withdraw our support their power disappears. They didn't have any power of their own....It is a great challenge, a very adventurous time. When the world is facing suicide, the possibility is that the world can be convinced — not intellectually but through your growing hearts, your love — to let the old world die and the new world with new values be born. You won't have such an opportunity again. In the past there was never such an opportunity. It is not to be missed. Osho (1987) NewD

Such perfection cannot be attained until all religions have become merged into one. This, the apparently "impossible," is every day becoming more and more probable. The sway and power of State-supported creeds is on the decline, or splitting into so many sects that they are "like sheep without a shepherd." Cheiro (1931) Cwp

Wise men have told their flocks in every age, be it golden or apocalyptic, "The truth will set you free." With all our pleas, penance and god-placating down the centuries, has it happened yet? Are we free of jealousy and envy, free from hatred and fear? And to those who immediately respond to such questions that they are free from some or all of the above, I have another question: Can we ever stop deceiving ourselves?

Can freedom be partial? Can one be partially pregnant with truth? Or is this an imaginary child we are gestating for thousands of years with no hope of birth?

The Eastern understanding is that this world is a classroom filled with near-eternal opportunities for us to examine its karmic curriculum for an endless semester of flunked incarnations — till nirvana do us part.

Just how much abuse can Classroom Earth endure for our growth? There's no more room in the trash cans for our spent class notes. The windows are fused and it's getting as warm as a greenhouse in here. There's too many classmates! There aren't even enough pencils or chairs for them. And the moral curriculum hasn't had a major revision for eons. Schoolmistress Gaia has her limits.

The question I must ask after considering prophetic trends is: Are we taking the trials of Earth beyond the breaking point? Will there soon be no classroom left where we can learn and evolve?

The Ramthas, Lazarises and Mafus of the channeled entity fad share the good news from the spirit realm that if the world ends we'll just find our spirits put on a better, more spiritually advanced planet. In other words, the new generation in Paradise-speak is a hip, Star Trek version of the Christian Rapture — that flight of spiritual fancy where believers are swept away into the clouds before doomsday gets too messy.

I wonder how long we can keep bending a callused knee, or *davening* a sunburned head to a Temple wall and continue hoping that God's got upwind of our prayers and will do a miracle to save Classroom Earth from our iniquities. There are over 300 cults (and counting) of God sending their prayers to him. Pity the poor angels who sort our mail!

Perhaps there's a new lesson waiting for the class — one we can't access unless we clear our desks of tradition's dog-eared, musty textbooks and throw them into the furnace.

If something from me must burn in the Great Purification, I'd rather it be my illusions, not my flesh.

The medieval religious scholar and seer, Giacchino de Fiore, in his famous twelfth-century work, *Vaticini del Vangelo (Prophecies of the Eternal Gospels)*, predicts that a new Age of the Holy Spirit will cleanse mankind with a flood of spiritual fire, love and justice.

Fiore says the final Pope of the Catholic church will vanish *because the reign of the Holy Spirit will be the reign of the free.* He could be saying that the Catholic church, if not all religions, will be transmuted into a new religiousness expressed by direct experience. In the Aquarian Age, freedom is the highest spiritual virtue. Religion will be a way of living rather than a dead dogma. It will follow the dictates of action and being.

The nineteenth-century German prophet, Johann Adam Müller, foresaw the end of all Christian sects. From their ashes, he said, would rise a *new religiousness*. Müller, like Cayce, promises that a "Christ"-ianty, a religion of the Christ essence, is waiting for survivors of the nightmarish nineties. A shift away from hierarchy to experiential religion is voiced by Asian prophets as well: the inner "Buddha" will flower out of the ashes of Buddhism, and inner Krishna consciousness will sever the ancient bonds of Hindu dogmatism.

260

THE DHARMA *Flame* WILL

The new epoch will deliver you from speech, because you will

When the founder of Tibetan Buddhism, the Guru Padmasambhava, bade farewell to his disciples twelve centuries ago, it was with a parting prophecy: *When the iron bird flies and horses run on wheels, the Tibetan people will be scattered like ants across the face of the Earth, and the Dharma will come to the land of the red men.*

Padmasambhava is speaking of modern times. Since the mid-twentieth century, when the Chinese began their systematic rape of Tibet and its religion, the fourteenth Dalai Lama, his monks and countless thousands of Tibetans have found themselves *scattered like ants* across the planet during the era of aircraft and trains. As a flower of Dharma, of the truth, Tibet will soon be no more. But the wheel of truth has no beginning or end. The Dharma will come to the land of the red man, to America. There are signs that the seed has already been planted.

There is a meditation celebration currently held every night in India by thousands of disciples of Osho. All true believers and doubting visitors are asked to wear white robes when they attend. It is also suggested that one wear dark red robes as an experiment in group meditation during daily activities. The founding guru of this Club Med(itation) explained the use of these collective color therapies as a spiritual purification process.

I cannot help wondering if poor St John and the First Isaiah might have seen these people in their visions (see below).

It is a common prophecy device of the Bible to say, "Those who have an ear — listen; and those who have an eye, see." But eyes and ears are tempered by the particular values of a visionary's belief system. St John sees all new evolution in consciousness in our future as solely Christian. The fellow-believers of this accepted sect do the same with their interpretations of prophecy. In the end, both groups run the danger of missing Christ-consciousness hiding in other religious paths.

Madame Blavatsky predicted that Eastern wisdom would experience a dramatic spread to the West in the year 1975. In that year, the Osho Commune enjoyed the recognition as the largest center for growth in the Human Potential Movement. However, it must be remembered that the Osho Commune is but one of many Dharma seeds floating westward. Many other movements, such as Maharishi Mahesh Yogi's Transcendental Meditation, or Da Avabhasa's Free Diast Communion are from the East or taking Eastern teachings westward. These new spiritual movements also experienced a sudden jump in Western disciples in the mid-1970s.

"Come now, let us reason together,"says the Lord. "Though your sins are like scarlet, they shall be as white as snow; though they are red as crimson, they shall be like wool." Isaiah 1:18

They will walk with me, dressed in white, for they are worthy. He who overcomes will, like them, be dressed in white... He who has an ear, let him hear what the Spirit says to the churches... Rev 3:4,5

SPREAD FROM THE EAST...

be able to feel what is in the thoughts of other men...

...THE DHARMA FLAME WILL USE RUSSIA AS ONE

...You have to understand: in those far mountains of the East

Russia

seems to be a land of destiny, not only for its own people, but for the whole world. It was the first to revolt against capitalism; it is going to be again the first to revolt — against dictatorial communism. The future is of a democratic communism, a communism rooted in the freedom of man...If [Gorbachev] can open the doors for a spiritual search, then certainly he can fulfill the prophecy of Edgar Cayce that Russia is the hope for all mankind.

Osho (1987) GFutr

OF ITS CHIEF STEPPING STONES TO THE WEST...

rests in the secret power...

In 1988 one of India's greatest contemporary astrologers, Shree Bhuveneshwari Panchang, predicted that in 1989 *someone from India's spiritual field will establish his name in Russia; it will be a significant event. [He] will go to Russia and will receive tremendous honor and respect. And, Russia's peculiar, strange, or indifferent attitude toward religion will change. Russia will turn toward religion, and the credit for this will go to the great spiritual figure and in effect to India.* (Gondal [Ephemeris] 1988-89, published in Gujarat province, India.)

As we have already examined, Nostradamus, Cheiro and Cayce view Russia as the hope of the world. In Gorbachev's second Russian revolution, many Russians are turning to religion, enjoying a new Christian renaissance. But they could eventually tilt eastward in their religious thinking.

In 1988 the Soviet government not only began reopening churches and monasteries, but many a dusty pew and altar was made available to Eastern religions as well. In that year, the Hare Krishnas of ISKCON (International Society of Krishna Consciousness) established a meditation center in Moscow. The following year, the neo-sannyasins of Osho's movement set up eight centers in Odessa, Moscow, St Petersburg, and Riga, and a retreat in the Caucasus mountains.

Though neither the Hare Krishna founder, Swami Prabhupad, nor Osho actually set foot in Russia, Panchang's astrological forecast is circumstantially correct: Both religious leaders (now departed) saw their message "go" to Russia. In 1989 Soviet TV news reporter Sergei Alekseev ran a documentary on Osho's Indian commune on "International Panorama," a prime-time Soviet television show with a viewing audience of seventy million.

Many Western prophets also say the next great teacher will come from Asia. American Indian seers, Jeane Dixon, Nostradamus, Cayce, Blavatsky — to name a few giants in the field — definitely pointed to a "man from the East," and India in particular, as the source of a change in world consciousness. Even the reference to the coming of the Judeo-Christian Messiah in Biblical scripture *coming from the East* supports the Asian source interpretation.

264

...BUT IT IS IN AMERICA...

...It will inexorably extend over the whole Earth and will tower

Perhaps in the near future, Russia will import American democracy and export to the US the "faith" of the next millennium. Prophecies from many different traditions say that America is destined to become the next seat of religious evolution.

In *My Journey with a Mystic*, Fritz Peters relates that his master, George Gurdjieff, a former citizen of Czarist Russia, foresaw a day when the Eastern world would again rise to a position of world importance and become a threat to the *momentarily all-powerful, all-influential new culture of the Western world, which was dominated by America* — a country, according to Gurdjieff, that was very strong, though very young.

Immaturity has its up side. Gurdjieff points out that the "old world" is in many ways too cultured, too set in its ways and moralities to welcome the new and radical changes required for the birth of the new man. On the other hand, America, though it is spiritually childish, brash and still capable of playing with nuclear fire, is fresh enough to take on a new religious dimension. Nevertheless, Gurdjieff warned that the span of man's continued existence will be "very short" unless a synthesis of the best qualities of East and West is attained. He believed that if the ultimate war comes, it will be caused by America's overreaction to an East-West crisis.

There are some tentative signs that the first Eastern seeds have already sprouted in the American field of dreams. For over two centuries, the world has exiled its misfits and rebels to America. And among this melting pot of incongruous races, minds and hearts has been a steady stream of experimental religious sects: The Quakers, Hutterites, Puritans, Mormons and Shakers came from the fringes of Christianity in the last century; the Hare Krishnas, the Rajneeshees, the Moonies and the Transcendental Meditators arrived in the present century. One of America's greatest attributes is its ability to give social and religious experiments a chance.

Some seeds have had to endure attacks even while planted in the land that boasts freedom of speech and religion. Americans burned Mormon cities to the ground in the last century. And in the last decade, the commune of Rancho Rajneesh in eastern Oregon was systematically persecuted. Only when Rajneeshpuram became a ghost town did the state government accept its incorporation as legal. In the twentieth century we don't burn communes; we "bend" the law to disband them.

But the tree of Eastern religious wisdom keeps releasing it seeds to the West. Rajneeshpuram is gone and in its place sprout dozens of smaller communes around America. The Maharishi Mahesh Yogi's transcendental meditators have established deep roots in middle America, establishing their Maharishi International University in the quiet farm town of Fairfield, Iowa. American Swami Sri Kriyananda's commune, Ananda (meaning "bliss"), set in the foothills of California's Sierra Nevada mountains, is still flourishing. The current spate of "Mormonization" of backwoods America is taking place in the Royal Teton Ranch, just outside of Yellowstone National Park, in Montana. There the followers of Elizabeth Clare Prophet are trying to synthesize Eastern wisdom with Western pioneer spirit, amidst considerable controversy. Their more orthodox neighbors have been attempting for years to metaphorically burn them out. If successful, their efforts might only succeed in crushing the dandelion and unwittingly spreading its seeds.

... the sky. Everything that recalls **end-times will collapse..**

A Pax Americana — a period of relative lack of war — should be soon upon us. Optimism should run high, decadence should run wild and the stage will be set for America to begin a search for new spiritual values.
Alan Vaughan (1973) Ptrns

Eastern culture will heavily influence American thought in years to come. Eastern cults and religions will gain strength here and finally supplant traditional Christianity. A new religion will combine Eastern and Christian concepts. Alan Vaughan (1973) Ptrns

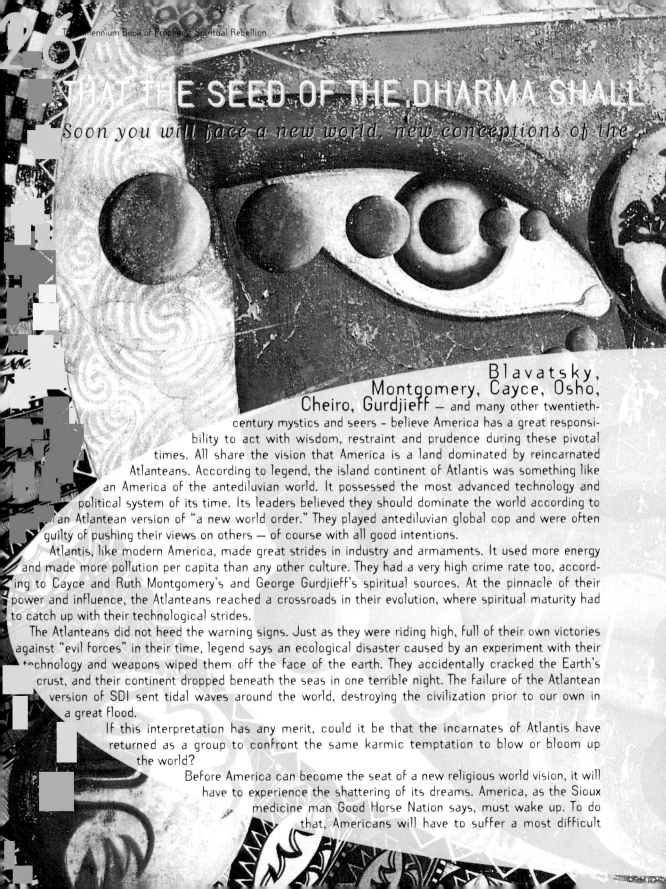

THAT THE SEED OF THE DHARMA SHALL

Soon you will face a new world, new conceptions of the

Blavatsky,
Montgomery, Cayce, Osho,
Cheiro, Gurdjieff — and many other twentieth-
century mystics and seers - believe America has a great responsibility to act with wisdom, restraint and prudence during these pivotal
times. All share the vision that America is a land dominated by reincarnated
Atlanteans. According to legend, the island continent of Atlantis was something like
an America of the antediluvian world. It possessed the most advanced technology and
political system of its time. Its leaders believed they should dominate the world according to
an Atlantean version of "a new world order." They played antediluvian global cop and were often
guilty of pushing their views on others — of course with all good intentions.

Atlantis, like modern America, made great strides in industry and armaments. It used more energy
and made more pollution per capita than any other culture. They had a very high crime rate too, according to Cayce and Ruth Montgomery's and George Gurdjieff's spiritual sources. At the pinnacle of their
power and influence, the Atlanteans reached a crossroads in their evolution, where spiritual maturity had
to catch up with their technological strides.

The Atlanteans did not heed the warning signs. Just as they were riding high, full of their own victories
against "evil forces" in their time, legend says an ecological disaster caused by an experiment with their
technology and weapons wiped them off the face of the earth. They accidentally cracked the Earth's
crust, and their continent dropped beneath the seas in one terrible night. The failure of the Atlantean
version of SDI sent tidal waves around the world, destroying the civilization prior to our own in
a great flood.

If this interpretation has any merit, could it be that the incarnates of Atlantis have
returned as a group to confront the same karmic temptation to blow or bloom up
the world?

Before America can become the seat of a new religious world vision, it will
have to experience the shattering of its dreams. America, as the Sioux
medicine man Good Horse Nation says, must wake up. To do
that, Americans will have to suffer a most difficult

weaning — from what is false
or destructive in the American Dream. It is all
too predictable that karmic lessons only get our attention
the hard way. Forecasters from Cayce and the Mormon prophets
to the aboriginal seers of North America say a second civil war may be
coming as soon as the latter half of the 1990s. Mormon visionary Orson Pratt
foresees something less like the battles between the northern and southern states of
the mid-nineteenth-century Civil War and something more like the drug and gang wars of
Harlem and South-Central Los Angeles, spread to every city and town. In 1940 Edgar Cayce
envisaged the erosion and breakdown of the American Dream when those who lead her proclaim
their might and power as being right. When the leaders of this land have brought *many of the isles of
the sea and many of the lands* under their influence, fearing *not man or the devil,* their own land will
see the blood flow as in those periods when brother fought against brother (the Civil War). №2976-24

In 1939, Cayce gave his future countrymen an alternative to civil war: *Unless there is, then, a more
universal oneness of purpose on the part of all, this will one day bring — here, in America — revolution!*
(№3976-25) Lytle Robinson and other Cayce scholars interpret these events as the struggle of black brothers against white during the 1960s. However, the Mormons and aboriginal prophets whose visions parallel
Cayce's point to a much more violent breakdown in American culture coming in the near future. It will be
considerably more disruptive than the political and social riots seen during the 1960s. In the 1870s, Pratt
described the coming Balkanization of America would be a war pitting *neighborhood against neighborhood, city against city, town against town, state against state, and they will go forth destroying,
and being destroyed. Manufacturing will almost cease, great cities will be left desolate...*

It may be that Russia is just the first of Madame Sylvia's fallen *Colossi* of the Cold War to
crumble from the strain of the arms race. America may follow in the near future. The
potential for social derailment is evident in the runaway pattern of crime, drugs and
violence of today's America. In the end, the coming social upheaval may be
necessary to shock America back to consciousness, before *the
Dharma* can move to the *land of the
red man.*

268 HOMO NOVUS

O Force-compelled, Fate-driven Earth-born race,
O petty adventurers in an infinite world
And prisoners of a dwarf humanity,
How long will you tread the circling tracts of mind
Around your little self and petty things?
But not for a changeless littleness were you meant,
Not for vain repetition were you built
...Almighty powers are shut in Nature's cells.
A greater destiny awaits you in your front
...The life you lead conceals the light you are.

Sri Aurobindo (1946-1948) Sav

J. Krishnamurti often stressed that there has been no true revolution in man's history. Like "civilization," it is only a great idea. It hasn't happened yet.

The minority prophetic view down through the ages points to the final seven years of this century as the seeding ground for a true and mystic revolution. The catalyst for this creative apocalypse is a new breed of human Being who is spiritually rebellious.

These early members of the genus Homo Novus (The New Man) will give birth to a fearless humanity, liberated from past and future obsessions. The species Homo Novus lives with alertness and creativity and delight in the present moment. If their rebellion is nurtured in the next seven years, then the following new millennium is predicted to see them spread and establish a global society that can work together to make a world so rich in health, technology and luxury that all individuals are free to discover and live their uniqueness to the fullest.

Who are the spiritually rebellious walking among us?

It would be rebellious if men and women no longer indulged or glorified misery and cruelty and ceased to shun the celebrants who enjoy life for no reason, and with no expectation of gain. It would be a mutiny against all we have been to see a humanity that was dedicated to protecting the freedom of others to be equally unique.

It would be avant garde to see laughter as a higher spiritual virtue than even prayer, and joyous fulfillment of humanity's highest potential the greatest value.

It would be spiritually rebellious if schools allowed children the freedom to explore their uniqueness while the teachers did their best not to pass off their hypocrisies and mistakes as "morality," "religion" and "truth."

The pundits of tomorrow's spirit rebellion teach our children about those men and women throughout our history who *didn't* conquer the world, establish Napoleonic Codes of dictatorship, or murder millions to establish "New World Orders." The prophecies of "blooms" day see a new age coming when the learned stop wagging their Genghis Khans and zip up their Tamerlanes and shelve their Hitlers and Stalins, relegating the whole rotten chronicle of wars, rape and inquisitions to the footnotes. Historians of a spiritual revolution will open children's minds and hearts to those people who dedicated their lives to silence, creativity and love. The new millennium's history lesson will focus on the happy, sane, and loving people and waste less time on our heroically insane.

It would be a revolutionary society that allowed its children to explore the stages of love from sex to superconsciousness. Loving would undergo a true revolution the day our teenagers are encouraged to freely explore their sexuality during its highest biological peak rather than sit on it for interminable hours spent at school and doing homework. There would be no need to thrust children into considering their career prospects at ages fourteen through eighteen at a time when all their attention is naturally focused on learning how to love and be loved.

Before marrying, and with care-filled instruction in contraception and safe sex from adults, the children of a new humanity would learn how to give and receive love; they would be encouraged to explore a wide range of unique young men and women before choosing their real soulmates. This would be a revolt in the extreme for those of us who believe we know whom to marry for life after a few random dates. Today, most men and women of the world don't even date. In the Third World, most people have their mates chosen for them.

It would be a new mankind that creates a universal pronoun embracing "man" and "womb-man." A revolution of the spirit would be a blessing, not an outlet to spill blood and spread misery in the fulfillment of its aim. Rather than cutting off heads, a true revolution's guillotine would slice off head-trips, conditioning, psychological wounds; it would chop off expectations of others, neediness, unhappiness. Fear. Misery would be sent to the *gulag* as counterrevolutionary behavior.

To allow each individual an equal right to be unique would be a revolution no George Washington, Bakunin, Simón Bolívar or Ronald Reagan could ever imagine. The commissars of tomorrow's Aquarian dispensation would attempt a real brainwashing of the human mind. There would be a hosing off of the ancient grit of nation-worship. The mind's mirror intelligence would lose the sweaty-with-political-piety fingerprint of state-sanctioned gods. Conditioning's paint strokes called the Pope, Pedagogue, Nuclear Parent, Priest and Politician would be scrubbed away. Such a positive wave of brainwashing has been predicted.

The coming spiritual rebellion in human consciousness is one of the largest collective forecasts in the minority prophetic vote for man's survival. It foresees a new mankind on the horizon. Its actual form is a mystery; prophets and mystics alike hint that it is neither completely a genetic mutation nor solely a psycho-spiritual change of mind.

The new man — Homo Novus — is collectively "fore"-scribed, rather than "described," as a synthesis of heaven and Earth, materialism and spirit. He/she is able to flow with the chaos and order of the paradoxical Aquarian millennium. S/he will be equally scientist and mystic.

In 1955, D.E. Stevens, narrator and editor of *Listen, Humanity,* recorded Meher Baba describing a future humanity that would heed science and its practical attainments. According to this Indian mystic, science helps spirituality rather than hinders it. Right or wrong science is a question of right use; or to put it in his words, *Just as healthy art is an overflowing of spirituality, so science when properly handled can be an expression and fulfillment of the spirit.*

The modern French seer, Mario de Sabato, like his compatriot of another time, Nostradamus, saw 1993 as the pivotal year for the beginning of the soul's revolt against the past. Not only will we see the flame of a new religiousness blossoming in the final seven years of this century, but also a *new evolution of man in every sense.* Thus will begin the slow fade-out or sudden nuclear burn-out of humanity as we have known it — the humanity of countless wars, division, competitiveness, and religious cock-and-bull stories.

The old-fashioned human who glories in death and destruction, who accentuates the conquerors over the Christs in his teachings — this life-negative creature that denies "huwomanity" their equality — is *Homo Moriens*. He has but one destiny — death. Some prophets call him the necessary cannon fodder for Armageddon, whether it is ecological or politically induced.

Regina, the German seeress, entertained her European blue-blooded guests of the Edwardian era with trances in which she pointed to — Homo Moriens expressing his destiny to be the terminator and the terminated through world wars. From his compassionately blunt point of view as the Zorba the Greek of mystics, George Gurdjieff views Homo Moriens, the man of death, as necessary "human shits" or fertilizer for the flowering of the new humanity. The black methane of their negativity, uncreativeness, their tradition-bound-and-blind believing, will act as the proper muck and muddle to trigger the germination and sprouting of a new man.

Edgar Cayce often stressed that if a soul doesn't reach a certain level of spiritual development, it will disintegrate and not reincarnate ever again. It seems that some souls transcend the wheel of life and death and others fall below it. Gurdjieff's insight is even harder to swallow. He says that we don't even have a soul. In other words, most of us belong to the class Homo Moriens, and death and dissolution of our souls is our only destiny. Our only hope then is to earn the right to have a soul. Only by the commitment to, as Gurdjieff says, "remembering self" every moment in every action, thought and feeling, can one "create one's soul."

There is a divergence of prophetic and mystical opinion as to whether those born into the genes and means of Homo Moriens can jump from fertilizer to flower. Forecasters like Blavatsky, the Biblical prophets, and Regina are of the "born a Homo-die a Homo Moriens school, while Osho, Da Avabhasa, Nostradamus and Meher Baba are visionaries of the transcending Homo Moriens school: Give birth to the Homo Novus within by using the manure of your own Homo Moriens personality.

Whatever way the garden of man is fertilized and seeded, several prophets throw a collective vision at us from many presents-past. In 1954 Meher Baba predicted a new world culture which would live an affirmative and creative life with meditation and love. He foresaw a new humanity with an "integral vision" which would perfect a comprehensive cultural synthesis between mind and spirit.

In a moment lived thirty years later, Osho foresaw an equally utopian synthesis resolving history's longest conflict, that between man and woman: *For the new age, for the new man, there are going to be new ways of loving too, that are more civilized and cultured....The bedroom will become a temple; now it has become a battlefield.* It seems that romance may not go to hell but go to giggling in the Aquarian Age.

The nineteenth-century American visionary, David Goodman Croly, could envision the Homo Novian celebrants on the future's horizon and see how they would handle the religion-thing: *Because Christianity and the other major religions are not compatible with scientific knowledge, man will satisfy his emotional/spiritual cravings with art.* Sunday church is replaced by Sunday in the sunflower fields, trying to grasp the subtle prayers of flowers with the paint and passion-play-fulness of a Van Gogh.

Perhaps J. Krishnamurti expressed in the clearest terms what qualities one needs to blossom out of Homo Morien manure, when in 1929 he said, *Those who really desire to understand, who are looking to find that which is eternal, without beginning and without an end, will walk together with a greater intensity, will be a danger to everything that is unessential, to unrealities, to shadows. And they will concentrate, they will become the flame, because they understand.* (From the Manifesto: *Truth is a Pathless Land.*)

One hundred years ago, Madame Blavatsky saw a future in which America becomes the cradle of the new mankind. Over 1,800 years before she set foot on North American soil, the Toltec mystic Kate-Zahl was carried in his meditations into a visionary dream: he saw the skyline of Tula — the present-day Toltec ruins of Teotihuacan in Mexico — being transformed sometime in our distant future from a ruin into the richness of a religious city rebuilt by Homo Novus:

The heavens parted and a rising golden sun shone down on another Tula. Plainly I could see the valley, but the city was one I knew not. I was lifted beyond the cold earth. No longer I saw the Age of Destruction. Gone was the terrible Age of Warfare. I was looking beyond the Age of Carnage. Walk with me though this Age of the Future. Tula shines in all its glory, but the metals are types we know not. Loving hands have rebuilt the parkways, have paved the streets, have reconstructed the temples. There is a great building where the books are kept for the scholars, and many are those who came to read them. Tula is a great center of culture. Shining again is my Father's temple. You will see again the same inscriptions which today your eyes are seeing, but now all people can read. Come to the metropolis of the future. Here are buildings unlike those we fashion, yet they have breathless beauty. Here people dress in materials we know not, travel in manners beyond our knowledge, but more important than all this difference are the faces of the people. Gone is the shadow of fear and suffering, for man no longer sacrifices and he has outgrown the wars of his childhood. Now he walks full statured toward his destiny — in the Golden Age of Learning.

This is not us. But it is up to us to make it so and live happily ever laughter.

HOMO MORIENS:

As we near the last decade of this century, we will encounter evil beings who are intent on taking advantage of everyone....This is the last desperate attempt by evil forces to control the Earth before they realize that their power will be eclipsed by the shift [of the Earth's axis] and the New Age. **Spirit guides of Ruth Montgomery (1986) Hrd**

The Atlanteans of the latter destructive period [ie, those responsible for the sinking of the continent] are making their last-ditch fight, albeit subconsciously, to deface the beautiful Earth and its peoples. They are wicked and have learned nothing through these long ages. They are a dying breed. **Spirit guides of Ruth Montgomery (1986) Hrd**

The old man, the way he has existed for centuries, is afraid of life — not afraid of death. Death, he worships; life he renounces... **(GFutr)**
The old man was basically taught to be a hypocrite; the greater hypocrite he was, the more honored, the more rewarded...because he had settled with society. **(GrCh)**
...the old man is determined to
die, committed to commit suicide. Let him die peacefully. **(DtoD)**
Osho (1987 & 1985)

A man who strays from the path of understanding comes to rest in the company of the dead.
Proverbs 21:16

A peculiar generation now exists on this Earth, which does not carry an urge for inner growth but only death for the whole race. And some day, at some future time, people will say: there lived a clan and here and there again — Germans, Britons, or Franks — the old, eternal law induced them to dig their own graves. They are digging graves also for their own souls. Britons, Franks or Germans or whatever the country, where they live: they are all united by an old law, which provides that they wither and die. When the sun will again rise over the graves in golden glory, a new generation will arise in the course of time and a new mankind.
Seeress Regina (early 20th century)

What Regina calls the *old eternal* law could stand for the outmoded religions and fossilized moralities people resist letting go of. Her cryptic use of *the sun* may be a dating for the death of the "old man" and an appearance of the new at the onset of the twenty-first century.

In 1989 Indian astrologer Bejan Daruwalla used the prophetic math of the Jewish Kabala to conclude that the sun stands for the twenty-first century and not the twentieth:

This is what the Kabala says about the number 21, that is the twenty-first century: The World Accession to leadership, Temporal and Spiritual. Prosperity Cycle in Mundane Affairs. Advancement of Backward People [ie, Homo Moriens]. Adept. Proper use of talent in arts, science, commerce. The power of Peace. The Hebrew Letter Schin, *Planetary Ruler, The Luminous One, the Sun.*

Tell me, readers, does this sound like Dooms day to you? To me, it sounds like the best, brightest, greatest century we will ever have: in other words, shades of paradise on Earth!

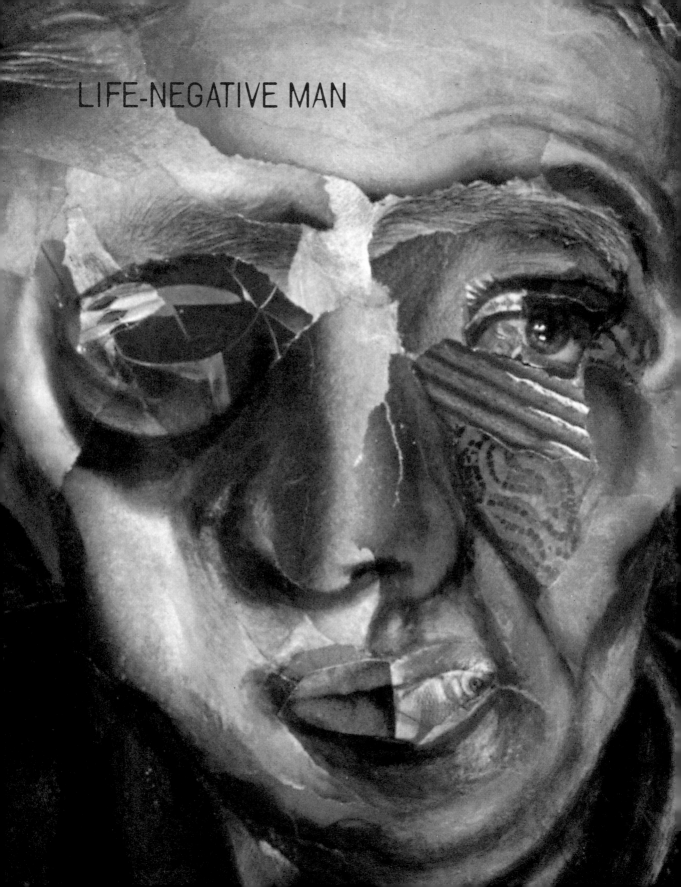

LIFE-NEGATIVE MAN

Zorba THE BUDDHA

The new man will stop all kinds of experiments which are increasing the heat of the atmosphere around the Earth, because the priority is life, not your experiments. [He] will not send rockets to create holes from which death rays can enter into our atmosphere.

Osho (1987) Razr

According to some of this century's most avant garde mystics, the best way to prevent people from attaining enlightenment is to send them into a monk's life of renunciation and celibacy. One of the new points of view arising from influences of the dawning Aquarian Age poses that a re-examination of the life of Lord Gautama Buddha — considered by most Asians to be the penultimate renunciate — will reveal that the greatest seekers begin their search first as over-fulfilled Epicureans. One of tomorrow's spiritual revelations will be that for twenty-five centuries millions of miserable monks have been living a formula for nirvana as upside-down as yogic headstands.

In Buddhist folklore it is said that upon Gautama's birth, an astrologer predicted that he would become either a great world conqueror or a great saint. His father, a king of the warrior caste, did not intend his son to wield a begging bowl rather than a sword. He conspired to make his son's life so luxurious and sensually gratifying that the young prince would never think of renouncing the world. Until Gautama was twenty-eight, he had all the sex, drugs and rock 'n' roll the fifth century BC could offer. He was a total hedonist, sensualist, an Epicurean far above and beyond Epicurus himself. But his father's plan backfired. Gautama became so satisfied that he was almost bored out of his mind.

Osho, one of Buddha's modern-day spiritual revisionists, argues that satiation was the chief cause of Gautama's renouncing the world and becoming a spiritual master. Like many mystics of this century, Osho foresees the coming of new men and women who will be a synthesis of East and West, of materialism and of the spirit, a new man who he predicts will be called "Zorba the Buddha."

To him a solely materialistic or solely spiritual man is not a whole man. The earthy, hedonistic man is like the fictional character Zorba the Greek: All body, all salt of the earth, but with no soul; whereas Buddha is all otherworldly and has lost touch with the body. If Osho's foresight is correct the coming centuries will see lusty monks of a different "habit." They will take a spin on life's wheel of fortune rather than spin a prayer wheel. Laughter will be the new mantra. The buddhas of the future will have their heads in nirvana's cloud and their feet planted firmly on the savory and sensuous earth.

I saw the sun-eyed children of a
marvelous dawn
...The massive barrier-breakers of
the world
...The architects of immortality
...Bodies made beautiful by the
Spirit's light,
Carrying the magic word, the
mystic fire,
Carrying the Dionysian cup
of joy Sri Aurobind (1946-47) Sav

HOMO NOVUS: THE NEW MAN

...even now, under our very eyes, the new Race and races are preparing to be formed, and that it is in America that the transformation will take place....Thus it is the mankind of the New World...whose mission and Karma it is to sow the seeds for a forthcoming grander, and far more glorious Race than any of those we know of at present. The Cycles of Matter will be succeeded by the Cycles of Spirituality and a fully developed mind.
Madame Blavatsky (1888) ScDoc III

A new world is born. At present we are right in the midst of a transitional period in which the two are mingled: The old world persists, yet all-powerful, continuing to dominate the ordinary consciousness, and the new one slips in quietly...unobserved to the extent that externally it changes little for the moment....And yet it works, it grows, till one day it will be sufficiently strong to impose itself visibly. **The Mother (1931) Conv**

Man is also a new stage in the event of time. His newness or uniqueness is hidden. This higher brain is the structural cauldron of the present and future evolutionary changes of Man and what is beyond Man in the scheme of the World. **Da Avabhasa (1978) Bdy**

[The new race] will silently come into existence...the peculiar children who will grow into peculiar men and women — will be regarded as abnormal oddities, physically and mentally. Then, as they increase, and the numbers become with every age greater, one day they will awake to find themselves in a majority. Then present men will begin to be regarded as exceptional mongrels, until they die out in their turn in civilized lands. **Madame Blavatsky (1888) ScDoc III**

"The most important need of humanity today is to be made aware that its past has betrayed it; that there is no point in continuing the past — it will be suicidal — that a new humanity is absolutely and urgently needed. And the new humanity will not be a society in the old sense, where individuals are only parts of it.

"The new humanity will be a meeting of individuals, where individuals are the masters, and society is to serve them. It will have many different aspects to it. It will not have so many religions, it will have only a religious consciousness. It will not have a despot God as a creator, because that implies the slavery of man. It will have godliness as a quality of ultimate achievement — a quality of enlightenment. God will be spread all over — in everything, in every being.

"The individual, for the first time, will not be programmed; he will be helped to be himself. He will not be given any ideals, any discipline, any certain pattern; he will be given only a tremendous love for freedom, so that he can sacrifice *everything* — even his own life — but he cannot sacrifice freedom. The new individual will not be repressive; he will be natural, with no inhibitions, expressive of everything that he has; just the way plants express themselves in different colors, in different fragrances, each individual will be doing the same.

"The new individual will not have the false idea that all human beings are equal. They are not — they are unique, which is a far superior concept than equality. Although the new individuals will not be equal, they will have equal opportunity to grow into their potential, whatever it is.

"There will be no marriage; love will be the only law. Children will be part of the commune, and only the commune will decide who is capable of being a mother and who is capable of being a father. It cannot be at random and accidental. And it will be according to the needs of the Earth.

...HOMO NOVUS: THE ONLY HOPE FOR

"The new humanity will have an ecology in which nature is not to be conquered, but lived and loved. We are part of it — how can we conquer it? It will not have any races, no distinctions between nations, between colors, castes. It will not have any nations, any states; it will have only a functional world government.

"The new man is an absolute necessity. The old is dead or is dying...cannot survive long. And if we cannot produce a new human being, then humanity will disappear from the Earth."

Osho (1986) Beyond Psychology

"It is hoping against hope — but I still hope that the danger of global death will be the shock which awakens humanity. If man survives after this century, it will be a new man and a new humanity. One thing is certain: Either man has to die or man has to change. I cannot think that man will choose to die. The longing for life is so great...just to think that the Earth has become dead — no trees, no humanity, no birds, no animals...it is such a great crisis...And if the third world war does not happen, that will mean a great change, a tidal change in human consciousness. We will see a new man."

Osho (1987) The New Dawn

THE FUTURE

Yet now, when all seems lost, miraculously a new dawn has
come. The sun shines bright again...
Earth rises a second time
from the sea, clad with green pastures and forests —
a thing of
beauty to behold. The morning air is filled with the sounds
of falling waters.

[This could refer to the seas falling after the
curtailment of global warming in the next century, or it may
indicate the end of floods after the axis shift around 2000.]

In this new Earth, Evil has ended and every ill has ceased.
...Pure are they, the members of this new race,
and without stain.
The food they share with one another in Time's second
morning is honey dew, and their children shall overspread
the Earth.

From The Ragnarök: Ancient Norse prophecy

[This is one of the few hopeful references suggesting there
will be a new flow of time. Time will run out for the old
man and his archaic ways, but not for humanity as such.]

...All nations should become one in faith, and all men as
brothers; that the bonds of affection and unity between the sons
of men should be strengthened; that diversity of religion should
cease, and differences of race be annulled.

Bahá'u'lláh (1890)

MEDITATION

While watching the changing world outside and the movement of thoughts and emotions within, I become more
aware of a presence that doesn't change. It is impossible
to define in words what this is, but I do know that it is

THERAPY FOR MADHOUSE EARTH

always the same presence; that when it comes, it is everywhere and nowhere at once; that nothing I'm thinking or
feeling can connect with it; that it is so still it doesn't
exist and so subtle that at times it is too alive to bear.

I remember first encountering this presence as a child. Then I

lost touch with it. The losing was a gradual process called growing up. I experienced it as "walling up." Gradually Pink Floyd's bricks piled up around me, blocking out the limitless view of the innocent and unnamable wonder that a child feels by just being alive. I was taught to hold on to thoughts and possess emotional expectations; in short, I was given recipes for accepted adult behavior. I painfully learned to live in a world where beauty and the art of being alive is pushed lower and lower on life's laundry list; I was taught to survive in a culture where cars, money, face-saving at all costs, and manipulation of others are the primary values. I had come into the world as a cosmos and it looked like I would leave the world as a spent commodity.

When it got too much, I got pushed to the edge of a nervous breakthrough. There were only two alternatives: rediscover what I had lost, or lose myself.

How can I tell you about this journey inward to find my self again, without tarnishing it with judgments, dialectics, words?

If I ever greet you beyond the veil of these words, we might find a way to share this mystery called meditation. I will not speak of it, I will sing it to you, dance it; we will hug meditation, we will "silent" meditation. Our sutras will be giggles. I'd rather not use words, but this is a book, after all, and this is the Kali Yuga: An age that uses the least adequate media to express the deepest truths.

With that said, let's stumble ahead in the darkness of print:

I do not yet know "who" I am but meditation allows me to often see "how" I am.

Through understanding the hows of my happiness-sadness-love-and-hate, I observe their rough-and-tumble within me with greater distance. Meditation helps me to watch the movement of my thoughts and emotions. I become more a spectator than a participant in stress, pain and denial. Through meditation I have been able to uncover the root cause of all my misery: The fear of change, and lurking behind that, the ultimate fear — the fear of death. Meditation has helped me observe the mechanics of misery and fear.

There's a Sufi metaphor about identification. Misery doesn't come to us, we unconsciously seek it out and hold onto it, like flinging our arms around a pillar. As we squeeze tighter we yell, "Oh, if I only could be rid of this misery and pain!"

This misunderstanding is our choice. As American mystic Da Avabhasa once remarked, we "do" misery, we "do" expectation. Hell is not a place, we "do" it.

We "do" predictability. We make prophecy work because we are so damned predictable. Caught in the cycles of time and unconsciousness, we have repeated again and again the behaviors that make it easy for the seers to prophesy us unto doomsday.

The crossroads in time where we find ourselves now demands a spiritual rebellion that can prevent us from "doing" an apocalypse of doom in all dimensions. The final years of this decade require that a significant number of people get some distance from themselves to see how they tick. There is a need for a global awareness of how, from the moment we emerge from the womb, we are programmed from birth onwards to imprint concepts that are totally divorced from our deepest natural understanding of life. Only when there are enough people ready to rebel against this ancient circle of programmed misery and predictability can it be broken. I take the hopeful view that no definite future can be clearly forecast after the millennium because mankind will have succeeded in accomplishing this.

The spiritual rebels will certainly be in the minority. Most of us are bound to avoid encountering the raw revelation that we actually love our misery and hold its pillar fast to our breasts while we wish and wail for a new age. In this decade, billions will discover that misery and fear is all they know. But unlike most people, the spiritual rebels will break out of their prison of conditioning and become the new humanity arising out of the rubble of the old.

The spiritual rebels will not pander to the death cults of current religious thought; they will live *this* life so fully that heaven will exist inside them, not somewhere in the afterworld. They will escape from their jail keeper called God. And they will slip from the bonds of national identification to become citizens of the world.

Meditation is the method to uncover all the illusions that keep humanity in bondage. It is the only hope this planet has to avoid the collision course so many seers down the centuries have predicted for us. Every misunderstanding and distortion of truth that has blindly dragged us to the brink of the precipice will have to be jettisoned, if we are not to plunge over the edge at the end of this decade.

This is why the emergence of the new breed, Homo Novus — the true strangers among us — is viewed with suspicion and fear. These people cannot be controlled by the priests or the politicians. They do not pray for happiness, they *are* happiness. In the midst of a suicidal world, their way of life exposes the death wish society must encounter and transcend if it is to survive.

The spiritual rebels are the soul and spirit of the new Golden Age. And meditation is their new science.

My own journey into meditation and spiritual rebellion

began from a nasty experience I had as a seven-year-old, when I moved to a new school in a new neighborhood.

I was in love with the little girl sitting next to me in my second-grade class. When she was moved to another spot in the classroom, I was brokenhearted. The teacher, like many adults I knew then (and now), liked to hide her fears behind a facade of power. She looked as big as her fear, and when she demanded to know what was the matter with me, I didn't speak in words but in pain, and sobbed into my hands. My expression of naked feeling elicited from kids and teacher alike an immediate wave of hostility and derision. For weeks after that event, I was treated with disgust and fear as some kind of "thing."

During an atomic air raid drill for World War III — so common in the years following the Cuban Missile Crisis — I accidentally bumped into the largest kid in the class while groping in the dark classroom for my place to "duck and cover" myself. His immediate reaction was to slug me in the stomach. Crying, doubled over in agony, I asked him why he hit me. Still a kid, and not yet completely formed into the proper masked and label-loving adult, he was struck by the blow of my existential question.

"I don't know!" he blinked, bewildered. "It's what dad told me to do. When you're hit, hit back."

That was my first hard lesson in programming.

It got worse. When he and a gang of kids would chase me off the playground every recess with tether balls and stones, I had to run my little ass into a nearby storm drain trench. As I huddled there, I was forced to face the reality that people were neither sane nor loving; they only pretended to be. The children would forget about me and wander back to the swings and sandboxes, but I could never forget this heartbreaking truth, heartbreaking because it set me apart from people. It made me aware that I am alone.

But no bitter experience is without its sweetness. Crouching in the trench, chin buried in the pungent grass, with tearful, wide eyes gazing at dancing clouds in a silent sky, I also became aware that Nature did not — could not — reject me. It was more than a friend, it was a beloved. As I became aware of my aloneness, Nature accepted it. Was it.

After that I could not see fear in Nature, only innocence. There is no judgment in Nature's stases and catastrophes. It is unnatural man, divided against the Self, who judges them. There is life, death, violence and peace flowing from animals, earth and plants. They don't judge or feel division like we do. The rose bush doesn't compare itself to the lotus and commit suicide. In fact, no animal except man commits suicide or indiscriminately slaughters its own kind. We compare, and throw our minds and hearts into the turmoil of division. This division becomes projected onto all of our relationships with other human beings and with the Earth. As we become more and more split off from our fellow humans and from the planet, we create all the conditions that draw us closer to death, personal and global.

The insights of my personal apocalypse made it hard for me to buy into all the ways people suppress the natural within and destroy the ecology of Earth with their fearful greed. A new and tender consciousness arose which at the time had no words. Looking back on it years later, I realized it was then I made the commitment that has forever sabotaged my efforts to embrace life as it is socially presented and commonly accepted. That is why I never succeeded in opera or fit with anyone's projections and expectations.

I somehow understood in my child-mind that a truly natural, spiritual person would be as silent as that sky, as playful as those eddying clouds, as rich with the fragrance of wisdom as the grass cushioning my chin. A natural human being, like the grass, could not dictate or push his or her fragrance on others but would simply be unable to contain it.

In the intensity of that terrible moment of rejection, Nature showed me how to sniff out an authentic member of the genus Homo Novus. These flowers in humanity's manure field would possess the silence of Nature and an equanimity in the face of Nature's two polar complementaries — destruction and creation. I would instinctively recognize these members of the new human race by their laughter and celebration uncaused, by the gleam of a second and consciously recognized childhood sparking in their eyes. I would know them if their silent gaze and presence was not disturbed by fame or infamy, riches or poverty, life or death. They would remain inwardly blissful, unaffected by life's vagaries or any attempts by those outside of their silence to abuse and disturb them. The Homo Novus would be happy in a palace or in the dirtiest holding cell. And if sadness on rare occasions came to their doors, they would watch it rather than indulge it, until sadness moved on.

I have spent the last fifteen years traveling around the world in search of such men and women. I have found them. They are my criterion for saying you and I are unnatural. They have also showed me — in their unique ways — that meditation, the science of self-observation, is the only medicine that can cure the insanity we have become and give us back a future.

I do not ask or expect you to believe me. In fact, there is no point in either believing or debunking what I'm saying without a sincere and intimate investigation on your own.

I am satisfied with the ongoing process of my own apocalypse. I have met a few members of the genus Homo Novus and their fragrance is meditation.

The words "meditation" and "medicine" have the same ancient root. One heals the body, the other, the soul. If we look from a more occidental angle, the words "meditation" and "mechanic" also have the same roots. If you can watch your entire mental-emotional engine without getting caught in its grinding gears, if you can see it as the dispassionate and watchful "mechanic," you will then find ways to fix your "engine." It will start working for you rather than disturb your ride through life.

I can thank **the apocalypse of meditation** for pushing me out of an operatic career. Nine months before I had my nervous "breakthrough," I became interested in meditation as a way to relieve stress and refresh my body-mind. But I soon found out that meditation was more than a mere exercise in positive thinking or an exercise in creative visualizations to find new and improved love, and abundant money and health. Taking twenty minutes a day to watch my breath turned my outward focus in. This turning *in* did more than slow the heartbeat and ward off high blood pressure of the upwardly mobile professional I had become. It reminded me of childhood's timeless time when trees fall and nobody is there to hear, when flowers grow with nobody there to see, and feelings flow with nobody there to feel. Through watching the simple witnessing of life's infinite movements I unearthed the pleasure in paradox.

I rediscovered moments when life became a poetry again.

When roots of silence sink where I sit so still soaking earth softly. And deep silence dives in skies caught cavorting behind closed eyes.

Meditation started washing my "looking" with eternity's twinkle.

After a few months of practicing simple Zen exercises of watching the breath, I couldn't understand why something so pleasurable and revitalizing wasn't universally practiced. Then a moment came when the new awareness reached deeper into my unconscious and threw a shattering light on my illusions.

"It" can happen at any moment. Especially if you watch your breath, if you are still, waiting. Something trips the existential switch and the screen of your personal id soap opera blinks out. A void fills the void, wiggling through a brief crack in the noise of the mind. It is the apocalypse of truth breaking the sliding bolt that locks away all the lies from one's sight. It is a thief in the night, stealth-like and silent, a wave, invisible, undermining one's cliff of solid ego.

In one unguarded moment I became transparent. And though the "guard" of moments — the personality — instantly returned, I could not completely forget the void's abiding and spacious sky of silence.

For me, this was and is the threshold of meditation. It is as much a death as a delight. Meditation's techniques of self-observation showed me my thoughts were no more "mine" to possess than a wind racing through empty dreams.

At Meditation's first penetration, I became aware that this "John Hogue" was a fiction written by many hands — none of them my own. A name, a religion, a country, and finally a personality had been applied like bricks, imprisoning the authentic being my mother and father had brought into the world. Early on, the label bricks were of soft and pliable mud, easy for a child to break free of, but between the ages of seven and fourteen, the bricks turned into unyielding stone. I had become my own memorial statue while still living. The child seized these brick labels as greedily as he seized the tit. What else could he do? That child needed the grownups, and the grownups felt they needed to condition him for the coming life of lies and limitations. The child of silence became a gullible youth who listened to society's learned hypocrites — the priests of impossible horizons — who, save for the noise of their roaring, have never encountered the things they taught:

gods, heavens, and hells.

The youth became imprisoned in adulthood's emotional and psychic castle. At the age of twenty-one, meditation's taste of disidentification made John aware that his "buddha" had atrophied. The Enlightened One reduced to "enlightened once". Fear had become his bed mate, denial, the sheets.

Like medicines, meditation can be bitter. Initially, it can give you worse pain than the disease itself. The cancer patient would like to escape the only therapies that might possibly save him, but if he chooses to fight for his life, painful chemotherapy or radiation will be risked.

After abandoning an operatic career, I began taking risks. I again started asking all those questions children ask and adults avoid. Essential questions: Why am I unhappy? Why do I fear? Who am I?

At first I tried the usual New Age assortment of meditations that heightened psychic powers. After four years of this, I could see auras, read minds, etc. Still, the essential facticity of my being was hidden. While astral traveling I had many fascinating experiences, but they didn't make me any more aware of "who" was zipping in and out of the astral realms. Who was seeing auras? Who indeed was opening his chakras? Who was reading minds? Who was this mystery that sometimes accurately saw the future?

Whether I am looking at a cup of coffee or seeing my past and future lives, how can any of these experiences be me? Who, after all, is the watcher?

Frustration led me away from the psychic seeker-sucking game to an exploration of many Eastern techniques of classical meditation such as Yoga and Vipassana — which is Buddha's technique of sitting watching the "suchness" of thoughts and emotions. I also had direct experiences with some new and radical seeds of Eastern meditation set to sprout in the West sometime in the next century.

Over the last decade, I have encountered what in my opinion were many charlatans and also a handful of authentic masters. An account of these spiritual examinations, meditation therapies and teachers would be too vast to describe here. A detailed account will be forthcoming in *The Second Coming Syndrome*, the third and final book in my prophecy trilogy.

In *The Millennium Book of Prophecy*, I can only touch on some of the radically new ideas about meditation that have been introduced in the latter half of this century. For instance, if you fly to the town of Poona, India, just 100 kilometers from the labyrinth city of Bombay, you will encounter the most striking examples of this. Nestled in the town that gave Tantra one of its greatest ancient centers, the birthplace of one of India's most significant twentieth-century mystics, Meher Baba, is the Ashram (spiritual campus) presently called Osho Commune International.

There you will find the disciples of the late Osho carrying on their master's vision of providing a Club Meditation for the creation of the new man. It is a thirty-two acre resort of luscious gardens, black granite and marble buildings and pyramids, a strange contrast to the surrounding squalor of a bustling Third World city.

It has undergone many alterations since I first entered its gates back in 1980, when it was known as the Poona Ashram of the notorious sex guru, Bhagwan Shree Rajneesh. I had gone there two years prior to my longer stay at the Rajneeshee Ranch in Oregon. While the later experiment allowed me the opportunity to sample social experiments in future living, the Poona Ashram offered me a taste of life at the frontiers of the Human-Potential Movement.

In the first volume of my prophecy trilogy (to be expanded and updated in 1994 under the title *Nostradamus. The New Revelations*), I examined predictions of Nostradamus regarding the loose fellowship of therapists and meditation movements of the last fifty years, known as the Human-Potential Movement. Nostradamus pegged this movement as the source of tomorrow's spiritual rebellion. I was determined to find out what it was all about. Frankly, when I did, it shocked me. Up until I became acquainted with these new therapy movements, I never knew that screaming, pillow beating, or openly exploring my sexuality in a therapy group could be the beginning of treading an authentic spiritual path. When I first heard about the Ashram, I was told they practiced the most cathartic meditation technique in the H.P. Movement. At first it was called Chaotic Meditation. Then the name was changed to Dynamic Meditation. I was about to find out what it was, firsthand.

Osho is famous in meditation circles for his controversial claim that modern man, particularly the Westernized variety, is the most restless and neurotic human that has ever existed. With enough forceful discipline, he may be able to keep his body still, but he cannot still his mind. Vipassana, Yoga and all the rest of the 112 techniques from the East are made for simpler people of more innocent and less complex times.

Before sitting in silence can happen, the accumulation of stress, anger, and repression packed away behind modern man's happy-face mask has to be creatively and safely expressed. Osho claimed to have a meditation technique which, if practiced all over the world every morning, could be used as a release valve for all the pent-up collective angers that periodically erupt in a binge of global slaughter — what I've coined as the will to catharsis.

The meditation has five sections and is done to a specially composed tape by the New Age composer, Deuter. During the first part, of ten minutes' duration, you breathe rapidly and deeply through the nose. This is supposed to build up the energy that can help you release the flame of pent-up repressions. Then, at the sound of a gong, the music changes into waves of sonic wildness. For the second ten minutes you are to cathart — laughter, anger, gibberish, fear, rage, madness — whatever comes up. You are to dance it, shake it, scream it, sing it, but you are absolutely not allowed to hurt others in the hall. The third gong brings on a ten-minute hop of heaven-hell. You stop catharting and reach your arms straight over your head and jump to the pulsing synthesizers and drums. Every time your feet hit the ground you yell "Hoo!" with all you've got, as if it meant life or death. This is a variation of a Sufi technique which is designed to bring your energies up out of your sex center and take them through the rest of your body.

At the last hop and "Hoo!" the pre-recorded voice of Osho yelling "stop!" cuts the music like splitting a thunderbolt. You then freeze in place like a statue for fifteen minutes and "watch" within. Finally, there is fifteen minutes of dancing and celebrating.

The first three sections are consciously constructed to completely exhaust you. In this way, Osho's techniques are similar to those of George Gurdjieff and the meditation schools of central Asia, who believed that man had deeper and deeper layers of energy — second winds, if you will — which must first be expended before real meditation can happen. The more total your exhaustion, the deeper the plunge within your being.

Many mystics, past and present, say that only when one reaches a crisis can an authentic spiritual journey begin. A state of extreme urgency is a must. Totality is the ultimate credential. Only when the inner search becomes a life and death issue can the tension be brought to the breaking point and send you into an altered state of deep relaxation.

Dynamic Meditation uses the first three sections to prepare you for the state of dispassionate witnessing that is the final preparation for meditation. The rapid breathing brings

up the repressed tensions; the catharsis stage then activates a good spiritual vomit; the hopping nearly exhausts you, bringing the body to the limit of its endurance, and then you can fall into an altered state — a meditator's version of a "runner's high," so to speak.

My understanding of mediation techniques is that they relax you into witnessing. These techniques themselves, however, are not true meditation, nor are all those so-called spiritual experiences one has through being still and silent. Meditation is not an experience. Meditation is not a thing one does to get something, but it does seem that some preparation for meditation is needed. The silent witnessing of meditation only blossoms from the waiting, the allowing, the parking of the body-mind, the deep relaxation without a goal or expectation, because to have goals and expectations is to be tense.

Back in 1980 when Dynamic Meditation was first described to me, it was enough to stir a volcano of rage and fear underneath my spiritual façade. The night before doing my first Dynamic Meditation was one of the darkest in my life. I experienced the essence behind the terrible words of St John's prophecy about people trying to pull the mountains over themselves to escape facing the "revelation of truth." That night moments passed like the peeling of skin. I tossed and turned, then ran to the bathroom and saw the puffy face and slit eyes of a man stunned by his own terror.

I never felt so stuck. I could not go back and I did not want to go forward into the unknown that a cathartic meditation would reveal. I writhed about in the damp fishing net of my bed covers in a tropical-fever night, cursing myself, Osho, meditation, and all the mystics that disturb people's sleep.

I could sense that if I went too far with this meditation experiment I would reach a point when I could no longer return to that deep sleep. I tell you, reader: Since my experience of that night I see a terrible revelation about everyone — we don't want to wake up. We don't want happiness, we don't want *real* freedom because to attain it we must confront all that is false in us, chaining us down. To be a meditator is to be mother to the birth of our own inner child. The master or the meditation technique is the midwife. They can help, they can hold your hand, they can indicate what you have to do, but the pain of giving birth to yourself is encountered alone. No one else feels the contractions of your womb like you do.

When 6 AM came, I somehow managed to drag myself out under the wide, wall-less dome of the meditation hall. There I mingled with several hundred groggy meditators. We blew our noses and blindfolded ourselves, digging bare feet into the cold cement floor. All braced themselves for the first gong, which would strip the pre-dawn air of its silence with Deuter's apocalyptic muzak.

At the sound of the gong, the knotted rubber band of my pent-up terrors released its prop and off went my model plane personality into the pre-dawn darkness.

By the end of the third stage of Dynamic, if I had any ambition for nirvana left, the hopping and "hooing" was squeezing it to the relaxing point. When the recorded blast of "STOP!" cut the sweaty air, I froze-fell to the cold floor. For fifteen minutes, I became a stillness floating on the waves of a gasping-for-breath — too tired to think, too cleaned by catharsis to be afraid.

What can I say to you about this heap of John Hogue lying on the cement floor? What words can convey the "down-down-down; deeper-deeper-deeper" he had become for those eternal minutes?

Clear, because nothing obstructs.
Soundless, because it has no end of depth.
No bottom for the sounding. No surface for the sounder.
"It" — looking without eyes and dying without death.

A cloud of darkness, I give my self in rains,
Letting fall showers of sorrow until a burning sky of joy remains.

The delicate notes of the flute heralding the final stage of Dynamic Meditation brought the first awareness of that inner sky to me. Drained limbs made an effort to move, twitching like a fresh corpse. The music caressed more movements out of my still pool of exhaustion until I was able to lift my heavy, blindfolded head. At that moment, I was drowned in an explosion of white light as bracing as a cold mountain stream. The light took me up in its embrace. Where one exhausted man lay a moment before, there appeared a dancing fool.

In my veins fired life, dyeing the darkness in countless fire clouds. To dance was to touch gold with eyes and bathe the world with sight. By the end of the celebration music, and as the rising sun cut shafts of light though bird calls and the tropical plants surrounding the hall, I had become the blue-viewing of sky.

Now when the world's misery pours tears out of my eyes, they are not only of suffering or the grieving spawn of expectations and desires, they are the realization that sanity is possible. Humans suffer because they cannot completely return to an animal's innocent state. I am one human who is convinced that all humans suffer life on Earth because to one degree or another they have sand chaffing their dreams. They hurt because they have the destiny — mostly ignored and repressed — to make within themselves a pearl called Homo Novus, the New Humanity.

Prophecy indicates that time is running out for the birth of this new humanity. The birth has to happen this very moment through a spiritual rebellion against the past. Man is destined for a catharsis, a psychic breakdown that can also become a psychic breakthrough. The choice is ours.

MEDITATION:

The words of the wise men are heard in quiet more than the cry of him that ruleth among fools.

Ecclesiastes 9:17

Science will be for making life more comfortable, more conscious, more beautiful; and meditation will become an absolute part of education all over the world. And the balance between [science and meditation] *will create the whole man. Without meditation you cannot have the clarity, and a grounding within yourself, and a vision which is simple and innocent....This* [synthesis] *can create a totally new science.*

Osho (1987) GrCh

This much we know: the two dimensions of spirit and physical being will become as one when universal law is more fully grasped. Feel the akinship with all of God's creations, and strive for that which is just. Banish fears, abolish angers, and work for the common good.

Spirit guides of Ruth Montgomery (1976) WbF

THE *Ancient*/FUTURE SCIENCE

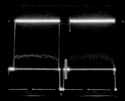

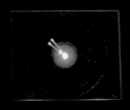

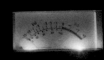

The search for religious truth in no way hinders the search for the objective reality, because both areas are absolutely separate.

Osho (1987) GrCh

"Science"

comes from the Latin word "scire," which means "to know." Over the last three centuries, the knowing which has replaced blind belief has broken humankind free from many of its superstitions. Without this revolution we never could have split the atom or reached to the Moon. Unfortunately, we are seesawing from one extreme to another, from a zealous subjectivity to measuring reality with a slide rule. Man can perform scientific miracles and walk on the waters of the Moon's Sea of Tranquillity, but he is forgetting his ultimate frontier, the subjective world within. It is not enough for man to live as a half-wit, either purely subjective or solely objective. The new mankind must be a synthesis of both.

Man's reality is set upon a metaphorical weighing scale. In the left dish is Aristotelian objectivity. Here, the science of logic, reasoning and argument requires that we take three doctrinal steps before discovering the truth of any "matter": The doctrine of *terms*, requiring correct definitions; the doctrine of *judgment*, relating to the correct affirmation or denial of the characteristics of concepts; and the doctrine of *inference*, the principle of correct reasoning represented by the syllogism, consisting of a major premise, a minor premise, and a conclusion. This is the basis for the current scientific pursuit of "knowing."

The objective discipline of science has met with great success when used to unlock the secrets of matter; however, when faced with the subjective world, the scientist is often in a dilemma. Should he deny what he thinks or experiences just because he can't see it or dissect it in his lab? This same difficulty extends to the realm of prophecy: If the "how" behind seeing future events is still a mystery, should we then deny the existence of a phenomenon we cannot explain with the objective faculty of our mind?

At no time does the discipline of objective reasoning express or give data about "who" is doing all of this reasoning. Objective thinking fails to define and measure "who" is seeing the world in dialectics. Or "who" is the judge of good and evil. Or "who" is defining Truth.

What is the quality, or essence, if you will, of the Being behind all thought, action and feeling? The "knowing" of who one is, is the "subject" of another science, the science of self-observation — meditation.

Perhaps the greatest subjective scientists of ancient times were Gautama the Buddha and the mystics of Zen. They have given man a science of subjective logic, which sits in the right-hand dish of man's metaphorical scale. It carries the reality of a subjective, trans-Aristotelian logic. The scientist is both the experimenter and the experimented.

Here, three doctrinal steps must be taken as well, before one experiences the truth of one's subjectivity. The doctrine of *terms* requires that one start with a correct recognition that the "subject" lives in disorder, pain and suffering because he or she is in an illusory state of identification with objects of matter and desire. To prove this, the subject must follow a doctrine of *judgment* and discernment called self-observation and self-remembrance. The mystics of meditation claim that through a non-judgmental observation of the suchness of thoughts, activities and emotions, one can *infer* that one experiences a state of being beyond personality, thoughts and emotions.

From this revelation a syllogism can be fashioned: Who one is is not an object but a witness of objects. By witnessing the suchness of a thought, emotion or activity, one automatically feels distance from that thought, emotion or activity. This understanding brings immediate transcendence from all division and suffering. One thereby concludes that consciousness is a freedom *beyond* the known. One can live in the world but not be of the world.

(Poor Aristotle must be barrel rolling in his tomb.)

Clearly, the source of such an awareness can never be explained by means of an Aristotelian dialectic. One cannot see or dissect consciousness, nor can the meditator objectively prove that his "experience" of consciousness is something beyond the biological mind. Objects and subjects are a universe apart. One can't make the other conform to its reality. However, the science of mysticism claims one can balance objective and subjective phenomena on reality's scales. You can't make water burn or fire wet; however, the two can brew a great cup of coffee. Polar opposites can become complementaries.

What, then, is Being? The question will remain unanswered. Instead, question and answer dissolve through witnessing. One encounters a trans-dialectic state in which one becomes amoral, or better, transmoral. If that elusiveness called Being is definable in words, it is a dialectic, an object. Therefore, nothing I have said so far can grasp the subjective. (Do you hear the ghost of Aristotle groaning?) At the onset of man's most scientific and technologically dominated century, 'Abdu'l -Bahá predicted a successful synthesis of the spiritual and material sciences in the near future:

This union will bring about true civilization where the spiritual is expressed and carried out in the material. Receiving thus, the one from the other, the greatest harmony will prevail, all people will be united, a state of great perfection will be attained, there will be a firm cementing, and this world will become a shining mirror for the reflection of the attributes of God.

Paris Talks of 'Abdu'l -Bahá (1911)

Even from a purely objective point of view, there is evidence that a revolution in the definition of science is at hand. In the latter half of this century, mankind is making friends with contradiction and paradox. Bantam Books reported a ten-fold increase in sales in its New Age/Meditation division during the 1980s. Though the 1960s are dead and buried in our celluloid memories, the mystique of Eastern religions and their disciplines of self-observation continue to attract the Western mind.

The first old guard gestalt to be undermined is what is sometimes called the newest priestly hierarchy of man, the psychologists.

MEDITATION: THE TWILIGHT OF "Primitive" PSYCHOLOGY

Within fifty years for the first time psychology will be really born. Freudian psychology is very primitive; it is like an aboriginal religion compared to Buddha. After a hundred years it will simply look silly. These people who are working in encounter, psychodrama, bio-energetics, gestalt, and others...

Their work is to contribute, to pool, all that is possible from every direction, and once the real psychology will start taking shape, they will start to disappear. Osho, (1976) Watr

This New Age will be an opening into awareness, with memories of previous lives on Earth and on other planetary spheres retained, as well as those of the spirit plane between. In other words, all minds will become open to the eternal Now. Spirit guides of Ruth Montgomery (1986) Hrd

In 1989 Dr Robert Michels, chairman of the psychiatry department at the New York Hospital Cornell Medical Center, wrote in the *Psychoanalytic Quarterly* that American psychoanalysis is "starved" for patients. He estimates that only "one in ten thousand Americans" is currently seeking solace on a shrink's couch confessional. The APA (American Psychoanalytic Association) admitted that its ranks have scarcely grown since the mid-1970s. Norman O. Brown, author of *Love's Body*, the Bible of sexual exploration during the 1960s, predicted that the therapies of the Human Potential Movement will eventually die out.

Author, playwright and meditator, Robert L. Coleman, refers to a "new gestalt that is shattering the very foundations of psychotherapy...For if the mind itself is to be ultimately transcended, why bother with all this needless psychic redecorating called therapy? One diseased mind counseling another diseased mind on the idea of health is not anyone's idea of sanity..."From the ID to the AUM": *Critique* magazine (1989).

MEDITATION:

Look then for a breakthrough in this field during the coming decade as science and medicine probe into inner man, and come to understand the importance of treating disease through ease and relaxation....Relax, meditate, and feel a part of the whole of mankind, loving and blessing all that is good, and praying for destruction of that which is evil in man.

Spirit guides of Ruth Montgomery (1976) Wbf

An enemy can hurt an enemy, and a man who hates can harm another man; but a man's own mind, if wrongly directed, can do him a far greater harm. A father or a mother, or a relative, can indeed do good to a man; but his own right-directed mind can do to him a far greater good.

Buddha (c. 500 BC) Dhm 3:42,43

Utopia IS possible. It is only a question of understanding the value of meditation.

Osho (1989)

The psychiatrist's couch may be replaced by the meditation cushion. And the new priesthood of meditation may find its ranks swelling, not with cultists but with the most disciplined scientists. Since the end of the 1960s, the number of scientists interested in finding objective evidence of meditation's benefits has continued to snowball. Esalen Institute, a mecca during the early growth of the Human-Potential Movement, published a review of over 1,200 accredited scientific investigations of contemplative activity conducted between 1931 to 1988, the majority of them after 1950.

John Sommers-Flanagan of the University of Montana and Roger Greenberg of the Syracuse University, New York, looked at forty-eight empirical studies conducted between 1979 and 1986 that linked hypertension to one's state of mind (*Brain/Mind Bulletin*, July 1989). Flanagan and Greenberg concluded that stress management was one of several remedies for the hypertense. In 1990 results presented at a meeting of the American Heart Association by Dr Redford Williams, a researcher in behavioral medicine at the Duke University Medical Center, reported a clear link between unremitting anger and heart disease.

Meditation is going mainstream in the 1990s. A major German health insurance company, AOK, ran an extensive advertising campaign on its new stress reduction program for businessmen. Their full-color ad, showing a businessman in tie and slacks meditating in the lotus posture, could be seen in all the major German magazines, on full-size billboards on the roads and in underground railway stations.

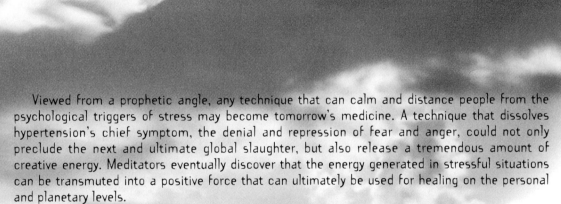

FROM "DIS-EASE" TO "Real Ease"

Viewed from a prophetic angle, any technique that can calm and distance people from the psychological triggers of stress may become tomorrow's medicine. A technique that dissolves hypertension's chief symptom, the denial and repression of fear and anger, could not only preclude the next and ultimate global slaughter, but also release a tremendous amount of creative energy. Meditators eventually discover that the energy generated in stressful situations can be transmuted into a positive force that can ultimately be used for healing on the personal and planetary levels.

Tomorrow's doctors of the mind and the body may prescribe meditation rather than drugs to heal the sick. In March 1988 *Science Today* published the report of the UK Medical Research Council's meditation experiments with 116 sufferers of mild hypertension. Chandra Patel and Michael Marmot of University College and Middlesex Hospital School of Medicine, London, divided the people into four groups. One group received drug therapy, the second received a placebo and were advised to lose weight, eat healthily, exercise, and stop smoking. The third and fourth groups took neither drugs nor a placebo. Some people were selected from each group to undergo meditation and relaxation therapy. This allowed the researchers to study the effect of drugs, placebos and relaxation therapy in various combinations. The blood pressure of people in all four groups who underwent relaxation therapy was reduced significantly. This held true whether the subjects had taken drugs for years before the experiment or only during the experiment.

MEDITATION: *Freedom* FROM CONDITIONING

As medicine becomes more costly, a session of muscle relaxation or deep breathing from the diaphragm, based on Eastern yogic and meditative techniques, will be considered a much less expensive and toxic dose of medicine to keep the doctor away.

Not only medical but also social diseases like crime might find their cure through "contemplating one's navel". Controversies about hopping yogis aside, the popularity of ancient Vedic mantra meditations, synthesized for the Western mind into a technique called Transcendental Meditation (TM), has not died out with the Doors and the Beatles. Independent studies show that Indian mystic Maharishi Mahesh Yogi's technique is more prevalent in the 1990s than at any other time.

TM is the closest thing to a mainstream meditation technique. A large majority of its adherents today are college-educated, with a significant number of scientists among them. TM has met with great success in the field of criminology as well. Allan Abrams, a part-time statistics professor at University of California at San Francisco, has co-authored a five-year national study of felons practicing TM. He concluded that of the meditating ex-cons, 35 percent were less likely to return to prison than the normal prison population. Abrams says that TM may provide former criminals with a successful way of dealing with the stress they experience on returning to society. Abrams relates that TM creates "a very restful state in the body." Stuart Moody, San Quentin TM program director, observed, "To some it seems silly that something so simple could be so powerful. Too often we try to make things more complicated and we completely miss the mark."

This inability to perceive the effectiveness of simplicity may also obstruct the possibility of medical breakthroughs. One case in point is the story of a French AIDS sufferer, Niro Asistent, who has undergone a seemingly miraculous recovery through meditation. Her story was first recorded in the *San Francisco Chronicle* (PEOPLE: "The Feisty Fighter of AIDS," 31 July 1989); and later in her book, *The Healing Yes*, published by Simon and Schuster.

In 1984 Niro tested positive for HIV virus at the Suffolk County Health Department in New York. Doctors diagnosed her as having AIDS-related complex (ARC) and told her she had little more than eighteenth months to live. Niro, a mother of two, had been infected with AIDS by a bisexual lover.

After hearing her death sentence, she went to a meditation retreat at the former Rancho Rajneesh in Eastern Oregon. There she began to feel the effects of terminal AIDS: "What happened was an incredible wake-up call," Asistent says. "I said, 'Holy shit! I have 500 days left to live. I cannot waste one.'"

She moved to San Francisco, changed her lifestyle, began eating healthy foods, and quit reading the news and watching violent movies. She began regularly practicing a meditative walk. She concluded that a stroll on the beach in silence was more important than all the "social crap." In March 1986, while doing her meditative walk, "something happened. I became kind of one with the universe, whatever that means. My boundaries disappeared. I had a deep knowledge that I was fine."

Our minds are so polluted with garbage and fears that have been passed on from generation to generation, that we have forgotten who we are. Our spiritual path is not complex, it is quite simple. It is not easy, it is not a romantic sacrifice to look at oneself, to be able to celebrate life. Yet, with this comes a feeling of joy, a sense of being, a connection with the flow of the universe.

Good Horse Nation, Visayan medicine man (1985)

I have said that my transmission is a process of unclothing. And the paradox is that the more clothes you take off yourself the richer and more well dressed you become. Roles and patterns are keeping you in a straightjacket. Freed from these you will come in contact with your inner being; with the one who doesn't see any limitations, who sees only the possibilities. Ambres (1986)

Watchfulness is the path of immortality: unwatchfulness is the path of death. Buddha (c. 500 BC) Dhm 2:21

But your dead will live; their bodies will rise. You who dwell in the dust, wake up and shout for joy. Your dew is like the dew of the morning; the earth will give birth to her dead. Isaiah of Jerusalem (eighth century BC)

Those who are watchful never die: those who do not watch are already as dead. Buddha (c. 500 BC) Dhm 2:21

We foresee a time of tribulation, yes, but those who are meditating and readying themselves for these strenuous times will find solace within and will understand how puny their individual worries seem in relation to the cosmos. Spirit guides of Ruth Montgomery (1986) Hrd

At present we are tinkering with results, with symptoms. We are not bringing about a vital change, uprooting the old ways of thought, freeing the mind from traditions and habits. It is with this vital change we are concerned and only right education can bring it to being.

J. Krishnamurti (1963) Liah

MEDITATION: "DON'T JUST DO

She was fine.

Three weeks after the incident on the beach, she tested negative for AIDS. All symptoms of ARC have vanished, and she has continued to test negative ever since. She has the documents to prove it.

Since then she has founded SHARE, The Foundation for Self-Healing AIDS Related Experiment, which is dedicated to exploring the fears of living and dying as they relate to disease. "I know the key to healing is acceptance," says Asistent.

Acceptance of the self and the other is a commodity in short supply in modern society. In spite of what the Christ is reported to have said about loving your enemies, it is not love that has brought this violent and competitive civilization to the nightmarish nineties. We are programmed to react to the slightest apparent affront and to make wars out of insults. Meditation helps us see ourselves from a greater distance; the grip of the conditioned mind is loosened and we are able to consciously respond to – instead of unconsciously react to – life situations.

The words from modern mystic, J. Krishnamurti, taken from his meditation classic, *Commentaries on Living*: *1st Series*, may be remembered as a prescient final verdict hurled at the misuse of the human mind: He says we are not only bound by the past, but also that we "are the past!" We are lost in a complicated labyrinth of memories, both happy and sorrowful. Krishnamurti viewed the past, the present and the future as tied together by a long string of dull memories:

"Thought moves through the present to the future and back again, like a restless animal tied to a post," he declared. "It moves within its own radius, narrow or wide, but it is never free of its own shadow."

Western civilization has taken as its own Descartes' statement, "I think, therefore I am." Mystics of the Aquarian Age like Krishnamurti, Maharishi Mahesh Yogi and Osho would say something more like, "You're so identified with your thinking, you don't know who you are." The constant cacophony of mind chatter — whether it is about sports cars or God — is a pettiness cut clear by the witnessing meditator. The capacity to think remains, but it is now a faculty to be used at will, not be enslaved by.

Osho defined the coming spiritual rebellion as a manifesto of silence: "Silence means: inside you, you are just spaciousness, uncluttered spaciousness," he says in his book, *The Wild Geese and the Water*. "Silence means you have put aside the whole furniture of the mind — the thoughts, the desires, the memories, the fantasies, the dreams — all you have pushed aside. You are just looking into existence directly, immediately. You are in contact with existence without anything in between you and existence...A tremendous transformation is needed to hear silence and to understand silence. Silence is the basic requirement for understanding God, the basic requirement to know Truth."

SOMETHING, *Sit There.*"

MEDITATION:

The Manifesto of the Coming Spiritual Rebellion

The day of your watchmen has come, the day God visits you. Micah (circa 721 BC): Mic 7:4

Then will the eyes of the blind be opened and the ears of the deaf unstopped.
Isaiah of Jerusalem (eighth century BC): Is 35:5

The sun will no more be your light by day, nor will the brightness of the moon shine on you, for the Lord will be your everlasting light, and your God will be your glory. "Third" Isaiah 60:19 (c. fifth to first century BC)

Be a light unto yourself. Buddha's last words (c. 483 BC)

So we fix our eyes not on what is seen but on what is unseen. For what is seen is temporary, but what is unseen is eternal. 2 Corinthians 4:18: (first century AD)

[To] those then, that are come into the new life, the new understanding — the new regeneration there IS then the new Jerusalem....not a place, alone, but as a condition, as an experience of the soul (№281-37)....The church is within yourself and not in any pope nor preacher, nor in any building but in self. For thy body is indeed the temple of the living God, and the Christ becomes a personal companion in mind and in body... Edgar Cayce (1944) №5125-1

Man will have to change within himself, not try to change others, in order to prevent wars. Spirit guides of Ruth Montgomery (1979) Amg

"No Knowing"

As It Was Collectively Foreseen Down Through Time.

The mistrust of the human being towards herself and everyone else is her greatest ball and chain anklet....She trudges under great strain. She is pulling herself around with her mistrust, with her inherited world of images from unlimited generations back in time. I want to say that if she only look down on her burden and started to watch it closely she would find that the strong metal chains are really only a thread as thin as a spider web and that her iron ball is only a red balloon. Ambres (1986)

Your existence is a carbon copy and you are clinging to it. Unless you drop it, the original, the real face of your being, will not show. And it is one of the most important things to remember: that if you can drop your ego, your personality, and allow existence to take its place, all the best and most beautiful qualities will follow on their own accord. You will not have to be good, you will find you are good. You will not have to be loving, you will find you are love. You will not have to meditate, you will find you are meditation. Osho (1987) RbSp

You must contemplate and enter into communion with that which is beyond the body. Beyond conditional existence. In one case you will be inherently free of fear and by that contemplation you must relinquish identification with that which is inherently afraid. Da Avabhasa (1988)

Dear friends, You are like a beautiful flower, one of a bouquet which falls like rain drops from the sky. Meet the true self in you. You are one of the sounds of the soundless symphony. Meet your real voice within. Today is the day that all the people in the world begin to see the Truth. You are one of the representatives of the world. Today. Tamo-san (1989) Awkw

The spiritual revolution can be reduced to a simple maxim: You disappear and let God be. Osho (1987) RbSp

The Critical Mass of ENLIGHTENMENT

Only when there are many people who are pools of peace, silence, understanding, will war disappear. **Osho (1979) ZnPr**

To speak the truth they will have closed mouths. **Nostradamus (1555) C5 Q96**

Out of thousands of seeds only one tree is born. Out of millions of sperm only one flips the ovarian switch to turn on an infant's life. Though the potentials for life are abundant, the critical mass of fulfillment of those potentials is atomically small.

The mystics believe the same law works in the evolution of human consciousness. Billions of humans have been born, each carrying within the shell of their personality the potential flower of Christ-consciousness. They are Gaia's near-countless seeds falling upon her earthly cradle. Billions live and die considering themselves blessed if the whims of existence scatter them upon barren, rocky fields of orthodox behavior. Only a tiny proportion of humankind ever reaches a full flowering.

The critical mass of enlightenment can be defined as the smallest number of awakened human beings whose collective influence can initiate a significant shift in global consciousness. The process of creating enough enlightened ones to achieve this critical mass can be likened to the transformation of coal into diamonds. The pressure of surrounding human unconsciousness creates an urgency in the potential enlightened one to awaken from illusion. The total weight of so much unconscious "carbon" exerts a tremendous pressure, through which a few coal stones reach the appropriate critical mass to become "diamonds." These awakened beings embody the crystal clarity of enlightened consciousness which can transform the level of consciousness of the entire planet.

Mystics who have used the metaphor of the mud and filth necessary to grow a lotus, like the sixth-century patriarch of Zen, Bodhidharma, say most of humanity has no other destiny than to live and die as compost and manure for the Bodhisattvas' (or spiritual teachers') flowering. The constant revelation of the rank odors of human consciousness, hidden behind society's manure of moralities and illusions, nurtures the urgency for a budding Bodhisattva's consciousness to grow. Once awakened, he or she shares his revelation with other seeds of buddhahood, encouraging them to seek their own flowering.

It doesn't seem fair that so few reach their ultimate potential. Yet such a small success rate is universal throughout Nature. Many a grain tower full of seeds must be produced by a great mother oak before one child from her wooden womb becomes a tree. We can accept or even overlook this simple law of Nature, but are offended upon discovering that the same rule applies to the blossoming of human consciousness.

The mystics say thus: Humankind arrives as billions of seeds filled with hope; in the end, almost all die as manure for others. A sterile grounding in tradition will preserve their hard shells of hope and dreaming from ever being shattered.

Even if a seed of Christ consciousness feels the urge to be blown out of his or her protected crevice in society, there's a one-in-a-million chance that that seed will land in the proper soil for a metamorphosis. There's even less chance that a wise and compassionate gardener will push one's seedy little self deep into the dark, wet earth to begin the germination process. One seed out of billions might be fortunate enough to receive such care and eventually give birth to a buddha lotus flower.

Never has mankind been so full of manure, or needed so desperately the proper soil to cultivate its higher consciousness, than in the coming few years.

Now I don't mind telling you that my ego hates the idea of being shit for someone else's buddhahood. Still, if my destiny is to be an untransformed seed-cum-manure of a man — or to put it in another way — if I can at least be the source of unconscious friction that triggers another Christ or Buddha's urgency to awaken, then so be it. Fertilize my ego!

Now I wish to take the narrative out of all this seedy talk and into a nuclear detonation best suited for a positive future.

The influence of self-awareness on the world seems to be a quality rather than quantity equation. The effect of the awakened ones on the mass of unconscious humanity is in proportion to the influence of an atom in a thermonuclear explosion. A split in the atom of awareness is predicted to be equally explosive in a spiritual sense. The detonation of meditation's silence expected between the years 1993 through 2000 could blow us into a golden future.

The forewarned end of the world may not see civilization go up in a thermonuclear holocaust at century's end. There may be another kind of atomic explosion — of human consciousness — in which the smallest mass of a fissionable material that will sustain a chain reaction is not uranium but "Uranian."

(Surprise! Uranus the ruler of the Aquarian Age is back. Blow the door off your prison of limitations and seek your freedom from the known.)

The number of enlightened people needed to set off the spiritual liberation of humanity has been bandied about by some of this century's visionaries as between five to 200 buddhatomic Christs.

The guru of TM, Maharishi Mahesh Yogi, who once counted the Beatles and Beach Boys as his disciples, predicts that only one-tenth of 1 percent of humanity is needed to create enough good vibrations to usher in world peace.

The end of the Kali Yuga is history's darkest moment. In her dark age, the population explosion has dumped more unconscious human burdens on the Earth than ever before. According to the Indian mystic, Osho, these darker times exert a higher pressure of unconsciousness, which could produce a greater buddhatomic detonation of joy and awareness. Osho estimates that at least 5 percent of the human seed base has the potential intelligence to germinate an awakening. Out of an expected manure pile of 5.5 to six billion people fertilizing earth during the nightmarish nineties, there are more potential buddha buds than there were people alive on the Earth at any time for most of man's four million year history — between 275 to 300 million spiritual rebels!

If only 200 of these found the right gardener to water them, this could turn out to be a great vegetable patch, shit and all, for the next twenty centuries.

Prophecy shares a collective vision of a Second Coming of a Christ figure. All of our soothsayers say his cloud is due to land from heaven during our time. Your guess is as good (or as biased) as mine about which promised Messiah (if any) will float down his divine father's cloudy gangplank.

The prophets who foresee the triumph of their choice for Messiah can't all be right. Their predictions about *their* favorite son of god being the herald of the new age are the most tainted by bias. In their defense, it must be said that in their groping they've grabbed hold of something, even if their bias can't quite interpret what they've seen correctly. In a sense, they all may be right as much as they are all wrong. There have always been messiahs walking among us. The Aquarian Age will make us aware that each human being is a messiah unto himself.

If the past is our criterion, many spiritual giants are still disturbing our sleep with new teachings and disturbing moral points of view. They are walking among us, teaching us, being stoned and poisoned by us. We may have already condemned a few as madmen and cultists.

Hindsight says we were wrong to stab Zoroaster, poison Socrates, burn Pythagoras and his commune, poison Mohammed, behead Sarmad and draw and quarter the Sufi mystic Al-Hillaj Mansoor; we were wrong to stone the Buddha and murder him by serving him tainted food. Was it not wrong to crucify Y'shua the Messiah and turn him into a fictionalized Jesus Christ?

The search for truth is neither new nor old....Nobody is a founder in it, nobody is a leader in it. It is such a vast phenomenon that many enlightened people have appeared, helped and disappeared.
Osho (1986) Soc

The Uniter is going to be born here and it is going to come in plenty. It is not going to be only one human being but many. And when the Uniter is born it is going to grow and more and more humans are going to be included in the thoughts of the Uniter.
Ambres (1985)

It is also true that the world is the Avatar. It is humanity as a whole that is the Avatar in human form, not some specific human individual....Only the whole is the Divine Manifestation without exclusion. Therefore, the Guru is not the Avatar in that exclusive sense. Mankind is the Avatar.
Da Avabhasa (1983) Garb

NAME THAT MESSIAH!

† "The Christian Messiah: Second coming of *Jesus Christ*

☼ The Islamic Messiah: (Orthodox Sunnis) *Muntazar:* The successor to Mohammed who at the "end of time" will unite the races of the world through understanding

✳ The Aztec/Mayan Messiah: The return of *Quetzalcoatl* -- an olive-skinned man with a white beard and followers in red

✦ The Sioux Messiah: A man in a red cloak coming from the East

✤ The Indonesian Messiah: the twelfth-century Indonesian prophet, Djojobojo, foresaw the coming of a great *Spiritual King* from the West to come after the Dutch and Japanese occupations, and what sounds like the severe end of the rule of Indonesian dictators, Sukarno and Suharto

※ The Hopi Messiah: *Pahána* the "true white brother" from the East will wear a red cap and cloak and bring two helpers holding the sacred symbols: The swastika, the cross and the power symbol of the Sun (atom?). He will restore the Indian version of the Dharma

◯ The Buddhist mainstream Messiah: *Maitreya:* Meaning either "The World Unifier" or simply "The Friend." A very human God-Man whom Buddha predicted will be a greater Buddha than himself

✳ The Mahayana Buddhist Messiah: *Amida:* A great Christ-like Bodhisattva

✤ The Japanese Messiah: Several sects of Japanese Buddhism and Shintoism foresee a variant of the Buddhist Maitreya appearing after 8 August 1988 (8/8/88)

✳ The Maori Messiahs: Over a dozen Maori chieftains in New Zealand from the nineteenth through the early twentieth centuries have laid claim to the title

✳ The Messiah of Central Asian nomads: *The White Burkhan*. He will come when the people of the steppes have abandoned their ancient gods (Communist Russia was atheist). He will come to offer them and the entire human race a spiritual rebirth

✡ The Jewish Messiah: *"The" Messiah:* The true messenger of Yahweh, the god of the Jews, who will restore them to their status as the Chosen People. Know his time has come when Israel is restored and the Temple of Solomon is rebuilt (interest in rebuilding the temple is at an all-time high during the 1990s)

✳ The Hindu Messiah: *Kalki* or *Javada* : The ninth and last Avatar of this yuga cycle. His final incarnation will appear from the West

✺ The Shiite Messiah: *The twelfth Imam*: The final religious leader of the Shiite sect of Islam. He has never died but will reappear beside Jesus prior to Judgment Day to complete the Holy Qur'an (Koran)

✲ The Sufi Messiah: *Khidr*, the mysterious guide of the Islamic spiritual underground. He is the Sufis' version of the Shiite twelfth Imam and Muntazar of the Sunnis

✸ The Zoroastrian Messiah: *Saoshyant*: Like Zarathustra, he's scheduled to come at the Zoroastrian twelfth millennium (AD 2000)

✿ The Eskimo Messiah: the prophets of the Arctic foresee him to be an olive-skinned man with long beard and white hair who comes from the East ☼ **etc...**

The "BUDDHAFIELD": The Temple of the

As time goes by, human after human will contribute to the growth of the Uniter....The Uniter is in opposition to the old thought and its ability to limit love. But the old thought was necessary for the new to be born [or, the necessary manure for the flowering]. Everything is a oneness. All the new is not really new. All this has been spoken before by different masters of different times, but it is only now in this new time that it will be understood that it will be lived. Together all of you who are listening to this are the body of the Uniter, the body and the limbs....Together you are the new thought of the new time. Ambres (1985)

Man has lived a long time the way he has lived [violently and unconsciously]. By the end of this century, a critical quantum leap is possible. Either man will die in a third world war or man will take a jump and will become a new man. Before that happens, a great Buddhafield is needed — a field where we can create the future. Osho (1977) DiSutra

Tuning in to a fully developed Master Field, where all these evolutionary processes have already taken place, permits those changes to be magnified and quickened or, in effect, lived into that system without its having to pass through certain of the processes associated with the individual struggle to evolve. Da Avabhasa (1978) Bdy

In the old days, evil things spread rapidly, but now good things spread rapidly. If you understand...everything begins to appear wonderful and beautiful, and it naturally makes people stop wasting or stop desiring unnecessary things. This awakening is contagious and it will be transmitted to everybody soon. Tamo-san (1989) Awkw

The Aquarian Age supports spiritual loners, not obedient sheep.
As misfits, what spiritual rebels have in common is their differences. Anarchy is their unifying bond. They will never be soldiers of any Christ — Hitlerian or holy.

The authentic gurus of the paradoxical Aquarian Age will not be Messiahs in the Piscean role of savior, they will simply be the way-showers for those who are rebellious enough to seek their own truth. The "Messiah" of tomorrow is not a man, nor even a son of man, but a spiritual force field generated by many human beings who share one thing in common — their individual search for themselves. Every seeker will be buoyed by the presence of the others' unique urge for spiritual transformation. Aloneness breeds togetherness. With their people, the Aquarian masters will dissolve themselves into a new phenomenon in the evolution of enlightenment, the mass presence of the greater Messiah called the Buddhafield.

Unlike ashrams and monasteries of the past, this field is less a place, more like a wellspring of shared consciousness, where the energies of many seekers pool together into a matrix of silent communion — a launching ground for a Buddhatomic chain reaction. Gurdjieff felt that each seeker is capable of influencing 100 others to each "turn on" 100 more seekers to an alternative, life-affirming state of awareness.

The mystic Osho believed that man's greatest chance for salvation was the creation of a collective and contagious awareness which he called a Noah's Ark of Consciousness:

"Impersonal" MESSIAH

Only amateurs in the field of spirituality can claim...that they are the center of the world, that they are the only begotten son of God, that they are the saviors of the whole world, that they are the messengers of God....They don't even understand a simple law, that everyone has to save himself, everyone has to be a savior unto himself. That is the only possibility.

But it is more than enough to be a center to yourself. Then your peace becomes infectious; then your silence starts spreading around, catching other people's hearts. Then your love starts overflowing and reaching unknown strangers, and giving their heart a new dance, a new song. But this happens naturally; you are not the doer of it. Osho (1987) Rebl

Suggested critical mass of Enlightenment

I want to do a certain thing in the world and I am going to do it with unwavering concentration. I am concerning myself with only one essential thing: to set man free. I desire to free him from all cages, from all fears, and not to found religions, new sects, nor to establish new theories and new philosophies. Then you will naturally ask me why I go the world over, continually speaking. I will tell you for what reason....If there are only five people who will listen, who will live, who have their faces turned towards eternity, it will be sufficient.

J. Krishnamurti

Only one-tenth of 1 percent of humanity is needed to usher in world peace.

Maharishi Mahesh Yogi

I do not want hundreds of thousands of disciples. It will be enough if I can get a hundred complete men, empty of petty egoism, who will be the instruments of God.

Sri Aurobindo

required by this century's maddest *scientists of mysticism:*

Even if only 100 people remember themselves the world can be saved.

G.I. Gurdjieff

...even if 200 people are aflame, enlightened, the whole world will become enlightened, because these 200 torches can give fire to millions of people. Those people are also carrying torches, but without any fire. They have everything, just the fire is missing. And when fire passes from one torch to another, the first torch is not losing anything at all.

Osho

...Splitting the

If in a single day everyone would now lay aside all animosities, and put aside selfish motives, the world would be revolutionized by nightfall. Such is the power of souls acting together to effect favorable change! If man elected to do so, he could bring the twenty-first century's wonders to this pathetic century overnight, by deliberately altering his thinking.

This will not occur in the present century, alas, but it will begin to occur in the next century....It is that manifestation [the shift of the Earth's axis, which Montgomery's Guides say is physical and other prophets claim is spiritual] *which will so shock humanity that man will devote himself to helping others as himself, and good thoughts will project to such an extent that it will seem like a new race of human beings. Actually, it is merely a demonstration of what right-thinking can do.*

Spirit guides of Ruth Montgomery (1979) Amg

ATOM of DHARMA

If we make good use of advances of science and we manage to avoid the destructiveness of science, then my understanding is the twenty-first century can be the most religious century on this Earth. The twenty-first century will give birth to so many buddhas, so many Siddhas, so many enlightened ones:

more than the whole history of

mankind has ever

produced.

The situation will be very much like that in science today: Do you know the ratio of scientists who are alive on Earth now to the number of scientists who existed in the whole of man's past? You will be amazed: 90 percent of all scientists are alive today. And in the whole history of man — for 10,000 years — only 10 percent existed. And today 90 percent are alive!

What happened? An explosion of science has happened. Precisely like this, the moment for an explosion in religion is drawing near. Ninety percent of all buddhas will be alive in the twenty-first century. And all the buddhas and enlightened ones of the past will account for only 10 percent. Osho (1979) Htmc

"WITHIN"

*This is the basis of all spiritual law; and to you would there be given as this:
There is no activity in the experience of man that has not its inception or purpose in a
spirit of those injunctions but what must fail: unless it is founded in the spirit of truth.
Hence each would ask, then: "What must I do about it; not what shall this, that or the
other ruler, other office holder, or the other individual do" but each should ask
"What must I do about the economic conditions in which we find ourselves?"
So live each day, each hour, as to put into practice those precepts, those influences in
thine own life, and in the life of all ye contact day by day.*

Edgar Cayce (1933) №3976-14

*Stop your quarrels, cease your preaching for a moment, withdraw a bit from your work,
and look here. You who are troubling others, you who are being troubled by others; you
who judge and you who are judged — look here. Troubling others and being troubled by
others — both are useless. Judging and being judged — both are ridiculous. Striving,
struggling, caught up in the day-to-day rat race. Why? For whose sake?*

Tamo-san (1960) Look

*I absolutely believe that no one wants to choose suicide. Up to now man has been
surviving without transformation because there was no urgency for change.*

Osho (1983) BofR

*The sole means now for saving of the beings of the Planet Earth would be...that every
one of these unfortunates during the process of existence should constantly sense and
be cognizant of the inevitability of his own death, as well as the death of everyone upon
whom his eyes or attention rests. Only such a sensation and such a cognizance can now
destroy the egoism completely crystallized in them that has swallowed up the whole of
their Essence.* G.I. Gurdjieff (1924-27) Beelzb

*I say unto you there is no evil, and there are no evil forces in the world. There are only
people of awareness and there are people who are fast asleep — and sleep has no force.
The whole energy is in the hands of the awakened people. And one awakened person can
awaken the whole world. One lighted candle can make millions of candles lighted
without losing light.* Osho (1986)

What haven't humans of good conscience done to try to save this world?

Yet all efforts to bring peace on Earth have failed; at best we have weathered and adapted to wars and disasters and dulled our pain with holy consolations. We have established laws to govern our actions because we are incapable of living according to our own consciousness. The imposed conscience of societal morality prevents us from ever living beyond the mechanical knee-jerk worship of duty and following orders. At best, our civilization has functioned but not flowered.

All the ingenious efforts to save the world have done nothing but bring us to this dangerous crossroads. One can despair at 10,000 years of failure, or see each disappointment as a step closer to success. Where we are now tells me that man must be very close to the answer.

We stand before a tomorrow of fear or a tomorrow of revelation. The seers of the future are trying to give us instructions on how to build a bridge to endless tomorrows rather than stumble along with our cherished traditions and beliefs to an all-too-predictable disaster.

Perhaps we are unable to save our planet because nearly all of us are missing the obvious and necessary first step to save it. And that first step can't even be considered because our past-oriented programming is preventing us from even knowing there's a first step to take.

The key must be right in front of our noses. Maybe even closer. That is why we've always missed it, life after life, eon after eon. Society has trained everyone not to see the key. I have seen this heartbreaking truth in every culture I've encountered, no matter how different its façade of morality and tradition.

There's an old Eastern tale:

God is sick and tired of listening to all of bleeding humanity's prayers. He tells the devil that he'd love to dash it all and hide somewhere on the farthest star.

"They will find you with time," says the devil, "and as you know, you have all of eternity so it won't be long before they catch hold of you again."

"Not to worry," the devil continues, "I have a simple remedy. Just hide yourself right behind their eyes. They will never look for you there."

The key to endless tomorrows is the realization that you, me, all of us, are the problem.

Stop running away from the seeds of every human misery.

Stop making excuses for the past. Your only home in the cosmos is on fire and every one of us is equally responsible for lighting the match and looking the other way.

You are the problem, and you are also the answer.

The first step toward saving the world is **within**.

Epilogue

There is no time to waste in any unconscious consolations. An immediate transformation is absolutely needed; it is an urgency which man has never faced before. In a way you are unfortunate that soon there will be no future. In another way, you are very fortunate because this crisis is so big — perhaps it may help you to wake up.

Don't think about the world, think about yourself. You are the world, and if you begin to be different the world begins to be different. A part of it, an intrinsic part, has begun to be different: the world has begun to change.

We are always concerned with changing the world. That is just an escape. I have always felt that people who are concerned with others changing are really escaping from their own frustrations, their own conflicts, their own anxieties, their own anguish. They are focusing their minds on something else, because they cannot change themselves. It is easier to try to change the world than to change oneself.

Osho (1987) HiSp, GrCh

In order to know the future it is necessary first to know the present in all its details, as well as to know the past. Today is what it is because yesterday was what it was. And if today is like yesterday, tomorrow will be like today. If you want tomorrow to be different, you must make today different.

G.I. Gurdjieff (1915) Mira

If you live each moment, that's the only way to live. And if you live this moment greatly, your next moment is going to be greater — because now you know how to live. You go on becoming more and more skillful, more and more artful. Each moment becomes a learning, how to get more juice out of life. And if man can live just one life fully, totally, he will have tasted something of truth, something of the eternal...the fruit that Adam and Eve have missed.

Osho (1986) Soc

EVER NOW

Prophecy is a window to the outcome of our present actions. But it is of little use if it only fuels our preoccupation with the future and does not frame this living moment.

As long as all things move, grow and die — be they great stars or the smallest sub-atomic particles — as long as there is life and its complement, death, there can be no real security. The illusion of security keeps drawing our attention away from the need to change. And the only moment we have to accept the challenge of change is the present.

THE PRESENT is eternity itself, waiting for us, opening its fields for our rest and enjoyment. But we go on missing it. We cannot see it for the smoke of a brush fire. That brush fire is our burning obsession with tomorrow.

I have given you this book as a backfire against your future obsessions. We have burned a lot of moments together with Utopian sparks and the firestorms of Armageddon.

All that is left is now.

And God is hiding right behind our eyes.

No matter where I have been and no matter what I have seen, I have always been in paradise....There is no other paradise but this. We are in the middle of paradise. To my eyes, all things appear as furnishings of paradise.
Tamo-san (1989) Awkw

This earth can be a splendor, a magic, a miracle. Our hands have that touch — it is just that we have never tried it. Man has never given a chance to his own potential to grow, to blossom, to bring fulfillment and contentment.
Osho (1987) GrCh

Finally, it will be understood that the end of the world was merely a kind of purification.
Mario de Sabato (1971)

Appendix:

'ABDU'L-BAHA' (1844-1921) The eldest son and successor of Bahá'u'lláh. Upon the death of his father, he assumed full authority for the Bahá'í movement as the interpreter of the teachings. Throughout much of his adult life, he spread the faith from its new religious seat on Mt Carmel, in present-day Israel. Like his father, he had a prodigious correspondence with believers and inquirers around the globe, and endured long years of prison life with cheerfulness, patience and compassion.

After the fall of the old Ottoman régime in 1908, 'Abdu'l-Bahá was released from prison and made extensive tours to Europe and America. In his travels he planted the seeds for the worldwide spread of Bahá'í. His inspiring correspondence to world leaders on the need for an international league of nations may have helped to fulfill his predictions of the formation of that governing body.

'Abdu'l-Bahá means "Servant of Bahá (glory)."

EVANGELINE ADDAMS (1865-1932) has been called "America's female Nostradamus." She shocked Boston high society by striking out on her own as an astrologer. She later moved to New York, where in 1914, she defended the integrity of astrology in court by winning a case filed against her for breaking a city statute against fortune telling. She proposed to put astrology on trial and make her defense stand on the horoscope she would make of someone totally unknown to her. "The defendant raises astrology to the dignity of an exact science," concluded the presiding judge. He was so impressed by her analysis of his son that he saw to it that astrology was no longer prohibited in the state of New York.

Addams became millionaire J.P. Morgan's personal astrologer and cast monthly horoscopes on the whims of the stock market. She also offered advice to millions of listeners on her national radio program.

Among her greatest predictive successes were the forecasts of the death of England's King Edward VII and the election of dark horse nominee Warren G. Harding over Herbert Hoover for US president. Death predictions were one of her best skills. She accurately calculated her own demise for the end of 1932.

AMBRES An entity purported to be channeled by a modern-day Swedish carpenter named Sturé Johansson. He is considered a Nordic Edgar Cayce for his ability to pluck highly successful medical remedies and other worldly insights out of trance states. This shy and humble man, living in a modest middle-class condominium outside Stockholm, obtained world notoriety during the 1980s through the patronage of Hollywood actress Shirley MacLaine. She introduced him to the greater world though her best-selling book and movie adaptation of her spiritual search entitled *Out on a Limb* (Bantam).

THE ARGHATI PROPHECIES Upon the high and freeze-dried Shang Tang plateau in Tibet, the leather-skinned nomads of Mongolian origin weave tales of a legendary kingdom deep within the earth called Arghati. Deep in the womb of the earth, a great ruler known as the King of the World awaits more enlightened times when he and his people can emerge from their great cavern cities and impart their wisdom to the survivors of a coming holocaust.

If the birds should fall silent in the Himalayan valleys and if the herds of horses should stand still and dumb, the nomads of Central Asia will tell you that King Arghati is making new prophecies.

SRI AUROBINDO (1872-1950) Bengali mystic and visionary. Born in Calcutta, India; educated in England where he graduated from Kings College in Cambridge in 1892. Afterwards he returned to India and became both a political and spiritual revolutionary. In 1908 he was arrested by the British government as a suspect in a bombing. It was while enduring the harsh life of prison that he crystallized his insights into meditation and yoga. He moved from Calcutta and established an ashram, or spiritual school, in Pondicherry after 1910. There he began publishing a monthly magazine and writing lyrical works. These writings delved into a wide range of spiritual and mundane themes, but they primarily suggested means for mankind's future physical and spiritual evolution — the birth of a new humanity.

In the final few decades of his life, Sri Aurobindo kept himself in seclusion, only rarely appearing before followers. He was succeeded by his long-time disciple, Mira Alfassa, who later became his spiritual successor, better known by Aurobindo devotees as The Mother.

DA AVABHASA (1939-) "I consciously decided to take birth in the West," says this unpredictable American mystic. A man of many names, he began life as Franklin Albert Jones in Long Island, New York. We are told that as early as the tender age of two, Franklin realized his mission was to open others to the way of the heart. He therefore made, he says, a conscious decision to enter normal, everyday life and renounce his enlightenment, his state of "the Bright" and enter totally into human suffering. His conscious fall was so successful that by his college years at Stanford University in California and Columbia University as a philosophy and religious major, he was totally consumed by doubt of God.

In 1964 he met his first guru, American Swami Rudrananda, and was later transferred to Rudy's guru, Swami Muktananda, in India. It was at Muktananda's ashram in Ganeshpuri that he underwent further expansions of con- sciousness, becoming a devotee of the goddess Shakti (the female principle of Tantra). After the reawakening of his original childhood state in 1970, Franklin Jones changed his name to Bubba Free John. During the first stage of his spiritual work, he led a growing following of Western seekers. But he was not satisfied with his disciples' progress toward silent communion with the master.

In 1973, he became Da Free John, inaugurating the

second, more tantric stage of his teaching work. Seeing that people were not ready for a devotional relationship with the master as the means to liberation, he "adopted" their lifestyle in an attempt to expose their inner emptiness. This was a time of wild parties, sometimes celebrating night and day for months on end, alternating with long periods of meditation, austerities and purification. He taught that the search for God is fruitless and that only understanding we are already free will liberate us.

By 1986, Free John had published forty books and established three ashrams, in Fiji, California and Hawaii. One night, his disciples in his Fiji ashram were awakened to his voice on the public intercom. He complained that after all of his efforts to help people, no one was "getting it" and there seemed to be no reason to remain in the body. It is reported that he collapsed in a death faint. His disciples relate that he literally died for a few minutes.

"That event was my true birthday," Free John later explained. "I achieved human likeness." The experience was something akin to a second enlightenment. Thus began the third stage of his teaching. He now called himself Da (Kalki) Love Ananda. Perhaps this is his declaration that he is the final avatar closing Kali Yuga. (In Hindu prophecy, Kalki is the name of the last avatar.)

He currently lives in semi-seclusion at Shree Love Anandashram — his spiritual campus on the Fijian island of Naitauba. He meditates in silent communion with an intimate gathering of devotees. On 30 April 1991, in response to his followers' confessed acknowledgements of what devotee and biographer, Saniel Bonder, calls "His Radiant bodily Revelation of God," Da (Kalki) Love Ananda announced his new name "Da Avabhasa", which essentially means, "The Bright." Bonder adds that the name points to Da Avabhasa's role as Sat-Guru: "meaning One who brings the light of Truth into the darkness of the egoic human world." (*Dawn Horse Testament*, 1991).

Da Avabhasa described in the briefest terms his path to enlightenment in his book *The Lion Sutra*: "There is not now and never has been any such thing as personal identity....You are happiness seeking happiness — be happiness! And witness only."

Devotees around the world live in communal houses, practice his teachings and meditate daily before his picture.

MEHER BABA (1894-1969) "Now I am going." These were the last words of one of India's greatest modern mystics. The last spoken, that is. His last words were not uttered on his deathbed, but forty-four years earlier. Meher Baba was a silent sage for most of his world ministry, communicating first by means of a spelling board and later with his own unique brand of lively hand signing.

He was born in Poona, India, to a Parsi family. He earned the nickname "Electricity" from his childhood friends because of his high energy. One night in January 1914, Babajan, a famous woman mystic from Afghanistan, opened the adolescent to the infinite bliss of self-realization with a kiss

on the forehead. For nine months, Meher Baba wandered like a somnambulist.

"When after the kiss from Babajan I knew that I was like the Ocean," says Baba, "I did not want to come back to the ordinary 'drop' consciousness from that Blissful State where I alone was." But despite his resistance, his guru, Upasni Maharaj, brought the "ocean" back to the "drop" by throwing a stone with great force right between Meher Baba's eyes. This sealed the divine enlightenment that Babajan opened with a kiss.

"That was the beginning of my present infinite suffering in illusion which I experienced simultaneously with my infinite bliss in reality," related Baba.

During the 1920s, Baba began regular trips to the West, attracting disciples in Europe and America. A mind reader in New York once tried his gift on Baba and was shocked. "I can't read any thoughts!" he stammered. Baba explained with his spelling board that he no longer had a mind, that his pure consciousness existed beyond the mind. Meher Baba was also known for his work with the *masts*, seekers on the path who suffer from "divine madness."

He died on 30 January 1969, sitting up straight with head raised heavenward. He signed his last words: "Do not forget that I am God."

ROGER BACON (1214?-1294) English Franciscan monk. Born of a wealthy family, it is recorded that he was a rebellious and precocious youth. Bacon's education explored the scientific frontiers of his superstitious time. He studied at Oxford and the University of Paris, becoming a master of alchemy, astrology, optics, astronomy and mathematics. In Bacon's medieval world, God was Big Brother and the theologian his infallible commissar.

Bacon remains one of history's greatest techno-prophets. One can open the yellowed and flaking pages of his *Epistola de Secretis* (c. 1269) and find descriptions, in clear and unmistakable language, of modern aircraft, cars and ships, and the advent of suspension bridges, submarines, and helicopters.

With time Brother Bacon felt the noose of orthodoxy tighten around him. He was sent to prison for his "suspected novelties," where he languished for fourteen years. He died soon after his release in 1292.

BAHA' 'U' LLA'H (1817-1892) AKA Mízrá Husayn 'Alí, Iranian mystic who took on the Persian moniker meaning "Glory of God" after assuming the role of chief patriarch and spiritual Messiah of Bahá'ísm, an offshoot of Islam. The founder of Bahá'ísm, Ali Mohammed — known as "the Bab" (the Gate) — had been martyred.

This declaration destined Bahá'u'lláh to suffer long years of persecution by orthodox Islamics. He was first imprisoned in Teheran for his missionary activities and later exiled from Persia. While living in Palestine he and his family endured further persecution from the Ottoman authorities, spending many years in the prison city of Acre. His disciples claim that he bore these many incarcerations with a cheerful, almost unearthly serenity.

Undaunted by the worst religious intolerance, he managed to spread his message of human unity to world leaders and laymen alike. This he did almost exclusively though the power of letters written in prison. Toward the end of his life, restrictions against his freedom were lifted by the Turkish Sultan, allowing Bahá'u'lláh to spend his final years establishing what has become the mecca of Bahá'ísm, near Mt Carmel, Israel.

THOMAS BANYACA (The Hopi prophecies) One of the contemporary Hopi elders entrusted with sharing specific parts of the heretofore secret Native American prophecy with the white man. This gesture is in itself a sign that we are living in the final days before the world as we know it is purified by either thermonuclear, greenhouse, or spiritual fire. The Hopi vision appears to be the earliest spiritual source for all ancient Native American prophecies.

PASTOR BARTHOLOMAEUS HOLTZHAUSER of Swabia (seventeenth century) professor of theology and pastor of St Johann Church in the Tyrol (Austria). At the age of fourteen he was already respected for his insights into religious matters. Often praying in seclusion, zealous and strict in his fasts and religious ardor, he was revered by the peasant folk of his congregation as a model holy man. Princes and kings praised him for the depth of his intellect. He was often seen as a guest in the court of Johann Philipp, Elector of Mayence.

Pastor Bartholomaeus accurately foresaw the French Revolution, Hitler, World War II, the Cold War, and rockets punching holes in the ozone layer.

BEROSUS (second century BC) Chaldean astrologer, historian, and one of the greatest magicians of his time. Fragments of his original writings are handed down to us through the surviving works of the Roman poet, Seneca, and the great Roman orator, Cicero. It is said of him by the ancient Greeks that almost all his predictions and astrological auguring proved to be accurate. The Greeks held Berosus in such high esteem that his statue was erected in Athens. Its tongue, sheathed in gold, symbolized the truth of his forecasts.

A man of many scholarly talents, he collected and translated into Greek a three-volume account of Babylonian history, which also chronicles the epic story of Gilgamesh (the Chaldean version of Noah's Flood).

WALLACE BLACK ELK Contemporary medicine man from the Lakota Sioux nation and grandson of the great Sioux medicine man, Black Elk. He is known as "The Eagle Man" because he always holds an eagle feather when he speaks. He would say that his uniquely slow and halting way of speaking comes from being a medium for the eagle spirits.

His predictions quoted in this book were made during a rare public gathering of Indian leaders and mystics in Portland Oregon in 1985. The topic was the ancient Hopi prophecy that the end-time of the human race is near. In 1990, Wallace Black Elk published *Black Elk: The Sacred ways of a Lakota* (Harper-Collins) with William S. Lyon.

MADAME BLAVATSKY (1831-1891) Famous nineteenth-century Russian occultist. Was born in Ekaterinoslav, Russia and at seventeen married Nicerphore Blavastsky, a counselor of state. Married life did not appeal to the future occultist and spirit channeler, and they soon separated. She then traveled extensively around the world, visiting the temples, ruins and centers of religious learning from Mexico's Mayan pyramids to the temples and cremation grounds of India. Her work remains one of the greatest bridges between Eastern mysticism and the West.

In 1873 she settled in New York City where she was the toast of spiritualist circles. During this time she met Colonel H.S. Olcott, with whom she founded the Theosophical Society. Later, the two moved the Society's main headquarters to Madras, India.

ST JOHN BOSCO (1815-1888) Born to a peasant family and raised by his widowed mother, he had an interest from an early age in doing religious work among boys and young men. This continued after his ordainment as a priest in 1841. He is responsible for establishing the nineteenth-century version of halfway houses for juvenile delinquents, as well as providing trade and agricultural schools and even hospitals and foreign missions. He is said to have provided food from thin air to his young charges during hard times. St Bosco's chilling letter written to Pope Pius IX in 1874, which presaged a Catholic apocalypse, is still kept in the Vatican archives.

BERTINE BOUQUILLON Nineteenth-century French nun, highly respected for her saintliness and piety, who devoted her life to nursing the sick at the Hôpital de St Louis in St Omer, France. Her prophecies concerned the coming of the Antichrist. She was convinced that the "latter days" before the Apocalypse would not take place in her century, but in our twentieth century.

BRAHAN SEER AKA Coinneach Odhar Fionsiche, a seventeenth-century Scottish clairvoyant who divined the future though the use of a piece of polished meteor. He worked as a simple farm laborer, giving prophetic readings on the side. Those who were acquainted with him say that he was quite clear-headed and practical. It wasn't long before his fame spread from the island of Brahan to the mainland, and Coinneach was collecting large sums for his seeings. His predictions mainly center around the future of Scotland. He foresaw the coming of tarmac roads, trains, piped gas and water, and the loosening of morals in the twentieth century.

Eventually his brutally honest predictions got him burned as a warlock. As he was led to the stake, the Countess of Seaforth declared he would most certainly go to hell.

He replied, "I will go to Heaven, but you never shall. After my death, a raven and a dove, flying in opposite directions, will meet for a second over my ashes, on which they will instantly alight. If the raven is foremost, you have spoken truly; but, if the dove, then my hope is well founded."

This so enraged her that the countess ordered him thrust head first into a barrel of burning tar that was laced with spikes on the inside. Later, as the legend goes, the countess and crowd saw a dove and raven descending from the sky to alight upon the Brahan Seer's ashes. It is said that the dove landed first.

BRAVE BUFFALO Amerindian medicine man from the Brule Sioux nation. His predictions quoted in this book were made during a rare public gathering of Indian leaders and mystics in Portland, Oregon, back in 1985. The topic was the ancient Hopi prophecy that the end-time for the human race is near. Other Indian prophets at the ceremonial conference were: Wallace Black Elk (Lakota Sioux Nation); Thomas Banyaca (the Hopi Nation); and Grace Spotted Eagle (Inuit Nation).

GAUTAMA BUDDHA (563?-483? BC) The founder of Buddhism. He was born Gautama Siddhartha near the town of Kapilavasta in what is now Nepal, near the border of India. He was the son of an aristocratic Hindu chieftain of the second warrior caste. Astrologers predicted that he'd either become a great world conqueror or a great Buddha (awakened master). At the age of twenty-nine, Gautama abandoned his protected, princely life and became a wandering mendicant. After six years of tremendous effort, he became enlightened, but only when he realized that all efforts to obtain realization are futile. He taught that buddhahood is a birthright of all people; it is not an achievement, it is merely a relaxation into the truth of one's being.

As a buddha, he wandered through Eastern India and Nepal for the next forty-five years, collecting as many as 10,000 disciples together at a time.

After eight attempts made on his life by orthodox Hindus, it seems Gautama was finally poisoned by tainted food. He pronounced his last words on the world's impermanence, exhorting his gathered disciples to meditate and witness the workings and illusoriness of the mind, body and desires.

"Be a light unto yourself" was the essence of his final message.

It is said that Gautama Buddha was born, became enlightened and died on the date of the full moon in May.

EDGAR CAYCE (1877-1945) One of the most significant prophets of the twentieth century. Cayce was born near Hopkinsville, Kentucky (USA). He was a simple farm boy, shy and good natured and deeply religious. He used to say he read the Bible once through every year. His sixth sense was awakened as a result of a learning impairment. At the age of nine, he was called an idiot by his teacher because he couldn't spell the word "cabin" correctly. Nor could his father teach the boy the rudiments of spelling. That evening he left

the boy's bedroom in frustration. Cayce later related that once left alone, he heard a voice say, "Sleep now, and we will help you." Cayce dozed off with his spelling book tucked under his head as a pillow. When his father woke him up thirty minutes later, both were amazed when Cayce could recite every lesson in the book.

A baseball can be thanked for awakening Cayce's healing powers. He was seriously injured when a childhood friend slammed a home run into his head. The unconscious boy was carried home. A trance-like voice stirred his lips, instructing his mother to apply a certain poultice on the nape of his neck. He soon recovered.

He dropped out of high school after the ninth grade. He married, fathered two children and scraped together a living, first as a clerk, then working at a bookstore, and later selling life insurance. With time, word spread around the country about an uneducated country bumpkin who lay down on a couch in a trance and prescribed down-to-earth medical cures. For instance, Cayce once prescribed Jerusalem artichokes for a diabetic years before it was discovered that they possess high concentrations of insulin. Scientists and reporters traveled to Hopkinsville to visit the man the Hearst Newspaper syndicate would label "America's Sleeping Prophet."

Thousands of readings were dated and documented throughout his life. For years he refused to take payment for his work but at last his wife convinced him to take a modest fee from those who could pay. He offered his services free to the poor.

In 1927 Cayce moved to Virginia Beach, Virginia, where wealthy supporters financed the construction of a modest hospital. As his notoriety increased, he suffered persecution from local authorities and was arrested twice: For practicing medicine without a license and "fortune telling" while visiting New York. All charges were dismissed.

Only on rare occasions did Cayce experience a conscious vision of tomorrow. On a sunny afternoon in June 1931, he was hoeing his garden. Suddenly he stood erect, and the hoe fell from his hands. Without a word, he rushed into the house and locked himself in the study. After several hours he came out and explained that he had seen a vision of a coming world war in which millions of men and women would be killed. The transcripts of thousands of sleep readings during the 1930s contain accurate dates and descriptions of the time and duration of World War II.

Cayce once recounted a dream in which he was standing on the fringe of time and space and he met a rosy-cheeked boy with a pair of scissors. Cayce asked the beautiful, smiling boy who he was. "I am Death," he replied.

The prophet was shocked, and said, "This is not how I expected death to be."

The boy laughed, and shrugged in understanding. "No one expects me to be a beautiful experience."

"And what are the scissors for?" asked Cayce.

The boy, Death, replied that when his time would come these scissors would snip him free from the silver cord that tethers the spirit to the body.

On 5 January 1945 the boy's scissors did their snipping; that day Edgar Cayce was laid to rest.

CHEIRO (1866-1936) A professional pseudonym (from the Greek word meaning "hand") used by British clairvoyant and palmist Count Louis Hamon. He was famous for his remarkable predictions made through palmistry, numerology and astrology. Hamon's life is filled with rich stories of intrigue and occult mysteries. He was a war correspondent during the Sino-Japanese War of 1895 and later during the Russo-Japanese conflict of 1905. It is said that he plied his gifts working for the British secret service during World War 1 and the sensuous spy Mata Hari was one of his lovers.

Hamon did not marry until late in life, preferring to use his hypnotic powers to seduce beautiful women, especially if they were married. He became an accomplished master of jujitsu and very handy with a revolver, just in case a cuckolded husband wished to take the matter of honor beyond the divorce court. The palmist did suffer being stabbed by a jealous husband all the same.

In 1930 Hamon moved to Hollywood to try his luck at screenwriting. There he established a school of metaphysics and perhaps is partially responsible for seeding the future fascination for all things New Age and occult in Los Angeles. Soon he could count as his palmistry clients many of Hollywood's shining stars, such as Lillian Gish, Mary Pickford and director Erich Von Stroheim.

In 1926 he wrote *Cheiro's World Predictions* which he updated in 1931. Nestled in a comfy chair with this book in the 1990s, one can find long passages which sound like a history of the last seven decades.

Count Louis Hamon died on 8 October 1936 at his home on Hollywood Boulevard. Many spiritualists and the metaphysically bent in "Southern Cal'" will tell you that his home at №7417 is haunted.

ST COLUMBCILLE (522-597) Irish saint. At forty-one, he sailed for Britain and landed on the island of Iona, where he and his twelve disciples established a monastery (the suffix *cille* — meaning monastic cell or church — was added to his name, Columba). He wrote many volumes of religious and prophetic manuscripts, poems, psalms and hymns. Columbcille set forth on a thirty-four-year pilgrimage, preaching his Christian ways to pagans in Scotland, the isles of the Hebrides, Orkneys, Shetlands, Faroes and all the way to the Vikings in Iceland.

His future eye remained affixed to the gloomy, moody tomorrows of his beloved Eire. Among his successful predictions were the Viking invasions of Ireland around AD 1000, the Anglo-Norman invasion to follow, the Irish Rebellion of 1641, and the great Irish Potato Famine of 1845-1850.

DAVID GOODMAN CROLY (1829-1889) American seer born in Ireland; grew up in New York. He was a respected journalist

working for the New York *Evening Post* and served as managing director of the *World* between 1862 and 1872. He married one of the first US female reporters, the women's rights advocate Jane Cunningham. Known by his contemporaries as a remarkable financial prophet, he foresaw the Panic of 1873 two years before it happened, and even named the first bank to fail (Jay Cooke & Company) and the first railroad company to collapse (Northern Pacific). In the 1870s, ill health put an end to his journalistic career. He finished life writing a regular prophetic column on business and politics, which he collected and re-edited into a book entitled *Glimpses of the Future*, in 1888. Croly advised his contemporaries to read it now and to let it be "judged in the year 2000."

DALAI LAMA The title stands for the political and spiritual leader of Tibet and is derived from Mongolian words which translate as "The Teacher whose wisdom is as great as the ocean." The pre-eminence of the Dalai Lama's rulership of Tibet was assured by the time of the fifth Dalai Lama, Lobsang Gyatso (1617-1682). Since then, each heir to the title is regarded as a incarnation of Chenrezi, patron saint of Tibet, who exists only in the spiritual plane as an oversoul. Chenrezi can manifest in the physical plane as one of five sub-soul aspects. Avalokiteswara, the soul aspect of compassion, incarnates as the Dalai Lama. Each Dalai Lama is considered a reincarnation of the preceding one. A few years after the death of the Dalai Lama, monks with special occult powers are sent throughout the land to identify the soul of their departed leader, which has been reborn into another body. Each candidate undergoes a spiritual interview of sorts. He is asked questions and is shown a series of articles. Some of them are the personal effects of the preceding Dalai Lama, some are decoys. If he correctly identifies his personal articles and passes other tests verifying his identity, he is taken back to the great Potala (temple) of Lhasa (capital of Tibet) and prepared for a new life as Tibet's president/pope, whose tenure usually begins at the age of eighteen.

THIRTEENTH DALAI LAMA (1876-1933) Each emanation of St Chenrezi as a compassion in human form in a new Dalai Lama is revered by the people of Tibet for his unique spiritual virtues and temporal actions. Thupten Gyatso was considered one of the greatest Dalai Lamas since the Great Fifth. He was an activist and reformer equal to the tasks of political statesman and awakened master. This was a rarity, as many Dalai Lamas were either great spiritual leaders and poor politicians or vise versa.

Thupten Gyatso was responsible for a series of far-reaching reforms. Under his guidance, the number of lay officials was increased and corruption in the lamaseries was exposed. He also overhauled the Tibetan penal system and abolished the death penalty. He is responsible for steering Tibet into the modern world, introducing electricity, the telegraph and telephone systems. A deeply spiritual man, the thirteenth Dalai Lama spent an average at least six hours each day in meditation and scriptural study. Shortly before his death, he uttered his famous prophecy accurately forewarning his people about the coming apocalypse of the Communist Chinese invasion of Tibet.

FOURTEENTH DALAI LAMA (1935-) Tenzin Gyatso is considered in Tibetan prophecy to be the last in the Dalai Lama lineage. He was forced to assume political leadership while still in his teens, when in 1950 the Chinese Communists invaded Tibet and began their systematic extermination of Tibetan culture and religion, along with an estimated one million Tibetans, under the slogan of "peaceful liberation." By 1958, an abortive Tibetan national uprising precipitated the young God-king's eventual self-imposed exile to Darjeeling, India. Since then, the fourteenth Dalai Lama has traveled the world, championing the plight of his oppressed countrymen. The 1990s have opened with his message receiving significant attention by the world's leading statesmen. He is compared with Mahatma Gandhi as the late twentieth century's most significant champion of non-violent religious and political activism.

DANIEL Old Testament prophet whose identity is as hard to piece together as a broken cruciform tablet. Daniel may actually be a composite of several people. The first could be a King Daniel in an Ugaritic legend of the fourteenth century BC; the second, the example (along with Noah and Job) of a righteous man in Ezekiel 14:14; and the third, the wise man who knows secrets in Ezekiel 28:3. In chapters 1-6 of the Book of Daniel, our prophet is a young Jew at a foreign court divining royal dreams as a vizier of kings, yet in chapters 8-12 it is his own dreams and visions which must be interpreted by angels.

As if that isn't enough of a time-traveling traffic jam, the stories and prophecies are set in the Babylonian and Persian periods between the sixth and fourth centuries BC, but they primarily describe the successors of Alexander the Great, one undoubtedly being the great oppressor of the Jews, Antiochus IV Epiphanes (175-163 BC), a demagogue of a much later time.

Whichever Daniels we are dealing with, this survivor of anti-Semitic lion's dens *did* accurately foretell the coming of the Christian Messiah Y'shua down to the year!

BEJAN DARUWALLA (1931-) Internationally renowned astrologer, born in India. His witty and accurate predictions are widely read in more than eight different publications throughout South Asia and the Middle East. He accurately predicted the deaths of Sanjay Gandhi and Indian mystic Osho (Rajneesh), and foresaw the defeat of Rajiv Gandhi by V.P. Singh. His August 1988 prediction dating the release of Nelson Mandela from South African prison was off by only thirty-four days. I found him to be a jovial and thoroughly entertaining conversationalist. He also has become a kind of Art Buchwald of the occult, writing a humor column that demystifies astrology.

ANDREW JACKSON DAVIS (1826-1910) America's greatest techno-prophet who was also a leading theorist of the Spiritualist movement. Predicted prior to 1856 the coming of air travel, gasoline, automobiles and prefab construction. He was born in 1826 in Orange County, New York, the son of a drunken shoemaker. His formal education consisted of five months in elementary school. Davis lived in poverty and survived through menial work. However, William Levingston, a journeyman tailor and amateur hypnotist, discovered this gifted clairvoyant and promoted him as a traveling faith healer. Davis gave over 150 lectures in New York City while in trance state. He also wrote numerous books on the future. Most of his greatest predictions about future inventions were made in his book *Penetralia*, published in 1856.

COUNTESS FRANCESCA DE BILLIANTE of Savoy was well known among fellow royals and the power brokers of the early twentieth century for entertaining them with flights of prophetic insight during her dinner parties.

GIAOCCHINO DE FIORE (1130-1202) Cistercian monk who lived in Calabria, Italy. He was a noted scholar and commentator on Biblical and Sibylline prophetic works. His predictions of the future rely heavily on these traditions. One of his more original interpretations of the future related in his work, *Vaticini del Vangelo* (Prophecies of the Eternal Gospels), labeled the Old Testament Era as the Age of the Father: a time of obedience and fear, slavery and tradition. Jesus marked the Age of the Son, an epoch of faith, symbolism, youthfulness and liberty. According to de Fiore, we are about to begin the third and final Age of the Holy Spirit which will blossom after a brief and violent apocalyptic period. It will be a time of mutual love, the brotherhood of man; the world will know only complete freedom, resurrection, meditation, and ultimately, spiritual transcendence.

DEGUCHI NAO (1836-1918) Japanese seeress and religious matriarch of the Omoto sect. She was considered by followers to be a manifestation of Kunitokotachi-no-mikoto, the God of Rocks (Earth). Late in life (1892), she claimed to channel the Japanese god Ushitora-No-Konjin, who moved her arm to write messages with Chinese brush and paper. It is said that Nao never learned to read or write. The quality of the brush strokes during her spirit sessions is that of a master calligrapher. She often put brush to paper in the middle of the night in pitch blackness.

With the collaboration of her son-in-law, Onisaburo (regarded as the physical representation of the God of Water, Susanoh), she became the matriarch of a new religious sect, which is an amalgam of various Shinto and Buddhist teachings and prophetic traditions. The Gods that Nao and Onisaburo represent are those that have been oppressed under State Shintoism.

MARIO DE SABATO (1933-) Contemporary French clairvoyant. This illegitimate son of an Italian father and French mother displayed great religious piety and devotion as a child. His prophecies have a strong Catholic influence similar to those of Jeane Dixon. During the 1970s, he was one of Europe's most well-known oracles.

JOÃO DE VATIGUERRO Thirteenth-century Christian seer, one of many who share a collective vision of the destruction of the Vatican in what sounds like either a thermonuclear or ecological holocaust some time around the turn of this century.

JEANE DIXON (Keeps her age a well-guarded secret.) She has been enjoying the prophetic limelight for over thirty years as America's first lady of prediction. She was born in a Wisconsin village as one of seven children to German immigrant parents. As a child, she couldn't decide whether to become a nun or an actress. Some might say she accomplishes both; she is quite a charismatic, fast-talking television personality as well as a non-smoking, teatotaling devout Catholic who regularly attends mass and dedicates much of her time to help old people and disadvantaged children.

In 1946 Dixon became a respected world-syndicated horoscope columnist for predicting the partition of India down to the very day, one month before it happened. She also forewarned the world of the 1964 Alaskan earthquake. Her predictions concerning the assassinations of John and Robert Kennedy score as some of the greatest pre-documented and pre-publicized forecasts in history.

EZEKIEL Biblical priest and prophet. Began his ministry in the final years of the Kingdom of Judah, before it ended in the Babylonian captivity following the destruction of the Great Temple in 587 BC. During his ministry, the Jewish nation underwent its greatest social transformation — from a society worshipping temple sacrifices and land to a faith identified with the Jewish people themselves. Scholars say this led to the formation of the synagogue and the study of Judaic law as it paramount tenet. Ezekiel dramatized his prophecies with actions and literary devices approaching the bizarre, or as some would dare say, the psychotic. The inclusive dates of Ezekiel's prophecies are the most secure of any Old Testament book. The first vision is dated 593 BC (1:2), and ends with an oracle for 571 BC. Scholars are at first confused by what appears to be Ezekiel's double ministry. Chapters 1:1-3:11 find him on occasion addressing his message to the Palestinian Jews (11:1-3). Bible watchers can speculate whether he is first speaking to the people in Palestine before the captivity and later to the captives in Babylonia after Jerusalem and the Temple were ashes. Some believe his message to the Palestinian Jews was made from captivity and was therefore a clairvoyant transmission rather than an earthly one.

Ezekiel's message stresses freedom of choice and human responsibility in one's relationship with God and with one's fellow man.

THE FLOWERING ALMOND TREE PROPHECY In the year 1944 Allied bombers were reducing Berlin into rubble. In the ruins of a gutted church, a lead tube was discovered which held a document entitled the Flowering Almond Tree, ostensibly penned by a nineteenth-century Benedictine monk. Upon the fading parchment is a list of cryptic predictions — one short prognostication for each year. Noted prophetic interpreter Peter Lemesurier, author of *The Armageddon Script* (Element Books), has said, "Clearly, it should not be beyond the wit of a man to link each of these predictions with some event or other during the year in question, though whether this would testify more to the ingenuity of the interpreter or the accuracy of the prophet is open to question."

BROTHER GENET A French Abbot of the convent of Clarisses in Fonjères, Bretagne. His prophecies, all made prior to 1798, were published in 1819 in Paris by Baucé. One of his most notable comments concerned the twentieth century, which he devoutly believed would not pass before witnessing the Lord's Final Judgment.

GOOD HORSE NATION (OYATÉ SUNKAWAKAN) Contemporary Native American mystic. He is a Visayan Medicine Man, Pipe Carrier and Sundancer of the Lakota Teton Sioux. Spiritual Advisor to Ableza Tiospaye Medicine Center.

G.I. GURDJIEFF (1877-1949) There could be many labels pinned on this modern mystic: Enlightened one, Sufi master, devil. Gurdjieff's favorite was simply, "a teacher of dance." He was born in Alexandropol in Russian Armenia and was known as a precocious child who grew to be an independent and rebellious young man. For some twenty years, Gurdjieff traveled throughout the most remote regions of Tibet, Central Asia and the Middle East in his obsession to understand the secrets hiding beyond all life's odd and mysterious phenomena. Gurdjieff began collecting disciples in Moscow just prior to World War I. However, his efforts to establish his mystery school were thwarted by the Russian Revolution.

Gurdjieff often told his disciples that one must first be a master of this world before one can master the other world. An example of this was his uncanny way of always managing to procure the worldly necessities to sustain his spiritual work. He and his flock of seekers left Russia destitute, yet by 1922 Gurdjieff managed to purchase the Château du Prieuré, near Paris, where he reopened his Institute for the Harmonious Development of Man. Much of his spiritual work at the Prieuré focused on the development of sacred dance techniques and often arduous physical tasks which pushed one beyond one's limits of endurance — or more accurately, resistance — to higher states of energy and consciousness.

In 1924 Gurdjieff crashed his car into a tree. The police found him comatose by the side of the wreck, neatly tucked under a blanket and with his head on a pillow. No explanation could be made how Gurdjieff, a man with a severe concussion and internal injuries was able to open the trunk, retrieve a blanket and pillow and lay himself down unassisted.

He recovered, disbanded the Mystery School and devoted himself to recording his teachings in three volumes: *Beelzebub's Tales to his Grandson, Meetings with Remarkable Men*, and finally, *Life is real only then when "I am."*

From 1933 onward he lived almost exclusively in Paris in a small apartment where he weathered out the Nazi occupation from 1940 to 1944. He spent his final years imparting his understanding of universal truth to a small band of dedicated disciples at nightly meetings in his flat.

HERMES The more objective ancient scholars say Hermes Trismegistus was a philosopher or a series of philosophers living in Alexandria during the first few centuries after Christ. His rebellious writings against the cut-and-dried, rote teachings of Greek and Platonic orthodoxy were compiled in the *Hermetica*.

More subjective sources place Hermes far back into antediluvian times as the great Atlantean adept, God-realized or actually a god in his own right. According to them, he founded the Egyptian mystery schools after the Atlantean island empire became "all wet" in one climactic inundation as far back as 12,000 years ago. This Hermes is credited with setting the foundation for nearly all Western mystical teachings. In his book *The White Goddess*, Robert Graves specifies Hermes' cosmic role as the "Leader of Souls." He is responsible for the creation of astronomy, and his teachings are even considered by occult researchers to be the root of the Tarot.

The prophecies used in this book come from a third dialogue to Asclepius attributed to an author using the *nom de plume* of Hermes. It foresees and bewails a future in which Christianity destroys all pagan virtues.

ST HILDEGARD (1098-1179) Called the "Sibyl of the Rhine," she was born at Bermersheim, Germany. She entered a Benedictine convent near Diessenberg, of which she became Mother Superior in 1136. She is considered one of the most remarkable women of medieval times. Some of her proliferous writing included expository works on the Gospels, the lives of local saints and even books on natural science and the human body, filled with careful and objective observations. Around 1147, she moved her convent to Rupertsberg, near Bingen, where she made her prophetic pronouncements in an apocalyptic work called *Scivias*. Her highly colored and allegorical "oracles" and "revelations" were received with equal belief and condemnation; however she had powerful friends and was never threatened with burning. In her long life of eighty years she corresponded at length with four popes, two emperors, King Henry II of England and with such eminent ecclesiastics as St Bernard of Clairvaux, the close friend of the Irish prophet, St Malachy.

HANS HOLZER'S "Survey of the Future" was compiled in 1971 by this eminent parapsychologist. It is a compendium of predictions by a selected group of British and American psychics and seers he was testing for accuracy. His findings were published in *The Prophets Speak* (New York: Bobbs-Merrill, 1971 — out of print).

GRANDFATHER SEMU HUARTE (1904-) Contemporary American Indian medicine man of the Chumash tribe of Ojai, California. This soft-spoken man of the earth has endured a lifetime of persecution by the white man with patience and humor. For example, he recounts that as a child he was continually beaten by the other kids at elementary school. The predominantly white-Christian children also used to beat another child who was Jewish, because the other kids believed he killed Christ. One day when Young Semu and the Jewish child were being hunted down for a beating after school, Semu asked him, "Why did you kill him?" "Kill him?" replied his bruised friend, "I didn't even know the guy!"

IRENE F. HUGHES Contemporary American clairvoyant from Chicago.

IRLMAIER Pseudonym for a contemporary Bavarian clairvoyant from Freilassing.

ISAIAH As in the case of Hellenistic seers like Hermes Trismegistus, this Old Testament prophet's name was used by several people and later consolidated into the illusion of one man. The "First Isaiah" is primarily responsible for chapters 1-39, though changes in narrative style hint that some passages were penned by his disciples. This Isaiah of Jerusalem, as he is called, was an adviser to four kings of Judah: Uzziah, 783-742 BC; Jotham 742-735 BC; Ahaz, 735-715 BC; and Hezekiah, 715-687 BC. History remembers him as an eloquent religious moralist and poetic genius, speaking against political treacheries. These intrigues threatened his southern kingdom of Judah by setting a course similar to that which precipitated the conquest of the northern kingdom of Israel by the Assyrian Empire in 721 BC.

Chapters 40-55 are thought to be authored by an unknown man generally identified as the "Second Isaiah," who made his prophetic mark toward the close of the Exile to Babylon (587-539 BC).

The final chapters (56-66) are descriptions from diverse authors using the "Isaiah" pseudonym. They are spiced with the hopes and discouragements of the post-exile period and describe Israel's effort to rebuild and restore the promised land to its former glory. This group of authors is often categorized under the title "Trito Isaiah" or "Third Isaiah."

JEREMIAH Jewish prophet who endured a long and frustrating ministry with patience and fortitude. He had undying faith that his beloved people of Judah would come through the darkest night and survive. He endured much persecution and ridicule for predicting the sack of Jerusalem and the destruction of the Holy Temple by the Babylonians, which did take place several years afterwards, around 587 BC. He is known to have been among the fugitives who escaped

330

into Egypt. There he made further gloomy predictions peppered with a few glimmers of hope and future consolation. It seems that few of his contemporaries believed his tidings of good news either. Yet he was again proven right when the Israelites eventually freed themselves from the Babylonian yoke.

Some scholars believe a number of the prophet's writings, such as "prophecies against the nations" (chapters 46-51), are authored by his disciple Baruch or other prophets of a later, happier era.

JOEL (c.600 BC) Nothing else is known about this Old Testament prophet but his dramatic eschatological visions of cosmic omens, plagues, divine wars, ruin and restoration. Scholars place Joel either as far back as 600 BC or as early as 350 BC. Most place him somewhere around the time of the Second Temple of Jerusalem, between 450 to 400 BC.

ANTON JOHANSSON (1858-1929) A simple Norwegian fisherman who was born in Sweden and moved to the fjords of Arctic Norway at the age of sixteen. Johansson was a deeply religious man who attributed his gift of future sight to the power and love of God. He worked as a shepherd, teacher, fisherman and later as a surveyor mapping the inhospitable wilderness and Arctic wastes of the Norwegian province of Finnmark. His fellow workers remember him as a man of honesty, courage and a simple faith in God, unencumbered by denominational crutches. Most of his early prophetic visions concerned friends and acquaintances in his town.

He accurately predicted calamities such as the great volcanic eruption in 1902 that destroyed the city of St Pierre on the Caribbean island of Martinique, the great San Francisco earthquake of 1906, and the tremor in 1908 that razed the Italian city of Messina. Like Morgan Robertson and Cheiro, he predicted the sinking of the *Titanic*, but he was also able to name the ship and one of the victims of the sinking, millionaire John Jacob Astor VI.

Most of his predictions about world events were revealed one midnight in November 1907. Johansson was awakened from a deep and dreamless sleep by a voice and a blinding shaft of light. First he was taken into the sky to look down on the assassination of Austrian Archduke Francis Ferdinand. He then hovered over the events of World War I, and the Russian (Communist) and German (Nazi) Revolutions which followed. He may even have seen the future superstorms arising from the greenhouse effect.

ST JOHN OF PATMOS The author of the New Testament's unique and thoroughly apocalyptic document, *The Book of Revelation*, written around AD 81 to 96, was the last in the line of Biblical prophets. The devout Christian convert probably wrote his revelations of doom in the gloomy confines of a prison cave on the Greek island of Patmos. There, he was the guest of the same Roman Empire he so psychedelically and accurately condemns to future collapse. He was paid for his efforts with a fatal nudge over a cliff.

It is popularly believed that John of Revelation and the Apostle John are the same. A closer examination of the two writing styles strongly indicates that they were different personalities.

There's also much debate about whether some of Revelation's prophecies are retroactive. Some scholars believe the "Beast" or Antichrist is not in our future but is long ago buried in our past. The number "666" in Hebraic numerals resembles the Latin spelling of none other than John's Roman contemporary, the bloodthirsty Emperor Nero.

KATE-ZAHL (first century AD) Considered the greatest prophet of the ancient Toltec Indians of Central Mexico. Kate-Zahl forecast the fate of the sacred Toltec city of Tula, the city modern scholars and archaeologists believe to be the recently unearthed ruins of Teotihuacan in Central Mexico. Among Kate-Zahl's remarkable successes were the forecasts of the coming of the Spaniard conquistadors wearing "suits of shining metal" who fired "thunder-rods" (muskets). He also described the coming Native American apocalypse caused by the white man's invasion; the fall of the Aztecs to Cortés; and detailed the Toltecs' own version of the Jewish Diaspora, which took place nearly five centuries after his death. He believed, as do many native seers across both Americas, that the "white Easterners" will busy themselves with the improvement of their infernal weapons until they are completely destroyed in a final war scheduled to take place in our near future. After this event, the Toltecs and those bound by living a life dedicated to the attainment of love and consciousness, will rebuild the sacred city of Tula. It will later become one of the spiritual and cultural centers of the coming New Mankind.

J. KRISHNAMURTI (1895-1986) South Indian philosopher and meditator, born in Andhra Pradesh. English occultist C.W. Leadbeater purportedly "discovered" the frail 13-year-old boy on a beach outside Madras. He later convinced Annie Besant and other leaders of the Theosophist movement that the young Brahmin's aura was of tremendous purity and innocence, making him a possible vehicle for the soul of Lord Maitreya, the great world teacher foretold by Theosophy's founder, Madame Blavatsky.

Leadbeater and Besant adopted the boy and set him down a course of arduous preparation of body, mind and spirit for the proscribed moment of Maitreya's advent. When Krishnamurti was thiry-four, this unique experiment in the annals of occult intrigue reached its climax. In 1929 he was to inaugurate the transmigration at a world gathering of Theosophists in Ommen, Holland. Rather than declare himself the Maitreya, he publicly ordered the disbanding of the Order of the Star of the East, the organization that had been established for his use as the Messiah. He resigned as its leader, stating, "I maintain that Truth is a pathless Land, and you cannot approach it by any path whatsoever, by any religion, by any sect. That is my point of view and I adhere to that absolutely and unconditionally. Truth, being limitless, unconditioned, unapproachable by any path whatsoever, cannot be organized; nor should any organization be formed to lead or to coerce people along any particular path. The moment you follow someone, you cease to follow Truth. I have only one purpose: To make man free, to urge him towards freedom; to help him break away from all limitations, for that alone will give him eternal happiness, will give him the unconditioned realization of the Self."

With hands clasped together bowing in farewell, Krishnamurti bade leave from the stunned audience at Ommen and spent the next five decades being a guru-less guru of un-following followers. He spoke regularly and untiringly about his experience of witnessing truth. He was deeply concerned with child education and oversaw the establishment of a series of Krishnamurti Schools by his un-disciples in America, England, Switzerland and India.

It is said that Krishnamurti did not obtain full spiritual enlightenment until 1948. However, he had already attracted and inspired with his discourses and numerous books many of this century's leading philosophers — eminent scientists such as David Bohm and Rupert Sheldrake, and writers of such stature as Aldous Huxley. He gave lectures right up until his death at the age of ninety-one.

EMMA KUNZ (1892-1963) Swiss seeress and mystic. Born in the village of Brittnau. At the age of nineteen, she traveled to America in search of a runaway lover she never found. She returned to her village and survived through menial jobs, working as a maid and laboring at a knitting factory. During that time, she also wrote and published poetry.

Her real career as a mystic and healer began at the age of forty, when she started curing people, using a pendulum as a diagnostic tool. She healed the ill and crippled primarily with a mineral substance she found in an alpine cave which she called AION A ("Aion" is Greek for "infinite"), along with herbal medicines. Many people in the surrounding countryside declared her healing successes miraculous. Emma Kunz would never use the word herself. She insisted that these natural forces are available to everyone; they are only hidden because people with materialistically-oriented minds keep their awareness turned away from their intuitive sense.

Eventually her healing practices attracted persecution and she was forced to move away from Brittnau to another Swiss canton. There she devoted herself to research into healing and the paranormal until her death at the age of seventy-one.

Frau Kunz also proved to be no mean predictor. She relates that often she saw past, present and future events "independent of time and space." She checked her visions through a pendulum and drawings of amazing geometric shapes of which she said, "My pictures will be understood only in the twenty-first century." Among her more notable predictions were the invention by America of a "weapon that could destroy the whole world (the atom bomb)" as well as the advent of manned rockets which would punch holes in the atmosphere. These, she said, would allow deadly rays from space to radiate upon the Earth's surface, which would "kill millions" if it wasn't stopped in time. Science has only caught up with her insights after fifty years. It is now known that rocket exhaust is one of the major factors in diminishing the ozone layer.

PROPHECY OF LA SALETTE Mélanie Calvat, a stonemason's daughter, born at Isère, France in 1831, had a vision of the Holy Virgin on 19 September 1846. The published report of the day declares that the fourteen-year-old was descending a slope with her companion, Maximine Giraud, heading for a small stream in the mountains of the commune of La Salette, near Grenoble. At first, Mélanie thought the sun had fallen next to the creek. The shepherdesses beheld a glowing ball which opened and issued forth "a beautiful lady, all light and flowers," said Mélanie. The lady sat on some stones lining the creek and huddled forward, her face buried in her hands in a gesture of great sorrow. The girls watched speechless as the lady suddenly floated into the air where she hovered motion-less in a nun's habit resplendent with pearls. She conveyed a prophecy bemoaning the decline of spirituality in the world, the fall of the Catholic Church and a litany of civil and world wars, destruction of cities, etc. She also gave what sounds like a close description of the greenhouse effect which would predate a global paroxysm of seismic and volcanic activity. The Bishop of Grenoble believed their story and sent Mélanie Calvat to Pope Pius XI to relate everything they had heard and seen. Many books have since been published concerning this mystical event.

ST MALACHY (1094-1148) Also known as Mael Maedoc Ua Morgair. Born in Armagh, Ireland, reportedly from noble lineage on his father's side. He was a product of the island's deeply ingrained legacy of Celtic mystery and clairvoyance.

Most of our information concerning this Irish abbot comes from his biographer and close friend, St Bernard of Clairvaux. In 1139, Malachy set forth from Ireland on a harrowing pilgrimage to Rome. According to another Malachy biographer, the Abbé Cucherat, while seeing the Holy City for the first time, Malachy experienced his famous vision predicting the future succession 112 popes unto doomsday.

Malachy stayed in Rome between 1139 and 1140 and received the title of Bishop and Papal Legate (ambassador). He returned to minister to the faithful in Ireland, where he ruffled the conservative feathers of many by introducing a foreign custom of building an oratory in stone rather than wood.

He fell ill while on his second pilgrimage to Rome and died at the monastery at Clairvaux, in the arms of his good friend St Bernard.

MARIA AND ELSA On 10 December 1937, two peasant women from Voltaga, in northern Italy, received stigmata (bleeding wounds on the palms and feet, imitating those suffered by Christ on the cross), which they claimed to be a gift from the savior himself. The "gift" they gave to the world at large was a lurid description of the next two world wars: The second and the third.

PROPHECY OF MARIA LAACH Sixteenth-century records from the monastery of Maria Laach in the Rhineland region of Germany.

PROPHECY OF MARIENTHAL North of Strasbourg, near the town of Haguenau, lies the thirteenth-century monastery of Marienthal. This famous place of Alsatian pilgrimage has been both a sanctuary for war's refugees and a billet for conquering warriors. It is a phoenix of wooden beams, faith and stone — often burned and razed, only to be faithfully rebuilt. The reason for its resilience is recounted from a legend which says that whoever visits this oasis from history's storms will never be oppressed by his destiny. The Marienthal monastery has within its walls a certain *Book of Pilgrimage*, printed in 1749 in Haguenau. It is something like a guest book for wondering monks and seekers; its pages also contain a prophecy in medieval verse which stands as a remarkably accurate chronicle of "coming events of the twentieth century."

MAYAN CALENDAR Archaeologists estimate that pre-Columbian soothsayers and astrologers of ancient Mexico had observed and recorded the movements of the heavens for 4,000 years and had developed a calendar so accurate that any given day could be ascertained without duplication for 370,000 years. The Mayans could calculate with an efficiency equal to that of their Chaldean contemporaries, long before the birth of Christ and 1,500 years before the birth of the Gregorian Calendar we use today.

MEISHU-SAMA (1882-1955) AKA Mokichi Okada, Japanese founder of Sekai-kyusei-kyo, a splinter Shinto sect which claimed to channel messages from the Japanese Sun God (or chief creator), as seen in the Shinto divine hierarchy.

MERLIN (fifth century AD) England's most illustrious prophet. Historical opinion is divided on whether the magician immortalized in the legend of King Arthur's court was a real or mythical person. Popular folk belief had it that Merlin was the devil's spawn from an unholy intercourse between a demon and a blushing nun.

MICAH (eighth century BC) A minor Old Testament prophet whose name in Hebrew means "who is like Jehovah." He was named after the Judean village of Moresheth, once a dependency of the Philistine city of Gath. He was a younger contemporary of Isaiah and something of a prophetic populist, seeing the future through the bias of a simple peasant wandering the countryside. He began his ministry just prior to the fall of Samaria in 721 BC. Micah's prophetic prejudice focuses on the sins of land-grabbing, the injustice of the powerful over the weak and the prophetic fraud of his pre-scient colleagues. He correctly foresaw (or at least cast his lot with collective Jewish forecasts) that all of Israel's iniquities

would cause the fall of Jerusalem and the destruction of the Temple of Solomon.

The prophecies included in this book are more than likely authored by Old Testament seers using the "Micah" pseudonym between the eighth and first century BC. Scholars believe only the first three chapters were written by the original Micah.

MOHAMMED (570?-632) The prophet and founder of Islam, born in Mecca. He spent much of his youth traveling with the Meccan camel caravans. He spent considerable time with the Bedouin tribesmen, from whom he learned much concerning the religions of ancient Arabia. Mohammed also met Nestorian Christians, who taught him about Jesus and the Christian scriptures.

At twenty-six, he married Khadijah, a wealthy widow nearly fifteen years his senior, who made Mohammed her business manager. It is said that she possessed exceptional intellect, and her integrity and devotion made her the strong woman behind the man who founded Islam. The poor caravan trader was elevated by marriage to the social heights of the rich and powerful, but this did not corrupt him. Mohammed was known around Mecca by the nickname "faithful and true" for his exemplary conduct.

He might have lived out his days just as one of Mecca's most upstanding citizens if it wasn't for that eventful day when, meditating in a cave in Mt Hira, he heard the voice of God. While he lay completely wrapped in a cloak, he experienced being bathed in an ocean of light. He lay there drowned in the all-pervading sense of perfect peace and tranquillity. When he awoke, Mohammed beheld the Angel Gabriel standing before him. The Angel spoke in a clear and wonderful voice and declared him to be the only Prophet of the living God.

He began his trance dictation of the Islamic holy book, the Qu'ran. Fearing Mohammed's growing popularity, many diverse pagan factions in Mecca planned to assassinate him. Mohammed heard of the plot in time and slipped away to join the rest of his followers journeying to Medina. This flight, or "Hegira," is the basis of the Islamic chronological system.

In the year eight he marched his army back into Mecca to make it his holy city, and ordered all 350 pagan images within the sacred Kaaba smashed to bits. He granted amnesty to all his enemies and dedicated the Kaaba to Allah, the monotheistic God of Islam. After his death at the age of sixty-two, as a result of being poisoned seven years earlier, Islam rapidly spread throughout Asia Minor and North Africa and became one of the great religions of the world. It seems that the enemies of any religion never learn from history. Crucify or poison a religion's founder and you ensure the spread of his religion.

KING MONTEZUMA II (1480?-1520) (See "Terror and Hope" page 7).

RUTH MONTGOMERY After many years as a syndicated

Washington columnist on politics and world affairs, Ruth Montgomery focused her attention on metaphysical and psychic matters. She has had international success as a reporter of the paranormal, first with *A Gift of Prophecy*, which explores the life of modern American seeress, Jeane Dixon, and wrote her own prophetic works later on as a medium in her own right. She has claimed to be, since 1971, a channel for the late trance medium, Arthur Ford, and for an assortment of "higher spirits" who she collectively calls her "Guides." She currently resides in Washington DC, where she invites her Guides to answer letters and spice her entertaining and thought-provoking books on popular New Age themes such as mass transmigration, UFOs, prophecy, and reincarnation.

"THE MOTHER" (1878-1973) The name devotees of the Indian mystic, Sri Aurobindo, use when addressing Mira Alfassa, his spiritual successor. She grew up in France as the daughter of a Turkish-Egyptian family. From 1920 she was the constant companion of the Bengali mystic. She helped establish the Aurobindo Ashram in Pondicherry, India. After his death in 1950 she founded her own ashram-city named Auroville and continued to apply her diligence and energy to propagate the teachings of Aurobindo until her death at the age of ninety-five.

JOHANN ADAM MÜLLER During the first decades of the nineteenth century, this simple farmer from Maisback, Prussia, accurately predicted the events of the Napoleonic Wars by means of a luminous, spectral figure. During 1807 the spirit woman and "other voices" commanded him to leave his farm, wife and five children and seek out the King of Prussia. The spirit promised to "send" Müller his important message at the moment of their meeting. After a long and difficult journey, he did at last receive an audience with the King. Müller overcame his shyness and pressed him to carefully read the chapters of Isaiah so the King could better rule his country. William III gave this humble man considerable attention and even paid for his journey home. In Müller's own opinion, the spirit's message was a bit of an anti-climax.

GURU NANAK (1469-1538) Indian religious leader, founder of Sikhism and compiler of the sacred texts. He grew up critical of formal ritualistic expressions of both Islam and Hinduism. In 1499 after his spiritual enlightenment — which he regarded as the commission to begin his work — he took to preaching Sikhism throughout the Punjab in India and beyond until 1521, when he settled in a village he himself founded, called Kartapur. There he lived until his death at the age of sixty-nine. Before he died he appointed a successor. There were to be nine more Gurus of Sikhism until Guru Govind Singh made it one of his last wishes that the final guru be the Sikh scriptures themselves.

NOSTRADAMUS (1503-1566) The Latinized nickname for Michel de Nostredame, whose enigmatic prophetic masterpiece, *The Centuries*, has made him the most famous and controversial prophet of the last four-and-a-half centuries. He was born to recently-"Christianized" Jews in the town of St Rémy, Provence. His father, Jacques, was a prosperous notary.

His mysterious talent for prophecy was first encouraged by his grandfathers, both learned men of the Renaissance and former personal physicians to the most free thinking king of the time, René The Good of Provence, and his son, the Duke of Calabria. Their eager pupil showed a superior aptitude for math and the celestial science of astrology.

His paternal grandfather deemed him ready at fourteen to study liberal arts at Avignon, the Papal enclave of Provence. There he angered his priestly teachers by openly defending astrology and Copernicus. Michel was then sent to study medicine in the University of Montpellier. He breezed through his baccalaureate examinations in 1525. Once he had a license to practice medicine, he dropped out of Montpellier to practice in the countryside throughout South France, where he could freely put his medical theories to the test.

Sixteenth-century France suffered from seasonal bouts of "Le Charbon," the black death. Nostradamus followed the plague's shadow, never leaving a town until the danger had passed. He honed his skills and availed himself of the knowledge and teachers of the Counter-Reformation's mystical underground of alchemists, Jewish Cabalists and pagans. By 1529 he returned to Montpellier where he received his doctorate degree. He remained a professor of medicine there for the following three years until he left to set up a practice in Toulouse.

He later moved to Agen, where he married into a wealthy family and sired a boy and girl. His patients where the rich and beautiful of Agen. However, in 1537 tragedy struck with such brutal intensity that the young doctor's spiritual and mental well being was forever changed. In that year, plague returned to Agen. The healing hands which cured thousands must have wrung themselves helplessly over the cooling corpses of his wife and children. Friends and family turned against him. He was ordered to face the Inquisition for making a chance remark years before: He had seen an inept workman making a statue of the Virgin in bronze, and commented that he was "casting demons." Nostradamus packed up his mule with a few belongings and stole away into the night to avoid the Inquisitors.

For the next ten years, the grieving doctor wandered through Southern Europe and Italy in a self-imposed exile. Tragedy and disillusionment turned his energies inward toward occult studies. At this time his prophetic "sight" began to manifest fully.

After many adventures, Nostradamus returned to Provence in 1544, when one of the century's worst bouts of pestilence was taking place. He almost single-handedly cured the city of Aix and Salon from the plague. In the little city of Salon, he married a rich widow and set up house at the end of town.

At this time he also plunged wholeheartedly into the

occult. He began an annual Almanac with a few cautious stabs at prediction. He was so encouraged by the reaction to the predictions that he embarked on an ambitious project: The future history of the world, told in enigmatic quatrains, using a polyglot smattering of French, Latin, Italian, Hebrew, Arabic and Greek — which has had interpreters of prophecy (including yours truly) scratching their heads ever since.

He began work on *The Centuries* on the night of Good Friday, 1554. A total of seven volumes, or "Centuries," of one hundred quatrains each (except for Century VII, which contained forty-one), were published between 1555 and 1557. The final three Centuries were published posthumously. (Further brushes with the Inquisition over the first edition of *The Centuries* had made him more cautious.)

After Nostradamus predicted the death in a jousting accident of King Henry II of France, he was summoned to Paris in 1556, where he became an intimate occult friend to Queen Catherine De Medici. Nostradamus was safely ensconced back in his Salon study when Henry II fulfilled that prophecy in 1559. Following quatrain 35 Century I to the letter, Henry received a wooden splinter from the jousting shaft during a tournament; it slipped through his helmet's golden visor and plunged behind his eye into his brain. On the night of his death, crowds gathered before the Inquisitors, burning Nostradamus in effigy — hoping the priests would burn him in earnest. Only Nostradamus's friendship with Queen Catherine saved him. This quatrain made Nostradamus the talk of the courts of Europe.

In 1564, while on a tour through the realm, Catherine (now the Queen Regent) and the adolescent King Charles IX visited the aging prophet of Salon. Before resuming their tour, Catherine had Charles IX honor Nostradamus with the title Counselor and Physician in Ordinary, with the privileges and salary this implied.

Nostradamus reached the high point of his prophetic career with only a year and eight months left to live. His last prediction concerned his own approaching death: *On his return from the Embassy, the King's gift put in place. He will do nothing more. He will be gone to God. Close relatives, friends, brothers by blood (will find him) completely dead near the bed and the bench.* At daybreak on 29 June 1556, the prophet's body was found, exactly as he predicted.

ST ODILE (died c. 720) Patroness of Alsace, France. Abbess of Hohenburg (Odilienberg) Monastery in the Vosges mountains. She began life in total blindness. Her father, Adalric of Alsace, believed this to be an evil omen and had the child banished to a nunnery. Her intense devotion to God was already apparent even at such a tender age. So was her ability to predict the future, which she said came as a result of having to learn how to live without sight. It is claimed her sight was miraculously restored by the intensity of her prayers and the healing powers of the local bishop. When he heard this, her father had a change of heart and ordered her brought home. She soon found the lifestyle of a princess unappealing

and finally persuaded her father to turn one of his castles into a nunnery, where she lived out her days as its abbess. St Odile's prophecies are said to be her final written testament before dying.

OSHO (Bhagwan Shree Rajneesh) (1931-1990) This controversial Indian mystic and founder of the Neo-Sannyas movement was a mystic of many names. Osho was born Rajneesh Chandra Mohan, in Kuchwada, a small village in central India. Stories of his early years describe him as an independent, rebellious child, who questioned all social, religious and philosophical beliefs.

On midnight of 21 March 1953, at the age of twenty-one, Osho claimed that he had become fully awakened. He described it thus:

"The past was disappearing — as if it had never belonged to me...as if it was someone else's story....All scriptures appeared dead and all the words that had been used for this experience looked very pale, anemic. This was so alive — it was a tidal wave of bliss....I felt a throbbing of life all around me, a great vibration almost like a hurricane; a great storm of light, joy, ecstasy....The whole universe became a benediction." (*The Discipline of Transcendence*, 1977)

He received his MA from the University of Sagar with First-Class Honors in Philosophy in 1956. He was a professor at the Sanskrit College in Raipur and later was appointed Professor of Philosophy at the University of Jabalpur. He soon became well-known throughout India as a powerful and passionate speaker, often challenging orthodox religious leaders in public debates.

Professor Rajneesh Chandra Mohan, now known as the Acharya Rajneesh, ("Acharya" means "spiritual teacher"), left the university in 1966 and began addressing gatherings of 50,000 to 100,000 all over India, and conducting and experimenting with new, more cathartic forms of meditation during camps attended by thousands.

At the beginning of the 1970s, he took the name Bhagwan Shree Rajneesh ("Bhagwan" means "the Blessed One"), a scandal which shocked Indian society. In 1974 he established a commune in Poona, India which attracted tens of thousands of seekers from the West. In those years, the Shree Rajneesh Ashram became the premier growth and therapy center of the world.

In 1981 Bhagwan traveled to the US allegedly to seek medical attention for a degenerating lower back condition. At that time, he began a three-year self-imposed public silence which he claimed was done to help clear off those followers who could only hear his words and not the existential truth hidden beyond them in silence. By the mid-1980s, Rajneeshpuram had become the largest and most controversial spiritual community ever pioneered in America.

Opposition to the commune was strong. Both sides were guilty of inflammatory behavior which worsened the situation. Heavy political pressure was brought to bear to prevent the expansion of the city.

Bhagwan broke his spiritual silence in the fall of 1984,

which ostensibly led to the defection of his personal secretary, Ma Anand Sheela, and her handful of lieutenants. Later they were found guilty of crimes that included poisoning, arson, wiretapping, and attempted murder. Bhagwan invited law enforcement officials to investigate the crimes of Sheela and her group. By late October of that year, a US federal grand jury in Portland secretly indicted Bhagwan and seven others on relatively minor charges of immigration fraud.

Assured by federal officials that there was no warrant for Bhagwan's arrest, his followers took him to Charlotte, North Carolina the night of October 27, to defuse rumorsofa National Guard invasion of his commune set for the following day.

Bhagwan was arrested at gunpoint, and without a warrant, by federal marshals after he landed at the Charlotte airport. He was held without bail for twelve days and held incommunicado for three. His followers believe that he was poisoned in jail with thallium, a heavy metal.

Fearing for his life, Bhagwan's attorneys agreed to an Alford Plea on two out of thirty-five of the original charges against him. (According to the rules of the plea, the defendant maintains innocence while saying that the prosecution could have convicted him.) Bhagwan was fined $400,000 and deported from America in November 1985.

He returned to India for only a brief respite, then began what he defined as a world tour to express his vision (February and July 1986). A total of twenty-one countries in Europe and the Americas either refused to grant him a visitor's visa or revoked his visa upon his arrival, and forced him and his jet-setting entourage to leave, in some cases at gunpoint. Bhagwan returned to India, and by January 1987 he was once again gathering tens of thousands of followers to a new and revamped Poona ashram. By September 1989 he was called simply "Osho," signifying his complete discontinuity from the past. It is less a name and more a sacred acronym for "Mr" derived from the Zen disciples' salutation to their masters; it also stands for the "oceanic" and orgasmic experience of spiritual enlightenment and refers to the one who experiences this state, the individual.

His health made a rapid decline after his US incarceration. By April 1989, nine months before he died, he set up an inner circle of twenty-one disciples who would make decisions about all the temporal affairs of the commune by unanimous vote.

"Never speak of me in the past tense," was one of his last requests. "My presence here will be many times greater without the burden of my tortured body." So far, his movement continues to flourish. The Poona Ashram has regained and, according to its adherents, exceeded its 1970s attendance records as the world's biggest therapy center relating to the Human-Potential Movement as well as for the study of meditation.

PADMASAMBHAVA (eighth century AD) Founder of Tibetan Buddhism. He was known as the Lotus-Born, or the Precious Guru who (in 748 AD) left the great Buddhist University of Nalanda to bring the Dharma to the Himalayas. He is also responsible for creating the Tibetan system of astrology.

MONK OF PADUA An eighteenth-century monk whose prophecies parallel those of St Malachy; however they only concern themselves with the last twenty popes before Judgment Day. Accounts of this monk's predictions surfaced in print around 1740. They correctly named a few twentieth-century popes and described their reigns with much more detail than Malachy.

PROPHECY OF PASSAU Arthur Prieditis, author of *The Fate of the Nations* (Llewellyn), discovered this prophetic fragment, which he says has been guarded by a family in Passau, Germany, for over a century. Its lurid accounts parallel scientific speculation on what life would be like in a nuclear winter.

MOLL PITCHER (c. 1731-1815) She has been called the Sibyl of the American Revolution. Born the daughter of a ship's captain, John Dimond, she apparently didn't use her second sight in earnest until after her marriage to Robert Pitcher, a shoemaker, in 1760. At the time of the American Revolution, Moll Pitcher's clairvoyant gifts were so widely recognized that the commander of the British garrison in Boston, Major John Pitcairn, came for a reading.

The American rebels also found Pitcher's forecasts quite reliable. After she dated three of General Washington's victories, he was heard to call her a sibyl and a saint. She also predicted George Washington's ascent as an American icon when she said to him, "Long after you are dust, you and your wife shall reign as king and queen in the hearts of your country's people."

Although she is best remembered for her accurate forecast of British troop movements and other psychic spying, Moll Pitcher had a special knack for seeing the future inventions which would make the yet unborn nation a pre-eminent world power.

Moll Pitcher's last prediction was made at the ripe old age of seventy-five. She declared her own death was waiting for the April 9 1815, and, with a little help from chance, she was right.

POPE PIUS X During an audience in 1909, the old Pope dozed off. He awakened with a start and exclaimed that he had had a horrible vision, a daydream no pope dare consider: He found himself or a future pope evacuating the Vatican, "stepping over the corpses of his priests."

PRINCESS PRANAZIN Aztec princess and seeress; sister of King Montezuma. See "Terror and Hope" (page 7).

ORSON PRATT (1811-1881) Early Mormon apostle, author, compelling debater and member of the first Quorum of the Twelve Apostles of the Mormon Church. Pratt was a store clerk in Hiram, Ohio, when converted to Mormonism by its founder, Joseph Smith. He went on to become a member of the earliest Mormon mission to England and Scotland (1840). He was appointed a city councilor of Nauvoo City, the first Mormon settlement, where he also held the post of Professor of Mathematics and English Literature at the city's university. In 1847 the Mormons abandoned Nauvoo because of persecution. Pratt acted as an advance scout for Brigham Young's trek to Salt Lake City, Utah. He later became head of the Mormon Church in England (1849) and was the first scholar to divide *The Book of Mormon* into chapters and verses with references. The prophecy concerning a future American civil war comes from *Orson Pratt, Journal of Discourses*, Vol. 20, pp. 151-152, 9 March 1879.

QUETZALCOATL Ancient American Indian philosopher, magician and Avatar. Lest the Christians think their Messiah has a monopoly on virgin birth, Quetzalcoatl was always known as "he who was born of the virgin." He established a school of sacerdotal initiates south of what is modern-day Mexico City, where he imparted his teachings as a priest-prophet-king.

Quetzalcoatl (which means "plumed serpent," the mystical symbol of the Aztec Indians) was thought to be the father of Amerindian astrology. He is credited with the creation of the sacred astrological calendar of ancient Mexico, the Tonalamatl, and for writing *The Book of Good and Bad Days*, also known as *The Book of Fate*.

GREGORY RASPUTIN (1871?-1916) Russian mystic monk, hypnotist and faith healer. For a time he became an influential favorite of the Russian imperial family because of his ability to heal the Czarevitch Alexei, the hemophiliac Romanov heir, from several life-threatening bouts of bleeding. Rasputin's court debaucheries and continued hypnotic power over Czar Nicolas and the Czarina Alexandria made him some dangerous enemies. Certain princes believed his advice to the Czar was causing Russia to lose its war with Germany. They conspired to have Rasputin assassinated in St Petersburg in late December 1916, as he himself had predicted. The English prophet-hypnotist, Count Louis Hamon (Cheiro) had described the assassination details in Rasputin's presence eleven years earlier, after each hypnotist had failed to stare down the other.

SEERESS REGINA German prophetess, popularly known as "the German Cassandra." She was perhaps the most famous German prophetess of the early twentieth century. Within her apocalyptic verse were the accurate forecasts of the time and duration of World Wars I and II. She warned Germany of Hitler: *King and emperor will disappear, and another will lash the whip. An iron crown is for thee, German nation, and it will press and weigh heavily upon thee for many years to come.* She also prophesied a coming ecological disaster which will decimate humanity, leaving only a handful to *build a new world*.

MORGAN ROBERTSON (1861-1915) At least nineteen people

had premonitions of the sinking of the Titanic at least two weeks prior to the disaster. Morgan Robertson, a retired sailor-turned-American-short story writer previewed the disaster in a fiction opus fourteen years before it happened. (See "Terror and Hope," page 12.) Robertson left the sea in 1894 and later tried his hand at writing. Distressed by the failing health of his wife and his fading creative powers, he had himself committed to a psychopathic ward of Bellevue Hospital. After his release he returned to writing but his stories lacked the former "punch." He was found leaning against a bureau in his Atlantic City hotel room dead on his feet from a heart attack.

EMELDA SCOCHY In 1933 a twelve-year-old girl in Ham, Belgium, shared a bit of spiritual bad news about antichrists and faithlessness which she said came to her from the spirit of Christ. Though her divine rave follows the usual heat and brimstone style of Christian doom proclamations, her particular reference to the ocean overflowing its banks may make her apocalypse in "sync" with the rising seas of the twenty-first century.

MOTHER SHIPTON (1488-1561) Any factual account of Ursula Southiel, the Yorkshire witch, better known as "Mother Shipton," suffers a heaping helping of legend and wives' tales. The same is the case for her poetic augurings, which suffer from a witches' blend of forgeries from would-be prophets. Be that as it may, our story begins with Ursula's birth in July of 1488 in a small Yorkshire village. It was whispered around that her mother had a winter visitor of superhuman origins — forked member, goat's head and what-have-you. Her mother Agatha, it is believed, was rewarded for her deflowering with a child destined to possess the same psychic powers as the old goat who done 'er down. The legend-weavers of Yorkshire will tell you that July of 1488 was marred by presages of thunderstorms, frog-voiced ravens and the like. The future Mother Shipton issued from the womb and "fell a-grinning and laughing, after a jeering manner, and immediately the tempest ceased." Hmm, why not? Perhaps the skies had recoiled with a thunderclap at the sight of her, for we are told that she was "larger than common, her body crooked, her face frightful; but her understanding extraordinary." (Thank the devil for small blessings.) At the sight of this "blessed event," her mother retreated to the nearest convent, where she dropped dead.

Little Ursula was given into the care of a nurse and was soon found applying some of her devilish powers to her school chums. The children were nibbled, pushed to the ground and kicked by invisible attackers whenever they dared push their taunts to the limit.

Ursula married at twenty-four. The lucky man was Tobias Shipton, a carpenter in the village of Shipton, near York. She became well-known in the area as a seeress. Her first success was the prophecy of Henry VIII's invasion of northern France in 1513. William Lilly, a seventeenth-century astrologer, claims in his *Collections of Prophecies* (1646) that sixteen out of eighteen predictions attributed to Mother Shipton were already fulfilled when he wrote the book. They mostly concerned the usual Counter-Reformation fare of plagues, famines, wars, fashions, and locally timed historical events. Other hits on the future's bull's eye include the destruction of the Spanish Armada ("The Western monarch's Wooden Horses/Shall be destroyed by the Drake's forces.") She also foresaw the London Fire of 1666.

The verses that made Shipton most famous surfaced in 1880 from the pen of an English editor, Charles Hindley. They more than adequately describe inventions, wars and events of the mid-nineteenth century. It gets a little foggy whether Hindley was actually a charlatan, since one of the "prophecies" he admitted he forged reads: "In 1936...shall mighty wars be planned." Hitler and his jack-booted friends were definitely planning their share of World War II by that time.

According to Mother Shipton/Hindley, World War III will be fought because of the situation in the Middle East. The US is destined to defeat the Arabs in four years of apocalyptica.

The good Mother died peacefully in her bed at the ripe (old crone) age of seventy-three.

SIBYLLINE ORACLES (second century BC-third century AD) In Greek and Roman legend, the name Sibyl is given to a woman inspired with prophetic insight by the god Apollo. The earliest known Sibyl was the Erythræan Herophile, who augured visions concerning the Trojan War. The number of Sibyls later increased to ten: The Erythræan, the Samian, the Trojan or Helespontine, the Phrygian, the Cimmerian, the Delphian (see "Terror and Hope" page 5), the Cumæan, the Libyan, the Babylonian, and the Tiburtine Sibyls. During the Roman Empire certain prophetic verses, known as Sibylline oracles, were attributed to the ten. Their utterances played an important role in Roman religious thinking.

A second wave of Sibylline oracles, written in Greek hexameter verse, came into the possession of Greek and Latin priests of the early Christian church. They are said to come from an inspired prophetess from Babylon, and contain accurate predictions concerning the rise of Christianity and the coming apocalypse. These oracles were quite popular during medieval times. Current scholarly opinion believes them to be composed by Jews, and later by Christians. They seem to imitate earlier pagan oracles in their attempt to win converts. Nevertheless, there are chilling references to present-day ecological disasters and their results, which make these verses more than a holy ad campaign.

TIM SIKYEA Canadian Denee Indian (Yellowknives Tribe) came to Europe in 1988 because of a vision which prompted him to warn Europeans of the consequences of their actions. He is a healer who believes 80 percent of all diseases are psychological and mainly caused by our stressful modern living. Like many aboriginal seers, Sikea doesn't see his prophecies as etched in stone, but more as warnings for Western man to change now, before it is too late.

JOANNA SOUTHCOTT English religious leader. Daughter of a Devonshire yeoman, Southcott gained attention and eventually gathered 100,000 followers because of her continued accurate predictions concerning events in late eighteenth-century England, the French Revolution, and the rise and fall of Napoleon Bonaparte. In her sixty-fourth year, she believed she had been impregnated by the Holy Ghost and would soon bear the child "Shiloh," a new Christ-figure destined to change the world. Seventeen out of twenty-one doctors agreed that she was pregnant. However, when she died just prior to the Battle of Waterloo in 1815, an autopsy showed no evidence of a child nor was there any clear evidence why she had died.

GRACE SPOTTED EAGLE Native American of the Inuit Nation, companion and translator for Wallace Black Elk. Her predictions included in this book were made during a special celebration ceremony for the public in Portland Oregon, back in 1985.

VESTRICIUS SPURINNA (first century BC) Respected augurer of the Roman Forum. During a religious ceremony, Spurinna examined the entrails of a slaughtered animal and discovered signs of great danger for the Roman dictator, Julius Caesar, which would culminate on 15 March 44 BC. Caesar ignored his warnings and met his death by assassination on the 15th. William Shakespeare immortalized Spurinna's prophetic warning, "Beware the Ides of March," in his play, *Julius Caesar*.

STORMBERGER (eighteenth century) Two centuries ago those dwelling in the Bavarian forests of Germany along the present-day border of Czechoslovakia might chance upon a solitary cowherd with the uncanny talent of throwing a disturbingly accurate prediction or two across their path. His contemporaries might listen in disbelief to his wild and morose nightmares of our century and the apocalyptic decades to come.

His utterances have been verified and written about by numerous Austrian and Bavarian prophecy scholars, but many of the documents, pamphlets and books they wrote were condemned to the furnaces by the Nazis in 1934. Hitler's propaganda minister, Joseph Goebbels, was no doubt angered by Stormberger's anti-Nazi premonitions about the War's disastrous results for Hitlerian Germany. Enough fragments survived to prove that he was one of the most frank and accurate seers of all time. He foresaw the invention of cars, trains and aircraft. He augured the very day World War I would begin, as well as its length (four years) and the infernal weapons of mustard gas, mines and tanks. Stormberger predicted the Great Depression, fascist dictators, the division of Germany and future inflationary trends. We might view him with as much hostility as his contemporaries did for his country-bumpkin bluntness concerning our own future: He declared that not one but three world wars will punctuate our century. The one after the end of the Cold War is predicted to be the worst.

MADAME SYLVIA The psychic nom de plume of one of Europe's most famous early twentieth-century clairvoyants, the countess Bianca von Beck-Rzikowsky of Vienna. Many of her clients were kings, princes, politicians and diplomats, mostly from Middle Europe. Many world prophecies lace her numerous correspondences. A sizable portion of them were compiled and printed in a book by Dr F.R. Liesche and have found their way to a larger audience through the dedicated scholarship of Arthur Prieditis, author of *The Fate of the Nations* (Llewellyn). Death brought her psychic career to a close in 1948.

MARIA TAIGI Italian peasant who in 1835 reportedly saw Christ in a vision which parallels other auguries by Swiss seeress Emma Kunz and the German prophet Bartholomaeus. All three warn of a great plague from the sky annihilating most of the human race, which could come from cosmic rays infiltrating the ozone layer of the atmosphere.

TAMO-SAN (1907-) Also known as the Reverend Ryoju Kikuchi of Kamakura. She is well-known in Japan as an enlightened mystic and early champion for the preservation of ecology. Tamo-san is the founder of the Buddhist sect named *Butsu gan syuu* (the eyes of the Buddha), which was approved in 1951. It remains the first new religious sect to be officially recognized by the Japanese government in 500 years.

I had the good fortune to meet Tamo-san during my last visit to India, in 1989. This diminutive woman of advanced years is remarkably strong; I have seen her pick up women twice her size in a loving bear hug. She is graced with a unique singing ability. She stands still as a statue, with her mouth slightly open, and fills an entire auditorium with penetrating and vibrant tones, that immediately send one into a relaxed and nurtured state.

Tamo-san says she was already self-realized before she gave birth to her daughter, Shizuru, who is currently her mother's translator and secretary. Tamo-san once gave some enlightened advice on how to raise children: "One thing I was very careful about was that my daughter was not to develop any fear. When she was a child, I told the people around her not to scream or to startle her, or show fear in her presence."

Shizuru added that Tamo-san never tried to educate or influence her at all. She always left her alone to find and live her own life as she chose. When she sees a child's innocent face, Tamo-san says, she wishes adults would not give all kinds of philosophies and ideas to them: "It spoils them and kills their wisdom inside."

On the subject of her own spiritual path, Tamo-san once said, "I never developed any desire to own anything or to impress others. I was born without anything and I grew up without anything. It was natural for me to live in tune with nature. I never really studied or set a purpose of life, but I lived as I felt was natural."

"Everything I see is shining and filled with love, and it looks beautiful. I just want to see that everything stays beautiful. I don't want to see things being spoiled by human hands."

Tamo-san's message to all simply is: "Everything is a buddha. Everybody is a buddha. You are the flower and I am the flower. We all form flowers and we are all one."

ALFRED, LORD TENNYSON (1809-92) English poet. One of the literary giants of the Romantic era. He wrote *Locksley Hall* in 1842, after a self-imposed period of silence and meditation. Tennyson is not usually known as prescient, however lines 120 through 130 of this poem are indeed a spark of prophetic insight into the future advent of air transport, aerial combat in world wars and the formation of the United Nations. The final lines of the passage promise that we shall live in global peace as a federation of humanity.

TIBETAN ASTROLOGERS Astrology was first introduced to Tibet from India in about AD 749 by Padmasambhava, the founder of Tibetan Lamaism. Although Tibetan astrology resembles the Indian and Chinese systems it is based on, it became a unique discipline of celestial augury rivaling the best Western systems. For centuries, one branch of lamas (priests) has accurately foretold events and counseled Dalai Lamas by calculating from fixed cycles, rather than planetary positions. Instead of an ephemeris, they have fashioned a mathematical process which has accurately predicted the dates of the English and Chinese invasions (1904 and 1950), the beginning and end of World War I and the birth of the last Dalai Lama (1935). Because of his lama astrologers, the thirteenth Dalai Lama was to partially prepare the priesthood for the systematic destruction of Tibet's religious scriptures and holy shrines by the Communist Chinese; the dates of their invasions were confirmed by court astrologers a century before. Astrology helped the lamas pace their efforts over many decades to place decoys of the gold-plated mummies of their spiritual adepts and mock copies of occult scriptures for the Chinese to destroy. The original artifacts and books remain hidden in Himalayan caves until Tibet is once again free.

ALAN VAUGHAN American seer, and one of the highest scoring predictors with the Central Premonitions Registry in New York City. Throughout the 1970s, he was a laboratory psychic at the Maimonides Dream Lab in Brooklyn, New York; Stanford Research Institute in Palo Alto, California; and the City College of New York. Vaughan holds an honorary doctorate in parapsychology for the Central Premonitions Registry and is the author of *Patterns in Prophecy*. He claims his book presents "a workable theory of how man can see into his future and fulfill — or even alter — his life 'blueprint.'"

PROPHECY OF WARSAW A document of unquestionable prophetic genius written by a Polish monk in 1790. It accurately dated and described events of the Polish Partition of 1793, the Napoleonic Wars, the 1848 European Revolution, World War II, and the resulting plague of little wars and struggles of indigenous nations that followed. It does contain one forecast of hope: What appears to be the beginning of a lasting global peace beginning "in 1986." This could represent the year Soviet President Mikhail Gorbachev initiated *perestroika*, triggering the thaw of the Cold War. However, the Polish monk warns us that this window for global peace could shut by the mid-1990s if the right decisions are not made by world leaders.

BRIGHAM YOUNG (1801-1877) American Mormon leader and prophet, born in Whittingham, Vermont. He became the guiding light of the fledgling Mormon religion when its founder, Joseph Smith, was martyred in 1844. Young led 5,000 disciples on a harrowing journey into the American West in search of a promised land far from persecution. They settled next to the Great Salt Lake, in Utah, where he established the Mormon Mecca of Salt Lake City.

Young's predictions examined in this book are from the *Brigham Young, Journal of Discourses*. Vol. 8, pp. 123:15 July 1860). These generally railed against another American wilderness, that of complacency. He warned that before the twenty-first century, America would fall into time of chaos, natural upheavals and civil strife. Some interpreters believe he had presaged the wild 1960s, while others see the upheaval coming in the mid-to-late 1990s, or during the first two decades of the twenty-first century.

Brigham Young was survived by his ninewteen wives and forty-seven children.

Y'SHUA BAR JOSEPH alias Jesus Christ (4?BC-AD 29?) Believed by Christianity's adherents to be the "only begotten son of God" and the Messiah. Many of the presumed facts about his life may have been added centuries later, around the time of the Council of Nicæa (AD 325), when Emperor Constantine organized and institutionalized the Christian priesthood, scriptures and hierarchy.

In the 1980s, a series of new revelations and insights concerning the life of Jesus Christ set the stage for a near-future revision of Christian thought. There is much debate over what Y'shua did between the ages seven through thirty. The Bible records nothing; however there is evidence supporting the theory that he spent most of those twenty-three years studying in the East. Legends say that the thirteenth tribe of Israel, lost during the Exodus from Egypt, settled in Kashmir. The tomb of Moses is purported to be in the valley of Srinagar. Miguel Serrano, in his book *The Serpent of Paradise*, speaks of one legend which says Y'shua returned to Palestine from a long sojourn in "Kashir", which means "equal to Syria." "Kashir" is the
original name of the Indian state of Kashmir. Two villages in Kashmir are named after Messiah of the Jews: Pahalgam, the "village of the shepherd," was built on the spot where Kashmiris say Y'shua rested from his spiritual studies and herded sheep for a time. Ishkuman, "the place of rest of Jesus," is a hamlet outside Srinagar which marks the spot where he rested and preached before making the long journey back to Judea.

Many of Y'shua's most immortal phrases, such as the golden rule, are distinctly Buddhist in nature. Nicholas Nattovisch, a nineteenth-century Russian explorer, discovered Buddhist scriptures in the Himalayan kingdoms of Ladakh and Tibet that included extensive mention of Y'shua studying at various Buddhist shrines and monasteries.

Y'shua the Christ reappears in Biblical chronicles at the age of thirty. After three years, his spiritually volatile ministry earned him condemnation and crucifixion in Jerusalem. The legend which says he rose from the dead after three days is the foundation of all Christian belief. As we enter the Aquarian Age of knowing rather than believing, new questions are being raised about the resurrection. Christian scripture tells us that a Roman soldier pierced Y'shua's side with a spear, and "blood and water flowed out of the wound" (John 19:34). The dead don't bleed. This brings up the question whether Y'shua actually died on the cross or was in a death-like coma when he was taken down. It has been theorized that Joseph of Arimathæa, a rich and influential disciple who had begged for Y'shua's body from Pontius Pilate and "laid it in his own tomb," had secretly nursed him back to health and smuggled him out of Judea. It is speculated that he was helped by the Essenes, an esoteric society of which Y'shua was a member.

There is intriguing evidence supporting the story that, after the trauma of being crucified, Y'shua retired from public religious life and returned to live out his days in Kashmir. He was known by the Kashmiris as Yousa-Asaf. Rather than ascending into heaven, the Kashmiris say, Y'shua remained in silent communion with a gathering of disciples at Pahalgam and died at the ripe old age of 102. One can visit his alleged resting place, a tomb outside of Srinagar reported to be around 1,900 years old. Upon the vault is a carving in stone of two feet pierced by a nail. The inscription, translated from Sharda to English, reads: YOUSA-ASAF (KHANYA, SRINAGAR).

Most of Y'shua's prophecies were not written down until many years following his crucifixion, and there is every possibility that they were extensively revised by the Council of Nicæa. However, this would make the revisionists prophets in their own right, since many of Y'shua's forecasts more than adequately resemble events in modern times.

ZECHARIAH One of the most enigmatic of the Semitic prophets, whose style foreshadowed the apocalyptic cadences and visions of Daniel and St John of Patmos. Scholars believe Zechariah's first and second books were written by two different men. The first chapters (1-8) were penned in Jerusalem during the time following the Exile to Babylon, when the city was once again rising out of its ashes and re-establishing itself as a living and religious city. The second book (chapters 9-14) was written at a much later time: After the Maccabean War, which drew to a close around the year 160 BC. Book two is a stylistic blender beyond any unified description: At one moment recalling the symbolic acts of earlier prophets like Jeremiah and Ezekiel; at another, threatening and promising the people of Zion a future of apocalyptic flames and divine redemption.

"Zechariah" means "the Lord remembers."

Alli, Antero. *Astrologik: The Interpretive Art of Astrology*. Seattle, WA: Vigilantero Press, 1990.

Ambres. *Ambres*. Torsby, Sweden: AB Sturid, 1992.

Anzar, Nadsherwan. *The Beloved: The Life and Works of Meher Baba*. North Myrtle Beach, SC: Sheriar Press, 1974.

Aurobindo, Sri. *The Future Evolution of Man: The Divine Life Upon Earth*. Wheaton, IL: Quest Books, 1974.

Aurobindo, Sri. *Savitri: A Legend and A Symbol*. Pondicherry: Sri Aurobindo Ashram, 1990, 13th printing.

Avabhasa, Da (Free John). *The Dawn Horse Testament*. Clearlake, CA: Dawn Horse Press, new standard edition, 1991.

Baba, Meher, and D.E. Stevens, ed. *Listen Humanity*. San Francisco, CA: Harper & Row/Colophon, 1971.

Bahá'u'lláh. *A Synopsis and Codification of the Laws and Ordinances of the Kitáb-i-Aqdas. The Most Holy Book of Bahá'u'lláh*. Compiled by the Universal House of Justice. Haifa: Bahá'í World Center, 1973.

'Abdu'l-Baha. *Paris Talks*. London: Bahá'í Publishing Trust, 1944.

'Abdu'l-Baha. *The Promulgation of Universal Peace*. Wilmette IL: Bahá'í Publishing Trust, 1982.

'Abdu'l-Baha. *The Secret of Divine Civilization*. Wilmette IL: Bahá'í Publishing Trust, 1957 and 1970.

'Abdu'l-Baha. *Selections from the Writings of 'Abdu'l-Baha*. Haifa: Bahá'í World Center, 1978.

Baigent, Michael; Richard Leigh, and Henry Lincoln. *The Messianic Legacy*. London: Corgi Books, 1987.

Batra, Ravi. *The Great Depression of 1990*. New York: S&S Trade, 1987.

Berlitz, Charles. *Doomsday 1999*. New York: Doubleday, 1981.

Bernbaum, Edwin. *The Way to Shambhala: A Search for the Mythical Kingdom beyond the Himalayas*. Garden City, NJ: Anchor Press/Doubleday, 1980.

Blavatsky, H.P. *The Secret Doctrine*. Madras, India: Theosophical Publishing House, 1888.

The New English Bible. New York: Oxford University Press, 1976.

Bonder, Saniel. *The Divine Emergence of the World-Teacher: the Realization, the Revelation, and the Revealing Ordeal of Heart-Master Da Love-Ananda: a Biographical Celebration*. Clearlake, CA: Dawn Horse Press, 1990.

Brown, Lester R. *The State of the World 1988*. New York: W.W. Norton, 1987.

Brown, Lester R. *The State of the World 1989*. New York: W.W. Norton, 1989.

Brown, Lester R. *The State of the World 1990*. New York: W.W. Norton, 1990.

Brown, Lester R. *The State of the World 1991*. New York: W.W. Norton, 1991.

Butler, Bill. *The Dictionary of the Tarot*. New York: Schocken Books, 1975.

Carter, Mary Ellen. *Edgar Cayce on Prophecy: His Remarkable Visions of the Future — and How They Can Guide Your Life Today*. New York: Warner Books, 1988.

Cheiro, Count Louis Hamon. *Cheiro's World Predictions*. Santa Fe, NM: Sun Books/Sun Publishing, 1981.

Crowley, Aleister. *777 and Other Cabalistic Writings*. New York: Samuel Weiser, 1973.

Edmonds, I.G. *Second Sight: People Who Read the Future*. New York: Thomas Nelson Inc. Publishers, 1977.

Esslemont, J.E. *Bahá'u'lláh and the New Era*. Wilmette, IL: Bahá'í Publishing Trust, 1966, reprint.

Fisher, Joe. *Predictions*. Toronto: Collins, 1980.

Forrest, Steven. *The Inner Sky: The Dynamic New Astrology for Everyone*. New York: Bantam, 1984.

Free John, Da (Da Avabhasa). *Garbage and the Goddess*. Lowerlake, CA: Dawn Horse Press, 1974.

Free John, Da. *The Enlightenment of the Whole Body*. Middletown CA: Dawn Horse Press, 1978.

Free John, Da. *Scientific Proof of the Existence of God Will Soon Be Announced at the White House.* Middletown, CA: Dawn Horse Press, 1980.

Forman, Henry James. *The Story of Prophecy*. Santa

Bibliography

Fe, NM: Sun Books/Sun Publishing, 1981, first printing.

Fromm, Erich. *To Have or To Be? A New Blueprint for Mankind.* London: Abacus, 1978.

Glass, Justine. *They Foresaw the Future.* New York: G. P. Putnam's Sons, 1969.

Goodman, Jeffrey. *We are the Earthquake Generation.* New York: Berkeley Books, 1978.

Graham, Lloyd M. *Deceptions and Myths of the Bible: Is the Holy Bible Holy? Is It the Word of God?* New York: Bell, 1979.

Green, Jeff. *Uranus: Freedom from the Known.* St Paul MN: Llewellyn, 1988.

Greene, Owen. *Nuclear Winter.* Cambridge, MA: Polity Press, 1985.

Gribbin, John. *Future Weather and the Greenhouse Effect.* London: Delta/Eleanor Friede, 1982.

Ground Zero. *Nuclear War: What's in It for You?* New York: Ground Zero, 1982.

Gunther, Bernard. *Neo Tantra: Bhagwan Shree Rajneesh on Sex, Love, Prayer and Transcendence.* San Francisco, CA: Harper & Row, 1980.

Gurdjieff, G.I. *All and Everything: Beelzebub's Tales to His Grandson.* New York: Arkana, 1985.

Gurdjieff, G.I. *Life Is Real Only Then When "I am": All and Everything/Third Series.* New York: E.P. Dutton, 1981.

Haich, Elizabeth. *Initiation.* Palo Alto, CA: Seed Center, 1974.

Hall, Manly P. *The Secret Teachings of all the Ages.* Los Angeles, CA: The Philosophical Research Society Inc., 1978.

Hazra, R.C. *Studies in the Puranic Records on Hindu Rites and Customs.* Delhi: Motilal Banarsidass, 1975.

Holzer, Hans. *The Prophets Speak.* New York: Bobbs-Merrill, 1971.

International Bible Society. *Holy Bible: New International Version.* East Brunswick, NJ: International Bible Society, 1978.

Ions, Veronica. *Indian Mythology.* New York: Paul Hamlyn, 1967.

Jochmans, J.R. *Rolling Thunder: The Coming Earth Changes.* Santa Fe, NM: Sun Books/Sun Publishing, 1986, tenth printing.

Kelly, J.N.D. *The Oxford Dictionary of Popes.* London: Oxford University Press, 1989.

Kidron, Michel. *The New State of the World Atlas.* 1989 New York: Simon & Schuster, 1989.

Kikuchi, Rev Ryoju Tamo-san. *Moor the Boat.* Kamakura, Japan, 1960.

Krishnamurti, J. *Commentaries on Living: First Series.* Wheaton, IL: Quest Books, 1967.

Lawrence, D.H. *Apocalypse.* London: Penguin, 1984.

Lemesurier, Peter. *The Armageddon Script: Prophecy in Action.* Shaftesbury: Element Books, 1981.

Loewe, Michael, and Carmen Blacker. *Oracles and Divination.* Boulder, CO: Shambhala Press, 1981.

Lovelock, James. *The Ages of Gaia: A Biography of Our Living Earth.* New York: W.W. Norton, 1988.

Mascaró, Juan. *The Dhammapada.* Harmondsworth: Penguin Books, 1983, reprint.

Mascaró, Juan. *The Bhagavad Gita.* Harmondsworth: Penguin Books, 1973 reprint.

Meredith, George. *The Choice is Ours: The Key to the Future.* Cologne: Rebel Publishing, 1989.

Mohammed M.H. Shakir, translator. *The Holy Qur'an.* Elmhurst, New York: Tahrike Tarsile Qur'an, Inc., 1988.

Montgomery, Ruth, with Joanne Garland. *Ruth Montgomery:Herald of the New Age.* New York: Fawcett Crest, 1986.

Montgomery, Ruth. *Aliens Among Us.* New York: Fawcett Crest, 1985.

Montgomery, Ruth. *A World Beyond.* New York: Fawcett Crest, 1971.

Montgomery, Ruth. *A World Before.* New York: Fawcett Crest, 1976.

Montgomery, Ruth. *Threshold to Tomorrow.* New York: Fawcett Crest, 1982.

Montgomery, Ruth. *Strangers Among Us.* New York: Fawcett Crest, 1979.

Mooney, Ted. *Easy Travel to Other Planets.* New York: Ballantine Books, 1981.

Murakami, Shigeyoshi. *Japanese Religion in the Modern Society.* Tokyo: University of Tokyo Press, 1983.

Noone, Richard W. *5/5/ 2000 Ice: The Ultimate Disaster.* New York: Harmony Books, 1971.

Ouspensky, P.D. *In Search of the Miraculous.* London: Harvest/HBJ Book, 1977.

Parker, Derek & Juliet. *The Compleat Astrologer.* New York: McGraw Hill, 1971.

Peters, Fritz. *My Journey with a Mystic.* Laguna Niguel, CA: Tale Weaver, 1986 reprint.

Prieditis, Arthur. *The Fate of the Nations: Nostradamus's Vision of the Age of Aquarius.* St Paul, MN: Llewellyn, 1982.

Rajneesh, Bhagwan Shree (Osho). *Socrates: Poisoned Again after 25 Centuries.* Cologne: Rebel Publishing House, 1988.

Rajneesh, Bhagwan Shree. *Beyond Psychology.* Cologne: Rebel Publishing House, 1987.

Rajneesh, Bhagwan Shree. *The Golden Future.* Cologne: Rebel Publishing House, 1987.

Rajneesh, Bhagwan Shree. *The Greatest Challenge: The Golden Future.* Cologne: Rebel Publishing House, 1988.

Rajneesh, Bhagwan Shree. *I am the Gate: The Meaning of Initiation and Discipleship.* San Francisco, CA: Harper & Row, 1977.

Rajneesh, Bhagwan Shree. *The Last Testament: Interviews with the World Press VOL 1.* Boulder, CO: Rajneesh Publications Inc, 1986.

Rajneesh, Bhagwan Shree. *The New Man: The Only Hope for the Future.* Cologne: Rebel Publishing House, 1987.

Rajneesh, Bhagwan Shree. *The Razor's Edge.* Cologne: Rebel Publishing House, 1988.

Rajneesh, Bhagwan Shree. *The Silent Explosion.* Bombay: Ananda-Shila, 1973.

Robinson, Lytle. *Edgar Cayce's Story of the Origin and Destiny of Man.* New York: Berkeley Books, 1976.

Russel, Eric. *History of Astrology and Prediction.* London: Citadel, 1972.

Satprem. *Sri Aurobindo: or the Adver_nture of Consciousness.* New York: Institute for Evolutionary Research, 1970 (second edition) third printing.

Schell, Jonathan. *The Fate of the Earth.* London: Picador, 1982.

Shoghi Effendi. *God Passes By.* Wilmette IL: Bahá'í Publishing Trust, 1944.

Stearn, Jess. *The Sleeping Prophet: an Examination of the Work of Edgar Cayce.* New York: Bantam Book, 1974.

Taherzadeh, Adib. *The Revelations of Bahá'u'lláh.* Oxford: Oxford Press, 1974.

Toth, Max. *Pyramid Prophecies.* Rochester, Vermont: Destiny Books, 1988.

Trismegistus, Hermes, and Walter Scot, ed. *Hermetica.* Boston, MA: Shambhala, 1985.

Vaughan, Alan. *Patterns in Prophecy.* New York: Hawthorn Books, 1973.

Wallenchinsky, David. *The Book of Predictions.* New York: William Morrow & Co, 1980.

Waters, Frank. *Book of the Hopi.* New York: Ballantine, 1963.

Ward, Chas. *A Oracles of Nostradamus.* New York: Dorset Press, 1986.

World Commission on Enviorment and Development. *Our Common Future.* New York: Oxford University Press, 1987.

Yatri. *Unknown Man: The Mysterious Birth of a New Species.* New York: Simon & Schuster, 1988.

Acknowledgements

DEDICATION:
To the "Blessed One" within.

I could not have seen this ambitious project through without the trust and support of many dear friends and colleagues. I am especially indebted to my agent, Ronald S. Tanner, for his abiding faith in this project and his financial support throughout this long and often difficult process of five years. Thank you Tanner! To my mother and life-long friend, Irene Hogue, I am equally indebted. Her support and patience is total. To fellow traveller, Nadine Joyau, I wish to thank her for all the times she provided love, laughter, generous financial support and the necessary friction for my soul to grow.

I also wish to thank: Linda Obadia for her initial proofreading of the manuscript; Kevin Bentley, Assistant Editor of HarperSanFrancisco, for his vision and faith to see this book through to publication; Mark Collen; Susan Gordon; Mark Blubaugh of Orb TV; Debra Chambers Buchanan; Catherine Binkley, for her feedback and her final edit of the book; Astrid Lundberg for her friendship and her translation of Swedish prophecies to English; Swami Chaitanya Kabir for all his songs and his translation of an important Hindi prediction into English; Monju; Plavan N. Go for his input and his translation of Japanese prophets to English; Marcel and Janine Joyau for their generosity; Dr George Meredith for his friendship (both mundane and mystical) and his insights; Dan Oldenburg for his astrological and Hopi Indian research and his magic; Robert L. Coleman; Madir; Bonnie Malmsten; J. Robertson; Akasha; Paul Cullen and Vicky Rhoades, and our healing bike rides; author, Max Brecher, my alter-literary ego; Prof. Roshani Shey, of Oregon State, for her research and humor; Sarita for her insights; and finally, Salvatori Zambito for his warm heart, joyous tears and challenging debating skills.

I wish to personally thank a number of the contemporary seers, shamans, medicine men, psychics and mystics who graced this book with their words and their personal blessing: Good Horse Nation, Osho, Tamo-san, Katsué Ishida, Alan Vaughan, and Sturé Johannson (medium for "Ambres").

I wish to thank all the permission managers and researchers of copyright, and in particular those people who offered extra editorial help so that the prophets and mystics quoted in this book should be accurately represented: Jeannette M. Thomas, Jeanette Rowden and Grace Fogg of the Edgar Cayce Foundation; Michael Macy of the Dawn Horse Press; Michael Shaeffer, Penguin USA; Skip Whitson of Sun Books/Sun Publishing; Kimberly A. Lewis and Jo-Anne Della Russo of Harcourt Brace Jovanovich; Mrs. Tatiana Nagro (granddaughter of P.D. Ouspensky) and Mr. William A. Simon of McGarry & Simon, Attorneys at Law; Ma Anando, Ma Rabia Prabhudasi, Ma Bodhitaru, Ma Amiyo, Swami Amrito and Swami Ramarshi of Osho International Foundation; Anna Lee Strasburg of the National Spiritual Assembly of the Bahá'ís of the United States; Carl M. Johnson of The Church of Jesus Christ of Latter-Day Saints; Lynn Newdome of Shambhala Publications, Inc.; Faith Barbato, of HarperCollins*Publishers*; Mark Lee, of Krishnamurti Foundation of America; Theresa Lynch of G.P. Putnam's Sons; and finally , Prof. Dr. Hans Holzer of the New York Committee for the Investigation of Paranormal Occurences.

In instances not extensively covered by fair usage, every effort has been made to obtain permissions from holders of copyright material. If however – either through a mistake or through circumstances beyond our control – any copyright owner has been omitted, the author and publisher extend their apologies and undertake to rectify the situation at the next edition.

Grateful acknowledgment is made for permission to reprint material:

to the Sri Aurobindo Ashram Trust for excerpts from *Saviti: A Legend and Symbol* by Sri Aurobindo, copyright © 1990 by Auromere, Inc.; *"Conversations"* from the *Bulletin of Sri Aurobindo* by Mirra Alfassa (The Mother), copyright © 1931 by Auromere, Inc.

to the National Spiritual Assembly of the Bahá'ís of the United States for excerpts from *A Synopsis and Codification of the Laws and Ordinances of the Kitáb-i-Aqdas. The Most Holy Book of Bahá'u'lláh* by Bahá'u'lláh (compiled by the Universal House of Justice), copyright © 1973 by Bahá'í World Center; for excerpts from *Paris Talks* by 'Abdu'l-Baha, copyright © 1944 by Bahá'í Publishing Trust; for excerpts from *The Promulgation of Universal Peace* by 'Abdu'l-Baha, copyright © 1982 by Bahá'í Publishing Trust; for excerpts from *The Secret of Divine Civilization* by 'Abdu'l-Baha, copyright © 1957 and 1970 by the Bahá'í Publishing Trust; for excerpts from *Selections from the Writings of 'Abdu'l-Baha.* by 'Abdu'l-Baha, copyright © 1978 by the Bahá'í World Center.

to the Edgar Cayce Foundation for excerpts from the Edgar Cayce Readings, copyright © 1971, 1993, by the Edgar Cayce Foundation, all rights reserved, used by permission.

to The Church of Jesus Christ of Latter-Day Saints for excerpts from *Brigham Young. Journal of Discourses Vol. 8* (pp. 123; July 15, 1860) by Brigham Young; for excerpts from *Orson Pratt. Journal of Discourses Vol. 20* (pp. 151-152 March 9, 1879) by Orson Pratt.

to The Dawn Horse Press for excerpts from

Garbage and the Goddess by Da Free John (Da Avabhasa), copyright © 1974; for excerpts from *The Enlightenment of the Whole Body* by Da Free John (Da Avabhasa), copyright © 1978; for excerpts from *Scientific proof of the existence of God will soon be announced at the White House* by Da Free John (Da Avabhasa), copyright © 1980.

to Doubleday, a Division of Bantam Doubleday Dell Publishing Group, Inc., and Grafton Book (a Division of HarperCollins*Publishers* United Kingdom) for excerpts from *Ruth Montgomery: Herald of the New Age* by Ruth Montgomery, as told to Joanne Garland, copyright © 1986.

to E.P. Dutton, Penguin Books USA and Arkana for excerpts from *All and Everything: Beelzebub's Tales to his Grandson* by G.I. Gurdjieff, copyright © 1985; for excerpts from *Life is Real Only Then When "Iam": All and Everything/Third Series* by G.I. Gurdjieff, copyright © 1981.

to Harcourt Brace Jovanovich Inc. for excerpts from *In Search of the Miraculous* by P.D. Ouspensky, copyright © 1949 by Harcourt Brace Jovanovich Inc., (copyright renewed © 1977 by Tatiana M. Nagro: Harcourt Brace Jovanovich Inc. and Penguin Books Ltd.).

to HarperCollinsPublishers, Inc. for excerpts from *Life Ahead* by J. Krishnamurti, copyright © 1963 by K & R Foundation. Copyright renewed 1991 by K & R Foundation.

to Prof. Dr. Hans Holzer of the Center for Paranormal Studies, to quote selected passages from *The Prophets Speak* by Hans Holzer, copyright © 1971 by Bobbs-Merrill (out of print).

to the Krishnamurti Foundation of America for excerpts from *TRUTH IS A PATHLESS LAND: The Dissolution of the Order of the Star* (KFA Bulletin №53) by J. Krishnamurti, copyright © 1986.

to Good Horse Nation, Visayan Medicine Man, for permission to quote various interviews given to *The Rajneesh Times.* copyright © 1982, 1985 by Good Horse Nation, Spiritual adviser to Ableza Tiospaye Medicine Center.

to W.W. Norton & Company Inc. for excerpts from *The State of the World 1989* by Lester E. Brown, copyright © 1989 by

Copyright Acknowledgements

Lester E. Brown (Worldwatch Institute).

to Osho International Foundation for permission to print excerpts of the books by Osho: *The Book of Rajneeshism*, copyright © 1984; *From Darkness to Light*, copyright © 1985; *The Diamond Sutra*, copyright © 1977; *From Death to Deathlessness*, copyright © 1985; *From the False to the True*, copyright © 1985; *The Golden Future*, copyright © 1987; *The Greatest Challenge: The Golden Future*, copyright © 1987; *Hari Om Tat Sat*, copyright © 1987; *The Hidden Splendor*, copyright © 1987; *Hansa To Moti Chugai*, copyright © 1979; *The Land of the Lotus Paradise*, copyright © 1984; *The Last Testament*, copyright © 1985; *The Path of the Mystic*, copyright © 1986; *The New Dawn*, copyright © 1987; *Om Mani Padme Hum*, copyright © 1987; *Beyond Psychology*, copyright © 1986; *The Rajneesh Bible*, Vol. 4, copyright © 1985; *The Rajneesh Upanishad*, copyright © 1986; *The Razor's Edge*, copyright © 1987; *The Rebellious Spirit*, copyright © 1987; *Socrates Poisoned Again After 25 Centuries*, copyright © 1987; *Transmission of the Lamp*, copyright © 1986; *The Sound of Running Water*, copyright © 1976; *A New Vision of Women's Liberation*, copyright © 1987; *Zen: Path of the Paradox, Vol II*, copyright © 1979.

to Penguin Books USA for excerpts from *The Book of the Hopi* by Frank Waters, copyright © 1963 by Frank Waters.

to G.P. Putnam's Sons for excerpts from *Aliens Among Us* by Ruth Montgomery, copyright © 1985; for excerpts from *A World Beyond* by Ruth Montgomery, copyright © 1971; for excerpts from *A World Before* by Ruth Montgomery, copyright © 1976; for excerpts from *Strangers Among Us* by Ruth Montgomery, copyright © 1979.

to Shambhala Publications Inc. for excerpts from *HERMETICA*, edited and translated by Walter Scott (reprinted by arrangement with Shambhala Publications), copyright © 1985.

to STURID AB for excerpts from *AMBRES* by "Ambres," copyright © by Sturid Johannson.

to Sun Books/Sun Publishing for excerpts from *Cheiro's World Predictions* by Count Louis Hamon, copyright © 1981. Reprinted by permission of Skip Whitson, publisher.

to the Theosophical Publishing House for excerpts from *The Secret Doctrine Vol. II & Vol III* by H.P. Blavatsky, copyright © 1962.

to Alan Vaughan for excerpts from *Patterns in Prophecy*, by Alan Vaughan, copyright © 1973 by Alan Vaughan.

A

Byron Bay Media

Production